THE ORDEAL OF
TOTAL WAR

1939-1945

*the text of this book is printed
on 100% recycled paper*

THE RISE OF MODERN EUROPE

Edited by WILLIAM L. LANGER
Harvard University

* *In preparation*

THE ORDEAL OF TOTAL WAR

1939 - 1945

BY

GORDON WRIGHT

ILLUSTRATED

HARPER TORCHBOOKS
Harper & Row, Publishers
New York, Evanston, and London

For Greg (1947–1965),
whose idealism, sensitivity, and
courage proved that an adolescent
can be a man

Acknowledgement is made to the Houghton Mifflin Company for permission to use various excerpts from Winston Churchill's *The Second World War:* Volume I, *The Gathering Storm*, copyright 1948 by Houghton Mifflin Company; Volume V, *Closing The Ring*, copyright 1951 by Houghton Mifflin Company; Volume VI, *Triumph and Tragedy*, copyright 1953 by Houghton Mifflin Company; Volume IV, *The Hinge of Fate*, copyright 1950 by Houghton Mifflin Company.

THE ORDEAL OF TOTAL WAR, 1939-1945

Copyright © 1968 by Gordon Wright.
Printed in the United States of America.

This book was originally published in 1968 by Harper & Row in The Rise of Modern Europe series, edited by William L. Langer.

Harper & Row, Publishers, Inc.
10 East 53rd Street, New York, N.Y. 10022.

First HARPER TORCHBOOK edition published 1968 by Harper & Row, Publishers, Incorporated, New York 10016.

LIBRARY OF CONGRESS CATALOG CARD NUMBER: 68-28221.

CONTENTS

CONTENTS

ILLUSTRATIONS

MAPS

INTRODUCTION

OUR age of specialization produces an almost incredible amount of monographic research in all fields of human knowledge. So great is the mass of this material that even the professional scholar cannot keep abreast of the contributions in anything but a restricted part of his general subject. In all branches of learning the need for intelligent synthesis is now more urgent than ever before, and this need is felt by the layman even more acutely than by the scholar. He cannot hope to read the products of microscopic research or to keep up with the changing interpretations of experts, unless new knowledge and new viewpoints are made accessible to him by those who make it their business to be informed and who are competent to speak with authority.

These volumes, published under the general title of *The Rise of Modern Europe*, are designed primarily to give the general reader and student a reliable survey of European history written by experts in various branches of that vast subject. In consonance with the current broad conception of the scope of history, they attempt to go beyond a merely political-military narrative, and to lay stress upon social, economic, religious, scientific and artistic developments. The minutely detailed, chronological approach is to some extent sacrificed in the effort to emphasize the dominant factors and to set forth their interrelationships. At the same time the division of European history into national histories has been abandoned and whenever possible attention has been focused upon larger forces common to the whole of European civilization. These are the broad lines on which this history as a whole has been laid out. The individual volumes are integral parts of the larger scheme, but they are intended also to stand as independent units, each the work of a scholar well qualified to treat the period covered by this book. Each volume contains about fifty illustrations selected from the mass of contemporary pictorial material. All noncontemporary illustrations have been excluded on principle. The bibliographical note appended to each volume is designed to facilitate further study of special aspects touched upon in the text. In general every effort has been made to give the reader a clear idea of the main movements in European history, to embody the monographic contributions of research workers, and to present the material in a forceful and vivid manner.

The present volume concludes *The Rise of Modern Europe* series, which undertakes to survey the evolution of European civilization from the late Middle Ages to roughly our own day. The appearance of several volumes in the series has been delayed, sometimes through death of the author but more frequently through diversions occasioned by the Second World War and the ensuing ructions. In the interval, however, the dozen or more volumes that have seen the light have made a real mark for themselves. They have enjoyed a steady sale among general readers and have been decidedly popular as collateral reading in colleges and universities, in literature as well as in history courses. Surely one of the reasons for their success lies in the fact that no other books in the English language provide so broad a portrait of the various periods of European history, nor give so penetrating an analysis. As for this volume, Professor Wright has, in his own preface, discussed the many problems with which he had to contend. To say more here would be supererogatory. But the editor may at least be permitted to say that Professor Wright has mastered a vast amount of diffuse literature and has put his own stimulating interpretations on a difficult and complicated subject. This book goes far beyond the usual military chronicle. It is a splendid synthesis of a tragic phase of recent European history.

WILLIAM L. LANGER

PREFACE

THERE is a certain paradox in a series entitled *The Rise of Modern Europe* that culminates (at least for the moment) in a volume on the Second World War. The war's destructive impact on the continent of Europe probably exceeds that of any previous disaster in the modern era; and for a time it seemed to mark the decisive stage in Europe's decline from its former dominance of the globe. A quarter-century after the conflict, one can no longer be so sure that Europe as a major locus of power and of high culture is extinct; the Jeremiahs of 1945 had failed to take account of the recuperative powers of an old continent. Even so, it would be difficult to argue that the series title is apt for this particular volume, or that the thirty-year conflict culminating in 1945 can be regarded as a phase in Europe's advance toward some higher destiny.

Unlike the previous contributions to this series, this volume is concerned with a brief six-year period—much too short to reveal the evolution of institutions and ideas, too short even to justify some sort of descriptive label for the era. Wars are periods of interruption rather than of development; their chief long-range significance lies in their causes and their consequences, and not in the vicissitudes of the struggle itself. To focus on the war years alone, therefore, is a somewhat frustrating exercise, if one's aim is not to recount the events of the period but to weigh its meaning for the development of European society and institutions. Perhaps, for purposes of this series, the war might better have been hitched onto the interwar period as a kind of caboose, or attached locomotive-fashion to the post-1945 era. When detached for separate study, the war years are bound to produce a volume somewhat different from the usual pattern of this series. I have tried, nevertheless, to conform to that pattern as closely as possible.

One purpose of *The Rise of Modern Europe* series is to synthesize the vast output of scholarly literature on a given period—an output so great that the informed lay reader can scarcely be expected to cope with it. Here too this volume must diverge a bit from the pattern. True, the list of books about the war has already reached formidable proportions. So great an upheaval could not fail to attract historians and journalists of both the serious and the popularizing sort; nor could it fail to produce a flood of memoirs by soldiers, statesmen, and common citizens who were caught up in the conflict. Hence Winston Churchill's ironic remark shortly after 1945: "I see that my generals are selling their lives dearly." Hence, too, Philippe Pétain's sardonic explanation of his refusal to join the rush: "Why should I write my memoirs? I have nothing to hide."

This torrent of books, however, has not covered the various aspects of the war in equal depth. On some topics—military events, resistance movements in certain countries, concentration camps—a great deal has been published. On others—economic and social developments, psychological warfare, the impact of the war on intellectual and cultural life—there are few serious studies, and much of the spadework remains to be done. No single scholar could possibly undertake all of that spadework. Some segments of this volume must therefore seem quite tentative and even superficial. Time will eventually allow both a longer perspective and a more thorough sifting of the evidence, and will permit more dependable judgments.

This series concerns itself with the history of Europe, not of the world. I have chosen, therefore, to say almost nothing of the war's non-European aspects. The role of the United States cannot be ignored, simply because American power and policy directly penetrated the continent during the war. But the Pacific and Middle Eastern theaters have been left aside, at the risk of distorting a historical epoch of great complexity. The struggle elsewhere undoubtedly impinged on events in Europe; but a short book imposes painful choices, and this omission is one of them.

I am heavily indebted to the American Council of Learned Societies and to the Center for Advanced Study in the Behavioral Sciences for grants that allowed me a free year (1962–1963) to begin reading and thinking about this project. The Stanford University Libraries provided me with most of the sources I have used; the librarians there were even more than usually helpful. My thanks are also due to a number of colleagues and friends who shared their knowledge and ideas with me: notably Thomas A. Bailey, Gordon A. Craig, Richard W. Lyman, Wayne S. Vucinich, Carl E. Schorske, Frank E. Manuel,

John Smith, Lancelot L. Whyte, Michael Howard, Alan S. Milward, Richard Pipes, and Val R. Lorwin. John G. Ackerman served as an efficient research assistant, while a number of participants in my graduate seminar—notably Gaines Post Jr. and Larry N. Horton—did some excellent prospecting into relatively unexplored territory. Help in running down photographs was provided by Hans Dollinger, Hans-Adolf Jacobsen, Henri Michel, J. F. Golding, Col. Grover Heiman Jr., R. A. Winnacker, Mme. Schürvy, and Peter K. Cline. I am indebted also to the trustees of the David Low estate, to the Tate Gallery, and to Henry Moore (for permission to reproduce one of his wartime drawings). Mrs. Beulah Hagen of Harper & Row did an exemplary job of seeing the manuscript through the press and dealing with a cantankerous author.

Like every author in this series, I am particularly grateful to Professor William L. Langer for his generous and constructive counsel and for his patient willingness to stretch deadlines when obligations piled high.

GORDON WRIGHT

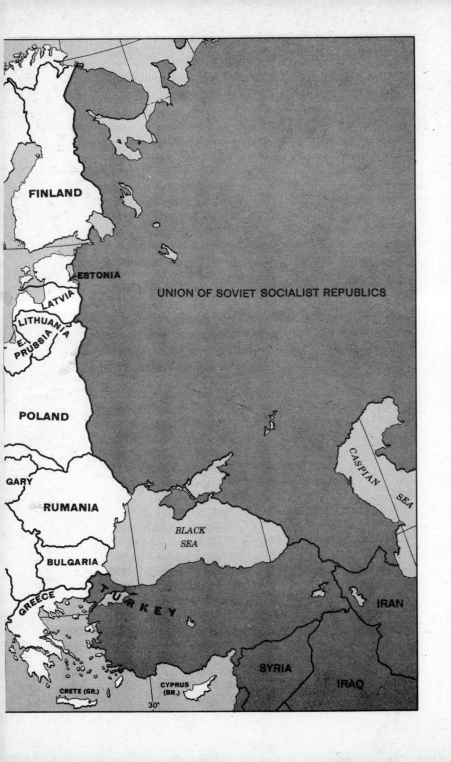

FINLAND

ESTONIA

LATVIA

LITHUANIA

E. PRUSSIA

POLAND

UNION OF SOVIET SOCIALIST REPUBLICS

CASPIAN SEA

GARY

RUMANIA

BLACK SEA

BULGARIA

GREECE

TURKEY

IRAN

SYRIA

IRAQ

CRETE (GR.)

CYPRUS (BR.)

30°

EUROPE
END OF 1945

ICELAND

NORWAY

SWEDEN

N. IRE.

NORTH SEA

EIRE

DENMARK

GREAT BRITAIN

Polish admin. POLA

ATLANTIC OCEAN

THE NETHERLANDS

BRITISH

Berlin W. U.S. E. SOVIET

N

BELGIUM

FR.

GERMANY

CZECHO-SLOVAKIA

BAY OF BISCAY

LUX. SAAR.

AMERICAN

AUSTRIA

U.S.S.R.

FR.

U.S.

HUN

SWITZ.

FR.

BRITISH

FRANCE

YUGOSLAVIA

PORTUGAL

SPAIN

CORSICA

BALEARIC IS.

SARDINIA

ITALY

ADRIATIC SEA

ALBANIA

Tangier

MEDITERRANEAN

SICILY

MOROCCO

ALGERIA

SEA

AFRICA

TUNIS

MALTA (BR.)

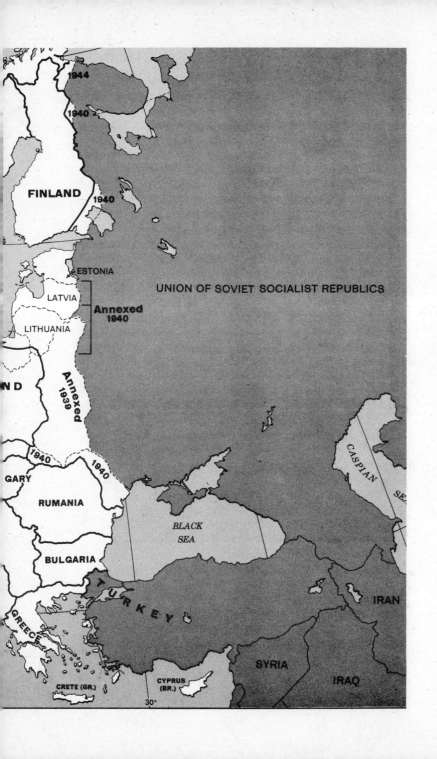

Chapter One

EUROPE ON THE BRINK

AT DAWN on the morning of September 1, 1939, the first units of a powerful German army crossed Germany's eastern frontier onto Polish soil. Two days later, the governments of Great Britain and France (followed shortly by the nations of the British Commonwealth) proclaimed the existence of a state of war with Germany. The long interlude in Europe's new thirty years' war was over.

Ten days of intense diplomatic activity had preceded this set of decisive actions. It is fashionable among scholars of our day to examine what they call the escalation of a crisis, and to seek the precise point at which the process became irreversible. Those historians who have studied the events of late August 1939 have not yet arrived at a clear consensus, and perhaps they never will. Their judgments must depend in part on the assessment of motives—a realm in which even the resources of depth psychology do not suffice to guide the historian's hand. Still, there is a fair amount of evidence to suggest that the European statesmen of 1939 were not mere victims of a process of escalation that somehow got beyond their control. Thinking in terms of such a process (or, better perhaps, such a metaphor) may illuminate the events of July 1914. But in 1939, the outbreak of war seems much less the product of unhappy accident and human frailty than of calculation—calculation that was in some cases willful, in other cases reluctant; in some cases shrewd, in other cases faulty. For Adolf Hitler, Germany's lone decision-maker, the fatal transition from war to peace was not the result of a last-minute decision to which he was driven by the failure of all peaceful alternatives and the rise of tension to the breaking point. Hitler's mind had been set for several months; so far as his quarrel with Poland was concerned, the sole alternatives were Polish capitulation or war (preferably against an isolated Poland, but if necessary against Poland's Western friends as well). In Warsaw, London, and Paris likewise, the conviction that force alone would

blunt Nazi aggression had lodged itself in the minds of leading statesmen well before the final denouement.

It might be argued, therefore, that the diplomatic activity of those
last ten days of peace has only marginal relevance, however rich it
may be in human interest. At that point in Europe's history, only a
drastic change in the stance of one of the great powers, or of Poland,
could have averted the outbreak of a general war. Hitler, it is true,
expected such a change in the stance of Britain and France, thanks
to his surprise move in negotiating a treaty with the Soviet Union
on August 23. This time his instinct, so often right as against his
critics, had betrayed him. He had gambled and lost; but he refused
to believe that his mistaken judgment might in the end destroy him
and much of Europe.

The diplomatic revolution of August 1939, which restored at least
the appearance of cordial relations between Germany and the USSR,
had dramatically isolated the Poles. Poland's dilemma henceforth was
of classic simplicity: either to capitulate to German demands for the
return of Danzig and a plebiscite in the region known as the Polish
Corridor, or to face Germany's armed might virtually alone (for the
first few months, at least). In most of the capitals of Europe, there
were men who devoted the last ten days of August to a futile search
for an alternative, a face-saving device that might avert a resort to
arms. But for the most part, the leading statesmen of Europe thought
the situation past the point of compromise, and fell back on bluff,
threat, or a show of calm assurance and determination in an effort to
overawe the potential enemy.

In Paris, Premier Edouard Daladier and his close advisers were
badly shaken by news of the German-Soviet pact, which had taken
them completely by surprise. France, Daladier told the United States
ambassador, was placed "in a most tragic and terrible situation":

The entire diplomatic structure which he had attempted to build up had
been destroyed. . . . He believed that in spite of their courage the Poles
could not hold out against the German armies for more than 2 months.
Thereafter the entire brunt of the war on land against Germany and Italy
would have to fall on the French Army. The British could not have a serious
army ready for another 2 years. . . . Under the circumstances he was faced
with the alternative of sacrificing the lives of all able-bodied men in France
in a war, the outcome of which would be to say the least doubtful; or the
worse alternative of abandoning the commitments of France to support

Poland which would be a horrible moral blow to the French people and would result in Germany swallowing one after another, Poland, Rumania, Hungary, Yugoslavia, Bulgaria, Greece and Turkey. In the end Germany would turn on France and England. . . .[1]

Yet despite his shock and his black mood, Daladier was determined to resist the almost hysterical pressure of many French politicians to arrange another Munich at Poland's expense. In the words of Daladier's chief foreign policy adviser, Alexis Léger, "It was exceedingly doubtful, to put it mildly, that France and England would be able to win the war. Nevertheless the chance must be taken since the chance would be even less if France should permit Poland to be destroyed."[2]

In London the pressure for abandoning the Poles was much less intense, and the government's resolve much stiffer. Prime Minister Neville Chamberlain immediately warned Hitler against misunderstanding British intentions, and strengthened his guarantee to Poland by completing negotiation of a long-suspended mutual-assistance treaty with Warsaw. The Polish government was even more intransigent. Foreign Minister Josef Beck and other high officials calmly shrugged off the German-Soviet pact, and talked recklessly of fighting the Germans alone if necessary.

Hitler on the twenty-third had ordered his generals to be ready for an attack on Poland on August 26. But Britain's firmness, and Italy's reluctance to join him in what might become a major war, led the Fuehrer on the evening of August 25 to postpone the invasion for a few days. The additional time, he thought, might still enable him to dissuade the Western powers from intervening. Mussolini was asked to help weaken Western morale by feigning an intention to fight alongside the Germans. Several days of feverish negotiation followed, in which Hitler with at least partial success managed to convey the impression that he might still be willing to settle his differences with the Poles without war. His attitude encouraged a mild revival of hope in London and Paris, and this in turn encouraged Hitler to believe that his strategy of driving a wedge between the Poles and their Western Allies might succeed. On the twenty-eighth he agreed to a British suggestion of direct German-Polish negotiations; but on the

[1] Bullitt to Hull, August 22, 1939. U.S. Department of State, *Foreign Relations of the United States 1939* (Washington, 1950), I, 301–02.
[2] *Ibid.*, p. 313.

following evening he demanded that the Poles send a plenipotentiary to Berlin within twenty-four hours to receive his still unstated terms. When the British ambassador protested that this appeared to be an ultimatum rather than an offer to negotiate, Hitler retorted that the moment was too urgent for delays and that "my soldiers are asking me 'Yes' or 'No.'" In fact, the Fuehrer had already ordered his high command to be ready to attack on September 1.

The British response to Hitler's demand arrived in Berlin on the evening of August 30; it sought to keep open the possibility of direct German-Polish negotiations, but pointed out that the terms and the arrangements for two-way talks must not be dictated by one party. Foreign Minister Ribbentrop rudely rejected these British caveats, read aloud to the British ambassador the terms of the "generous offer" which Hitler had intended to present to the Poles, and announced that there could no longer be any question of direct negotiations since no Polish plenipotentiary had been sent to Berlin for the purpose. The German terms would have called for the immediate transfer of Danzig to the Reich, a plebiscite in the Polish Corridor, and an extraterritorial corridor through that area for whichever nation lost the plebiscite. This whole episode was doubtless designed to sow division between Poland and the West rather than to serve as a serious basis for possible settlement of "the Polish problem."[3] If the latter had been Hitler's purpose, he could easily have approached the Poles directly through their ambassador in Berlin, and could have set forth his terms before his own deadline had expired. At any rate, Hitler by the evening of the thirtieth had clearly given up the idea of any further maneuvers to keep the British and French neutral, though he continued to believe that they would stay out, or that the Western powers would at least confine themselves to a *pro forma* declaration of war. Early on August 31 his armies were ordered to take up attack positions along the frontier, and at 4:45 the next morning they struck into Poland.

Mussolini had meanwhile been mounting a last-minute attempt to arrange a second Munich conference that might add to his own stature and might give Hitler what he wanted without war. On the thirty-first he proposed a five-power meeting on September 5, and he continued to urge this plan even after the invasion of Poland had begun.

---

[3] Hitler remarked privately a few days later, "I needed an alibi, especially with the German people, to show them that I had done everything to maintain peace. That explains my generous offer about the settlement of Danzig and the Corridor." P. Schmidt, *Hitler's Interpreter* (New York, 1951), pp. 153–54.

It won enthusiastic support from French Foreign Minister Georges Bonnet and other strongly anti-interventionist politicians in Paris, but the British coldly replied that there could be no talks unless Hitler would first withdraw his armies from Polish soil. On the morning of September 3, Britain's ultimatum to this effect was delivered to Hitler; that of France followed at noon. For the first time since he arrived in power, Hitler's diplomatic scheming had gone awry. If the British and the French really meant what they said, the day of easy victories over isolated victims was over.

II. AIMS AND EXPECTATIONS OF THE BELLIGERENTS

Four hours after launching the attack on Poland, Hitler appeared before the Reichstag to offer a public justification for his decision. His sole purpose, he declared, was to respond to the provocation of the Poles, who had not only refused to discuss Germany's just demands, but had actually violated the German frontier and had fired on German troops. This curious accusation rested on a sham "incident" arranged on Hitler's orders by an SS unit; on the evening of August 31, a group of SS men wearing Polish uniforms burst into a German radio station at Gleiwitz near the frontier, broadcast a brief but violent manifesto in Polish, and departed leaving behind a dead concentration-camp inmate as a simulated victim of the attack. In his Reichstag speech, the Fuehrer described his pact with the USSR as "a turning point of tremendous consequence for the future. And it is final. . . . [It] excludes the use of force between us for all time to come." He made one last attempt to forestall Franco-British intervention by proclaiming the purity of his intentions toward them. "I have given the solemn assurance and I repeat that we neither demand nor will we ever demand anything from these Western states."[4] If Western intervention should occur nevertheless, he had persuaded himself that it would be merely nominal. "In two months," he remarked to an aide on August 29, "Poland will be finished, and then we shall have a great peace conference with the Western Powers."[5]

That Hitler anticipated a quick and easy victory over Poland is clear. Much less clear is the question of his long-range aims and expectations at this moment of decision. His lack of rigidly prefabricated war aims has sometimes been viewed as evidence that his intentions were essentially peaceful. In fact, that lack ought to be viewed

[4] A. Hitler, *Speech Delivered in the Reichstag on Sept. 1, 1939* (Berlin, 1939), pp. 7–8.
[5] E. von Weizsäcker, *Memoirs* (Chicago, 1951), p. 208.

as evidence of Hitler's bent toward improvisation—of his flexibility in tactics and goals, both of which he was always ready to adapt to changing circumstance.

The scope of Hitler's foreign policy ambitions has been much debated, and probably will never be defined beyond doubt. Did he dream of world domination, or of the conquest of Europe alone, or of dominion over a more limited German sphere in central and eastern Europe? Those who believe that *Mein Kampf* contained a rough sketch of intentions from which Hitler never diverged are likely to conclude that his immediate goal was a limited one. In *Mein Kampf*, Hitler focused on the conquest of living space to the east—specifically the Ukraine and the Baltic region, and possibly beyond. He asserted the need to break France's military power, but seemed to indicate no desire for territorial expansion in the west. He expressly rejected the idea of a challenge to Britain's position on the ocean or overseas, and ruled out the acquisition of a colonial empire as a diversion of Germany's energies. True, *Mein Kampf* suggested that a Greater German Reich in command of eastern Europe would inevitably become a world power rather than merely a Continental one. But the vagueness of the phraseology left the nature of that future world-power role ambiguous.

Did *Mein Kampf* still reflect the general character of Hitler's expansionist aims when war finally came in 1939? On the whole, and despite some modifications in detail, that appears to be the case. The most notable modification was a somewhat halfhearted decision, midway through the thirties, to try to rebuild a colonial empire. On Hitler's orders, a *Reichskolonialbund* was formed as a substitute for the old colonialist pressure groups, and was given a monopoly of "colonial indoctrination and enlightenment." Demands for the return of Germany's lost empire began to be advanced in Hitler's speeches and in diplomatic negotiations. But Hitler made it clear early in 1939 that *Ostpolitik* still preceded *Weltpolitik* in his list of priorities—in part because postponing *Weltpolitik* might keep Britain neutral while he moved east.[6] As for the precise content of Hitler's *Ostpolitik*, it remained almost as cloudy as it had been when *Mein Kampf* was writ-

[6] The probability that he would have to fight the French and British before accomplishing his broader aims in the east was cheerfully accepted by Hitler in 1938-1939; it is demonstrated by a number of private remarks to his intimates, his generals, and his ally Mussolini. He believed, however, that he could postpone that confrontation for as much as three or four years.

ten. It is true that by 1937 Hitler had committed himself to the outright absorption of both Austria and Czechoslovakia; but beyond that, his goals were flexible. Even Poland's future role in Hitler's plans remained uncertain until at least the spring of 1939, and perhaps even until the completion of its conquest. Hitler's contempt for the Slavs seems to have allowed a partial exception for the Poles, and if they had been willing to accept satellite status, he would probably have been ready to accept Poland as a junior partner in his *Ostpolitik* design. It was the vast reaches of Soviet territory that continued to fascinate Hitler, despite the apparent reversal of purpose contained in the pact of August 1939.[7]

Not all Germans shared their Fuehrer's aims at the outbreak of war; but by 1939, few of them were able or willing to express contrary views. Privately, skeptics and critics in the foreign office or the army might voice their doubts either about Hitler's goals or about the risks involved in trying to attain these goals; but they had lost all influence over decision-making. Whether German citizens in general sensed where Hitler was leading them is uncertain. There is no doubt that the great bulk of Germans enthusiastically approved the foreign policy successes of 1936–1939, and hoped for more of the same. There is greater doubt that most Germans wanted further successes badly enough to face a general war. Foreign correspondents in Berlin during the days of crisis reported a depressed and defeatist mood: "Everybody against the war. People talking openly."[8] When Hitler drove to the Reichstag on September 1, the streets were emptier than usual, and the Fuehrer's appearance attracted only silent stares. When the loudspeakers on September 3 announced Britain's declaration of war, Berliners seemed stunned, and listened without a murmur. "No excitement, no hurrahs, no cheering . . . There is not even any hate for the French and British. . . ."[9] The day of popular wars, it seemed, was over.

Poland stood out as a sharp exception. Tension had been building

[7] Two private statements by Hitler demonstrate the stubborn consistency of his aims in the east. On February 3, 1933, four days after taking power, Hitler told a group of his generals that Germany's future lay in "the conquest of new *Lebensraum* in the East and its ruthless Germanization." *Vierteljahrshefte fuer Zeitgeschichte*, II (1954), 435. On April 29, 1945—the day before he committed suicide—Hitler's last directive to his military staff read: "The aim must still be to win territory in the East for the German people." H. R. Trevor-Roper, *The Last Days of Hitler* (New York, 1947), p. 195.

[8] W. L. Shirer, *Berlin Diary* (New York, 1941), p. 191.

[9] *Ibid.*, p. 201.

up there for several months, and the outbreak of war brought a sense of relief. "Enthusiasm ran high," recalled a student in Cracow some months later. "Groups of students and members of national organizations marched through the town with bands and sang patriotic songs. Everyone was infected with the optimism of youth."[10] Although Poland's governing clique shared, in varying degrees, some of the prejudices of the Nazis—notably their dislike of democratic processes, their hatred of Bolshevism, their anti-Semitism, and their corrosive nationalism—these Polish leaders were determined to stand firm against German territorial demands. Western visitors to Warsaw found a spirit of admirable courage that verged on bravado. Polish officials insisted that their army could if necessary hold off the Germans without external aid. Few of them imagined that they could defeat the Germans all alone; but they believed that they could resist successfully for six months—long enough for French and British power to be brought to bear on Germany's other flank. The fact that neither of the Western powers could come to Poland's relief for at least the first two weeks was known to Polish leaders. They faced the prospect with a kind of reckless insouciance. Poland, after all (as they had been asserting for twenty years), was a great power.

In France, the dominant mood was quite the reverse; it amounted to gloomy resignation. Like the Poles, Frenchmen thought of their country as a great power; but unlike the Poles, they had few illusions about their ability to face Germany alone. Through the summer they had desperately sought a Western pact with the Soviet Union; in contrast to the British and the Poles, they had been prepared to pay almost any price. The sudden collapse of their hopes had shaken even those French leaders who were convinced that appeasement had failed. A large and influential segment of parliament, and even some cabinet ministers, were eager to continue appeasement. Some of them hoped that if Hitler were allowed to swallow Poland and establish a common frontier with the USSR, his next blow would be eastward rather than westward. But Daladier and the other reluctant resisters managed to outmaneuver the appeasers, and the country acquiesced in a mood of grim resignation that contained no touch of enthusiasm. French army leaders, on the other hand, were inclined to overestimate Poland's ability to fight back, and to exaggerate the invincibility of the French armies so long as they stayed behind their Maginot Line.

[10] D. Wegierski, *September 1939* (London, 1940), p. 19.

British morale, though certainly not buoyant, was firm and high when compared to that of the French. Few prominent Englishmen any longer doubted the necessity to take a stand. Hitler, they felt, had not played the game; he had betrayed Britain's confidence by destroying the Munich settlement only six months after it had been signed. Through the summer of 1939 some British officials had continued, via private contacts, to urge the German government to take just one step backward (out of Czechoslovakia) as a demonstration of its good will, after which they suggested that the British would be ready to forgive and forget. Even these late appeasers, however, were unwilling to see Britain retreat again without a prior gesture by Hitler to attest his honorable intentions. To Neville Chamberlain and the men around him, the outbreak of war represented the dismal failure of a policy based on a combination of admirable motives and false illusions. "Everything that I have worked for [said Chamberlain in the House of Commons on September 3], everything that I have hoped for, everything that I have believed in during my public life, has crashed into ruins."[11] This was hardly the kind of talk to inspire Britishers with a crusading spirit. Yet the public mood, if not enthusiastic, was marked by a quiet determination. That it rested on a continuing substructure of illusion was to be proved by the conduct of the war in its first few months. That it could survive the destruction of those illusions was to be proved in 1940 and beyond.

III. ATTITUDES AND HOPES OF THE NEUTRALS

Of the twenty-seven nations of Europe, twenty-three stood aside at the outset of the struggle, desperately hoping to avoid involvement or shrewdly awaiting the moment when intervention might bring the richest advantage.

The Soviet Union, most powerful and most enigmatic of the neutrals, had astutely calculated the tactics best suited to divert German power from itself toward the west. Soviet leaders, convinced that "the capitalist world" intended the forcible destruction of the Soviet state, had nevertheless detected rifts and rivalries within that capitalist world, and had set out to exploit them. Their immediate purpose was undoubtedly defensive; they sought to protect their beleaguered Communist island against its presumed enemy besiegers. In the longer-range future (if they still took their own doctrine seriously), they

[11] Great Britain, *Parliamentary Debates: Commons* CCCLI (Sept. 3, 1939), 293.

hoped to take the offensive against the decadent capitalist world. After an initial attempt in 1933–1934 to maintain a formal friendship with the new Nazi regime, the Kremlin had shifted to the opposite tactic: the forging of a bloc of anti-fascist states, with the Soviet Union as a participating member. The sincerity of Soviet intentions during this Popular Front phase remains one of the great debated issues of the interwar era; but sincere or not, the Soviets could plausibly contend that the Western nations were playing their own hypocritical game. To the men around Stalin, the Munich settlement seemed clear confirmation of their belief that the West hoped to isolate the USSR and to unleash German power against her, leaving the Western powers in the comfortable role of applauding spectators. The fact that many Western leaders suspected the Kremlin of playing the same kind of game in reverse did not make it easier, in the year after Munich, to forge a ring of military power around Germany.

The sudden Soviet reversal in August 1939, whether inspired by suspicion of the West or by clever calculation (or both), ensured that German power would surge eastward right up to the Soviet frontier. As the Kremlin saw it, however, that would be no worse than the continued existence of an independent Poland tied to the West, which provided no effective barrier against capitalist encroachment. A pact with Hitler would enable the Soviets to buy time, to push their own border somewhat farther to the west by a new partition of Poland, and even, perhaps, to precipitate a serious civil war within the capitalist world. Such tactics, of course, involved a genuine risk: the "capitalist civil war" might end not in deadlock but in an overwhelming triumph for one of the warring camps—after which the threat to Soviet security would be graver than ever. But a long deadlock seemed a more likely prospect in August 1939; and there was always the prospect that if one side should eventually begin to prevail, Soviet intervention might then be timely and decisive. At least the gamble appeared to be preferable to an immediate confrontation between German and Soviet power, in which effective assistance from the Western nations would be an uncertain hope at best. News of the outbreak of war, therefore, was received with outward calm in Moscow. The Supreme Soviet on August 31 ratified the pact with Germany after hearing Foreign Minister Molotov explain that "August 23 must be regarded as a date of great historic importance . . . a turning point in the destiny of Europe." As for the complaints of the British and

French, Molotov added this taunt: "If these gentlemen have such an irresistible desire to go to war, well then—let them go to war by themselves, without the Soviet Union. (*Laughter and cheers*)."[12] But a wave of panic buying soon swept the stores of Moscow clean of the necessities of life, suggesting that ordinary Soviet citizens were only partly reassured.

Calculation also entered strongly into the behavior of the other great-power neutral, Italy. In May 1939, Mussolini had accepted Hitler's proposal to turn their Axis pact of friendship into a full-fledged military alliance—the so-called Pact of Steel. Mussolini had made it clear, however, that he would not be prepared to enter a general war until 1942 at the earliest, and Hitler had not demurred. The thunderbolt of the German-Soviet pact and Hitler's attempt to invoke the Pact of Steel unsettled and angered the Duce, who wobbled badly during the last ten days of August. At one point the Italians demanded as the price for their belligerence the prior delivery of an astonishing list of essential war materials—"enough to kill a bull," said Foreign Minister Galeazzo Ciano, "if a bull could read it."[13] Ciano and others managed to restrain Mussolini during his moments of warlike ardor, so that the Italians were left standing on the sidelines when the conflict finally broke out. For Mussolini and the more ebullient Fascists, it was an unnerving situation. They were aware that Italians generally lacked any enthusiasm for entering the war, yet Mussolini was strongly possessed by the itch for military glory and by a nagging sense that perhaps he had failed to leap aboard the locomotive of destiny.

Elsewhere in Europe, the middle or smaller powers watched nervously as war began; for war, like a prairie fire, might at any moment shift its course and engulf them. Belgium and the Netherlands lay in the most exposed position, for the existence of the Maginot Line and the German West Wall almost ensured that any land attack in western Europe by either the Germans or the French would be launched across their soil. The Dutch, who had managed to ride out the First World War without invasion, clung to their traditional neutrality and hoped that they might be spared again. The Belgians, who had lost most of their illusions in 1914, had allied themselves with France after that war, but had shifted back to a neutral stance in 1936, even though they no longer enjoyed the dubious protection of an international treaty guaran-

---

[12] A. Werth, *Russia at War 1941–1945* (New York, 1964), p. 74.
[13] M. Muggeridge (ed.), *Ciano's Diary 1939–1943* (London, 1947), p. 135.

teeing that neutrality. When war broke out in September, the French and British governments immediately sought to persuade the Belgians to discuss plans for the eventuality of a German attack. King Leopold and his government flatly rejected the proposal, asserting their determination to give no provocation to any of their neighbors.

For the Scandinavian nations, location and tradition made neutrality an even more natural choice. Eire likewise, because of its unsolved conflict with Britain over Ulster and over trade relationships, could not have been expected to adopt any other line. Spain, licking its wounds after the bloodiest civil war modern Europe had known, was in no position to take up arms again, even though General Francisco Franco's government owed much to the Axis powers which had contributed to the Franco victory and which seemed at the time to be doctrinally congenial to the new Spanish leadership. In southeastern Europe, the situation was more complex. Domestic strife and border feuds in the Danubian and Balkan regions had made the whole area susceptible to great-power rivalries and intrigues. The resurgence of German power after 1933 had gradually undermined French influence in the Little Entente countries (Yugoslavia, Rumania, and Czechoslovakia) and had threatened Italian ambitions as well. Shrewdly conceived German trade policies had created a strong new economic tie with Berlin; Hitler's military strength and diplomatic successes had impressed the political leaders of the region. Although Chamberlain in the spring of 1939 committed Great Britain to send aid to Greece and Rumania if attacked, both the Greek and the Rumanian governments adopted a straddling policy designed to placate the Axis powers and to avoid being drawn into a general conflict. Yugoslavia and Bulgaria adopted a similar line, while Hungary leaned more perceptibly in the direction of Germany after sharing the spoils of Czechoslovakia in March 1939. With the outbreak of war, all of southeastern Europe stood nervously aside, fearful of the consequences of neutrality yet even more fearful of being drawn into the struggle.

IV. STRENGTHS AND WEAKNESSES OF THE ADVERSARIES

German armed might in September 1939 outweighed that of any single adversary. In absolute numbers of men under arms, however, that margin was not overwhelming. Hitler could mobilize in short order approximately five million men—roughly the same number of regulars and reservists available to France. Only about half of Germany's 105 divisions were suitable for attack warfare; 54 divisions were used in the invasion of Poland. The Polish forces totaled 40 divisions (30 active and 10 reserve); the French, 94 divisions (67 "field divisions" and 27 "fortress divisions"). Alongside these figures, Britain's land army seems ridiculously small; prewar plans for a 19-division field force had scarcely begun to be implemented, and only 4 divisions were available for service in France when the war began. Conscription had been in effect only since May 1939, and was so restricted in scope as to be a symbolic gesture rather than an operative reality.

Even more important than numbers of troops was the German advantage in modern equipment. Hitler had six armored (panzer) divisions ready for use in September 1939, and had assigned the bulk of his 3200 tanks to those divisions. The French late in 1938 had reluctantly decided to organize two armored divisions, but had not yet implemented this plan when war came. Their total force of about 2200 modern tanks combined with Britain's 1100 matched the strength of the Germans, but a larger proportion of the French and British tanks were light models designed for infantry support rather than massed attack. The Polish army was much less adequately equipped; mechanization had been neglected in favor of horse-drawn equipment, and a sizable portion of defense funds had been wasted on an almost useless navy. The Poles possessed only about 200 modern tanks, and only a few antitank guns.

In the air as on the land, the Germans enjoyed a clear margin of superiority against any single enemy, though not against the combined strength of the Western powers. In absolute numbers, Germany possessed some 3600 planes (mostly first-line craft); Britain had 1500 first-line and 2000 reserve planes; France, slightly more than 1000 first-line planes. Poland had only 350 combat aircraft, some of which were obsolescent. But these raw figures provide little indication of relative air strength for the kind of war that was impending, nor do they allow for differences in quality. The German *Luftwaffe*, about evenly balanced as between fighters and light bombers, was designed for tactical action in support of the advancing ground forces. Anticipating a rapid campaign, the Germans assigned the bulk of their planes for immediate use, retaining only a small reserve for replacement or training purposes. Their operational strength was thus not far below their total strength. Although the quality of the German bombers was higher than that of their British and French equivalents, there were no heavy aircraft designed for long-range strategic bombing, nor did the Germans have any plans for such a strategic air offensive. German fighters, like their light bombers, were of high quality, and could be matched only by certain new British models just beginning to come off the production lines.

Both Britain and France were seriously handicapped by prewar decisions to alter their plans for aerial warfare or to substitute new aircraft models for outmoded ones. Throughout the interwar years, British planners had looked ahead to a war of attrition in which strategic bombing plus a sea blockade would be the decisive weapons. By 1937 it had become clear that the existing type of British light bomber could not carry out such a mission in central Europe, and that the Royal Air Force would have to build a new fleet of heavy four-motor bombers with longer cruising range and larger bomb capacity. But the cost of the program, and sharp controversy about its wisdom, caused severe cutbacks in the heavy bomber program. The emphasis was shifted toward fighters rather than bombers, on the theory that defense against a German bomber attack must now take top priority. If the *Luftwaffe* could be destroyed in the air over England (so ran the new argument), Britain could then resort to its traditional methods of warfare, with emphasis on sea power and the blockade. By the time war came, the new Spitfire and Hurricane fighters were beginning to come off the production lines. But Bomber Command was quite unprepared to embark on a major air offensive over Germany, both because it lacked heavy bombers and because it had not yet worked out the difficult tactical problems posed by a large-scale strategic offensive.

The French, whose air force had been the admiration of Europe a decade earlier, had fallen on evil days by 1939. Government officials realized by 1937 that French planes were dangerously outmoded, and reluctantly decided to begin the costly and time-consuming task of re-equipping the air arm. The process of factory retooling was further complicated by labor strife and political feuds; during 1938, production fell almost to zero. By the time war came, fighters were coming out of the factories at a rate of between two and three hundred monthly, though bomber production still lagged at about a dozen per month. The French bought some modern fighter planes in the United States, but their air force in September 1939 was in no condition to meet the Germans on anything like even terms.

It was only on the sea that the Western Allies enjoyed a heavy margin of superiority. By the Anglo-German naval agreement of 1935, Britain had agreed to let the Germans build up to a ceiling of 35 percent of British tonnage, and to parity in submarine strength. Until 1938 Hitler had avoided any significant naval expansion, partly because he clung to the hope of Anglo-German cooperation, partly because Britain's lead was simply too great to be matched. After Munich, however, Hitler had approved the so-called "Z-program" advocated by his admirals. It called for the construction of a large fleet of both submarines and fast, powerful surface ships designed for commerce-raiding; it would pose a serious challenge to Britain's command of the seas. The target date for completion of this program was 1944–1945; but in fact, its execution was suspended almost at once. The prospect of an early war forced a shift in priorities toward more submarines and the speedier completion of two partially finished battleships. In no other realm did Germany enter the 1939 war so underprepared. Germany possessed 3 pocket battleships, 2 old battleships, 2 battle cruisers, 5 light cruisers, 17 destroyers, and 56 submarines. The strength of the French navy alone was more than twice as great in most categories (except submarines), while Great Britain had 12 battleships and battle cruisers, 6 aircraft carriers, 35 fleet cruisers, 200 fleet or escort destroyers, and 57 submarines.

Behind the fighting forces proper, the material and human resources of the belligerents varied considerably, and helped shape different attitudes toward the war. The Germans, outnumbered by the combined populations of their enemies, deprived of access to certain essential raw materials, and easily cut off from the world by sea blockade, counted on their more highly developed organization to ensure a short war. The British and French, with potential resources at hand but with inadequate prior preparation for the demands of warfare, naturally hoped for a war of attrition, in which time would work in their favor. The Poles, possessed of few valuable assets save the quality of stubborn courage, hoped merely to hold on for six months until help from their Western Allies could offer relief.

Plans for conversion to a war footing had matured only in Germany, where a quasi-militarized system had been developed since 1933. Mobilization there involved far less confusion than in the Western nations, which were forced to improvise under pressure. In both France and Britain, a great many specialists and technicians volunteered or were called up for service, but soon had to be demobilized in order to prevent a breakdown in industrial production. A start toward civil defense planning, on the other hand, had been made in both Britain and France. Because the British had anticipated an immediate German air blitz on London and other cities, they had already drawn up detailed plans for the mass evacuation of women and children, and for the establishment of civil defense units to control fires and possible public hysteria. Some three million persons were evacuated from Greater London during the first few days of September; the process went off with remarkable efficiency. A much smaller evacuation of school children (only about thirty thousand in all) occurred in Paris, while almost the whole civilian population of Strasbourg was ordered to find its own way out of the city. In Germany and Poland, civil defense planning was almost nonexistent. Luckily, no nation needed it during the first phase of the war—except the unfortunate Poles.

Chapter Two

THE EXPANSION OF GERMAN POWER

I. THE DESTRUCTION OF POLAND

THE storm of fire and steel that struck the Poles during the first few days of September left that unhappy people stunned and shattered. At the end of ten days, the German mechanized spearheads had sliced through the Polish defenses all the way to Warsaw. Most of the inadequate Polish air force had been destroyed on the ground before it could even get into action; the fighter planes and Stuka dive bombers of the *Luftwaffe*, acting in tactical support of the advancing ground forces, disrupted Polish communications and spread terror and destruction from the skies. "The Germans," reported an American journalist, "are today crushing Poland like a soft-boiled egg."[1] In a desperate attempt to gain time, the Poles on September 14 transferred their government and military headquarters to the remote southeast, adjacent to the Rumanian frontier. But their last hopes vanished when on September 17 the Soviet armies suddenly struck from the east, and flooded across the plains almost unresisted. On the eighteenth, the Polish political and military leaders fled across the frontier into Rumania, hoping to direct resistance from that more sheltered spot; but they were immediately interned by the nervous Rumanian government, which feared to offend Hitler. Warsaw stubbornly held out for another ten days against battering artillery and dive-bomber attacks. By September 27, food supplies and ammunition were exhausted; the city was surrendered to the encircling Germans, and Poland lay prostrate.

The Soviet intervention surprised the Poles and their Western Allies, but not the Germans. By a secret protocol attached to the German-Soviet pact of August 23, the two powers had agreed that if Poland should undergo a "territorial-political transformation," the line between German and Soviet "spheres of interest" would be drawn along a series of rivers a hundred miles east of Warsaw. True, the protocol had not specified active Soviet participation in the process of "trans-

---

[1] O. D. Tolischus in the *New York Times,* Sept. 12, 1939.

forming" Poland. But the Kremlin was evidently startled by the speed of the German conquest, and thought it wise to ensure possession of its share of the spoils. Ten days later a revised German-Soviet agreement confirmed the secret protocol, and broadened the Soviet sphere of interest to include Lithuania as well as Latvia and Estonia. On October 6, Hitler, with Stalin's endorsement, called on the Western powers to accept the *fait accompli* and to meet the victors for a negotiated settlement of the remaining problems that obstructed a durable peace in Europe.

Probably neither Hitler nor Stalin expected the British and the French to respond to this peace appeal. Surely Stalin cannot have hoped for peace now; for if what he called the capitalist world had really set a high priority on destroying the Soviet Union, he could wish for nothing better than the continued division of the capitalist nations, and an eventual armed struggle in the west. Hitler, on the other hand, may have hoped that the Western powers might rise to his bait. Neither the British nor the French had provided any effective aid to their Polish ally, even in an effort to relieve the German pressure; the French confined themselves to a few border raids, the British to dropping leaflets over Germany. Perhaps this encouraged Hitler to believe that the West had entered the war only as a *pro forma* gesture required by existing commitments. Still, at the height of the Polish blitz Hitler had begun to talk privately of preparing an immediate attack on France as soon as Poland fell. On September 12, he confided this intention to his aide-de-camp, and on the twenty-seventh he informed his top military commanders that this second campaign would be launched without delay.

There were some in the west who welcomed Hitler's peace offer and eagerly pressed for its acceptance. In France, an influential minority of politicians had opposed the initial decision for war, and now hoped that their government's quixotic "mistake" could be corrected. In England, Chamberlain received almost nineteen hundred letters in three days, begging the government to stop the war. Indeed, Chamberlain feared that Hitler's peace offensive might prove to be a more effective psychological weapon than the air raids on London that were still expected. Fortunately for Chamberlain and Daladier (both of whom were determined not to withdraw from the war), Hitler's proposal was not seductively phrased or uttered, and it calmed few suspicions. Neither London nor Paris made any formal acknowledgment of Hitler's peace offer; and on October 9 the Fuehrer issued a secret directive for the preparation of an early offensive in the west. Germany's aim, he declared, was "to destroy the preponderance of the Western powers and to clear the way for the German people's expansion in Europe." He cautioned, however, that this aim must be revealed only "little by little, and accompanied by such propaganda correctives as are psychologically necessary."[2]

II. THE TWILIGHT WAR

Several tense weeks followed the abortive peace offer. As the Germans rapidly shifted the bulk of their forces from east to west, rumors spread that a massive German attack was imminent, and that it was likely to be launched before the rains and snows of winter could intervene. The French were particularly edgy; the highest permanent official in the foreign ministry considered it "98 percent certain" that two thousand Soviet bombers would be sent to join the *Luftwaffe* in a blitz of unprecedented horror.[3] The British were less inclined to take the threat seriously; they suspected that Hitler might prefer to strike through Rumania toward the Bosporus. In an effort to check such a drive to the southeast, the British endeavored to develop a neutral bloc in the Balkans, and redoubled their efforts to ensure Mussolini's continued neutrality. The French, on the other hand, were more inclined to favor military action in the eastern Mediterranean in order to divert some German manpower from the western front. As the weeks dragged on, both London and Paris began to suspect that the Germans had merely been conducting a war of nerves by spreading empty threats of an attack in the west. They were wrong; Hitler was not indulging either in mere bluff or in pure psychological warfare. In October, he had set November 12 for his attack; but bad weather forced a postponement, and a second D-day (January 17) also had to be canceled for the same reason. By mid-January it was clear that both armies would remain dug in for the duration of the winter. Impatient journalists seeking news began to complain of "the phony war," or of what some of them called the new doctrine of *Sitzkrieg*.

The focus of action meanwhile had shifted eastward. Stalin, looking

---

[2] H. A. Jacobsen, *Dokumente zur Vorgeschichte des Westfeldzug 1939-1940* (Goettingen, 1956), p. 6.

[3] Bullitt to Hull, Sept. 30, 1939. U.S. Department of State, *Foreign Relations of the United States 1939* (Washington, 1956), I, 459-60. The same official, Alexis Léger, added despairingly: "The game is lost. France stands alone against three dictatorships. Great Britain is not ready. The United States has not even changed the Neutrality Act. The democracies again are too late."

to the longer future, had begun immediately after Poland fell to but-
tress Soviet defenses in the small neighboring countries along the USSR's
western frontier. Mutual assistance pacts were forced on the small Baltic
states, and demands for similar pacts were made upon Finland, Rumania,
and Turkey. The Finns stubbornly resisted the Soviet demands, particularly those which would have established military and naval bases on
Finnish soil and would have ceded certain strategic territory to the USSR.
After almost two months of fruitless negotiation, the Kremlin at last sought
to break the stalemate by force; on November 30, Soviet armed forces
suddenly attacked Finland. Stalin evidently expected that an initial air
raid on Helsinki would terrorize the population, leaving the capital almost
undefended against the invading ground forces. But the expected triumphal parade turned into a bloody three-month war; the Finns, who could
muster only nine divisions against a Soviet force three times as large,
fought back with a doggedness that won the astonished admiration of the
world.

For a time the Western powers hoped that the "Winter War" might
cause serious strain between Germany and Russia; but that hope was
quickly extinguished by Hitler's hands-off policy. Meanwhile public
opinion in France and Britain, inspired largely by considerations of
sentiment, was beginning to press strongly for aid to the Finns. The
result was an embarrassing dilemma for the Western Allies. They
could scarcely provide the Finns with enough help to defeat the USSR;
and if they did send some assistance, they would risk involving themselves in outright war with the Soviet Union as well as with Germany.
The British, who had been quietly trying to improve their relations
with Moscow in the belief that the Soviet-German pact would eventually break down, were especially reluctant to tweak Stalin's beard.
The French, on the other hand, urgently favored an expedition to Finland, even though it might mean war with the USSR.[4] They proposed
to send help either by sea to Petsamo or overland across neutral Norway and Sweden.

At this point, the Finnish problem became entangled with another
Scandinavian issue: the supply of Swedish iron ore to German arms
factories. Germany's war machine depended heavily on imports of

---

[4] The top career official in the French foreign ministry, Alexis Léger, "expressed the
opinion that the British were entirely idiotic in believing that they could detach the
Russians from the Germans and that they could finally obtain the support of the Soviet
Union against Germany." Bullitt to Hull, Jan. 15, 1940, U.S. Department of State, *Foreign
Relations of the United States 1940* (Washington, 1958), I, 277.

iron ore, about 40 percent of which came from mines in the far north of Sweden. During the winter months, Swedish ore was shipped by rail to the ice-free Norwegian port of Narvik, whence it came by ship through Norwegian coastal waters to north German ports. During the summer, a much more protected route from the Swedish port of Luleå through the Baltic Sea was available to the Germans. Soon after the war began, First Lord of the Admiralty Winston Churchill had begun to campaign for sowing mines in Norwegian coastal waters, and perhaps in the port of Luleå as well, in order to choke off this vital flow. The Finnish war opened a larger possibility: someone suggested that troops to aid the Finns might land at Narvik and proceed across Norway and Sweden by rail, seizing the ore fields en route. The French leaped at this scheme; the British were sharply divided by it. Such a violation of the rights of small neutral nations troubled many British leaders, though Churchill argued in *Realpolitiker* fashion that "small nations must not tie our hands when we are fighting for their rights and freedom. . . . Humanity, rather than legality, must be our guide."[5]

After weeks of dithering, the Western Allies at last decided early in February 1940 to risk the larger plan: an expedition to Finland by way of Narvik and the ore fields. But the British insisted on two prior conditions: that the Finns make a formal appeal for aid, and that the Scandinavian neutrals grant transit rights across their territory. On the assumption that both conditions would be fulfilled, they began to assemble a Franco-British expeditionary force in Scotland. But in spite of Allied pressure, the Norwegian and Swedish governments flatly refused the right of transit; they were determined to cling to their neutrality, and were convinced that aid to Finland would be a futile gesture. By the end of February, the impatient Allies had virtually decided to land at Narvik and at other west coast ports even without Norwegian permission. Now, however, it was the Finns who balked their purpose. The Finns had reached the end of their endurance, and knew that their only recourse was to seek a settlement with the Russians. On March 12, as the Anglo-French expeditionary force was on the verge of embarking, news came from Helsinki that the Winter War was over. The Finns were forced to cede more territory than they would have lost by accepting the Russians' initial demands; they retained their independence, but emerged in an embittered mood. As for the Western powers, they had balanced precariously on the edge

[5] Winston Churchill, *The Second World War* (Boston, 1948–53), I, 547.

of an adventure that might have changed the whole course of the Second World War.

The fiasco of Western aid to Finland led almost at once to a cabinet crisis in Paris; Daladier fell, and was replaced by Paul Reynaud, a man of more vigor and determination. The Finnish failure also led to the revival of Churchill's scheme for mining Norwegian territorial waters. Late in March the Western Allies decided to act, in this case without seeking Norway's prior consent. They assumed that the Germans might retaliate by invading Scandinavia, but the British were blithely confident that their sea power would permit them to overwhelm any German landing force. Churchill had even asserted some weeks earlier that "we have more to gain than to lose by a German attack upon Sweden and Norway," and Chamberlain on April 4 added his classic remark that Hitler, by delaying so long, had "missed the bus." The Allied expeditionary force that had been assembled in Scotland was kept on the alert for action, but was to be used only in case the Germans should land first in Norway. On April 8, the British began to lay their mine fields. Twenty-four hours later, the operation was interrupted by a startling German coup—the lightning occupation of Oslo and five other Norwegian port cities ranging all the way to Narvik. For good measure, Denmark was taken over in a simultaneous action.

Hitler's new-style blitz had been in the making for three months. Ever since the fall of Poland, his naval advisers had been urging him to occupy Norway; they warned that Britain would eventually be tempted to intervene there, and argued that "losing Norway would be tantamount to losing the war." Furthermore, they coveted the western ports as an invaluable chain of U-boat bases from which to harass the British sea approaches. But Hitler was reluctant to divert strength from his intended blow against France. In January he finally ordered that plans be prepared, but a firm decision did not come until March 1, when the Fuehrer became convinced that the British really intended to land in Norway, and soon. His Scandinavian flank, he decided, would have to be safeguarded before risking the great offensive in the west. The German plan was remarkably ingenious and daring in both concept and execution. Small landing detachments of elite troops were crowded onto fast warships that might elude British surveillance. They were dispatched at the last possible moment, preceded by their equipment, which had been concealed in apparently innocent merchant vessels. Paratroop units were dropped on the key Norwegian airfields to coincide with the surprise landings; reinforcements were scheduled to follow in forty-eight hours. All went almost exactly as planned; every key point along the Norwegian coast was soon in German hands.

In Denmark, the take-over was almost bloodless; there were only thirteen Danish casualties. The Norwegians, on the other hand, resisted vigorously and called for British aid. There followed one of the most inglorious episodes of the war. Small British forces were landed in central Norway in an effort to recapture Trondheim, but German command of the air made their mission hopeless, and after two weeks they were evacuated. A combined force of British, French, and Polish troops was put ashore near Narvik with a view to cutting the iron ore route and preserving a free Norwegian enclave in the far north to which the king and government could retreat. But before it could take the town, word came of the launching of Hitler's attack on the Low Countries, and the Narvik operation became expendable. The town was finally captured late in May, only to be abandoned a week later. From the Allied point of view, the Norwegian venture had been a masterpiece of muddled improvisation. As a by-product of this failure, the Chamberlain government lost its grip on Parliament and the country, and was replaced on May 10 by a Churchill cabinet (even though, ironically, Churchill had been technically in charge of the Norwegian operation). In Paris too, grave dissension was racking the Reynaud cabinet, and a new governmental crisis was imminent. Hitler's western blow was struck at a moment when Western morale had fallen to its lowest ebb since the outbreak of war.

III. VICTORY IN THE WEST

During the winter of the twilight war, both sides speeded the expansion of their military power, though which side profited most from the respite would be hard to calculate. By May 1940, the Germans had massed 134 divisions on the western front. Confronting them were 94 French and 10 British divisions, which might be supplemented, if the Low Countries were invaded, by 22 Belgian and 8 Dutch divisions. In sheer numbers of men, therefore, the two sides were almost evenly matched; but the German troops were better trained and equipped, and their morale was higher. In tank strength, the Western Allies had a slight numerical advantage: about 2500 French and 700 British tanks to 2500 for the Germans. Here again, however, the Germans possessed an advantage in organization and experience; they had built up ten armored divisions compared to the Allies' three. In the air, the Germans possessed a decided margin. By May 1940 they had 3500 planes ready for use in a western campaign; the French had 800 in the battle area, the British approximately 400 stationed on the Continent (though some additional British aircraft would eventually be shifted from their British bases at the height of the battle).

Repeated rumors of a German invasion of the Low Countries during the winter months had impelled the British and French planners to try to anticipate such an event, and to seek Belgian and Dutch participation in shaping defense plans. Although the Belgians at times were tempted to engage in talks, they chose in the end to cling to the hope that Hitler would spare them, and resisted the Western appeals. The Dutch even more flatly refused to consider joint discussions. The Western Allies therefore developed their own plans for moving up to defense lines in Belgium; two alternative lines were envisaged, with the choice to be made if and when a German invasion came.

Franco-British staff talks over this issue were not always harmonious; but this was only one of several problems which raised the temperature of Franco-British relations and offset the outward appearance of mutual confidence between the Western Allies. These problems all clustered about a central question: how was the war to be fought, where, and by whom? To the French, it seemed increasingly evident that "perfidious Albion" had not changed its ways. The British, they complained privately, wanted to remain aloof from the nasty business of war, utilizing the traditional British weapons of sea blockade and economic pressure, relying on time to dull the enemy's claws, and depending on French soldiers to shed most of the necessary blood. The French resented Britain's insistence on keeping the bulk of its air force in the British Isles; they attributed unworthy motives to Britain's long hesitation to act in Norway and Finland.

This French irritation and distrust was reciprocated in high British quarters. The British soon concluded that the French were eager to open as many fighting fronts as possible, provided that all such fronts were a long way from France and that British naval and air power would have to bear the weight of the operations. The French insistence that more British planes be sent to the Continent, and that the entire Royal Air Force be used to attack a German invasion army, struck the British as quite unreasonable. British planners were not prepared to denude their island of aircraft at a time when Hitler might mount an air offensive against Britain rather than a ground offensive against France; and they considered it senseless to use their bombers against an advancing army rather than against Germany's industrial nerve center in the Ruhr. Through the winter and spring, the French steadily opposed the strategic bombing of German industry and communications for fear of reprisals against French cities; likewise, they rejected a British scheme to release floating mines from the French bank of the Rhine, on the ground that the Germans might retaliate against France. Six months of not very dignified squabbling over these and other issues left tempers frayed, and augured badly for the success of the common defense.

German planning, meanwhile, had undergone an important change during the winter. The original plan of attack, as developed for use in November 1939, bore some resemblance to the Schlieffen Plan of 1914. It placed the main striking force on the right wing of the German front, while farther south the German units would engage in a holding and diversionary operation. The mission of the right wing would be to drive across the Belgian plain into northern France, and to conquer a large block of territory along the Channel as a base for air attacks on Britain and an eventual drive on Paris. During the months of idleness, Hitler's attention was caught by a scheme advocated by General Erich von Manstein and others, and designed to make full use of Germany's powerful armored divisions. The main blow would be struck in the south rather than the north. Motorized infantry units, spearheaded by the panzer divisions with their heavy tanks and air support, would break through the hilly Ardennes region of southern Belgium, would rupture the French defense lines near Sedan, and would then make a right turn directly toward the Channel, in the rear of the main Franco-British armies. This daring maneuver was expected to disrupt Allied communications and to sow general confusion. The risk, of course, was that the French and British might improvise a counterattack that would pinch off and destroy the German armored spearhead.

For an adequate response to this kind of attack, the Western powers needed not only imaginative commanders but a flexible communications system and their own striking force of armored units that could move rapidly to the proper battleground. In the event, all of these things were to be found wanting. In May 1940 the French possessed two armored divisions, the British one; but the British unit had not yet crossed the Channel, and the French divisions were too newly-organized to be effective under fire. Most of the Allied tanks were still scattered in packets along the lines, attached to infantry divisions; they could not be converted into an effective "riot squad" on the spur of the moment. The French army's wireless communications system had been set up to operate behind the shield of an unbroken front; no emergency alternative had been prepared to cope with a major breakthrough. In retrospect, the French commander-in-chief expressed regret that his armies had possessed no supply of carrier pigeons! As for imaginative leadership at Allied headquarters, it was in distressingly short supply.

The attack began at last on May 10. In the north, a powerful German force drove into the Netherlands with devastating effect. Five days sufficed to knock out the Dutch army, which suffered heavy casualties before capitulating on May 15. To hasten the surrender, the *Luftwaffe* on May 14 wiped out the center of Rotterdam in the first major air blitz aimed at a city; forty thousand civilians died in the attack. Meanwhile in Belgium, a crack unit of highly trained German troops carried out a different kind of blitz by capturing the key to the Belgian defense system, the supposedly impregnable fortress of Eben Emael. On the thirteenth, the first German spearheads crossed the Meuse and drove straight on through the Ardennes hills toward Sedan.

The French and British forces at the outset of the attack had moved up into Belgium to assume their planned defensive positions. Before they had even reached those positions, disturbing news began to arrive of the progress of Kleist and Guderian's mechanized forces; but the Allied command was too rigid to improvise a new strategy quickly. By the time it awakened to the danger on May 16, Guderian had smashed through the French lines at Sedan and had pushed fifty miles beyond. At that point, he was ordered by German headquarters to stop and consolidate his forces. But the headstrong tank commander ignored the order; seeing his chance, he continued at full speed toward the Channel coast, driving a narrow wedge between the main Allied forces and their rear headquarters. By the evening of May 20, he had reached the sea at Abbeville.

The speed of this unorthodox threat produced near-chaos in the Allied camp. Liaison between the French and the British, as well as with the Belgian army, virtually broke down. Masses of civilian refugees began to clog the roads; rumors of treachery by fifth-column agents began to spread. On May 18 Premier Reynaud made a desperate effort to restore morale by removing commander-in-chief Maurice Gamelin in favor of Maxime Weygand, and by bringing Marshal Philippe Pétain into the cabinet as vice-premier. For a brief moment, it seemed that the Allies might regain the initiative; the French and British forces in northern France attempted to strike southward, with a view to severing Guderian's corridor. There was mild panic at Hitler's headquarters, where some members of the Fuehrer's entourage had been nervous about the whole risky operation from the outset. But the Allied move was not coordinated with an equivalent blow from the south, which might have changed the whole course of the battle. The Allied offensive bogged down, and on May 22 Guderian resumed his advance toward the main Channel ports of Boulogne and Dunkirk, threatening to cut off the last possible path of retreat for the Allied armies in the north and in Belgium.

Throughout these critical days, Premier Reynaud with growing desperation and anger pleaded with the British government to send more planes. Prime Minister Churchill vainly sought to explain that the R.A.F. was "in effect our Maginot Line." For a time, nevertheless, the British did reduce their home strength to thirty squadrons of fighters, far below the essential minimum required to defend the island, but by early June the bulk of Fighter Command had been pulled back to British bases. Already, on May 28, the Belgian king had ordered his armies to lay down their weapons, while the British government had authorized its commanding general in France, Lord Gort, to evacuate as many of his troops as possible from the beaches around Dunkirk. The eight-day naval operation that followed was astonishingly successful; 200,000 British and 130,000 French soldiers were taken off the beaches, though all their equipment was lost. While German dive bombers harassed the embarking troops, German tank forces along the perimeter of the Dunkirk beachhead failed to move in for the *coup de grâce*. A legend later materialized that Hitler had overruled his generals on this point, and had intentionally spared the escaping British in an effort to arrive at an early peace settlement with London. In fact, the German high command was sharply divided over the wisdom of risking its tanks in the difficult terrain around Dunkirk; Hitler took the side of the cautious faction, partly because he believed that the *Luftwaffe* could do the job alone. This error in judgment permitted the British to carry out a salvage operation of inestimable military and psychological importance.

The Germans, surprised at the extent of their success, lost no time in striking at the scattered remnants of the French army. On June 5 they began to drive westward and southward toward Paris and toward the unprotected back door to the Maginot Line. On June 11 the French government abandoned Paris for Tours, whence it shortly moved on to Bordeaux. Meanwhile, on June 10, Mussolini had leaped to the aid of the victor by declaring war on France and Britain. Until now, "Mussolini's position [had been] that of a turkey buzzard soaring and peering and hoping for something dead to eat."[6] That the Italian public was unenthusiastic about entering the war was well known to Mussolini; but he could no longer risk exclusion from the glory of victory and the partition of the spoils. "To make a people great," he told his son-in-law Count Ciano, "it is necessary to send them to battle even if you have to kick them in the pants. This is what I shall do."[7] But his armies were not ready to move until the twenty-first, by which time French resistance had virtually ceased. To the Duce's chagrin, the Italian attackers on the Alpine front were met by a stubborn French defense, and managed to penetrate barely a hundred yards onto French soil before the war in the west ended.

Ever since the French government left Paris, a defeatist faction had been pressing hard for an armistice. The British desperately sought to counter this mood by assurances that Britain would not give up the fight, and by a last-minute proposal that Britain and France be merged into a single state with common citizenship. The British, and some French leaders as well, hoped that some French troops and equipment might be ferried to North Africa, to be joined by the French navy and the French president and cabinet. These plans were frustrated when the cabinet, on June 16, voted to ask Germany for armistice terms. Premier Reynaud immediately resigned his post in favor of the aged war hero Marshal Philippe Pétain. The armistice was signed a week later (June 22) at Compiègne, in the same railway car that had been used for the German capitulation on November 11, 1918. Hitler's triumph, and revenge, were complete.

IV. DEFEAT IN THE SKIES

Ten months elapsed between the defeat of France and the next major land action of the German Wehrmacht. It was to be the longest interlude in almost six years of war. In part, it was the product of

[6] Bullitt to Hull, Jan. 25, 1940. U.S. Department of State Archives (740.0011 Eur. War 1939/1556).

[7] Muggeridge, *Ciano's Diary*, p. 236.

Hitler's hesitations; where did his destiny beckon him to turn next? In part, it was the result of Britain's unexpected stubbornness in continuing an apparently hopeless fight.

There can be no doubt that after the fall of France Hitler expected an early internal crisis in London, to be followed by prompt capitulation. He had no plan for a Channel crossing, and it was not until July 2 that he ordered his military staff to begin drafting such a plan. When Mussolini urged prompt action and eagerly volunteered to send planes and men to share in the next triumph, Hitler politely put him off. But as the weeks passed without the expected overthrow of the Churchill government—as the British instead gave every evidence of intensifying their war effort—Hitler reluctantly informed his commanders-in-chief on July 16 that he had decided "to prepare, and if necessary to carry out" a landing in the British Isles. Probably he still continued to hope that in the end a Channel crossing would be unnecessary. Some of his advisers sensed that his heart was not in the enterprise, and that he clung to the belief, strongly expressed in *Mein Kampf*, that Britain and Germany might yet collaborate as allies. But whether willingly or not, Hitler had to face up to the hard fact of British resistance, and to plan accordingly.

His military and naval advisers, however, were sharply at odds over how to carry out the operation. Admiral Raeder much preferred a blockade to an attempt at invasion, and insisted that any landing force would have to be concentrated at a single point on the south coast where impregnable air cover could be provided. Army leaders argued that the invasion force must be put ashore at widely separated beaches along the southern coast, in order to scatter and thin out the defenders. But the army and the navy were agreed on one point: that air superiority was an absolute prerequisite for the operation. Such superiority the commander of the *Luftwaffe*, Marshal Hermann Goering, confidently promised to provide. Goering's certainty that air power could win campaigns even without help from the other arms had been reinforced by the *Luftwaffe*'s easy triumphs in Poland and France. He knew that the R.A.F. was heavily outnumbered; he was sure that British morale was ready to crack. Four days of concentrated attacks, he promised, would destroy the air defenses of southern England; four weeks of more generalized bombing would create havoc, and would open the way to victory with only a token landing. Early in August Hitler adopted Goering's plan, and on the thirteenth the

Battle of Britain—the greatest air battle in human history—began. The army had meanwhile assembled thirteen picked divisions at French Channel ports, while Raeder began to collect the necessary ships and landing barges for Operation Sea Lion. SS officials assigned to police the conquered island drew up lists of British notables to be imprisoned, and plans for deporting certain categories of males to the Continent. Goebbels' propaganda services prepared two months of radio programs to be broadcast over British stations after the victory.

By now the British had emerged from the relative lethargy in which the country had slumbered during the twilight war. Heretofore, in Bruce Lockhart's harsh phrase, they had seemed to be suffering from "gangrene of the soul."[8] The French defeat, the Dunkirk miracle, and the inspiring leadership of Churchill combined to transform the nation's mood. If any Britons believed at this point that it would be wise to give up the fight, they were not to be found in high office. Churchill later recalled with some pride that the question of fighting on alone was not even put on the War Cabinet's agenda in 1940. There was much—indeed, almost everything—still to be done. On the morrow of Dunkirk, the island stood virtually stripped of effective land defenses. The Continental disaster had left the army with barely enough modern equipment for two divisions. Coastal defense works were almost nonexistent. Fields near the coast contained no obstacles against glider landings. One Oxford undergraduate, newly commissioned a lieutenant after a hasty training course, received as his first assignment the defense of Southampton, for which purpose he was given sixty men and a bus in which to transport them to the point of enemy landing. Some of these shortcomings were corrected during the summer, but by August the British still could rely on little save the Royal Navy and a barely adequate Fighter Command. The Germans had 1200 bombers and approximately 1000 fighters in France and the Low Countries; Britain's first-line fighter strength stood at only 900 planes. Besides, the Germans were now flying from airfields just across the Channel rather than from the more distant German airports.

Against these seemingly overwhelming odds, the R.A.F. enjoyed a few advantages of its own. Its newest fighter planes—the Spitfires and Hurricanes—were faster and more heavily armed than any *Luftwaffe* plane except the short-range Messerschmitt-109, which could operate only in the area south of London. British pilots were flying almost di-

[8] Robert Bruce Lockhart, *Comes the Reckoning* (London, 1947), p. 72.

rectly over their own bases, and had to waste no time and fuel getting to the scene of action. The R.A.F.'s radar screen provided early warning, and its tested radio ground-control system permitted the most efficient use of British planes. Furthermore, the Germans' great numerical advantage was less fearsome than it seemed. The German bombers were slow and vulnerable, and required constant protection from the *Luftwaffe's* fighter force. There were not enough ME-109's to support more than 300–400 bombers on any given day. The British, on the other hand, could put 600 modern fighters into the air, and might thus be able to counter the *Luftwaffe's* numerical advantage—especially if the Germans were to dissipate that advantage by serious blunders.

Thanks to Goering's arrogance and amateurish interference, the Germans contributed the necessary blunders. Goering's four-day attempt in mid-August to destroy British air defenses in the south failed, in part because the British refused to commit all their fighters to the struggle there, in part because the Germans scattered their energies by hitting at a variety of targets. During late August and early September the *Luftwaffe* switched to a concentrated effort to knock out Britain's fighter force. The strategy almost succeeded; R.A.F. fighter bases were badly shot up, and British losses (especially of pilots) reached the danger point. Another week or ten days of sustained attacks on the fighter bases might have driven the R.A.F. out of the air. But at this moment of supreme crisis, Goering shifted back to unessential targets: aircraft factories (whose destruction could not affect the immediate battle) and the city of London (whose magnetic attraction Goering could not resist). Berlin had been raided late in August by the R.A.F., in retaliation for German bombs dropped accidentally on London on the night of August 24–25. Hitler, furious at this British action, publicly threatened on September 4 to "exterminate British cities." On the seventh, round-the-clock attacks on London began, providing Fighter Command's bases with welcome relief. "Like an indestructible sponge, [London] absorbed punishment and diverted what might have been the death blow."[9]

Although British losses were heavy, so were those of the *Luftwaffe;* and Hitler repeatedly postponed a final decision on a Channel crossing until victory in the air had been assured. On September 15, in a supreme effort, the *Luftwaffe* swarmed over London in massive force;

[9] D. Wood and D. Dempster, *The Narrow Margin* (London, 1961), p. 116.

and at the end of the day, the British triumphantly announced that 185 German planes had been shot down. The toll was in fact only 60; but that was enough to decide the issue for 1940. On the seventeenth, Hitler postponed Operation Sea Lion until further notice; a day later, he ordered the dispersal of the invasion fleet in order to avert further damage by British air and naval attacks. The Battle of Britain had been won; it marked "the triumph of foresight and organization over improvisation and muddled thinking."[10]

V. THE RESHAPING OF GERMAN STRATEGY

Balked in his designs for the first time since the war began, Hitler gave no clear indication of his future course. His naval advisers assumed (and Hitler did nothing to disabuse them) that Sea Lion would be revived with the return of good weather in the spring. The *Luftwaffe* continued to blast away at British cities in destructive night raids that continued from September 1940 until May 1941, and that seemed to be designed to wear down British resistance. But already, events in eastern Europe and the Mediterranean had begun to divert Hitler's attention to other possible theaters of action. The relatively quiet months of autumn and winter 1940–1941 gave Hitler a chance to savor his new role as master of Europe, and provided him time to weigh alternative strategies. It was an opportunity wasted; the record suggests not careful planning, but a tendency to drift, to improvise and to rely in the end on impulse.

Immediately after the fall of France, the alarmed Russians had begun to take their own precautions. Stalin sent troops into Estonia, Latvia, and Lithuania, and announced that the three Baltic republics had been annexed to the USSR. On his southern flank, he forced Rumania to hand over the two border provinces of Bessarabia and northern Bukovina. His successful ultimatum there aroused other appetites as well. Rumania's neighbors, Bulgaria and Hungary, thought they saw their chance to despoil the Rumanians of long-coveted territory. But the threat of war in the lower Danube led Hitler to intervene; for an upheaval there might have offered Stalin an excuse to occupy Rumania and to seize the oil fields so essential for the German armed forces. On August 30 Hitler (and Mussolini *pro forma*) dictated the so-called Vienna Award which forced Rumania to hand over half the province of Transylvania to Hungary. In the wake of these

[10] B. Collier, *The Battle of Britain* (London, 1962), p. 23.

humiliations King Carol abdicated, and Rumania under a new strong man, General Ion Antonescu, slipped completely into the German orbit.

Stalin meanwhile had done his best to convince Hitler of his continued loyal adherence to the 1939 pact of friendship. To Churchill's new ambassador, Sir Stafford Cripps, who had been sent to Moscow in an effort to detach the USSR from Germany, Stalin privately explained that he could not afford to change his policy for fear of inviting a German attack. But the Fuehrer was not appeased by Stalin's caution and expressions of good will. Late in July 1940, just as the Battle of Britain was about to begin, Hitler told his military staff that he had decided to make war on the USSR as soon as the strategic position should be favorable; and during the late summer and fall he began to move troops from France to the east. Although his initial impulse had been to attack in the autumn of 1940, he quickly realized that more time would be needed to prepare, and therefore postponed a firm decision on the date of the operation.

While the army general staff busied itself with drafting an invasion plan, some of Hitler's advisers (e.g., Admiral Raeder and General Guderian) were attempting to persuade him to shift his attention to the Mediterranean. There, they believed, was Britain's weakest point; and there lay a possible route to the Middle East and even into southern Russia. Mussolini was already massing an army of some 300,000 men in Libya for an attack on the small British garrison in Egypt. German support to the Italian army would ensure the capture of the Suez Canal and a clear road eastward; a German blow at Gibraltar would pinch off the western end of the Mediterranean and would lead to Axis control of all North Africa and west Africa. Hitler apparently toyed with the idea, but adapted it to fit his own inclinations. He was not prepared to make a major investment of German power in the Mediterranean; the magnetic attraction of *Lebensraum* in the east was too great. But he was willing to send some aid to Libya, and to see what could be done about persuading Spain and Vichy France to join his crusade, so that they (along with the Italians) might take on the task of driving the British out of the Mediterranean and North Africa.

Late in October, Hitler made the long journey to Hendaye on the French-Spanish border for a conversation with General Francisco Franco. Hitler proposed a joint attack on Gibraltar in January 1941, with the Germans providing some technical aid and the Spanish providing most of the troops. But Franco, who in June 1940 had been eager to enter the war, had grown more wary since Britain refused to collapse. His price for participating in Hitler's scheme was high: he demanded French Morocco and part of Algeria as his share of the spoils. Furthermore, he expressed disagreeable doubts about Germany's ability or willingness to provide all the necessary aid. Hitler, unaccustomed to such arrogance from the spokesmen of lesser nations, later told Mussolini that rather than repeat the Hendaye conversations "he would prefer to have three or four teeth taken out."[11] En route home, Hitler stopped at Montoire for an interview with Marshal Philippe Pétain and Pierre Laval. This conversation went more smoothly; the French leaders assured the Fuehrer of their warm desire to collaborate with Germany, and a vaguely-worded agreement was reached expressing France's "interest in seeing Britain defeated as soon as possible." Laval was evidently encouraged to hope that Hitler might be prepared to make France his favorite ally in Axis Europe, replacing Italy in that role; and later apologists for both Pétain and Laval were to claim that the Vichy leaders had won a great diplomatic victory at Montoire by dissuading Hitler from undertaking a major German-Spanish operation in the Mediterranean. In fact, the Montoire conference produced no measurable results; France did not re-enter the war, and there is no evidence whatsoever that Hitler changed his Mediterranean plans because of Pétain's or Laval's blandishments.

Shortly after Hitler's fruitless journey to Hendaye and Montoire, he received another visitor in Berlin: Soviet Foreign Minister Vyacheslav Molotov. The Kremlin for some time had been expressing nervous concern at German activities in Rumania and Finland and at the content and purpose of the new Tripartite Pact between Germany, Italy, and Japan signed in September.[12] During this conference, Hitler and his foreign minister Ribbentrop proposed to associate the USSR with the tripartite powers through mutual guarantees to respect each party's natural sphere of interest in the world. The Soviet sphere, according to this proposed agreement, would lie "in the direction of the Indian Ocean." Not only was this phraseology vague, but it clearly implied that the USSR would have to leave Europe to the Axis powers. Molo-

[11] M. Muggeridge (ed.), *Ciano's Diplomatic Papers* (London, 1948), p. 402.
[12] Hitler's purpose in negotiating the Tripartite Pact seems to have been to strengthen his tie with the Japanese and to encourage the isolationist element in the United States.

tov entered strong objections before returning to Moscow to report. Nevertheless, the Kremlin on November 25 expressed its willingness to sign the pact, provided that the Soviet sphere of interest were more sharply defined and extended to include bases in Bulgaria and Turkey, an end to German activities in Finland, and certain rights in the Far East. The Soviet counterproposal drew no reply from Berlin. Instead, Hitler on December 18 secretly ordered his Wehrmacht planners to be ready by May 15, 1941 "to crush Soviet Russia in a quick campaign even before the end of the war against England." Operation Barbarossa, Hitler's oldest dream of conquest, thus moved from the preliminary into the final planning stage.

The chronological sequence of events might make it seem that Hitler's decision to act was triggered by Soviet quibbling about the terms of the pact proposed in November. It is doubtful, however, that Hitler intended that offer seriously. A long-term agreement with the Kremlin ran counter to all of the Fuehrer's deepest prejudices, and could not be harmonized with Hitler's repeated expressions of intent since July 1940. Probably the proposed sphere-of-influence arrangement was designed as a smoke screen behind which to prepare Operation Barbarossa. Neither does the record support Hitler's later explanation, accepted by some historians, that the attack on Russia was a preventive war made necessary by the USSR's massive military buildup and Stalin's alleged intention to strike at Germany in 1942. That Stalin desperately sought to avoid a confrontation is quite clear; that he fulfilled his commitments under the 1939 pact and later trade agreements is equally plain. Hitler had convinced himself that the quickest way to London lay through Moscow; that if the British were deprived of the hope of eventual Soviet intervention, their will to fight on would crumble. And, deeper still, he was driven by a primitive urge to settle once and for all with what he once had called "that degenerate Jewish sponge-fungus, Marxist Russia."

While Hitler's plans were thus taking firm shape, his attention was partially diverted by events in the Mediterranean and the Balkans. In mid-September the Italian army in Libya had attacked into Egypt, and had driven the outmanned British forces back sixty miles before being checked at a well-fortified defense line. Mussolini was so elated that he decided to launch a second campaign: an invasion of Greece. Part of his purpose was revealed in his private comment to his son-in-law, Count Ciano: "Hitler always faces me with a *fait accompli*. This time I am going to pay him back in his own coin. He will find out from the newspapers that I have occupied Greece."[13] On October 28 his armies based in Albania struck into the Greek hill country. The Greek army's response was startling; the invaders were held at the frontier, and even thrown back into Albania at some points.

The British, who were bound by Chamberlain's 1939 guarantee to Greece, responded to Greek appeals for aid, even though they were hard pressed at home and in Egypt. They occupied the island of Crete, sent some aircraft to the Greek mainland, and eventually (in March 1941) dispatched a sizable expeditionary force to fight alongside the Greeks. Adding to Mussolini's misery, in mid-December a small British mechanized force in Egypt suddenly struck back at the Italian invaders, who retreated in a demoralized rout. By the time the front was stabilized in February 1941, the British had driven halfway across Libya and had captured 130,000 prisoners.

A chastened Mussolini swallowed his pride and agreed to accept the German reinforcements which he had until now refused to consider. In February Hitler sent General Erwin Rommel with a German panzer division and a few aircraft to Libya, where British supply lines were now badly stretched across five hundred miles of coastal desert. By April Rommel was ready for his countermove; within two weeks he had driven the British all the way back to the Egyptian frontier, where the accordion-like front was stabilized once more. But Hitler would not consider sending further reinforcements that might have led to the rapid conquest of Cairo and the Suez. The great adventure in Russia was all-important now.

Before Barbarossa could be launched, however, it was essential to remove the threat to the German flank caused by Mussolini's fiasco in the Balkans. In December 1940 Hitler ordered the Wehrmacht to prepare a powerful blow across Bulgaria and Yugoslavia into Greece as soon as good weather returned. Heavy pressure was put on the two Balkan countries to permit the transit of German troops, and both eventually capitulated. But in Belgrade, news of their government's craven concession outraged a group of Yugoslav army officers who, in late March 1941, forced the resignation of the cabinet and repudiated the agreement with Germany. Retribution followed swiftly; the enraged Hitler massed his troops along the northern and eastern frontiers of Yugoslavia, and attacked in force on April 6. In eleven days—

[13] Muggeridge (ed.), *Ciano's Diary*, p. 297.

the most rapid blitz action of the war—all organized resistance was broken. A week later the Greeks capitulated, and the British troops there were hastily evacuated. The island of Crete soon fell to a spectacular airborne attack, the first of its kind in history. But this new evidence of Germany's awesome military power cost Hitler a six-week delay in his larger plan, for his tanks and planes required overhaul after the Balkan diversion. When the Russian winter descended some months later, the Germans would have reason to regret that they had lost the use of those favorable weeks in the spring.

VI. VICTORY IN THE EAST

In planning Operation Barbarossa, Hitler had encountered only mild doubts on the part of his military command. The blitzkrieg technique had succeeded so remarkably to date that the skeptics now hesitated to speak out. Still, there were some who sensed that in Russia, with its almost infinite space in which to recoil, a knockout blow might be harder to deliver. Old-line army officers grumbled silently, and even suggested that it would be wise to plan an invasion by stages: an initial drive, followed by a stabilization of the lines during the winter, and then a renewed advance when good weather returned. Hitler, however, brushed aside these reservations, which in any case were not advanced with much vigor. He insisted that the Russian war could be won within three months by driving a series of mechanized spearheads deep into the country and pinching off the bulk of the defending forces for easy capture or destruction. Furthermore, he declared, his intimate knowledge of the Soviet political scene assured him that after the initial defeats, a violent revolution would sweep the men in the Kremlin out of power. It was likely too, he predicted, that the Japanese would seize their chance to strike into Siberia and would thus destroy the last hope of Soviet resistance. There was no need, therefore, to lay plans for a winter campaign, or even to lay up a store of winter equipment and clothing.

Not every doubt was quelled by these arguments, but no responsible German military leader was prepared to challenge the Fuehrer. The tradition of unquestioning obedience was too strong, and the reluctant admiration for Hitler's intuitive judgments too deep. Nor was there much vocal protest in the armed forces at Hitler's directives on the conduct of the war in the east: that Soviet political officials and army commissars should be liquidated on capture, and that "collective measures of force" might be carried out against the civilian population as reprisals against "malicious attacks." By June 22, the most powerful striking force ever assembled in Europe stood poised along the Soviet frontier: approximately four million men, thirty-three hundred tanks, five thousand aircraft. Yet even Hitler's self-assurance faltered for a moment as he confronted his self-chosen destiny: the vast Russian plains, defended by an army that outnumbered his own in men, tanks, and aircraft. On the evening before the attack, he admitted to a strange sense that he was "pushing open the door into a dark room without knowing what lies beyond it."[14]

For the first few weeks, it seemed that Hitler's moment of doubt had been unjustified. The Soviet frontier forces, taken by surprise, were decimated; two thousand planes were destroyed on the ground during the first forty-eight hours; the Germans intercepted a plaintive wireless signal from one Russian unit to its headquarters: "We are being fired on. What shall we do?"[15] Hitler's mechanized units raced eastward at full speed, turning at intervals to join in vast pincers movements. By mid-July, the Germans had captured Smolensk, two-thirds of the way to Moscow, and had taken more than a million prisoners. All was proceeding on schedule, save that Soviet resistance had not collapsed and revolution had not broken out in Moscow.

Hitler's top commanders now urged an immediate all-out drive toward the capital, where the Russians would doubtless mass their remaining reserves. A sharp controversy ensued; Hitler insisted that the armored divisions be diverted north toward Leningrad and south into the Ukraine, in order to bolster the German drives there. His will prevailed against an almost solid front of military advisers; and the stunning sequence of successes continued. The northern armies now drove all the way into the suburbs of Leningrad, and virtually surrounded the city. The reinforced southern armies carried out a vast encircling maneuver in the Kiev region, trapping another 600,000 Soviet troops before they could escape to the east. The triumph at Kiev, Hitler boasted, constituted the greatest victory in the history of the world; and he claimed full credit for it, since the strategy had been forced on his reluctant generals by the sheer power of his will and his genius.

[14] H. Heiber, *Adolf Hitler* (London, 1962), p. 160.
[15] J. Erickson, *The Soviet High Command* (London, 1962), p. 587. Headquarters responded, "You must be insane. And why is your signal not in code?"

After the fall of Kiev on September 19, Hitler rapidly shifted his panzer divisions back to the central front for the final assault on Moscow. It was launched on the last day of September, and again the German advance was dazzling. The Soviet command expected no major German offensive so late in the year, and was taken by surprise. Within ten days another great trapping maneuver caught two-thirds of a million additional prisoners, and the road to Moscow seemed open. Hitler publicly announced that the Red Army had been destroyed; he ordered immediate steps to demobilize part of the German army, and directed that when Moscow fell, the Kremlin should be blown up as a symbolic gesture.

A brief moment of panic ensued in Moscow. For three months now, disaster had piled on disaster. Preparations to meet an attack at the frontier had been totally inadequate; Stalin, warned repeatedly by British and American intelligence and by his own agents that Hitler was about to strike, had refused until the end to believe these warnings, and for four hours after the invasion had even denied his armies the right to return German fire. No plans whatsoever had been made for a strategic withdrawal to take advantage of Russia's great resource—space. The early weeks of the war glaringly revealed the near-fatal effects of the great army purge of 1937–1938; the ranks of field-grade officers had been decimated and most of the political generals proved to be incompetent. Three months after the invasion began, the Soviet armies had lost some 2.5 million men (of a total of 4.5 million) killed, wounded, or captured, and had seen their tank force reduced from 15,000 to 700. Some Soviet officers were shot after the initial rout, and the first hesitant steps were taken to substitute able professionals for the political generals. Georgi Zhukov, for example, was made commander of the western front on October 10.

In Moscow the approach of the Germans, and the evacuation of many government offices to Kuibyshev, produced a real breakdown of morale. For three days beginning on October 16, there was a mass flight from the city, and total collapse seemed imminent. On the nineteenth, however, the government declared a state of siege, and order was quickly restored. Rumors that Stalin had fled proved untrue; he remained in the capital and shared in directing the city's defense. Civilians were mobilized by the thousand to construct earthworks in the suburbs. But more important still was the arrival of fresh troops from the Soviet Far East. At first, Stalin had maintained a large force there to meet a possible Japanese attack; but on the basis of information about Japanese plans sent by his remarkable secret agent in Tokyo, Richard Sorge, he felt it safe to risk a gradual denuding of the Far Eastern province. The flow of troops began in summer and was speeded in the autumn; by November, about twenty divisions from the Far East had arrived in the Moscow area.

The German attackers meanwhile were near exhaustion from their long-sustained effort. Their dead and wounded approached 25 percent of their initial force, and the proportion of tanks out of action was even higher. Icy rains followed by sub-freezing temperatures were beginning to hamper operations. In mid-November some members of the army high command began to press for suspension of the offensive until spring, and the withdrawal of advance units to defensible winter lines. But Hitler would have none of this, and insisted on a final effort. It was met just north and south of Moscow by a powerful Soviet counterblow (December 5–6) that was made even more effective by a drop in temperature to thirty below zero. The fresh divisions from Siberia were the decisive factor; they smashed deep into the German lines at several points. Hitler on December 8 reluctantly ordered his armies to go on the defensive, but to refuse retreat anywhere along the line. Units that were bypassed were ordered to organize "hedgehog" defenses, and were promised air supply so long as they could hold out. Marshal von Brauchitsch promptly resigned as commander-in-chief of the army, and was replaced by the most eminent of German strategists, Hitler himself. Other dismissals (von Rundstedt, von Bock, Guderian) preceded or followed Brauchitsch's fall, beheading the army of its top professional commanders. Hitler's no-retreat order was later justified by the argument that it saved the German army from the kind of disintegration that had destroyed Napoleon's forces in Russia when they chose to retreat from Moscow. Still, it is doubtful that morale in the German armed forces was fragile enough to produce that kind of disintegration. And the "hedgehog" policy proved costly to the Germans both in men (through illness and frostbite) and in aircraft (lost in the airlift operation).

Hitler nevertheless remained confident that 1942 would bring him final victory in the east. Soviet losses had been vastly greater than those of Germany so far, and a high proportion of the USSR's best agricultural land and most productive industry lay under German occupation. Furthermore, Hitler's hopes were reinforced by the spread of the war from Europe to the Pacific, where Japan's surprise attack on Pearl Harbor (December 7, 1941) seemed likely to dry up the flow of United States aid to the British and the Russians.

Japan's sudden entry into the war was in no sense the response of a loyal Axis partner to Hitler's appeals or advice. Rather, it was the product of tension between Japan and the United States that had been building up since 1937, when Japanese armies invaded and occupied a large part of north China. The Americans had stubbornly insisted that the Japanese evacuate China, and had placed an embargo on the sale of certain essential war materials to Japan. In Tokyo, an expansionist faction in the government and the armed forces pressed strongly for a showdown, and from 1940 onward its spokesmen argued that the war in Europe offered Japan an unparalleled opportunity. When Hitler invaded Russia, the war party faced a choice between striking into Siberia or driving south toward the vital raw materials of southeast Asia and Indonesia. Although Hitler would have preferred the first alternative, the Japanese military and naval faction found the second much more tempting. The Pearl Harbor scheme, devised in 1941 by Admiral Yamamoto, was designed to knock out American striking power in the Pacific so that conquest in southeast Asia could proceed at leisure.

Yamamoto's plan went off with astonishing success, thanks to a combination of careful planning, sheer luck, and American negligence. On the day after Pearl Harbor, Japanese troops went ashore in Malaya; two days later, in the Philippines; on December 17, in Sarawak. For the British and the Americans, calamity piled on calamity. By mid-February 1942, the Japanese had fought their way down the Malay peninsula to the almost undefended back door of Singapore, whose forts had been constructed to face an attack from the sea. The British garrison of 85,000 men, cut off from reinforcements and food supplies, surrendered on February 15 in what Churchill was later to call "the worst disaster and largest capitulation of British history." In April and May, as the last American resistance ended in the Philippines, the triumphant Japanese undertook to gamble for even higher stakes; they decided to move on the Aleutians, on Midway Island in the central Pacific, and on the island chain just north of Australia. At the same time a strong Japanese fleet raided Ceylon, and it began to seem that India itself might be in mortal danger. Most of the British fleet in the Indian Ocean was pulled back to bases in east Africa.

Heartened by the news from the Pacific, Hitler pushed ahead with his plan for a clinching blow at the USSR in 1942. By spring, German and satellite reinforcements had rebuilt the Axis armies in the east to almost the level of June 1941. For the Germans, the question was not whether to strike but where to strike. The strongest Soviet units guarded Moscow, and the German high command favored a strategy of grappling with them at once on the theory that wars are won by destroying the enemy's armed forces. But Hitler chose instead to aim at economic and political targets; he planned to direct his main thrust toward the Caucasus, in an effort to seize the oil fields there and to deny that essential resource to the Russians. A secondary blow would be dealt in the north at Leningrad, which had been virtually surrounded by the Germans since late 1941, and which had lost at least 600,000 of its inhabitants by starvation during the winter.

The new offensive, delayed by an abortive Soviet attack in the Kharkov region, was finally launched late in June. As in 1941, the initial successes even exceeded the Fuehrer's expectations. Only three weeks were needed to bring the Germans to the northern gateway to the Caucasus (Rostov, at the mouth of the Don); and on August 9 they captured the first of the Caucasian oil fields. Farther north in the Ukraine, the Wehrmacht was meeting somewhat stiffer resistance, but was crunching forward with unrelenting power. Hitler was strengthened in his conviction that the Soviet army's terrible losses in 1941 had left it little resilience, and that a few more hammer blows would bring complete collapse. He was not concerned at the fact that few Soviet prisoners were falling into German hands this year; the Soviet high command (and Stalin) had learned the painful lesson that timely withdrawal was wiser than the old policy of stand-and-fight. So confident was Hitler that he began to divert forces from the south; two panzer divisions were sent to western Europe, and the bulk of one entire army to reinforce the siege of Leningrad.

Encouraging news also reached German headquarters from the Libyan theater. During the previous winter, Rommel had suffered a severe setback when the British struck at his overextended positions along the Egyptian border and drove the Axis forces back several hundred miles. Hitler had immediately bolstered Rommel by sending an entire air corps from the Russian front. Late in May 1942, just as the German armies in southern Russia were preparing their great new offensive, Rommel returned to the attack in Libya. A furious ten-day fight ended in a clean breakthrough and a near-collapse of British resistance. Tobruk fell to the Axis on June 21, and the remnants of the British and Commonwealth forces retreated across the Egyptian frontier. Rommel, promoted to field marshal, persuaded Hitler to let him pursue the British without reprieve; he promised the imminent fall of Cairo and the Suez Canal, and talked of pushing on into the Middle East. Hitler's more cautious advisers favored a delay to permit the overhaul of Rommel's tanks, only a handful of which were still fit for action. They also insisted that the first priority must be a long-planned knockout blow at Malta, which had been dispatching submarines and aircraft to harass Axis convoys crossing the Mediterranean. Mussolini strongly favored the Malta operation, but was overruled by Hitler. "Destiny," wrote the Fuehrer enthusiastically, "has offered us a chance which will never be repeated. . . . The main military objective must be, in my opinion, to exploit it as totally and rapidly as possible. . . . Order operations to be continued until the British forces are completely annihilated. . . . The goddess of fortune passes only once close to warriors in battle. Anyone who does not grasp her at that moment can very often never touch her again."[16] Mussolini, swept away by Hitler's rhetoric, concurred; he crossed to Libya in person, and prepared for his triumphal entry into Cairo. While the German forces in southern Russia delivered the final hammer blows at the Red army, and beleaguered Leningrad seemed about to succumb at last, Rommel's armored units drove across the frontier into Egypt.

Only in the Pacific were there the first ominous signs of a possible shift in the fortunes of war. Japan's risky attempt to push out the perimeter of conquest had run up against the obstacle of resurgent American naval power. Early in June 1942, the American fleet had turned back a strong Japanese striking force near Midway Island, and had dealt a crippling blow to Japan's carrier strength. In August, the Japanese invaders of Guadalcanal Island in the Solomons chain (just north of Australia) found themselves confronted by a force of American marines that checked, for the first time, their southward advance. But these setbacks in the Pacific appeared unlikely to influence the outcome of the struggle in Europe. Everywhere in the European and North African theaters of war, as harvest time approached, victory seemed to be within easy reach of the Axis dictators.

[16] F. W. Deakin, *The Brutal Friendship* (New York, 1966), I, 21.

Chapter Three

THE BROADENING SCOPE OF WAR:
THE ECONOMIC DIMENSION

I. GERMANY: THE ECONOMICS OF BLITZKRIEG

"Modern warfare," Adolf Hitler once asserted, "is above all economic warfare, and the demands of economic warfare must be given priority."[1] The remark was a shrewd one; for the war of 1914–1918, the first of the modern industrialized wars, had proved how outmoded was the traditional concept of war as a simple conflict between rival armed forces. Since the First World War, no government could any longer ignore the need for imposing rigid and comprehensive controls over virtually every aspect of economic life, and for reorienting production toward goals determined by the state. Nor could any government ignore the potentialities of economic warfare in its more active and aggressive form, as a technique for undermining the enemy's military strength and will to resist. During the earlier war, the European nations had arrived at such conclusions gradually, reluctantly, by a process of improvisation. In 1939 they could draw on that earlier experience to move much more rapidly; and thanks to the increased sophistication of economic science (particularly after the shocks and experiments of the 1930's), they could use economic devices much more efficiently.

At the outset, the Germans seemed to enjoy a marked advantage in the economic as in the strictly military sphere, for Hitler had already instituted extensive state control of peacetime economic life, and had converted part of German industry to armaments production. The Western Allies, on the other hand, still possessed relatively liberal economic systems, and had been late in tooling up for rearmament. Yet the test of protracted war was to demonstrate the greater adaptability of the Western nations—and, perhaps, of the Soviet Union as well—in almost every aspect of economic warfare. In part, that was because protracted war must become in large measure a conflict be-

---

[1] "Hitler and His Generals," *Times Literary Supplement*, May 24, 1963, p. 366.

tween rival industrial complexes, so that the side with access to greater economic resources enjoys a growing advantage as each month passes. But in part, it was also because Adolf Hitler and most of the Nazi establishment never really understood the nature and requirements of economic warfare, and waited much too long before they grudgingly converted to an economy of total war.

To most outside observers in September 1939, it seemed that the German economy had already been thoroughly militarized. From 1936 onward German armaments production considerably exceeded that of any other power; in 1938, indeed, the Germans outspent the British on armaments by five to one. "No nation," remarks a British historian, "had ever previously spent so vast a sum in peacetime on preparation for war."[2] Hitler's Four-Year Plan, inaugurated in 1936, was openly designed to make the country more nearly self-sufficient and less vulnerable in case of war. Most of the new plants built by the Four-Year Plan Office were concentrated in central Germany, at a safe distance from the frontier; local low-grade iron deposits were exploited for the first time; a crash program of developing synthetic oil and rubber was undertaken; and stockpiling of key raw materials was begun. Hitler's bellicose behavior reinforced the impression that the German economy must be approaching peak production for purposes of war.

The reality was far different. Since 1933, Hitler had carried out no basic reorganization of the economy as a whole; he had stepped up armaments mainly by restoring German industrial production from the depression level to full capacity, and by checking the rise of consumption after about 1936. Indeed, Hitler was instinctively hostile to the idea of an overall economic policy, rationalized and efficient in character, for such a policy would have restricted his own freedom of action. Besides, it would have run counter to the unsystematic and disorderly structure of the Nazi state bureaucracy, whose overlapping character and neo-feudal spirit could scarcely be harmonized with a rationalized state-controlled economy.

Some German officials—notably those of the army armaments branch, headed by General Georg Thomas—had begun to grow uneasy during the immediate prewar years. They had advocated, in General Thomas' phrase, a policy of armament "in depth"; a drastic expansion of Germany's basic heavy industry to ensure a continuous output of munitions and equipment during a long war. Such a policy

[2] A. S. Milward, *The German Economy at War* (London, 1965), p. 27.

would have dictated a postponement of any major conflict until at least 1943, during which time Germany's steel output could be channeled into building additional plant rather than a stockpile of weapons. It would also have dictated a sharp increase in the authority of the Wehrmacht's planning branch—a sweeping militarization of the economy, approaching that of the First World War. Hitler, however, ignored these suggestions, preferring a policy of armament "in breadth." He proposed to utilize the existing industrial structure rather than to expand it, and to pile up a sufficient backlog of armaments to permit either a diplomatic victory or a lightning conquest of an inadequately prepared enemy. If it should come to war, a series of blitzkriegs could be mounted without serious drain on the nation's munitions reserves; in fact, the losses in each case would be at least partly offset by captured booty from the conquered enemy. Furthermore, between one blitzkrieg and the next, armaments priorities could easily be altered to fit changing circumstances; certain campaigns might require an emphasis on tanks and artillery, others might call for an expanded air force or submarine fleet. Meanwhile, the bulk of German industry would continue on a business-as-usual basis, quite unaffected by changing needs for war materials. And most important of all, Hitler's elbows would be free from the constraints imposed by an overall economic plan designed to fit a single type of war—the protracted kind.

For two years after September 1939, the course of events seemed to confirm all of Hitler's expectations. Armament "in breadth" provided the Wehrmacht with a fully adequate supply of equipment for each successive campaign, and permitted rapid shifts in the items of production to fit each successive enemy. Overall, the production of armaments continued at a fairly steady rate—a rate scarcely higher than that of the immediate prewar years. The output of consumer goods likewise remained steady, and in some items even increased. Spoils from the occupied territories more than offset the losses incurred. A very complete rationing system and effective wage and price controls maintained financial stability. No manpower controls had to be applied during those years; Hitler was even able to continue such pet projects as the construction of the Autobahnen, despite their drain on labor and materials. It is not surprising, then, that Hitler could twice order sharp cutbacks in arms production: in 1940, after France fell, and in the autumn of 1941, when victory seemed assured in Russia. Thus for more than two years, Germany could avoid the strains of total war, and could operate a semi-mobilized economy scarcely different from that of the prewar Nazi state.

II. THE WESTERN ALLIES: FROM COMPLACENCY TO ACTION

In theory, the Western powers also might have chosen between armament in depth and armament in breadth. In actual fact, however, the moment for such a choice had long since passed. In 1939, Britain's underpreparedness combined with France's fixation on a defensive strategy ruled out any chance of a quick Western victory, and dictated the kind of gradual industrial expansion and conversion which Hitler had already rejected for Germany. Psychologically, too, the French and British were more inclined to a policy of slow buildup. Time seemed to be on the Allies' side, as it was during the First World War; and postponement of military action might in the end reduce the military phase of the war to a mere final mop-up. For—so ran the theory—the Germans, squeezed by a crippling blockade, would eventually be softened up for easy conquest. The idea of war fought primarily at a distance with economic weapons had a natural appeal to a people like the British, especially in an era when the horrors of war had been amply demonstrated and publicized. One nagging question, however, plagued the more perceptive Western leaders: could the Germans be fended off long enough to permit an adequate buildup of Western armed might? The question was raised, but not really confronted.

True, both the French and the British seemed to be moving with admirable promptness and efficiency to establish the machinery for a real war economy. The French government in September 1939 immediately invoked the wartime powers authorized by parliament a year earlier; Britain had already established a ministry of supply, and now added new cabinet posts to deal with food and shipping. Furthermore, steps were taken to coordinate the inter-allied economic buildup. Only three months after the war began, an Anglo-French Coordinating Committee chaired by the Frenchman Jean Monnet went into operation. During the First World War, it had taken four years rather than three months to arrive at this degree of cooperation. But if the machinery of economic mobilization was impressive, the manner of its use during those early months left much to be desired. Both Britain and France neglected the opportunities provided by the respite of 1939–1940; and their formal collaboration led to no effective pooling of economic resources. Neither government had real confidence in the intentions of its partner;[3] neither one provided a vigorous lead.

Viewed in retrospect, the twilight war provided an invaluable interlude of quiet during which the Western powers might have built up stocks of essential raw materials and foodstuffs from overseas sources, and might have begun to experiment with the kinds of compulsory controls over imports, consumer goods, and manpower that are required by a system of planned economic mobilization. Instead, the two governments lulled their respective publics (and perhaps themselves as well) with assurances of long-range victory, and with comforting contrasts between the Anglo-French and the German standards of living. There was little serious talk of a fundamental reorganization of the economy, except as persuasion and voluntary action might bring about gradual changes in the industrial system. The two governments shied away from rationing, import controls, the direction of manpower. Consumption patterns remained almost unaffected; indeed, imports into Great Britain of some nonessential items actually increased during the winter of 1939–1940. Western political leaders seemed more concerned to protect the pound and the franc than to build up the Allied arsenal; financial considerations plainly outweighed production goals. To the extent that Anglo-French armaments production did increase during the early months of the war, it was achieved not through the planned mobilization of resources but through such simple devices as lengthening factory hours and drawing on the large pool of unemployed.

Hitler's western blitz shattered not only the armed resistance of the French but also the comfortable illusions of the British. Time no longer seemed so surely on the British side, for the Axis powers, bloated with the spoils of most of western Europe, now far outweighed Britain in economic resources as well as in organized military strength. Suddenly, the war had taken on a totally different aspect; full economic mobilization became a matter not of choice but of necessity. It was not a case of switching from armament in depth to armament in breadth, from a long-range buildup to a crash program for immediate production. Crash programs might (and did) succeed for one or two

[3] A French cabinet minister who had been negotiating a financial agreement with London privately expressed the opinion that the British government's object was "to have France exhausted before Great Britain should become seriously weakened so that Great Britain could control the situation absolutely at the end of this war." U.S. Department of State Archives, Bullitt to Hull, Nov. 3, 1939 (851.51/2749).

critically-needed items—notably fighter planes—but the general re-arming of Britain still required time: two or three years, at best. The difference between the pre-Dunkirk and the post-Dunkirk periods was, therefore, primarily a difference in mood rather than in program or purpose. Symbolizing the altered temper of the government and of the nation was the figure of the new prime minister. The cartoonist Low depicted Churchill, sleeves rolled up and cigar clenched in teeth, at the head of a mass of Britons in serried ranks, all striding forward in ca-denced and purposeful step. A spirit of grim yet hopeful determination replaced the "muddled cheerfulness" that had marked the months of the twilight war.

The transition from laissez faire to all-out mobilization was not, however, an immediate and dramatic one. It was worked out calmly, in piecemeal fashion, by a government that was determined to act only with public consent, and by a nation that refused to lose its aplomb on the edge of the abyss. A few emergency decisions were taken, notably a decision to concentrate temporarily on the production of only five types of aircraft—mainly fighters. Thanks to this measure, the delivery of new fighter planes almost doubled between April and September 1940; indeed, the R.A.F. emerged from the Battle of Bri-tain with more fighter aircraft than it had when the battle began. But spectacular improvising of this sort simply could not be generalized. It was a far more complex matter to organize and equip a mass army, to expand the navy and the merchant fleet, which would ensure a steady flow of essential raw materials and foodstuffs, and to construct an armada of massive heavy bombers that might some day carry the war to the enemy.

On the last day of the Dunkirk evacuation, economists attached to the War Cabinet presented a policy paper sketching the outlines of a thorough going war economy. It proposed sharp restrictions on civil-ian consumption, rigorous control of imports, mobilization of all avail-able manpower, equalization of the financial burdens of all-out war, and concentration on those export items that would earn desperately-needed dollars. To attack these problems, Churchill moved at once to tighten and rationalize the machinery of economic decision-making. Heretofore, some sixty interdepartmental committees had attempted, under the overriding authority of the War Cabinet, to deal with limited and often overlapping segments of economic activity. The new gov-ernment promptly abolished many of these committees, and assigned general supervision of the nation's economic effort to a small ministerial group called the Lord President's Committee. This body, composed for the most part of members of the War Cabinet, and headed by a skillful civil servant, Sir John Anderson, gradually enlarged its sphere of authority. That sphere included all the "large questions of economic policy" that had to be answered if the nation were to develop a real war economy instead of a patched-up peacetime system. Over the next eighteen months the Lord President's Committee successfully supervised this conversion, and by the end of 1941 had laid the groundwork for the most thoroughly coordinated war economy of any warring nation.

The process of conversion was gradual rather than brusque, and rested on the principle of popular consent rather than compulsion. At the outset, a few voices had been raised for more drastic measures: for example, the immediate establishment of a "siege economy," in which the entire population—in uniform or out—would be mobilized, disciplined, fed, and housed by the state. Such voices had found no echo among government officials, who relied on the nation's civic spirit to accept the necessary sacrifices. That reliance proved to be well founded; at times, indeed, public opinion actually ran ahead of the government in demanding the establishment of rigorous controls. The idea of general rationing of consumer goods, for example, was accepted by the public even before the government established a system of points rationing in 1941. Since austerity was unavoidable, most consumers wanted it parceled out in fair shares.

Controls over imports and exports, over the allocation of raw materials, and over profits had been adopted piecemeal after war began, and were sharply tightened after Dunkirk. But the central problem as the war moved on was that of manpower. The supply of skilled labor was already growing short by 1940; thereafter, Britain was threatened by a general labor famine. With a population markedly smaller than that of Germany, and without Germany's access to a huge supply of voluntary or conscripted foreign workers, the British could compete in armaments production only by the most stringent manpower mobilization. The need to expand the British armed forces after Dunkirk further intensified the problem. Over the next eighteen months, the government gradually established a system of manpower budgeting that culminated in December 1941 in the National Service Act. By that act, Britain's leaders ". . . demanded for the State the services of men and women on a scale that Britain's totalitarian enemies never dared to ask of their own people."[4] Men aged from eighteen to fifty were subjected to call for either military or essential civilian war service; women aged twenty to thirty were placed under the same obligation. The government was thus empowered to divert labor from nonessential pursuits into the armaments factories or other areas of critical need. In subsequent years, the age group subject to conscription was extended still further, until eventually it included even women aged fifty (the so-called grandmother category). The total increase in gainfully occupied persons during the war years was 2.8 million; of these, 2.2 million were women. No other warring nation (except perhaps the Soviet Union) imposed so great a burden on its female population, or so ruthlessly diverted labor from peacetime to wartime employment. By mid-1944, 33 percent of Britain's total labor force was in civilian war employment—a figure that far exceeded the proportion in either Germany or the United States. Indeed, the control of manpower came to be, after 1941, the key device in the direct central planning of the total-war economy.

After Dunkirk, production replaced financial solvency as the British government's primary concern. Still, the question of how to pay for the war and how to avert a runaway inflation could not be ignored. If the government was to mobilize all of the nation's resources and to plan their most effective use, it needed an accurate X-ray photograph, a statistical overview of the whole economy. Such an official overview was provided for the first time in April 1941, thanks to the work of John Maynard Keynes and his disciples attached to the Treasury and the War Cabinet. Their white paper on national income and expenditure—the first such analysis in any warring country—provided the government with a base from which to reckon the nation's needs and capacities. "Thus . . . was scientific budgeting born into the world."[5] During the next few months, a variety of anti-inflationary techniques were inaugurated. Taxes were sharply increased; Keynes's scheme of deferred pay or "compulsory savings" was adopted; consumer rationing was made general. In addition, such traditional devices as bond drives (dressed up as campaigns to purchase warships or weapons) were mounted to sop up part of the excess buying power.

[4] W. K. Hancock and M. M. Gowing, *British War Economy* (London, 1949), p. 314.
[5] P. Wiles, in G. D. N. Worswick and P. H. Ady (eds.), *The British Economy 1945–1950* (Oxford, 1952), p. 157.

Britain thus averted financial disaster, though at the price of rigorous austerity. The proportion of governmental expenditure borne out of current revenue actually increased as the war progressed: from 39 per cent in 1940, it rose to 55 per cent in 1944. No European nation had approached that figure during the First World War; no other warring state did so well during the Second.[6]

Clearly, however, the British could not have continued for long to carry the full burden of protracted war against such powerful enemies. The economic and financial collaboration of the United States after 1941 brought a large measure of welcome relief (although it also brought some additional burdens, as the war spread to new parts of the world). It must be said, too, that Britain's war economy had its flaws; production often fell short of both targets and needs, per capita productivity remained dismayingly low (especially as compared to that of the United States), and the overall results probably fell short of the unprecedented effort made by the British people. The reasons for these deficiencies were varied: the archaic nature of much of British industry, the lack of complete coordination in procurement for the three armed services, a tendency for British leadership to cling to their empirical tradition and to distrust too much planning. Yet the British record in the realm of economic mobilization for total war still stands out impressively. Operating by consent rather than compulsion, utilizing a partially antiquated industrial complex, and working with limited resources, the British government managed to convert a loosely articulated peacetime economy into a fully mobilized economy for total war. From 1940 to 1942, British production of tanks, aircraft, and self-propelled guns surpassed that of Germany. In a time of severe manpower shortage, British farmers increased the area under cultivation by half, and augmented the native-grown portion of Britain's food supply from 30 to 40 percent of the total. Whatever the long-range costs of such an effort, it stands out as one of the most notable accomplishments of the war years.

III. ECONOMICS AS AN OFFENSIVE WEAPON

Modern wars are fought and won with a wide variety of weapons. Hitler's aim was to use the traditional weapons: victory would be

[6] In Germany, sharply increased taxes in 1939 enabled the government to pay almost 50 percent of expenses out of current receipts. But by 1942–1943 the figure had fallen to 34 percent, and by 1943–44, to 23 percent. Exactions from the conquered countries (especially France) eventually exceeded tax income, but these sources dried up after mid-1944.

achieved on the battlefield through the use of men and guns. Britain's aim, on the contrary, was to concentrate on economic warfare: to undermine the enemy's war-making potential, and to postpone as long as possible the clash of arms on the battlefield. Indeed, during the early part of the war some British leaders showed a tendency to view the economic weapon as a substitute for, rather than a supplement to, the use of military force.

In part, this British attitude was the product of interwar folklore. The Germans after 1918 had fostered the legend that the so-called "hunger blockade" of the First World War had in the end starved out the country and destroyed its will to resist. This legend, which contained just enough truth to make it plausible, had found fairly wide acceptance in the Western nations as well. When combined with a measure of wishful thinking, it encouraged the idea that in the coming war, a long squeeze might be as effective as a short clinch—and considerably less bloody. So one of Britain's first acts after war began in September 1939 was to establish a new ministry of economic warfare.

The term "economic warfare" was of recent coinage; it appeared to transcend the older concept of mere blockade, and to imply a broader and more positive conception of the role of economics as a weapon. Direct air attacks on selected economic targets, the forcible rationing of neutral countries adjacent to the enemy, pre-emptive buying of essential war materials in order to keep them out of enemy hands—all these devices had been considered by British planners during the prewar years. But when war came, an attitude of cautious reserve prevailed; during the first year, the Western Allies confined themselves to the long-range blockade tactics of the first World War, and scrupulously avoided infringing traditional neutral rights. Through British control of the Atlantic sea lanes, they sought to choke off Germany's direct trade with overseas suppliers, and to control "contraband" en route to European neutral ports. In an effort to limit Germany's trade with adjacent European neutrals, the British and French offered war-trade agreements to these neutral countries; they proposed to prohibit the re-exportation to Germany of goods cleared through the Allied blockade, and to limit the sale of other goods beyond the "normal" prewar level. After lengthy negotiations, trade agreements of rather limited scope were signed with the Scandinavian powers, the Low Countries, Switzerland, and Greece; but Italy, the Balkan states, and the Soviet Union constituted sizable leaks in the attempted blockade.

Despite some complaints from tough-minded critics, the British government hesitated to go beyond its "soft blockade." Its confidence was bolstered by intelligence estimates that Germany was dangerously short of key strategic items. Indeed, the Minister of Economic Warfare publicly declared in January 1940 that the Germans were already in straits as severe as those of 1916. In a few respects Germany's position *was* precarious; the stock of oil, for example, was sufficient for only three to five months' needs. But Hitler's astounding victories of April-June 1940 transformed the situation. Not only did the Germans prove that they lacked nothing required to fight a major campaign; in addition, they improved their position so far as essential war materials were concerned. In France alone they captured more oil than they had used in the Polish, Norwegian, and French campaigns combined. More important still, they now had direct control of the economic resources of most of western and central Europe, and their ability to overawe the remaining neutrals was sharply increased. To make things worse, German possession of sea and air bases in Norway and France seriously threatened British control of the Atlantic sea lanes, and seemed to suggest that the blockade, in somewhat altered form, might be turned against Britain itself.

The disaster of 1940 shook the confidence of British leaders in the economic weapon. But in the general mood of consternation just after the fall of France, it seemed unwise to admit to such a change of heart. Publicly, therefore, the government continued to assert its calm confidence in the blockade as the instrument of ultimate victory. Privately, however, British war planners embarked during the next few months on a drastic overhaul of their economic warfare strategy. They could no longer control Axis supply routes through adjacent neutral territory; instead, commodity control at the source had to be tried. This system of "blockade at a distance," though difficult and costly to operate, was gradually forged into an effective weapon, thanks in considerable part to United States cooperation after 1941. Ironically, it was only after the British ceased to regard economic warfare as the main instrument for victory that it began to produce results.

The renovated system was built mainly upon improved techniques of contraband control, the vastly expanded use of preclusive buying, and an increased tempo of air attacks on Axis industry and communications. The key device for contraband control was the compulsory navicert—a document provided by the British to neutral shippers at the source of supply, certifying that the goods in transit were not contraband. Violators were penalized by being denied access to British-owned shipping facilities (coal, water, insurance, stores) in ports throughout the world. In addition, the British now adopted a tougher attitude toward the few remaining European neutrals; they established import quotas of essential goods, barely sufficient to provide for the neutrals' domestic consumption. There were some leaks in the blockade still—notably through the Soviet Union until June 1941, and through Vichy France, which managed to carry on a fair amount of clandestine trade with its colonies in North Africa and West Africa. Until Pearl Harbor, the British were also embarrassed by pressure from certain American groups to relax the blockade by permitting food relief shipments to the conquered countries of western Europe. This pressure they resisted, however, on the ground that relief shipments would ease Germany's burden and would permit the Germans to seize equivalent food stocks in the occupied countries.

By 1941, the British were also using the costly device of preclusive buying in neutral countries. Hitherto, the Treasury, for financial reasons, had blocked the use of this technique for it knew that preclusive buying would quickly drive prices up to astronomic heights, and would force Britain to buy certain raw materials not for their own usefulness but simply because the Germans desperately needed them. Chrome in Turkey, wolfram in Spain and Portugal, became the objects of frantic bidding by both sides. Luckily for the British, the United States Treasury came to the rescue from 1941 onward, and thenceforward carried the principal burden of the preclusive buying program. The effect on Germany's war effort was, however, dubious—at least until the last year of the war. The Germans had built up three-year stockpiles of such key materials as ferroalloys and managed to stretch them over an even longer period. There is little evidence that Hitler was hampered by shortages of any mineral except oil in 1942 (before the breakthrough in synthetic oil production) and in 1944–1945.

Meanwhile, ever since the German conquest of France and Norway, the Axis had been attempting to tighten its own noose about the British Isles. Its weapons—the submarine, the bomber, and the surface raider—were of the orthodox military sort, but its purposes in this campaign were essentially economic. As in the First World War, the Germans believed that if they could cut the sea route between Britain and the United States, the Atlantic powers would be rendered helpless.

In both wars, Germany seemed at one point to be approaching its goal. During the early months of 1943, when Allied shipping losses were averaging 400,000 tons a month, the British War Cabinet estimated that both food and raw materials were so dangerously short as to threaten Britain's capacity to carry on the war. In retrospect, the judgment was probably too gloomy. In any case, the U-boat threat was shortly broken, and by the summer of 1943 the Germans' wager on economic warfare had been lost.

As for the Allied effort to strangle Germany, its results seemed even more uncertain—at least until 1944. Neither preclusive buying nor pressure on the European neutrals materially reduced neutral trade with the Germans until the last year of the war. It was only when the outcome became clear beyond doubt that the Swedes, Swiss, and Spaniards bent to Western demands. Even more disappointing was the impact of the bomber offensive; until mid-1944, German war production continued to rise despite heavy British and American air force sacrifices. After that date, however, the doubters found their case crumbling beneath them. The devastating decline in synthetic oil production after June 1944 was the most disastrous blow; the disruption of transportation facilities and the crippling of much Ruhr industry were almost as serious. When Germany surrendered in May 1945, no one could doubt that the combined forms of economic warfare had been a major factor in the victory.

IV. THE SOVIET ECONOMIC EFFORT

Throughout the interwar years, Soviet leaders had steadily asserted the superiority of their state-controlled economy to systems based on private ownership. The test of war offered them an unparalleled opportunity to attempt to prove their case. By 1939, a decade of experience in economic planning had enabled the Kremlin to correct many of its initial errors, and to develop reasonably effective machinery for centralized decision-making. In no other nation was it so easy to convert an economy from peacetime to wartime needs—to reduce consumer goods in favor of military hardware, to carry out massive transfers of labor, and to limit the scope of currency inflation. As economic systems go, the Soviet system undoubtedly had a special adaptability to a time of total war. Perhaps that was in part because the line separating peace and war was, in Soviet theory, an indistinct and porous one.

During the two years of the USSR's uneasy alliance with Germany, the Kremlin was painfully careful to fulfill its economic commitments to Berlin. The treaty of August 1939 provided for a broadening of trade relations between the two countries, and formal negotiations to that end followed during the autumn. The outcome was a trade agreement signed on February 11, 1940, embodying concessions by both parties. The USSR committed itself to deliver, during the next eighteen months, large quantities of such essential raw materials as oil, grain, timber, iron, and various nonferrous ores. In addition, the Soviet Union promised to provide transit facilities for certain raw materials from the Middle East and the Far East—notably rubber, and a million tons of soybeans from Manchuria. In return, Germany was to furnish manufactured goods—including munitions, naval equipment, and a nearly completed cruiser—plus sizable shipments of coal. By mid-1940, the USSR had become Germany's leading supplier of grain, and Germany's second supplier of oil, timber, and base metals. A new trade agreement in January 1941 further increased Soviet oil deliveries during the last months before the invasion.

That this trade policy reinforced German more than Russian military strength seems almost certain. On the other hand, it enabled Stalin to buy valuable time, which he used with considerable wisdom. The third Five-Year Plan, inaugurated in 1938, had already given new impetus to the industrial development of the heretofore neglected eastern regions, notably the Urals and western Siberia. Iron, coal, and nonferrous ore mines were opened there; railways and power plants were built; new factories burgeoned. By June 1941, the Soviet east was already producing 39 percent of the USSR's steel, 35 percent of its coal, 25 percent of its electricity, 50 percent of its tractors. In nonferrous metallurgy, the east had moved ahead of any other section of the USSR. Only in oil production was there a serious lag; the east accounted for only 12 percent of Soviet output by 1941. A powerful new industrial base, geographically secure against enemy attack, had thus been created between 1938 and 1941. In addition, the third Five-Year Plan had more than doubled the share of the budget devoted to defense industries, and had provided for the stockpiling of certain strategic items. By 1941, both aircraft and tanks were being turned out by production-line methods. Post-Stalin critics were to complain that even more ought to have been done in these years of grace, both to speed arms production and to convert to more up-to-date models of planes and tanks. Right up until 1941, the older industrial regions in the west continued to receive almost as large a share of the industrial-expansion budget as the underdeveloped east. In the view of these critics, Stalin simply would not face the painful prospect that Hitler might strike soon, and without warning.

The blow, when it came, would surely have been fatal if the USSR had lacked the new Ural and trans-Ural industrial base. Even with that base, it came near to being fatal. By the end of 1941, most of the old industrial regions had been overrun; total industrial output was down by more than half. Even though the German drive was checked at Moscow in December, the Russian armies faced the threat of a supply famine. Their tank force had been decimated; ammunition reserves were virtually exhausted; aircraft production had dropped by two-thirds; foodstuffs and raw materials were at dangerously low levels. A trickle of equipment and supplies was beginning to arrive from Britain and the United States—a trickle that would eventually become a torrent; but it was still far from enough to pull the Russians through this dangerous crisis.

Yet the crisis was surmounted; and not surprisingly, this economic feat was to become part of the heroic legend of what Soviet historians and citizens call "The Great Patriotic War." The most dramatic aspect was the massive transfer, under conditions of appalling difficulty, of a considerable number of large Soviet factories from the threatened western regions (and from Leningrad and Moscow) to the Volga area, the Urals, and beyond. This process began two weeks after the initial attack, and continued until the end of the year; during that time, 1360 large enterprises and some 200 smaller ones were disassembled, hauled eastward by rail (along with most of their workers), and reassembled in new buildings hastily put up for the purpose. To illustrate the scale of the operation, one such plant required eight thousand railroad cars to transport it, yet it was again in production within four months' time. In a number of cases, the evacuated plants were merged with new enterprises recently constructed in the east. The consequence of this remarkable hegira was that total industrial production, after falling to an all-time low in December 1941, began to rise again thereafter, and increased almost without interruption throughout the rest of the war. New plants continued to be built in the eastern regions—2250 of them in the years 1942–1944. Soviet authorities were therefore able to set, and to fulfill, astonishingly high quotas for the production of military equipment from 1942 onward. Tank output averaged about 2000 per month in 1942 and 1943; aircraft output rose from less than 1000 to 3000 per month in the same period. In a few basic items, notably coal and oil, recovery continued to lag until 1944; yet despite this handicap, Soviet industry was able to provide the bulk of the armaments required by the nation's huge fighting forces. The contribution of British and American industry (especially after 1943) was of vital importance too, but for the most part it took the form of vehicles, foodstuffs, and clothing rather than weapons.

As in all warring countries, the manpower problem was a central one for the Soviet Union. The mobilization of millions of men for the armed forces, combined with the loss of many workers in the German-occupied western regions, reduced the Soviet labor force in 1942 to 59 percent of the prewar figure. Desperate measures were needed to man the new and the uprooted plants in the east. A decree in February 1942 ordered total mobilization of men aged sixteen to fifty-five and women aged sixteen to forty-five; many thousands were combed out of jobs in the cities, and were sent off to the east. By 1943, almost half of the total labor force was employed in the eastern regions. Most important of all was the recruiting of women and teen-agers for the factories. The proportion of women in the labor force rose from 38 percent in 1940 to 53 percent in 1942. Even though the new workers had to be retrained for factory jobs through speed-up courses, and were forced to adjust to difficult and unfamiliar living conditions, Soviet figures show that labor productivity rose each year from 1942 onward. Both better management and generally high morale contributed to that result. A nation invaded and fighting for its existence is no doubt more likely than any other to make a superhuman effort, whatever the form of its economic organization.

This effort extended to agriculture as well as industry. Here too, the initial impact of the German invasion was catastrophic. By mid-1942, 42 percent of the USSR's cultivated soil was under enemy occupation, and this included the country's richest land. Those collective farms which lay behind the front were stripped of much of their skilled manpower by mobilization; tractors as well were often requisitioned by the army. By early 1943, the total farm labor force had been reduced by one-third. Again it was women and young people—particularly the former—who partially filled the gap. Answering the cry of "Women to the tractors!" recruits poured into the crash programs established to train tractor operators. During the war years, 2 million such recruits were trained, and 1.5 million of them were women. Indeed, the proportion of women in the total farm labor force reached 71 percent in 1943. Young people, refugees from the western provinces, and labor draftees from the cities made up the remainder.

Recovery in agriculture was nevertheless slower and more limited than in industry. Some new acreage was opened up in the east, but it could not match the lost Ukraine in productivity. Tractors remained in short supply, for tanks took a higher priority. Even after the reconquest of the Ukraine in 1943–1944, the restoration of the kolkhozy there was slow, and the rebuilding of the livestock herds even slower. When the war ended, grain production still lagged at only half the 1940 figure, while livestock numbers varied from 38 percent (for hogs) to about 75 percent for cattle and sheep. For its essential foodstuffs, the USSR depended heavily on supplies from its Western allies to survive the war.

Although the USSR's managed economy was well adapted to the demands of war, it was not immune to one "capitalist" danger—that of financial dislocation. To meet its budgetary deficit, especially in 1941 and 1942, the government had to increase the amount of currency in circulation; the total volume rose 2.4 times during the war years. At the same time, all consumer supplies and services were cut to the bone. As in other nations at war, the Kremlin imposed rigid rationing and utilized higher tax rates and bond drives to soak up some of the excess buying power. But conditions dictated the emergence of a kind of legal black market, especially in foodstuffs: collective farmers were allowed to sell their excess produce on the open market. Some items skyrocketed to one hundred or even two hundred times the rationed price; members of collective farms near the large cities briefly attained the status of Soviet millionaires. Beginning in 1944, Soviet authorities undertook a series of corrective measures that was to culminate in 1947 in a forced currency exchange at the rate of ten old rubles to one new ruble. No other nation dared to handle the financial stresses of the war in quite such brutal and effective fashion.

There can be no doubt that the Soviet Union's overall achievement in the economic realm was impressive. No other warring nation had to fight on with almost half of its industrial and agricultural resources in enemy hands, and with much of its transportation system disrupted. The men in the Kremlin proved their ability to improvise under terrible pressure; the Soviet people proved its energy and endurance. These traits, combined with the courage of the Soviet soldier, enabled the nation to meet the test of invasion and total war.

Meanwhile, gradually and reluctantly, Hitler had been abandoning blitzkrieg economics for something closer to total mobilization for war. The change began at the end of 1941; it was forced on Germany by the refusal of the Soviet Union to collapse on schedule. Heretofore, sudden spurts of economic effort had sufficed to support a series of blitzkrieg actions. The successful resistance of the Russians dictated a fundamental change in Berlin.

Although the Wehrmacht's War Economy and Armaments Branch under General Thomas had been urging this solution since the beginning of the war, it was not the Wehrmacht that now moved in to take control. Rather, it was a civilian ministry headed by the engineer Fritz Todt. Todt, an old Nazi, had built up a kind of private empire in prewar days through contracts to build the Autobahnen. Early in 1940 he had been named Reichsminister for Armaments and Munitions, but his powers at first had been narrowly restricted, and the army had jealously resisted his efforts to introduce greater efficiency into armaments production. Todt's aim was to cut back the role of the Wehrmacht bureaucrats, and to put production in the hands of the industrial technicians. To this end, he had begun in 1940 to set up a series of production committees with at least theoretical powers to reorganize industry, allocate raw materials, and place orders for various types of armaments. A series of development committees was soon added; their function was to standardize and simplify designs.

So long as Hitler clung to blitzkrieg economics, however, Todt's reforms were relatively ineffective. Todt's ministry lacked real power to enforce its will, mainly because the system of allocating raw materials lacked teeth. Factory managers, aided by the gauleiters of their districts, continued to scramble for the available stocks, and political pressures rather than economic necessity usually decided the outcome. No conversion to a full war economy was possible until Hitler vested real control in either the Wehrmacht or the Ministry for Armaments and Munitions. Early in January 1942, the Fuehrer at last took a decisive step; he ordered vast increases in armaments production of almost every kind, together with an expansion of the army. The problem of implementing this order led to a sharp but brief struggle between Todt and the Wehrmacht, both of whom sought control of the stepped-up war economy. By February, the contest had been won by Todt; the army's authority thereafter was to be progressively reduced as the Ministry of Armaments and Munitions invaded one realm after another.

Todt did not live to enjoy his victory; before the final decrees had been signed, he was killed in an air crash. But his successor, Albert Speer, proved to be a man of even greater talents. Under Speer's guidance, armaments production rose in dramatic fashion: the overall figure trebled during the next two years. His achievement indirectly demonstrated the casual and wasteful character of Germany's economy during the earlier blitzkrieg era, when armaments production had grown hardly at all.

The Speer miracle was not achieved without numerous difficulties, however. At the outset, Speer had been given authority only over production for the army; naval and air force production remained outside his realm, as did those segments of the economy not engaged in war production proper. The Wehrmacht's War Economy and Armaments Branch, though stripped of much of its power, was still a potential source of rivalry and interference. So was Goering's Four-Year Plan Office, for Goering sporadically attempted to reassert his prerogatives in the economic sphere. Some influential party officials, strongly anticapitalist in temper, looked with suspicion on Speer's tendency to rely heavily on the industrialists in rationalizing the economy. And the issue of manpower controls, evaded until now, was still unsettled, though its central importance was henceforth clear.

Speer dealt with these problems piecemeal and, on the whole, successfully. During the spring of 1942, the teeth of several rival agencies were pulled, and Speer's ministry was able to assert its clear predominance in the economic field—subject always, of course, to Hitler's personal veto. The Wehrmacht's War Economy Branch was swallowed up, being transferred bodily to the Ministry of Armaments and Munitions. The Four-Year Plan Office was reduced to a largely ornamental role, though Goering continued to balk from time to time. In April, Hitler agreed to set up a small Central Planning Board with real power to allocate raw materials. Speer also managed to get some voice in naval and air force production by extending the authority of Todt's production committees into those areas. Thus by mid-1942, the basic structure of the new total-war economy had been established; and after the shock of the Stalingrad defeat, Speer could undertake a more fundamental reorganization involving the more rational use of German industry.

This is not to say that the new system worked without hitches, or that Speer now enjoyed unrestricted freedom of action in the economic sphere. Hitler still hankered after the old blitzkrieg economy which had given him greater freedom of decision; he interfered sporadically with Speer's plans, and often had to be cajoled or persuaded. The navy clung to its right to the last word on naval production until mid-1943, when Admiral Doenitz at last handed over the task to Speer in an effort to get more submarines. The air force was even more stubborn, thanks in part to Goering's influence. Aircraft design and production remained a prerogative of the air staff until March 1944, when Speer at last attained substantial control in this crucial realm. In addition, Himmler's SS went on building up its own separate economic empire both within Germany and in the conquered eastern territories; it remained autonomous to the end, despite Speer's efforts to coordinate its activities with the rest of the economy. The SS used labor in inefficient as well as barbarous ways, and its diversion of certain scarce raw materials interfered with Speer's production plans.

One other chronic problem was never fully solved—the problem of manpower. At the very outset, Speer had pushed hard for a manpower agency under his direct or indirect control; but here he had failed to get his way. Instead, Hitler entrusted the new agency to the old Nazi and long-time gauleiter Fritz Sauckel, a potential rival rather than an ally. Speer and Sauckel had sharply different ideas about how to allocate available labor and about how to utilize workers from the occupied countries. Speer believed that foreign labor could be used most efficiently at home, through operating industrial plants in the occupied countries to produce for German purposes. Sauckel insisted on rounding them up for transportation to Germany, where his office controlled their distribution without much reference to Speer's priorities. The Speer-Sauckel controversy went much deeper than personal rivalry or technical differences; it reflected a conflict over the very nature of the Nazi state. Sauckel, along with Martin Bormann and many of the gauleiters, belonged to the "revolutionary" wing of the party; they complained that Speer was in league with the big industrialists, who were being given far too much power and freedom. Speer's system did in fact involve a degree of industrial self-government; the industrialists were key figures in most of the production committees, and in some cases Speer had to check their tendency to favor their own firms. Speer was convinced, nevertheless, that only through their cooperation could an efficient war economy be run. The "revolutionary" Nazis, on the other hand, distrusted the business group and advocated a system of strict party control.

In spite of all these difficulties, Speer achieved impressive results. From 1939 until he became minister in February 1942, Germany's total armaments and munitions production had remained almost stationary. Thereafter, it increased in jerky but dramatic fashion. Using February 1942 as the base month, the overall index rose to 153 in July 1942, to 229 in July 1943, and to 322 a year later. The output of weapons, ammunition, and aircraft went up more than threefold; of tanks, almost sixfold. Yet no drastic drop in civilian consumption levels accompanied this growth in arms production, at least until the last year of the war. Not that guns *and* butter was Speer's aim; he worked steadily (with strong support from Goebbels) for harsh restrictions on the consumer, for real total war. But his efforts were largely frustrated by Bormann and the gauleiters, who steadily resisted cuts in civilian consumption and who usually won Hitler's support. There were actually increases in the output of some civilian items during 1944.

Speer's inability to get control of aircraft production until 1944 also handicapped his effort to create a fully rationalized war economy. The air staff's insistence on building too many types of planes (thirty, as late as mid-1943) and on introducing constant modifications slowed up production markedly; monthly targets were rarely reached. Adding to the difficulty was Goering's stubborn refusal to stop building expensive bombers in favor of fighter planes, even after the scene of the air war had shifted to the skies over Germany. Goering clung to the belief that his bombers could still knock out Britain, or could at least seek revenge for British raids. Not until 1944 was Speer able to impose a drastic reduction in the number of models produced, and the complete abandonment of bomber production. From 2316 planes in June 1943, Speer raised German production to 3538 in September 1944— and this in spite of allied air attacks and the growing stringency of raw materials and skilled labor.

By mid-1944, there could be no doubt that only the most desperate measures could save Germany from total defeat. In June, Speer at last persuaded Hitler to funnel all resources into quantity production of a few standard items. No more time or energy could be spared for the development of new weapons or the improvement of old ones. But the potential effects of this decision were soon blunted by Hitler's decree in October creating the *Volkssturm*—a conscript home defense force of youngsters and old men for the last-ditch protection of the homeland. All males from sixteen to sixty, save a few skilled workers, were placed under Wehrmacht control, thus diverting from arms production virtually all the potential manpower that remained. But Speer's last gesture was an empty one at best. Stocks of essential raw materials were at last running dry, and could no longer be replenished from Hitler's European empire. Round-the-clock air bombardment was finally producing results in the form of disrupted transportation facilities and damaged factories. Even those planes and tanks that continued to come off the production lines in surprising numbers stood idle for lack of fuel. As a miracle-worker, even Speer had his outer limits. The hard facts of economic power, expressed in the form of military equipment and the men to operate it, in the end overwhelmed both him and Germany.

Chapter Four

THE BROADENING SCOPE OF WAR:
THE PSYCHOLOGICAL DIMENSION

I. PSYCHOLOGICAL WARFARE, NAZI-STYLE

"PROPAGANDA," asserted Adolf Hitler a week after the outbreak of the war, "is an important instrument of the Leadership for forwarding and strengthening the will to victory and for destroying the enemies' morale and will to victory."[1] Indeed, Hitler's whole political career offered living testimony of the central role of mass persuasion in a totalitarian movement, whether at war or at peace. Hitler was of course not alone in recognizing the importance, in an age of mass communications, of the struggle for men's minds. Indeed, some propaganda specialists during the interwar years undoubtedly exaggerated the potential role of what they were beginning to call "psychological warfare." This new term, coined in Germany, reflected the deep conviction of many Germans that Allied propaganda rather then military power had brought about Germany's defeat in 1918. As evidence that propaganda would be even more important in the next war, the exponents of psychological warfare could point to the explosive development of advertising and of mass communications media since 1918. Furthermore, advances in the field of psychology as a theoretical and empirical discipline suggested (at least to some laymen) that psychological techniques might be developed into a kind of secret weapon even deadlier than the new forms of military hardware. Some publicists contended that the possibilities of mass manipulation through propaganda were almost infinite.[2] When war broke out, therefore, every participating nation moved at once to set up some kind of official agency designed to undermine enemy morale and to persuade neutrals and the home population of the justice of its own cause.

In this realm even more than in economics, the Germans had a long start over their enemies. For almost twenty years the Nazi leader-

---

[1] "Command of the Fuehrer," Sept. 8, 1939, *Documents on German Foreign Policy 1918–1945*, Series D, VIII (Washington, 1943), p. 30.

[2] See, for example, Serge Chakotine's *Le viol des foules* (Paris, 1939), translated as *The Rape of the Masses* (London, 1940).

ship had been testing and adapting its methods of mass manipulation within Germany, and it had experimented extensively with propaganda aimed at foreign audiences as well. Joseph Goebbels, Hitler's Minister of People's Enlightenment and Propaganda, was widely regarded as a kind of genius in his field. Goebbels shared that estimate, and was convinced that his ministry's wartime role would equal that of the Wehrmacht in achieving Germany's goals. Yet in the sphere of psychological warfare as in that of economics, the Germans were gradually to lose much of their initial advantage, and were eventually to be outmaneuvered by their rivals. Only in the sphere of home propaganda did Goebbels' persuasion machine remain effective until the very end.

As in the realm of economics, the central error was Hitler's certainty that victory would be quick and cheap. Goebbels, who willingly accepted Hitler's assurance of a short war, took it as his task to hasten that early triumph. In the war of words as well as that of weapons, the Germans relied at first on the blitzkrieg technique; their principal aim was to divide, mislead, and terrify the enemy, and to overawe neutral bystanders. Using radio (supplemented by film) as their chief medium of penetration, the Germans reminded their hearers in western and southeastern Europe of the fate of Poland—a fate that was sure to confront any nation that challenged the Wehrmacht. A powerful feature-length documentary film of the Polish campaign, complete with screeching dive bombers laying waste to Warsaw, was circulated not only in Germany but in the nearby neutral countries; special showings were arranged for important officials who might be suitably impressed by the display.

Through the winter of the twilight war, Goebbels' services also concentrated on the justice-for-Germany theme, and on stimulating dissension between the Western Allies. Britain, they repeated daily by radio and via loudspeakers along the western front, was prepared to fight to the last Frenchman. When the great western offensive began in May, German broadcasters worked in close cooperation with the military command to sow panic and confusion in the fighting zone, and encouraged swarms of refugees to block the roads leading westward. These open broadcasts from German soil were supplemented by "black" propaganda stations, purporting to operate clandestinely somewhere in France and Britain and to represent the domestic opposition. Three of these "black" stations were beamed toward Britain; one claimed to speak for the oppressed British workers, another was billed as "the voice of Scotland," and a third (managed by the British fascist William Joyce) was designed to arouse the latent fascist sympathies of Englishmen generally. Joyce, who was promptly nicknamed Lord Haw-Haw by a London journalist, also spoke over the regular German stations, and won a wide audience for a time in 1940. His techniques aroused some fear that an extensive fifth column was operating in England; a London tabloid went so far so to organize the "Anti-Haw-Haw League of Loyal Britons" whose members were sworn to counter Joyce's false rumors.

During the years of Germany's triumphs, the Goebbels blitz-propaganda tactic succeeded admirably. Within Germany, any early skepticism about the government's claims and predictions was quickly dispelled, for those predictions were fulfilled and even exceeded. On the home front, victory always makes the task of the propagandist easy, and even unnecessary. The impact on neutral countries also seems to have been profound; German newsreel shots of the Polish and French campaigns caused a salutary shiver of fear to run up neutral backbones. In the countries at war with Germany, however, the effectiveness of German psychological warfare even during these early years was more debatable. "Justice for Germany" was a slogan that had influenced a good many Frenchmen and Englishmen before 1939, but it had now lost most of its potency. "Germany, bulwark of the West against the Bolshevik menace" would have been a tempting substitute, but it had to be shelved temporarily because of Hitler's pact with Stalin. The concept of a new united Europe under German guidance did not emerge as a serious propaganda motif until after the fall of France: and then its persuasiveness was offset by the oppressive nature of German occupation policy. The most effective theme in 1939–1940 was the encouragement of Franco-British dissension, since it rested on a genuine substratum of mutual distrust. But Goebbels' effort after the defeat of France to use the same divisive tactics within England failed dismally, for it stemmed from a basic misunderstanding of British attitudes. The Berlin radio's vicious personal attacks on Prime Minister Churchill served only to reinforce the bond between Prime Minister and ordinary citizen.[3] Here was a classic case of propaganda that boomeranged.

[3] The British Gallup poll showed that the nation's confidence in Churchill stood at 88 percent in July 1940, 89 percent in October, and 85 percent at the end of the year, when the German night-bombing blitz was at its height. L. Thompson, *1940* (New York, 1966), p. 146.

Goebbels' real test, however, was to come in the later years, when triumph turned into stalemate and stalemate into impending disaster. As the war dragged on, the German generals could fall back on alternatives to blitzkrieg; but the propagandists were entangled in their own web. They had confidently predicted a short war, then the collapse of British resistance, then the disintegration of the Soviet armies and regime. Repeated paeans of triumph (complete with Wagnerian fanfares) and announcements that the war was as good as over (the last and most damaging of which came in October 1941, when Hitler's press chief Otto Dietrich proclaimed the final defeat of the Russians) exposed the German propagandists to disbelief and, eventually, to ridicule. British psychological warriors took full advantage of these errors; they obtained a copy of the *Voelkischer Beobachter* headlining Dietrich's rash statement, and dropped facsimiles over Germany at intervals during the rest of the war. Likewise, when Hitler failed to speak in public on the tenth anniversary of his accession to power (January 30, 1943), the British put together a composite of his earlier boasts and beamed it at Germany as a substitute. Excessive reliance on blitz-propaganda led the Germans to indulge in flagrant exaggerations and contradictions, useful in the short run but damaging to Berlin's long-run reputation for reliability.

Goebbels himself was shrewd enough to sense this danger, and had tried to avoid falling into such a trap. When Russia was attacked, his services carefully refrained from spreading the impression that this campaign would be a short and easy one, and Goebbels was shocked and infuriated at Dietrich's *faux pas* in October. But in the realm of psychological warfare as in so many other spheres, jurisdictional rivalries seriously hampered the Nazi regime's effectiveness. Hitler's penchant for what someone has called "authoritarian anarchy" within his own bureaucracy was clearly revealed here. No clear boundary separated Goebbels' powers from those of Press Chief Dietrich, who had long been a member of the Fuehrer's close entourage and who operated semi-independently as an undersecretary within Goebbels' own ministry. There were rivalries of somewhat similar nature with the army; the Wehrmacht's propaganda warfare branch[4] had sole authority in the battle zone and among the German armed forces, while Goebbels' propaganda ministry was responsible for the home front and for broadcasts to enemy and

---

[4] A curious innovation by the army was the creation of "propaganda companies" made up of war correspondents and cameramen who, as full-fledged soldiers, accompanied the troops into combat and reported or filmed each campaign for the home public.

neutral countries. The foreign office had still another spoon in the soup; Ribbentrop was authorized to issue general policy directives for all propaganda directed at foreign countries. After the invasion of the USSR, a new Ministry of Eastern Territories headed by Alfred Rosenberg was assigned control of most propaganda activities in the conquered east. Thus the possibilities of contradiction and personal conflict were almost infinite. Goebbels pressed steadily for supreme authority over every branch of propaganda, and at one point won Hitler's promise to put the Wehrmacht propaganda branch under his control; but the promise remained a dead letter. He also won a partial victory over Rosenberg in 1943, too late to profit very much by it.

The internal tug of war was worst with respect to the conquered east, where personal jealousies were complicated by sharp policy differences. During the first stage of the invasion of Russia, Goebbels adopted the extreme-racist line of Hitler and the SS; the term *Untermenschen* made its way into common usage in propaganda destined for both German and Western consumption. Photographs of hairy, beetle-browed Soviet prisoners studded the pages of the German press, alongside shots of handsome, earnest Teutonic soldiers in field gray. The crusade against Bolshevism, which had already struck a responsive chord in certain circles of central and western Europe, thus took on strongly racist overtones. This propaganda line had been opposed from the start both by Rosenberg and by the army. Rosenberg advocated a softer line toward the non-Russian minorities in the USSR, in order to split them away from the Great Russians; the army preferred a softer line toward the Russian masses generally, in an effort to undermine their loyalty to the Kremlin. By the end of 1941, Goebbels began to realize the potentially disastrous consequences of his hard line; but his jurisdictional feuds with Rosenberg and the army, along with Hitler's prejudices and his own as well, made it difficult for him to switch. He began to play down the *Untermensch* thesis, but it was not until 1943, after the Battle of Stalingrad, that he finally brought himself to order a basic change. Thereafter, his services set out to rally all the "eastern peoples" to the crusade against "Jewish Bolshevism." But it was far too late for this lip-service change to produce results. Only a drastic alteration of German occupation policy itself could have made the new line believable; and that change would have had to come long before Stalingrad. Instead, Hitler continued to stand firm against any softening of occupation policy, and consented to changes in the propaganda line ". . . only under one condition: that not the slightest practical consequences will ensue. . . ."[5] If consistency between words and acts is the *sine qua non* of successful psychological warfare, it was more egregiously violated during the later stages of the Russian campaign than during any other phase of the war.

During the last two years of the war, Goebbels was confronted with a set of problems quite different from those of the triumphal period. Propaganda had formerly ridden on the back of military success; now it had to try to provide a substitute for success. The earlier effort to spur dissension among the Allied powers had to be continued and intensified; but far more important now was the necessity to maintain German morale, and to preserve a sense of unity between the widely dispersed armies and the home front. It was in this latter enterprise that Goebbels achieved his most remarkable success. Somehow he managed to fuse the sufferings of the nation and the sacrifices of the combatants; his weekly articles in *Das Reich* and his occasional public speeches to huge but select audiences were designed to intoxicate the nation, to create "a palpable fellowship of the German people . . . and a world impregnable to enemy attack."[6] During 1942 he shifted from assurances of certain victory to somber, hard-headed realism on the Churchillian model to arouse the Germans to desperate effort. Even Soviet victories were utilized as a kind of asset; reports of Russian advances were allowed to go out unchallenged, in order to terrify those who might eventually become Russia's victims. Goebbels' appeals now were principally to those most basic of emotions, hatred and fear: between Russian savagery and Anglo-American rapacity, he warned, there was no exit for Germany save endurance and a distant victory. The Western policy of unconditional surrender, enunciated by Roosevelt at the Casablanca conference in January 1943, provided Goebbels with a convenient slogan to support his case.

In Goebbels' campaign of "strength through fear," he received little active help from Hitler. After Stalingrad the Fuehrer shunned the spotlight, remained almost constantly at his remote headquarters in the east, and spoke publicly only twice. Goebbels therefore carried the additional burden of furbishing the absent Fuehrer's image, and justifying his virtual disappearance from the home front. Although Ger-

[5] G. Fischer, *Soviet Opposition to Stalin* (Cambridge, Mass., 1952), pp. 178–79.
[6] M. Mégret, *La guerre psychologique* (Paris, 1963), p. 55.

man morale was seriously affected during the two years after Stalingrad, the impairment was one of mood rather than overt behavior. Goebbels was even able to persuade the nation, after the attempt on Hitler's life in July 1944, that the plotters had acted on such contemptible motives as defeatism and aristocratic prejudice.

At home, Goebbels' efforts probably did much to avert any real collapse of morale. Outside Germany, however, his services had long since lost their effectiveness. Germany's psychological warriors were paying the price of their risky blitz tactics during the early years. Too much boasting, too many unfulfilled promises, too many blatant lies— these might have been powerful weapons in a short war, but they proved disastrous in the longer haul. Nor could Goebbels escape the painful truth that propagandists cannot win battles when the soldiers are obviously losing the war.

II. PSYCHOLOGICAL WARFARE, WESTERN- AND SOVIET-STYLES

Any nation's methods of psychological warfare tend to reflect its particular national style and system of values. Yet the pressures of protracted war can add a strongly distorting factor, and may in the end outweigh differences in style and values. To the degree that sheer efficacy becomes the principal measure of propaganda techniques, those techniques are likely to become homogenized as the conflict continues; each side learns from the enemy's mistakes as well as from its own errors, and each side copies its enemy's successes. As war drags on, totalitarian and democratic styles of psychological warfare thus tend to become more alike than different. Yet efficacy rarely becomes the only test of any nation's propaganda policies. Values and prejudices that are deeply held by the political leadership set limits to what the professional manipulators of opinion can do. Totalitarian and democratic styles may come to run in parallel grooves, but they never really merge.

Unlike the Germans, the Western powers started virtually from scratch in 1939, and gradually improvised their own version of psychological warfare. Part of the problem was to overcome widespread skepticism about the utility and morality of such techniques. To most Western political leaders, propaganda was a disagreeable word, and the idea of government-managed information a repellent thing. No Western leader had written, or could have written, a shrewd and tough-minded essay on propaganda like Adolf Hitler's notorious

chapter in *Mein Kampf*; no peacetime democracy could have tolerated
a Goebbels in high office, even if the society had managed to produce
one. Nevertheless, both the British and the French recognized the
need to try to counteract Goebbels, and when war came both governments were quick to establish Ministries of Information. At first, both
were appallingly ineffective. The French were largely content to resurrect the methods of the First World War. Their emphasis was on
censorship rather than on active psychological warfare; their idea of
constructive action was to publish high-flown pamphlets by such literary figures as Minister of Information Jean Giraudoux, extolling the
primacy of French culture and of Western values. They overempha-
sized the written word at the expense of radio, and generally neglected
the growing fund of knowledge about mass communication techniques.
Underlying their problem was the government's failure to provide essential directives on such questions as war aims. Until the Ministry of
Information was told whether the enemy was Nazism or the German
people en masse, no effective propaganda line could be developed. As
for domestic propaganda, the French high command shrewdly observed early in 1940 that there ought to be less talk about universal
freedom and more effort to prepare the minds and spirits of Frenchmen for a blitz like that of Poland.

The British, on the other hand, showed considerable talent in the
realm of what they preferred to call "political warfare," though it
took time—more time than was allotted to the French—for this talent
to mature. For the first year or so, groping and confusion characterized
the effort to develop an effective propaganda machine. Three newly-
created agencies shared the task in overlapping fashion: the Ministry
of Information (set up in 1939), a highly secret Department of Propaganda to the Enemy and Enemy-Occupied Territories, and the British Broadcasting Corporation's European Services (which dated from
late 1938). For a time, one high official later recalled, there was more
political warfare on the home front than against the enemy. Gradually
a system of coordination was worked out, though some jurisdictional
conflicts persisted throughout most of the war. A new Political Warfare Executive (PWE), established in 1941, was entrusted with policy
control over all broadcasts and pamphlet operations directed at enemy
and occupied territory. Its chief problem was to satisfy various agencies whose views did not always coincide: the Ministry of Information,
the Foreign Office, and the Chiefs of Staff. A further complication was

the fact that Prime Minister Churchill, a man of the old school, had scant respect for psychological warfare except as it might be used for purposes of deception; he professed to prefer deeds to words.

Despite these handicaps, PWE under the former career diplomat R. H. Bruce Lockhart gradually developed a range of techniques that successfully counterbalanced Goebbels' operations. Lockhart insisted from the outset that the efficacy of Britain's propaganda would be in direct proportion to its accuracy. In a long war, he believed, a reputation for truth and consistency would pay high dividends, for it would allay the natural skepticism of audiences both at home and on the Continent. The BBC strongly shared this view, and consistently sought through its news broadcasts to provide as much solid information as was feasible in wartime. Its programs—sober, restrained, even a bit dull—avoided the temptation to excite or amuse. Some British propagandists, impressed by Goebbels' blitz techniques, were critical of this attitude during the early war years; and they received sympathetic support from high military quarters during the period of Hitler's unbroken victories. In the end, however, restraint paid. As confidence in the accuracy of German broadcasts diminished, the British news services shone by contrast. In spite of vigorous German efforts to jam British programs and to punish clandestine listeners, the audience both in Germany and in the Western occupied countries grew steadily during the latter half of the war, and probably ran into the millions.

Along with straight news reporting, the British propagandists also aimed to undermine enemy morale and to bolster that of the occupied nations. During the first year of the war, some amateurish efforts were made to drive a wedge between the German masses and the Nazi leadership, but by 1940 the futility of this line had become clear. The British broadcasters then shifted to an emphasis on the strength and determination of the British and their allies, the broadening stream of aid from the United States, and the relative ineffectiveness of German attempts to terrorize or starve out Britain by air or submarine attacks. At first, such talk seemed empty bravado, and inspired sarcastic responses from Goebbels' services. But by 1941, and increasingly thereafter, Continental listeners began to be impressed. Most effective of all were the BBC's programs beamed to occupied countries, where appeals for moral and active resistance to the Germans struck a responsive chord. The BBC played a major role in organizing a mass resistance movement in Denmark, and its broadcasts to France (both by regular BBC speakers and by facilities provided to de Gaulle) were almost as important. It was a BBC official who hit on the V-for-victory sign, with its accompanying musical motif, the first four notes of Beethoven's Fifth Symphony. No other wartime symbol was as effective; Goebbels was eventually driven to try to take it over as a German symbol. During the latter part of the war, BBC broadcasters were working round the clock, transmitting 160,000 words daily in twenty-three languages. The British also steadily expanded the use of printed propaganda dropped from the air, and directed at both civilians and enemy soldiers. Millions of leaflets, miniature reproductions of periodicals, and "air newspapers" were dropped by the R.A.F. and, later, by the American air force. The impact of this campaign, though impossible to measure, seems to have been less great than that of the broadcasters.

After the first year of the war, the British also turned to imitating the German technique of "black" propaganda. The idea ran into sharp opposition in British official circles, on the ground that it might eventually undermine confidence in the dependability of Britain's "white" or open broadcasts. But in 1941, authorization was granted for an experiment in "black" propaganda with a special twist. The new British station, manned in part by German prisoners-of-war, pretended not only to be located in German-controlled territory but to be run by Germans sincerely loyal to Hitler. As the alleged voice of a group of patriotic Wehrmacht officers sickened by the schemers who surrounded the incorruptible Fuehrer, the station sought to propagate subversive rumors under cover of patriotic clichés. The author of this scheme, the British journalist Sefton Delmer, described the technique as "psychological judo." It continued to operate until 1943, when it went off the air with a flourish: a burst of machine-gun fire interrupted a broadcast, and the station was never heard again.

As a substitute, the British now moved into a new field of "gray" propaganda. A more powerful new station, aimed primarily at the German armed forces, also pretended to be a clandestine German enterprise, but in this case the pretense was rather opaque. Most of its listeners knew it to be British-operated—hence the label "gray." *Soldatensender Calais* built up a sizable audience by offering lively programs of popular music, together with detailed reports of British bombing raids in Germany and "doctored" news items designed to whet the curiosity of soldiers a long way from home. The more orthodox "white" propagandists were never reconciled to these "black" and "gray" operations, which they considered risky and ineffective; the clandestine broadcasters retorted that they were reaching a virgin audience that would have scorned the more staid BBC offerings. Debate over the utility of clandestine broadcasting was to continue into the postwar years, with neither side able to marshal convincing evidence to prove its case.

The entry of the United States into the war further complicated the organizational problems of the British psychological warriors, but it also added immensely to their physical facilities and their skilled personnel. An amicable merging of effort was eventually arranged, though the American operation contributed its own internal tensions between two rival agencies, the Office of War Information and the Office of Strategic Services. The British and Americans joined forces to form a Psychological Warfare Division, attached to Eisenhower's headquarters, that operated in the battle zone in North Africa and later on the Continent. It received policy directives from a combined committee of the British PWE and the American OWI; its principal function was to prepare leaflet and other printed propaganda designed to impair German army morale and to encourage desertions. For this purpose, the need to establish credibility no longer held; any kind of deception was in order.

Some abortive attempts were also made to coordinate Soviet psychological warfare with that of the Western Allies. Soon after the invasion of Russia, the British had proposed such collaboration, but without success; Moscow preferred to shape its own line in broadcasts and pamphlets aimed at the German invaders.[7] During the early months, that line consisted of an attempt to drive a wedge between the German common soldier and his government. Its failure was total. Such an appeal to an army in the full flush of victory would be unlikely to find hearers in any case; but the clumsiness of Soviet proceddure ensured its miscarriage. Soviet propaganda materials, heavily loaded with Marxist-Leninist phraseology, summoned the presumably class-conscious German troops to stop sacrificing themselves for their plutocratic masters. By 1942 the futility of this effort was becoming clear to the Russians, and the emphasis slowly shifted toward a more

[7] For a brief period in 1944, Soviet representatives were sent to London to participate in weekly policy meetings on psychological warfare; but they soon took offense at the proceedings, and brusquely returned to Moscow.

persuasive set of themes: appeals to the patriotic sentiments of German soldiers, and to their instinct of self-preservation. Beginning in 1943, Soviet propagandists made great use of the Free Germany Committee, an organization of émigré German Communists and prisoners of war set up under Soviet sponsorship. But its primary purpose—to encourage German desertions—was not achieved. More effective were Soviet ventures into "black" propaganda. Leaflets purporting to be from official German sources, but containing one or two cleverly-inserted propaganda items, were showered over the German lines. Goebbels was sufficiently concerned to take special measures to counteract their impact.

Soviet domestic propaganda underwent even more drastic changes in the course of the war. During the early months, the government's lack of confidence in its own citizens produced a fully reciprocal lack of trust among those citizens. Shortly after the invasion, all private radios were called in by the police, to ensure against clandestine listening to enemy broadcasts; news was circulated by public loudspeakers. But the government hesitated to admit what was often public knowledge: the fall of Smolensk, for example, was not announced until almost a month after the city had fallen. A serious credibility gap developed for a time, and doubtless contributed to the morale crisis in Moscow in mid-October 1941. By autumn, the Kremlin had begun to adapt its tactics; ideological and class themes rapidly gave way to an increased stress on Soviet and even Russian patriotism. The emotional power of national sentiment could no longer be ignored—though it caused some embarrassment to Soviet propagandists when they sought to stimulate loyalty and the war spirit in the Ukraine and other minority regions. Films and newspapers resurrected epochs of the Russian past when strong political or military leaders, supported by the courageous masses, had saved the motherland from alien enemies. Partisan groups operating behind the German lines were allowed an even greater degree of flexibility in adapting their psychological warfare techniques to local needs. Some were even permitted to go so far as to preach the doctrine of land for the peasant; but the commoner theme was German brutality—a theme that won credibility wherever the German occupation authorities had been seen in action.

The effects of psychological warfare are never easy to assess; indeed, the very nature of the operation probably rules out any accurate assessment. After the war of 1914–1918, there had been a widespread tendency to exaggerate the role of propaganda in the final defeat of Germany. As a result, too much was probably expected of it during the Second World War, so that many postwar estimates were colored by disillusionment. A noted British historian has observed that since each nation followed its own leaders to the bitter end, psychological warfare in the years 1939–1945 must be adjudged a disappointing failure. An American scholar adds that nations under Hitler's heel—occupied France, for example—proved immune to the Nazis' mass manipulation through propaganda, demonstrating thus that built-in psychological defenses are tougher than mass-manipulation theorists like Chakotine had led men to believe. Yet who can be sure that the dogged loyalty of the Germans to their government was not traceable in part to the persuasive home propaganda of Goebbels? How can one know that the occupied countries would have resisted Goebbels' blandishments as staunchly if there had been no psychological countermeasures by the Allies? And is it not possible that postwar Germany would have followed a quite different course if no German citizen during the war years had been exposed to the ideas smuggled in via radio from London and Moscow? The experience of the Second World War demonstrated once again that propaganda cannot win wars, but that it can supplement military action to speed and shape the outcome. Possibly it suggests as well that psychological warfare, like radioactivity, may have its side effects, its hidden consequences, that will emerge unsuspected in the years that follow.

Chapter Five

THE BROADENING SCOPE OF WAR: THE SCIENTIFIC DIMENSION

I. SCIENTISTS, SOLDIERS, AND STATESMEN

As THE Second World War ended in Europe, the British physicist Sir Henry Tizard noted in his diary: "I wonder if the part that scientists have played will ever be faithfully and fully recorded. Probably not."[1] Tizard had some reason to be morose; historians of warfare have traditionally tended to concentrate on soldiers and strategies rather than on the technical advances that may have contributed to victory. But with the coming of technological war, the scientist's role became far more vital than ever before. When victory or defeat might hinge on the application of new theoretical discoveries, soldiers and statesmen could no longer afford to treat scientists as minor bureaucrats of a highly specialized type. In the forcing-ground of total war, a new and more intimate partnership was likely to grow up. And the product of this partnership, despite Tizard's gloomy forecast, was to be too important for either historians or informed citizens to ignore. That great phrasemaker Winston Churchill was to dramatize the scientists' contribution by labeling it "the wizard war."

In a sense, of course, the application of technology to warfare was centuries old. Until recent times, however, this effort had rarely transcended the rather elementary level of weapons development. Pure science, as contrasted to applied science, had seemed to have little direct relevance to war. The beginnings of change could be seen in the 1914 conflict, when chemists made a particular contribution in developing improved explosives, poison gases, and synthetics, and when aeronautics experts succeeded in building the first combat air force. That war left behind it a residue of military respect for the scientist's contribution; in all major nations, the armed forces maintained scientific research staffs during the interwar years. In general, however, these staffs were small and their prestige limited. Their function was seen as useful but essentially menial—rather like that of the black-

---

[1] C. P. Snow, *Science and Government* (Cambridge, Mass., 1961), p. 4.

smith in cavalry days, except for the fact that weapons development required somewhat greater expertise than shoeing mules.

There were, of course, some exceptions; in a technological age, not all soldiers and statesmen were unaware of the mysterious potentialities of burgeoning science. German military leaders, relying on their nation's long pre-eminence in many scientific fields, took for granted that German science would continue to outpace that of any rival power. Hitler himself had a passionate interest in weapons of a new and dramatic kind; but his enthusiasms were somewhat volatile, and were guided by his moods rather than by the opinions of technical experts. In Great Britain, during the interwar years, the greatest receptivity to new scientific ideas was to be found in the air force command. Lacking a long tradition, this branch of the service was less hidebound than the army or navy; and besides, its very existence depended on recent and continuing scientific advances.

Shortly before the war began, the Royal Society (Britain's most renowned association of scientists) undertook a kind of census of scientific manpower, and developed a central register of some seven thousand specialists willing to do war work in case of national emergency. When war came, the register was used in rather haphazard fashion by the various branches of the armed services to recruit scientists for a variety of ad hoc problems that needed solving. At the end of the first year, the pool of available talent was threatening to run dry, and complaints about the unsystematic use of scientific manpower began to be voiced. Since the summer of 1939, officials of the Royal Society had been urging a more sensible allocation policy; they stepped up their campaign in 1940. They were also disturbed at the lack of direct communication between the scientific community and the government. The War Cabinet, they believed, needed direct and continuing access to the best possible scientific advice instead of the informal and limited contact that had been the rule to date. Somewhat reluctantly, Churchill agreed in October 1940 to set up a Scientific Advisory Committee attached to the War Cabinet. The Prime Minister saw to it, however, that the committee's powers were narrowly restricted; he warned its members at the very outset not to "meddle with our innards."[2] Churchill preferred to depend for advice on the man who had long been his intimate consultant in matters scientific: Professor F. A. Lindemann of Oxford, who was soon to be elevated to the peerage as Lord Cherwell.

[2] R. W. Clark, *The Rise of the Boffins* (London, 1962), p. 158.

The presence of this eminent scientist at the elbow of the Prime Minister, though unprecedented in ·time of war, by no means sufficed to relieve all tensions between scientists and government. Cherwell was a highly controversial figure, and his long feud with Sir Henry Tizard, the government's most influential scientific adviser prior to Churchill's accession to power, increased the division in the scientific community. By 1942 this dissatisfaction was spreading to Parliament, one of whose committees urged the creation of a full-time scientific and technical board "to coordinate research and development in relation to the war effort and to ensure that the experience, knowledge, and creative genius of British technicians and scientists exert a more effective influence over the conduct of a highly mechanized war."[3] But none of these complaints produced any significant results; until the war ended, Cherwell was to remain a kind of one-man advisory committee enjoying (as his bitter critic C. P. Snow was later to put it) "more direct power than any scientist in history."[4] Churchill refused to be budged from his conviction that no board of scientists should be allowed an imperious voice in directing the war.

Below the cabinet level, on the other hand, relations between scientists and soldiers grew increasingly friendly and intimate. Although one officer remarked ironically to Tizard that "he could hardly walk in any direction in this war without tumbling over a scientist who had got in his way," and another protested that wars were won with weapons, not with slide rules, most of the old barriers between the two professions were eroded as scientists and fighting men worked together on a wide variety of joint problems. A notable example of this new sense of partnership was the series of informal weekly sessions at the home of the radar expert A. P. Rowe. These so-called "Sunday Soviets" attracted a mixed group of high officers, technicians, and pure scientists who met on terms of complete equality and discussed all kinds of topics without restraint. This kind of mutual relationship undoubtedly increased the effectiveness of scientists in the war, for when the theorists and the practitioners were in constant collaboration, problems could be raised and solved with minimum delay.

Germany's utilization of scientists during the war took a quite different form. Despite the prestige that scientists had always enjoyed in German society, their wartime influence and effectiveness fell considerably short of that achieved by either British or American scien-

[3] *Ibid.*
[4] Snow, *Science and Government,* p. 63.

tists. In part, this may have been a consequence of the Nazi leadership's lack of understanding of, and respect for, pure science. Hitler's intimate knowledge of weapons was not accompanied by any true comprehension of scientific method or its possibilities. Obsessed by the idea of a panacea weapon, he wanted no expert to frustrate his desires. More serious still, both Hitler and the German general staff believed until midway through the war that victory was just around the corner, and could be won by orthodox methods. There seemed to be no need, therefore, to organize German talent and resources for anything beyond *ad hoc* scientific projects of the short-term sort. At one point, after France fell in 1940, the general staff ordered the suspension of any program of scientific research or development that would not produce usable military results within four months; a number of scientists were drafted into regular units for the impending invasion of Britain. Not until the latter half of 1942 did the Germans make a desperate effort to spur scientific activity—and by then it was too late.

At the working level, too, the Germans apparently failed to develop the cordial scientist-soldier collaboration that marked the British war effort. Much remarkable research was carried out in Germany during the war, but regular communication between the scientists and the operational leaders was quite inadequate. Too often, the soldiers were inclined to view the scientists as subordinate technicians rather than as partners in a common enterprise. Even at the developmental stage, scientific advice was neglected; the various development committees set up by Speer were dominated by representatives of industry and the army, with only a small sprinkling of scientists. It is true, of course, that the inclusion of scientists in the Third Reich's policy-making machinery might not have altered things very much, for scientists, like other specialists, are frequently fallible and occasionally naïve. Still, there were moments during the war when a rational and objective voice was desperately needed to arbitrate the factional feuds within the Nazi system, and to point out the possible consequences of neglecting scientific knowledge in the midst of war.

II. RADAR AND ITS REFINEMENTS

If any scientific device were to give its name to the Second World War, that device would probably be radar. In the air and on the sea, its importance for both defense and offense was to be crucial. Unlike the atomic bomb, it came into use at the beginning rather than the end of the war, and wartime improvements were to render it steadily more effective.

The idea of using the reflected echo of radio waves for locating a distant object was first tried in a primitive way in the 1920's; but it was not until the next decade that scientists in a number of countries—Germany, Italy, Great Britain, and the United States—began to experiment seriously with the idea. The most dramatic chapter of the story (and, for the outcome of the Second World War, the most significant) was that written by the British. Soon after Hitler took power and set out to build up a German air fleet, some British political leaders and air force officers began to worry about the future defense of London and other highly vulnerable cities. Air force exercises over London in 1934 suggested a gloomy prospect: the simulated attackers, given the House of Parliament and the Air Ministry as their targets, demolished both. It seemed that Stanley Baldwin had been right when he had said resignedly in 1932, "The bomber will always get through." The Air Ministry promptly set up a small committee of scientists to study possible methods of air defense; it was headed by the physicist Henry Tizard, rector of the Imperial College of Science and Technology. At its second meeting in 1935, the Tizard committee heard a report from Robert Watson-Watt, director of a small team of government radio experts, suggesting the use of radio echoes to detect approaching planes. The committee seized on the idea and assigned the experimental work to Watson-Watt who, within a month, demonstrated the feasibility of the idea by carrying out an experimental flight with rudimentary equipment. The work continued secretly and steadily. In 1937 the first coastal radar station was ready; and by spring 1939, a chain of twenty stations along the south and east coasts went into regular operation. The scientists had succeeded in "making England an island again."[5]

German intelligence made some sporadic efforts to find what the British were up to; in 1939 they even sent the dirigible *Graf Zeppelin* over the area with special listening devices, but these failed to work well. A year later, victory in the air Battle of Britain was to depend in considerable part on the early warnings provided by the new radar chain. Yet even during that battle, the German high command was to show a strange indifference or lack of understanding;

[5] J. G. Crowther and R. Whiddington, *Science at War* (London, 1947), p. 10.

the *Luftwaffe* soon shifted its attacks away from the radar stations, and left them largely intact during the height of the blitz. The Germans, remarks one historian, "chose to ignore the advent of science in warfare."[6]

Radar alone, however, would not have sufficed to win the Battle of Britain. The R.A.F. also needed an effective ground-control system to direct fighter planes on the basis of the early warnings that radar would provide; and such a system could not be hastily improvised. Tizard had been the first to foresee this need, and with his remarkable skill at interpreting scientific conceptions to military men, he had persuaded the air force to attack the problem of ground control even before the radar screen became operative—indeed, even before anyone could be sure that it would ever be operative. Beginning in 1937, the air force undertook exercises based on the presumption that radar would work; and by 1940, it had solved most of the initial difficulties. Thanks to these timely preparations, British fighters were employed so effectively in 1940 that German intelligence decided it must have seriously underestimated the R.A.F.'s strength. Gadgetry and foresight were thus combined with courage and daring to save Britain from defeat, and to alter the course of the entire war.

That the Germans failed to recognize the importance of British radar is the more surprising since their own scientists had been working in the field in prewar years, and had in fact outpaced the British in certain respects. Their "Freya" device was successfully tried as early as 1936, and by 1938 it could detect approaching aircraft at a distance of sixty miles, with greater accuracy than the British radar system. Indeed, the Germans won the initial radar victory of the war. In December 1939, they spotted a group of twenty-two British bombers approaching the north German coast, and shot down twelve of them.

More serious still, the Germans were far ahead of the British in the use of radar for offensive purposes. They had developed a radio directional beam that could be used to guide their attacking bombers to the target. Two of these beams from widely separated transmitters were laid so as to intersect at the target city; when the German plane reached the intersection, it dropped its bomb load. The device was first used during the summer of 1940, but the British quickly learned to jam or "bend" the beam so that many bombs fell in open fields. The Germans were prepared, however, with an even better sub-

[6] D. Wood and D. Dempster, *The Narrow Margin* (London, 1961), p. 20.

stitute device: the so-called X-Gerät. a complex beam which could be operated on various frequencies in order to avoid jamming. It was first used in a night raid on the great industrial city of Coventry in November 1940, with terrifying results; and for several months Britain reeled under successive blows to one city after another. Once again, it was radar that came to the rescue. Since 1939 the British had been experimenting with small airborne radar sets that could be installed in fighter planes in order to search out attacking bombers. These sets, combined with radio ground control, came into general use during the winter blitz of 1940–1941, and contributed more than any other single factor to blunting the effectiveness of the enemy's night attacks.

Meanwhile, the Germans had been losing their initial advantage in radar development. Hitler and his generals had their minds fixed on the Russian campaign, where manpower and machines far outweighed electronics in importance. A psychological factor doubtless operated here too; for the Germans, unlike the British, had not been saved from probable defeat in 1940 by a purely scientific device, and had less reason to view the contribution of the radar experts with healthy respect. Eventually German leaders were to recognize their error; late in 1942 they re-entered the "radar war" in vigorous fashion, granting vastly increased authority over manpower and materials to their top radio expert, General Martini. But the decision had been too long delayed; henceforth it was the British and Americans who maintained the initiative, while the Germans were kept busy countering one new weapon after another.

By this time the Atlantic powers had shifted their attention from the defensive to the offensive use of radar. Their bomber force had met unforeseen difficulties in the skies over Germany; planes often failed to find their targets, and even more often failed to hit those targets. They needed navigational aids to carry their aircraft through murky weather or darkness; bombing devices to permit them to strike accurately; techniques to frustrate the Germans' radar defenses. By 1942, all of these needs had been at least partially met by British scientists. A navigational system called "Gee" utilizing three radio pulse transmitters went into use early in 1942, but within six months the Germans had learned to jam it successfully. A blind-bombing device code-named "Oboe" was soon added; radar transmitting stations dispatched the attacking bomber along a beam, and kept track of its location by means of a device that measured its ground speed. On arrival over the unseen target, the ground station notified the crew by a special signal, so that in effect the bombs were dropped by a technician back on English soil. With the introduction of "Oboe," the age of visual bombing virtually came to an end.

Although "Oboe" was used until the end of the war, it was susceptible to German jamming, and it could be used for only limited numbers of aircraft. For mass raids, a new blind-bombing device was shortly added to the British arsenal: the so-called H_2S system, an airborne radar set whose downward-looking transmitter allowed the air crews to "see" through clouds and darkness below them. The key component in H_2S was the cavity magnetron, a small and simple device invented in 1940 by two physicists at Birmingham University. The magnetron, it has been said, "probably had a more decisive effect on the war than any other single new weapon."[7] It produced a powerful high-frequency beam which made possible microwave radar, a vastly improved type which replaced the old longer-wave radar in fighter planes and ships as well as in bombers. H_2S enabled Bomber Command to find certain types of targets at night with remarkable accuracy. Used for the first time over Hamburg in January 1943, it produced devastating results. It was soon utilized in the antisubmarine campaign as well. Heretofore, British bombers on Atlantic patrol had carried old-style radar to locate U-boats, but its effectiveness was lost as the German navy found ways to detect approaching planes. The new microwave radar, first used in search planes in March 1943, led to a slaughter of U-boats during the next three months. German scientists eventually devised countermeasures, but by that time the Battle of the Atlantic had been won by the Allies.

Once the main battlefield in the air war had shifted to the skies over Germany, the British had to seek ways to frustrate the Germans' radar defenses. Their most successful device, remarkably simple in conception, bore the code name "Window." It involved dropping tin foil or aluminum strips over a target city; each strip caused a blip on the German radar screens, exactly as though it had been an aircraft. For many months, however, the British hesitated to use this technique for fear the Germans might retaliate in kind over Britain. When "Window" was eventually employed for the first time over Hamburg in July 1943, British bomber losses were cut to one-tenth of those normally expected in such a raid. The device worked effectively

[7] Crowther and Whiddington, *Science at War*, p. 39.

for almost a year before the Germans developed adequate counter-measures. And while the Germans had worked out their equivalent of "Window" even earlier than the British, they could never utilize it, for they could no longer spare bombers and gasoline for raids on Britain.

III. SLIDE-RULE WARFARE

Traditionally, scientists had been used in war to provide ideas for new weapons or to suggest improvements in old ones. The war of 1939 added a new function: the use of scientists in connection with actual military operations, with a view to greater effectiveness or economy of effort. For this function the British in 1940 coined the term "operational research." The term is not easy to define, but the physicist C. P. Snow sums it up as simply "thinking scientifically about operations."

Operational research began as a kind of accidental by-product of radar development. Scientists not only devised the new equipment; they then proceeded to join with air force personnel to test it out in team fashion. The essential contribution of the scientists impressed itself on the Air Ministry and the R.A.F., who became aware that hit-or-miss methods were no longer good enough in a technological war. During the early war years, operational research sections were quietly introduced into many different branches of the air force; and from 1941 onward, the other armed services and the civil defense authorities began to imitate the practice. Statistical techniques combined with the scrupulous habits of observation of the trained scientist provided a check on the effectiveness of current operations, and proved invaluable in working out better ways to do things.

As early as 1940, for example, the army called on operational research to study the complexities of applying radar to anti-aircraft fire. A team that carefully analyzed anti-aircraft operations during the Battle of Britain quickly spotted serious deficiencies, and proposed a regrouping of batteries and an altered firing pattern that yielded far better results. Highly detailed studies were made of bomb damage in British cities, both to improve civil defense measures and to help plan the eventual bomber attacks on Germany. When those attacks got under way, scientists tackled the problem of the traffic pattern involved in sending a thousand bombers over a target city. For the army, laboratory tests were run on the effects of various weapons in different sets of circumstances; and eventually, operational research teams accompanied the troops during actual military operations, studying battles in some cases from the initial assault to the end of the action. For the navy, the scientists studied the proper depth at which to detonate depth bombs; the best color to camouflage aircraft assigned to Atlantic patrol; and the optimum size of convoys as they passed through the danger zone. Indeed, operational research may have rivaled microwave radar for top honors as the most important single factor in winning the Battle of the Atlantic.

Of the other warring powers, only the United States developed the practice of slide-rule warfare to a degree that paralleled the British effort. The Germans' lesser interest in operational research techniques may seem surprising in light of their traditional excellence in science and their taste for the systematic. It may be that the neoromantic flavor of Nazi doctrine had something to do with it; for operational research tended to reduce war to a rational process, coldly analytical rather than subjectively heroic. Perhaps there is some truth in the epigrammatic remark of a British historian: "One reason why Hitler failed is that he was out-of-date."[8]

IV. WEAPONS TECHNOLOGY

A much more traditional aspect of the application of science to warfare is the realm of weapons technology: the refinement of old weapons, the development of new ones. Here engineers and technicians played a considerably greater role than pure scientists, and their collaboration was more readily accepted by the soldiers. Military hardware was easier to comprehend than theoretical talk about bouncing radio waves off aircraft or calculating probabilities by the use of statistical method.

In weapons technology, the Germans enjoyed a clear lead over other European countries when the war began. Their military buildup had begun late, so that none of their equipment was outmoded; and the Spanish civil war had provided a practical testing ground for German planes and tanks, some of which were modified after that experience. Qualitatively as well as quantitatively, the German arsenal was an awesome sight when paraded before foreign visitors; motorized equipment, tanks, guns, bombers, fighters were the equal or the superior of the best models possessed in 1939 by any rival power.

[8] *Ibid.*, p. 120.

If the Germans at the outset regarded any device as their miracle weapon, it was probably the magnetic mine. The British had used a primitive version of the device during the latter part of the First World War, but the new German model was vastly improved. Sown in the Channel and the North Sea, these mines would be exploded by the magnetic attraction of passing ships, and seemed likely to disrupt Britain's commercial shipping. Acoustic and water-pressure mines were available to supplement the magnetic variety. For a brief period, it appeared that the Germans' hopes were well founded: during the first three months of the war, Britain lost more than 200,000 tons of ships per month to mines alone. But British scientists soon hit on a simple countermeasure in the form of the demagnetizing or "degaussing" of ships, and rendered the magnetic mine virtually useless. During the Dunkirk evacuation in 1940, which cost the British over two hundred vessels, only two were sunk by magnetic mines.

As the battlefield shifted from sea to air, the British experimented with a number of schemes to interfere with German air attacks. A balloon barrage anchored about London proved relatively ineffective. Free balloons trailing networks of wire and bombs were then projected, but the Battle of Britain ended before the equipment was ready. For a time, the British devoted much time and energy to developing aerial mines: drifting bombs on the end of long wires, to be sown in the path of approaching German bombers by British planes or artillery. Lord Cherwell was the most vigorous advocate of this scheme, but his confidence in it was misplaced. It was never effectively used during the war; nor was a similar device which the Germans later developed.

Perhaps the most widely used new weapon of the war was the simple short-range powder rocket, fired in many cases from multibarreled launching devices. Although powder rockets had been used in warfare during the Middle Ages and again for a time during the early nineteenth century, they had long since been displaced by modern artillery. The war of 1939 reintroduced them on a large scale; rocket guns were installed on aircraft and naval vessels, or were hauled to the front on trucks. During the early weeks of the German attack on Russia, the Nebelwerfer and Wurfgerät rocket launchers were among the most effective weapons the Nazis possessed; but the Soviet armies quickly retaliated in kind with such devices as the "Stalin organ," which could fire forty-eight rockets at once. The Americans in Tunisia first introduced the small antitank rocket gun called the bazooka, and similar weapons came into prompt use everywhere. In 1944 the Germans began to install on their fighter planes a rocket launcher so effective that its use might have posed a serious threat to Allied bombers if the war had continued for another year. German scientists also experimented in 1942 with launching powder rockets from submerged submarines; but this promising idea was blocked by interservice rivalries. A radio-controlled rocket for anti-aircraft defense was also proposed by German weapons developers, but failed to get official sanction and remained in the theoretical stage.

Rivaling the rocket in importance, but developed much later in the war, was the proximity fuse. This ingenious device, produced in quantity in the United States on the basis of research carried out in Britain, and invented independently by the Germans as well, greatly increased the effectiveness of anti-aircraft defense. Shells from ground batteries and fighter planes no longer had to score direct hits on the target; the proximity fuse exploded the shell when it came near enough the enemy craft to be activated by the noise.

One vital wartime race—the development of jet engines for aircraft—ended in a virtual dead heat between the Germans and the Anglo-Americans. Young free-lance engineers had been working on applications of the jet principle in both Germany and Britain during the 1930's; the Germans achieved a slight lead by putting a Heinkel turbojet into the air five days before Hitler's invasion of Poland. But the *Luftwaffe* authorities lacked interest in the project, and failed to press ahead with further experiments. In England, on the other hand, Tizard and later Lord Cherwell lent official support to Frank Whittle, the engineer who had been a lonely pioneer for jet power. Government subsidies kept Whittle's small company alive during the difficult early years of the war, and he achieved a successful trial flight in 1941. Churchill was persuaded to authorize a speedup in development both of the Whittle engine and of a plane to carry it. But technical difficulties and rival demands for resources slowed the work, and it was not until the summer of 1944 that the first Gloster Meteors became operational. Since their range was short, they were used primarily to shoot down the German V-1 missiles.

By this time, the Germans had made rapid strides toward catching up in jet development. In 1942 the Messerschmidt firm successfully flew an experimental ME-262 turbojet, and proposed to begin immediate mass production of both that plane and an even more advanced ME–163 model. Once again the government failed to press its opportunity; competing demands for tanks and U-boats were severe, and the rocket program offered an alternative temptation to Hitler in his search for a panacea weapon. It was not until the summer of 1944 that the first ME–262's and ME–163's became operational. During the last year of hostilities about two thousand jet planes were built, though half of them were never used due to lack of fuel. A factory for the mass production of ME–262's was scheduled for completion in April 1945, with a capacity of 1250 planes a month. The Messerschmidt, armed with rocket launchers, might have had a formidable effect on the course of the air war if perfected two years earlier. By 1944, however, the Germans' margin was too narrow; both the British and the Americans were only slightly behind in the mass-production jet race.

V. THE MEDICAL SCIENCES

Improved devices for killing are natural by-products of warfare. Improved techniques of healing follow along at some distance in the rear; yet they too are likely to be stimulated by wartime needs. In earlier wars, the problem was simply to maintain armies at the peak of fighting fitness through control of epidemic diseases and better methods of battlefield surgery. The Second World War broadened the concerns of doctors and medical researchers to include the civilian populations as well, for home-front fitness and morale were almost as important as the physical state of the fighting forces. The strain of a long war, the unprecedented ratio of civilian casualties, and the need to ensure adequate nutrition in a time of consumer shortages confronted medical science with a greatly expanded list of problems. On the other hand, these same factors also provided medical scientists with unprecedented opportunities for experimentation and statistical analysis of disease. Even though most long-range research had to be suspended in favor of meeting immediate needs, medicine nevertheless profited by the fact that some governments devoted so large a share of their available resources to the advance of the healing arts.

Great Britain and the United States set the pace in this realm. In Britain, a government-sponsored Medical Research Council had been functioning since 1920; it immediately assumed most of the task of coordinating wartime research, and vastly broadened its work by establishing many new committees to tackle particular problems that ranged from the treatment of wounds, burns, and traumatic shock to the control of infectious hepatitis and the feeding of the nation at war. In most branches of medicine, notable progress occurred under the stimulus of war; in a few cases, the progress was spectacular. For its short-run effect during the war years, improved malaria control was probably most notable; for the longer future, the development of the sulfa drugs and of penicillin undoubtedly ranks first in importance.

German chemists had made the initial breakthrough in malaria control during the First World War, when they were cut off from supplies of quinine and succeeded in synthesizing atebrin as a substitute. The Second World War brought the same problem home to the Western Allies, who lost their source of quinine (Java) in 1942, and who faced a major campaign in malarial regions. British and American chemists promptly came up with their own version of atebrin (mepacrine), which proved far superior to quinine. New insecticides and repellents soon followed, and did much to reduce the incidence of malaria. The most effective insecticide, DDT, had been known since the late nineteenth century, but its insecticidal properties were not discovered until Swiss chemists happened onto the fact in 1939. Their work went unnoticed for a time, and was not picked up by the British and Americans until 1943. Thereafter, DDT was produced and used in large quantities by the Western powers. Its effectiveness extended beyond malaria to a number of other damaging diseases, notably certain forms of dysentery and typhus.

A beginning in the use of the sulfonamide drugs had also been made before the war; they had been in limited clinical use for about five years. The most rapid strides, however, were made under the impact of the war. Dozens of new sulfa compounds were developed in British and American laboratories, and their use was extended to a broad spectrum of ailments and injuries. Still more important was the discovery of penicillin's curative properties. Alexander Fleming had been the earliest pioneer in 1929, but for a decade its usefulness in medicine had been pretty well discounted, even by its discoverer. Shortly before the outbreak of war, Howard Florey at Oxford began a new investigation of this and other similar substances. By 1941 he and E. Chain had succeeded in extracting penicillin in active and stable form, and had found through experiments that it possessed great antibacterial potency when circulated in the blood stream. Because British industry was too busy to undertake its commercial production, Florey went to the United States in 1941 and persuaded American firms to do so. Most of the wartime penicillin was therefore American-produced, though smaller amounts began to come out of Great Britain by 1945. Its first use was in the treatment of war wounds during the North African campaign in 1943; as production increased, it came into broader military and even civilian use, though the supply had to be strictly controlled throughout the war. Penicillin marked a kind of revolution in chemotherapy—the arrival of the antibiotic age.

In the field of nutrition, British experts were offered an unusual chance during the war to experiment with the national diet and to measure the results. Severe shortages of fats, animal protein, and fresh fruits might have been expected to cause a decline in health standards; instead, those standards improved somewhat during the latter part of the war. This result was achieved by careful management of the national diet to distribute available supplies more fairly among all groups and to ensure the enrichment of such basic foodstuffs as flour and milk with the essential vitamins.

One curious medical phenomenon of the Second World War, both in Britain and throughout most of the Continent, was the high incidence of peptic ulcers both in the armed forces and among civilians. The contrast with the First World War was striking: in 1914-1915 ulcers caused only 709 discharges from the British armed forces, while in 1939-1941 the figure was over 23,000. A similar increase occurred among workers in war industries. In the Soviet Union, factories provided special dietetic facilities for ulcer sufferers, while the German army set up special units to which they were assigned. The highest incidence among civilians was reached during and after periods of intense air bombardment; among soldiers, it was during periods of static rather than active warfare. British studies suggested that even more important than the altered character of warfare was the steady rise in the tensions of twentieth-century life. Most wartime ulcer victims in Britain had prior medical histories dating from the interwar years, and quickly suffered recurrences under the pressures of the conflict. The later years of the war brought a marked decline in the incidence of peptic ulcers, probably because of improved morale and reduced tension.

Little is known of wartime medical advances in Germany, the occupied countries, or the Soviet Union. Apparently the Germans made no attempt to develop penicillin, though they did a little experimenting with the sulfonamides. They also made some progress in the control of typhus, which was a serious threat on the eastern front. But until the last year of the war Germany suffered neither serious epidemics nor grave food shortages that might have stimulated crash programs of medical research. In the occupied countries and the concentration camps, on the other hand, such diseases as typhus were common toward the end, and German doctors were evidently unable to check their ravages. The British are said to have found sixty thousand typhus cases in the Bergen-Belsen camp alone when they liberated it in 1945. Malnutrition was also severe in many of the occupied countries, notably in eastern Europe and the Balkans. Infant mortality and the incidence of tuberculosis rose sharply there during the later war years, though the lasting damage from malnutrition was less grave than might have been expected. That permanent damage could result from wartime strain and shortages has been amply demonstrated, however, by follow-up studies of men who spent the war years in prisoner-of-war camps. Twenty years after the end of hostilities, specialists reported that ex-prisoners showed an abnormally high incidence of nervous and psychiatric disorders, of premature aging, and of susceptibility to such diseases as tuberculosis and hepatitis.

One notorious footnote to the story of wartime medical research in Germany was the use of concentration camp inmates as human guinea pigs. These unwilling victims were subjected to a wide variety of experiments designed to determine the effects of high altitude, low pressure, freezing, and exposure, and to test various types of vaccines and drugs. "Euthanasia" techniques were also tried out on prisoners, as a prelude to organizing programs of either mass sterilization or direct elimination of "racial inferiors" and "undesirables." The distorted motives behind many of these experiments would suffice to condemn them by any civilized standard. What made the procedure even more reprehensible was that it evidently failed to push back the frontiers of medical knowledge in any useful way. After the war, a number of SS doctors were convicted of war crimes for these concentration camp activities.

VI. THE COMING OF THE MISSILE AGE

For a generation before 1939, a handful of unorthodox scientists and a few widely-scattered lay enthusiasts had been fascinated by the idea of long-range self-propelled rockets. Few of these theorists and tinkerers had a new weapon in mind; their real interest was in rapid transportation or space travel. The earliest pioneer of the missile age was a self-educated Russian physics teacher named K. E. Tsiolkovsky who, beginning in 1903, preached the possibility of travel in space and worked out many of the theoretical problems of rocket construction. During the 1920's, Hermann Oberth in Germany and R. H. Goddard in the United States retraced Tsiolkovsky's theoretical steps, and Goddard moved from theory to practice by firing the world's first liquid-fueled rocket in 1926. Societies of rocket fanciers were organized in several countries, and their members were hard at work trying to build a workable rocket motor.

It was only in the Soviet Union and Germany, however, that such dreamers were given much official encouragement during the interwar years. In Russia, where a successful rocket motor was tested in 1933, the Soviet government in 1934 took over official control of all rocket research, and clamped a tight secrecy lid on all subsequent activities in the field. By 1939 the Soviet scientists had progressed far enough to launch the world's first two-stage rocket; but thereafter the pressures of war apparently diverted Soviet energies from long-range missiles to improved versions of the simpler short-range powder rocket for battlefield use.

In Germany, the government had taken an even earlier initiative. The Army Weapons Department in 1930 set up a small experimental station near Berlin, headed by Captain Walter Dornberger, to investigate rocket weapons. By 1934 the Germans had caught up with the Russians by building a successful motor, and had fired several small models. In 1937 a sizable grant of government funds enabled Dornberger's team to build a much larger experimental station at Peenemünde, on a remote island in the Baltic.

Hitler, however, remained skeptical about the rocket as an operational possibility in the next war. Although he finally agreed to visit one of the rocket stations six months before his attack on Poland, he departed without committing himself to increased support for rocket development. But Marshal von Brauchitsch, commander-in-chief of the army, was an enthusiastic convert, and in September 1939 he assigned the highest military priority to the rocket program. In the spring of 1940, Hitler brusquely intervened to reverse that decision; indeed, rocket development was removed from the priority list, and many of the rocket scientists and technicians were called up for regular army service in preparation for the invasion of Britain. The program might have disintegrated at that point save for Brauchitsch's continued support; privately, he arranged to assign four thousand highly trained army technicians and laborers to the Peenemünde station.

Thanks to this fortunate lease of life, the rocket scientists pushed forward until, late in 1942, they achieved their most important success: a new model was launched, soared to a height of almost sixty miles, and hit a target more than a hundred miles distant. Nevertheless, Hitler still refused to invest scarce manpower and materials in such a costly and uncertain enterprise, especially at a time when the Russian campaign had made his need for tanks and planes more desperate than ever. Early in 1943 he allegedly told Albert Speer, "I have dreamed that the rocket will never be operational against England. I can rely on my inspirations. It is therefore pointless to give more support to the project."[9]

Meanwhile, the German air force had been hard at work developing its own long-range missile: a "flying bomb" or small pilotless plane powered by a jet-propulsion engine, far cheaper and easier to build than a rocket. Work on this weapon had been under way since 1940 at a research station only a mile from the army's rocket laboratories at Peenemünde. By the end of 1942 the air force had overtaken the army; its first experimental flying bomb was successfully launched in December 1942, only two months after the rocket scientists' great success. Shortly thereafter, one of Speer's industrial development committees studied the two programs, observed tests, and recommended that both weapons be given top priority, since both had reached about the same stage of development. Hitler, in July 1943, at last changed his mind. He agreed to watch films of the 1942 rocket launching, told Dornberger he had been wrong in failing to appreciate the work earlier, and ordered that top priority be assigned to rocket development. Nazi propagandists shortly began to drop public hints that some sort of miracle weapon would soon turn the tide of war.

By this time, British intelligence had begun to piece together bits of information about the German flying bomb and rocket programs. During the prewar years, British officials had shown no interest in rocket research; the Air Ministry had been satisfied that heavy bombers would be sufficient if war came. This lack of interest doubtless

[9] W. Dornberger, *V-2* (New York, 1954), p. 206.

contributed to the failure of British intelligence, in the period 1939–1942, to follow up some scattered items of evidence about the Peenemünde enterprise. In 1942–1943, however, air photographs revealed what appeared to be launching sites for missiles across the Channel, together with torpedo-shaped objects at Peenemünde and elsewhere that might be the missiles themselves. In August 1943 the R.A.F. carried out a massive raid on Peenemünde, which partially wrecked the facility and killed several hundred technicians and workers. Most of the key technicians survived, however, and were transferred to safer underground quarters in the Harz Mountains of central Germany. There, and at a new testing ground in occupied Poland, work on the rocket continued at top speed. The raid on Peenemünde had left the *Luftwaffe's* flying-bomb station unscathed, and its work proceeded without interruption.

Although the rocket experts now had Hitler's full support, they confronted other difficulties almost as serious. The Nazi state was a jungle of overlapping agencies, and a bitter struggle for control of the rocket program soon set in. Himmler's SS eventually emerged on top, but at the cost of much bitter feeling and some delays in the program. There were also serious tensions between Dornberger and his staff on the one hand and Speer's bureaucrats and industrialists on the other. The enormous problems of development and production had been tackled much too late, thanks to Hitler's indifference; it was not enough to assign a top priority to the program, now that manpower and materials were in short supply and now that the Fuehrer's demands for production of all kinds had become flagrantly unreasonable. Nevertheless, the program continued somehow to move ahead, and by mid-1944 both rockets and flying bombs were beginning to be turned out in some quantity.

British and American intelligence, meanwhile, remained uncertain about the nature of the new German weapon and the imminence of the threat it posed. As insurance, they did their best to obliterate the launching sites along the Channel; but until the eve of the Normandy landings, General Eisenhower and his staff feared that a sudden rain of rockets or flying bombs might disrupt the cross-Channel operation. The British government grew nervous, too; for several weeks it discussed the possible evacuation of a million Londoners and the transfer of the government itself to a less threatened city. But D-day came and went without interference by any kind of miracle weapon, comforting those who had always insisted that the whole thing was a German hoax, designed to mislead the Western Allies.

Then, just a week after the Normandy landings, the first German missile struck near London. It was not a rocket, but the *Luftwaffe's* pilotless plane, promptly labeled "V-1" by Goebbels' propaganda machine, and "buzz bomb" by the British. During the next three months, 9300 V-1's were fired toward England, and about two-thirds of them reached the English coast. Their effect, however, was much less grave than the Germans had hoped. Their slow speed and their telltale buzz enabled the British to improvise defensive measures, and before long a large proportion were being shot down by British fighters and anti-aircraft batteries using the new proximity fuse. It was clear that V-1, though a dangerous nuisance, was not the kind of weapon that could win a war.

Meanwhile, Dornberger and his staff were pushing desperately to perfect what Goebbels was to call "V-2"—the larger, longer-range supersonic rocket. Almost three hundred of these had been built by the summer of 1944, but the German scientists were aware of certain defects in them, and wanted time to make some final improvements. Dornberger's superiors, despite his protests, ordered their immediate use. Employing a cleverly devised movable launching device that could easily escape the vigilance of British bombers, the Germans on September 8 fired the first long-range military rocket ever used in warfare. It fell without warning in London, only hours after a high British official, encouraged by the slacking-off of the V-1 attack, had announced that the Battle of London was at last over.

The new blitz continued intermittently for almost seven months, until the Allied advance into the Netherlands at last drove the Germans back out of firing range. During that period about 4300 V-2 rockets were fired: 1500 of them toward England, 2100 toward the port of Antwerp which had been captured almost intact by the Allied forces. Their effect was far more devastating than had been that of the flying bomb. Furthermore, the British had found no way to counter this new weapon: rapid and soundless, it could not be overtaken or shot down by any existing aircraft or system of ground fire. If perfected a year or two earlier, Hitler might have had the "miracle weapon" of which he dreamed—the weapon that might have determined the outcome of the war. But if the German rocket scientists had failed to play the decisive role in the Second World War, they had possibly helped to reshape the character of all future wars.

VII. THE ATOMIC BREAKTHROUGH

In the September 1939 issue of the British scientific magazine *Discovery*, its editor C. P. Snow speculated on the possibility of building an atomic weapon. Opinion among British scientists was divided, declared Snow; some of them even thought that such a weapon might be devised within a few months. If so, he concluded, "science for the first time will at one bound have altered the scope of warfare."[10]

The most eminent scientific figures of the time were, however, skeptical. The greatest of the early pioneers of nuclear research, Lord Rutherford, shortly before his death in 1937, had said that all talk of using nuclear energy for any purpose whatsoever was "moonshine." The future Lord Cherwell told Churchill in 1939 that for several years at least, there was no danger that the enemy might develop a dependable chain reaction. Henry Tizard was equally bearish about the prospects. Yet less than six years later, barely two months after the end of the war in Europe, the first atomic bomb was to be successfully tested, and its operational use was soon to follow at Hiroshima.

Much of the scientific knowledge on which the atomic weapon was based had been building up during the first four decades of the twentieth century. From Roentgen's accidental discovery of the X ray in 1895 there followed a long series of experiments with the radioactive elements found in nature. By 1914, thanks to the work of such scientists as the French-Polish couple Pierre and Marie Curie, the New Zealander Ernest Rutherford, the Englishman Frederick Soddy, and the Dane Niels Bohr, the atom had taken on a new look. In place of the solid billiard-ball concept there had emerged a new model, resembling a tiny solar system, composed of a positively-charged nucleus surrounded by negatively-charged electrons circling in orbit. The experimenters had also discovered that as radioactive elements disintegrated or "decayed," they sometimes produced variant atoms that were chemically identical with the standard atoms at that stage of the process, but that possessed a different atomic weight. These "identical-but-different" atoms they christened isotopes.

But scientists still knew almost nothing about the composition of the atom's nucleus, nor did they know why some elements were self-destroying. During the First World War, Rutherford sought to solve the mystery of nuclear structure by bombarding atoms of simple elements such as nitrogen with alpha particles (one of the rays emitted by the

---

[10] Quoted in R. W. Clark, *The Birth of the Bomb* (London, 1961), p. 25.

radioactive element uranium). He succeeded in disintegrating the nuclei of various elements in this fashion, and in the process discovered one component of the nucleus which he called the proton. Through the interwar years European and American physicists made further laboratory observations of nuclear structure and propounded more sophisticated theories to explain what they discovered. In 1928 the Russian-born scientist George Gamow suggested the possibility of using a stream of accelerated protons to bombard nuclei, on the theory that these projectiles would be more effective than the rays from naturally radioactive materials. In 1932 both a British team headed by J. D. Cockcroft and an American team under E. O. Lawrence succeeded in building accelerators capable of disintegrating atoms by artificial means.

Meanwhile, a number of related discoveries were deepening man's knowledge of atomic structure. In 1932, James Chadwick at Oxford demonstrated the existence of the neutron, an uncharged nuclear particle that would soon become the key to nuclear fission. Two years later, Enrico Fermi in Rome used neutrons to bombard a large number of non-radioactive elements, and succeeded in producing isotopes that were themselves radioactive. These experiments and others led to a new theoretical analysis of nuclear reactions by Niels Bohr. The paper which he published in 1936 has been called "the decisive influence on the analysis of nuclear reactions for the next twenty years"; it sought to explain the process of change produced within the nucleus by an impinging particle.

The work of Fermi and Bohr inspired a whole series of new experiments in Europe and the United States. One scientist, the Berlin chemist Otto Hahn, in 1938 achieved a surprising result: by bombarding uranium with neutrons, he produced radioactive isotopes not of uranium itself or of a neighboring element (as had been the case in the past) but of quite different elements possessing roughly half the atomic weight of uranium. It appeared that the nucleus in this case must have split into two approximately equal fragments, and that if such fission had really occurred, a great quantity of energy must have been released in the process. Tests run in Copenhagen by the refugee German physicist Otto Frisch soon confirmed this hypothesis. The news created a sensation in scientific circles everywhere. For, if the theory was sound, the fission of a uranium nucleus caused some free neutrons to be thrown out; these in turn might impinge on other nuclei, causing fissions in them as well; and thus a self-sustaining chain reaction might be set off, releasing enormous energy for constructive or destructive purposes. The next problems were to find out what kind of fissionable material would be most susceptible to use, and how much of the material would be required to permit the chain reaction to proceed. These problems were under intensive study when the war broke out; but theory was then still well ahead of experimental verification.

The outbreak of war temporarily slowed experimentation everywhere. Most of the prominent scientists in the belligerent countries were quickly drawn into war work of a more pressing nature. In Paris, a team of physicists under Frédéric Joliot did push ahead with its attempts to produce a chain reaction, and achieved a partial success in the autumn of 1939. They artificially induced a chain reaction but were unable to make it self-sustaining. In Germany, two groups of government-employed scientists had been looking into the question of atomic development during the prewar months, and a few more specialists were assigned to the project when the war began. But there was little sense of urgency in Germany either among the scientists themselves or in high political and military circles. The war, after all, was expected to be short. In England meanwhile, atomic research fell rather by default into the hands of younger scientists, and notably to those who were refugees from Hitler's bigotry. These enemy aliens, excluded from other war work for security reasons, thus found themselves accidentally entrusted with much of the responsibility for what eventually became the greatest of wartime secrets.

Niels Bohr had suggested just before the war began that the likeliest material for a successful chain reaction was the rare uranium isotope called U–235. Since uranium ore contained only infinitesimal quantities of U–235, Bohr's idea put a serious damper on the idea of an early development of atomic energy. But early in 1940 two German refugee scientists working at the University of Birmingham, Rudolf Peierls and Otto Frisch, set out to calculate, by purely theoretical analysis, the probable amount of U–235 needed for a chain reaction. This so-called "critical mass," they concluded, would not be several tons (as had heretofore been assumed), but less than one pound.

This encouraging hypothesis led to a sudden revival of interest in atomic research. The Peierls-Frisch memorandum, a remarkably prescient summary of how to make what they called "a radioactive superbomb" and of the probable effectiveness and dangers of such a weapon, was sent to Sir Henry Tizard, the most influential of the government's scientific advisers. Tizard was skeptical. ". . . The scientific and industrial resources of the country are strictly limited," he wrote, "and it is essential to use them in such a way as to produce a decisive result as soon as possible, and to avoid dissipation of effort on things that do not matter much. . . . If we try to do everything, we may do nothing in time."[11] He nevertheless arranged the appointment of a small committee of scientists (the so-called Maud Committee) with instructions to examine atomic possibilities and recommend a policy. After fifteen months of careful study by groups of scientists under its sponsorship, the committee brought in its report in July 1941. Its view was that a nuclear bomb could be built within two years at a cost of five million pounds; it recommended that work begin at once, with the bomb itself to be built in the safe haven of Canada.

Although investing vast resources in such a project seemed a dubious venture, Britain's situation in the late summer of 1941 was sufficiently grave to convince Churchill and his scientific adviser Lord Cherwell that it must be tried. The defeat of the Soviet Union appeared imminent, and if it came, most of Europe and Asia would be under Nazi control. Should that happen, Britain's hope of an eventual victory might depend on the development of a new weapon, decisive enough to shape the final outcome. Besides, the British suspected that the Germans might be ahead of them in atomic development, in which case Britain must catch up or face defeat. The decision was made, therefore—made so secretly, indeed, that it was not even discussed in the War Cabinet, and Deputy Prime Minister Attlee himself remained almost completely uninformed. Under the cover name "Directorate of Tube Alloys," an all-out effort to produce a nuclear weapon was mounted late in 1941.

Within a year, however, the British found themselves outpaced by the Americans. Atomic research had been proceeding in the United States also, though at a more leisurely pace. As the prospect of American entry into the war became imminent, the Americans suggested that the two nations pool their talent and their facilities in a joint project. The British government, perhaps because it then enjoyed a clear lead in atomic development, failed to respond to this approach. After Pearl Harbor, the Americans threw their vast resources into the enterprise and quickly forged ahead. Too late, the British in 1942 attempted to revive the partnership plan; it was the Americans who

[11] R. W. Clark, *Tizard* (Cambridge, Mass., 1965), p. 210.

now evaded, on the ground that establishing joint machinery would delay progress. By the time a partnership agreement was finally worked out in August 1943, the American lead was so great as to ensure that if the bomb were to be built in time for use during the war, it would come from an American rather than a British plant.

Britain's most difficult problem involved production techniques: how could a sufficient supply of U–235 be turned out by Britain's over-worked and partially outmoded industrial plant? Scientists and engineers were not even agreed on the proper method to use for the separation of U–235 from uranium; three different industrial processes had been proposed, each one expensive and difficult. While the British wrestled with the problem, the opulent Americans pushed ahead on all fronts. They built plants to separate U–235 by all three methods, plus still another plant to produce a second fissionable element—plutonium—which American scientists thought to be potentially superior to U–235. By 1945, enough of both materials was on hand to permit bombs of both types to be built. The first plutonium bomb was successfully tested in the New Mexico desert in July 1945; the first U–235 bomb fell three weeks later on Hiroshima. A new age in warfare had begun.

One of the most powerful drives behind the British decision to push wartime atomic research had been the fear that Germany might win the race for nuclear weapons. It was in Berlin, after all, that nuclear fission had first been achieved; and German science and industry seemed particularly well equipped to carry through such an enormous enterprise. When Lord Cherwell in 1941 advised Churchill to invest Britain's scarce resources in the development of an atomic bomb, he observed ominously: "It would be unforgivable if we let the Germans develop a process ahead of us by means of which they could defeat us or reverse the verdict after they had been defeated."[12] Not until Germany was invaded in 1945 could the Western Allies be sure that their fears had been exaggerated. By that time the Germans, despite their initial advantages, had fallen far behind. Worse still, they were not aware that they had fallen behind; the progress of atomic development in the West largely escaped the German intelligence services. When the news of the Hiroshima bomb was announced in August 1945, several of Germany's top nuclear physicists who had been captured by the Western armies refused at first to believe the report, and insisted that it must be a propaganda trick.

Until 1942, German scientists had kept pace with the progress of their

[12] David Irving, *The Virus House* (London, 1967), p. 90.

Western rivals. Indeed, at the outset Germany was the only nation whose army had set up a nuclear research office. In December 1939 the eminent physicist Werner Heisenberg proposed the construction of a nuclear reactor, and asked for a supply of heavy water for that purpose. After the German conquest of Norway, the government responded by ordering Norsk-Hydro—the only plant in Europe capable of producing heavy water in industrial quantities—to increase its output sharply. The Germans also seized Europe's largest stock of uranium compounds when they overran Belgium. During the next two years, the German physicists pushed ahead steadily toward solving the theoretical problems involved in nuclear development.

Progress was hampered, however, by several factors. The scientists were divided by factional rivalries; their penchant toward theory led them to neglect the more pragmatic experimental side; a serious error of calculation by one noted physicist seemed to rule out the possibility of using graphite in a reactor. In addition, the Germans in 1943 lost their source of heavy water when the Norwegian underground, aided by the British, carried out a daring sabotage raid on the Norsk-Hydro plant and destroyed most of the accumulated stock. Worse still, most members of Hitler's military and civilian entourage were dubious about the prospect of developing a nuclear bomb, and the scientists muffed their chance to convert them. At a meeting with Albert Speer and high military officials in June 1942, Heisenberg and his colleagues were reluctant to urge an all-out effort in the atomic field; the non-scientists naturally decided, therefore, to give the missile program a higher priority.

From 1942 onward, the German attempt to build a reactor stagnated. The heavy drain of the eastern front on men and supplies, plus the cost of beating off Allied air attacks, diverted the bulk of Germany's industrial resources. In August 1944, during a conversation with Marshal Antonescu, Hitler talked vaguely of a prospective atomic weapon, but the moment was far too late. Only a sense of desperate urgency felt early in the war could have driven any government to strike out energetically on such an uncertain and costly path. Of the European nations, the British alone felt that sense of urgency in time to profit by it.

Unknown to either the Germans or the Western Allies, one other competitor had entered the wartime nuclear race: the Soviet Union. In 1939, Soviet physicists had shared the excitement in the scientific world over the prospect of nuclear fission, and had embarked on some theoretical studies of the problem. Hitler's invasion had diverted their attention to more pressing things; but one physicist, G. N. Flerov, maintained his interest and became a kind of one-man lobby for an effort to build what he called a "uranium bomb." The government by this time had somehow learned that urgent secret work on nuclear fission was under way both in Germany and in the United States. This knowledge, together with Flerov's urging, led the State Defense Committee in June 1942 to appoint the physicist Igor Kurchatov head of a crash program to develop an atomic weapon. Kurchatov and Flerov began their work at the height of the Battle of Stalingrad; despite the critical situation, they were given laboratory space and top priority to requisition a team of physicists. Early in 1945 the team had finished building a cyclotron, and Soviet plants were beginning to turn out the necessary graphite and uranium in some quantity. But they remained well behind the Americans in the race; their first successful chain reaction was not achieved until eighteen months after the end of the war in Europe, and their first atomic bomb not until 1949.[13]

No atomic bomb was ever dropped in the European theater of war. Would it have been used against the Germans if completed in time? There is no adequate evidence to permit a sure answer, though the readiness of both British and American governments to pulverize German cities with "conventional" bombs suggests that they would not have hesitated to try the new weapon on fellow white men. The effects of certain "conventional" bombing raids were, after all, just as devastating as those by the first atomic bombs; indeed, the destruction of Dresden in February 1945 cost more lives than the nuclear attack on Hiroshima. Any doubters would probably have been reminded that the Nazis, if they had won the nuclear race, would not have let moral scruples deter them from using it on London, Moscow, or Washington.

More striking, perhaps, is the fact that the American and British officials in charge of developing atomic weapons were too preoccupied with their task to think very much about the long-term implications of this revolution in warfare. Despite the warnings contained in the Peierls-Frisch memorandum of 1940, there was evidently little concern about the possible genetic effects of radioactive fission; and when a few scientists (notably Niels Bohr) developed strong qualms of con-

[13] The story of the USSR's wartime atomic project was a closely guarded secret for more than twenty years, and was first revealed in 1966 when a Soviet paper published excerpts from I. N. Golovin's biography of Kurchatov (*Sovetskaya Rossia*, Aug. 3–16, 1966).

science about their brainchild, their concern found little echo among the statesmen and soldiers who shared the secret. Bohr, who escaped from Denmark in 1943 and came to England, sensed that the new weapon might fundamentally change the world. Along with some fellow scientists, he warned both British and American leaders that the Russians could almost certainly develop their own bomb within a few years after the war. On Bohr's urging, Sir John Anderson suggested to Churchill in the summer of 1944 that the Foreign Office begin at once a study of the postwar international control of atomic energy, and that it seek Soviet collaboration in this enterprise. Anderson was sharply rebuffed by the Prime Minister; thereafter until the war ended, Bohr pursued his desperate but futile effort to get a hearing in the Allied capitals.

"Under pressure of war," declared Sir John Anderson in a broadcast to the British people just after Japan's final surrender, "development has been compressed within the space of a few years which might normally have occupied a century or more. . . ."[14] Perhaps Sir John underestimated the speed of "normal" scientific advance in our day, even in time of peace. One can scarcely doubt, however, that the coming of the atomic age was materially hastened by the circumstances of the Second World War. Perhaps it was that war's principal contribution to the future, ensuring that there would never be another conflict on the lines of the war of 1939–1945. Henceforth the world would know only lesser wars—or greater ones.

---

[14] J. W. Wheeler-Bennett, *John Anderson, Viscount Waverley* (London, 1962), p. 298.

Chapter Six

GERMAN RULE IN OCCUPIED EUROPE

I. SCOPE AND STRUCTURE OF HITLER'S NEW ORDER

DURING the middle years of the Second World War, the map of the new German empire almost coincided with that of Continental Europe. From the Pointe du Raz in Brittany to the mountains of the Caucasus, from the arctic tip of Norway to the shore of the Mediterranean, Hitler's word was law. True, there were a few surviving islands of autonomy: the six middle-sized neutral states Spain, Portugal, Eire, Switzerland, Sweden, and Turkey, plus the Pope's Vatican City. There were the three Danubian junior satellites Rumania, Bulgaria, and Hungary, which maintained a precarious kind of national sovereignty by joining Hitler as military allies; there was Finland, which slipped from neutrality into a kind of quasi-alliance with the Axis. And there was Italy, a theoretically equal partner in the domination of Europe. But if Mussolini had once imagined that he might restrain or influence Hitler, or might fight his own "parallel war" alongside that of the Germans, his illusions ought to have vanished by 1941. Even in the Italian homeland itself, the Fascist regime's decisions were only in appearance the decisions of an independent government. For the materials of war and for the security of the peninsula, the Italians depended on Hitler's good will. Mussolini and his henchmen might grumble privately, but they could not presume to ignore the voice of Berlin. Even before the dramatic events of 1943 when the veil was torn away, Italy had sunk to the status of an uncomfortable satellite.

The outward thrust of German power toward all four points of the compass proceeded so rapidly as to outrun the Nazis' plans for empire. Hitler's immediate goal was military victory, not the reorganization of conquered Europe according to some predetermined blueprint. The structure of his new order (which would endure, he boasted, for a thousand years) could be worked out at leisure after the conquest. Besides, so long as the war continued it seemed wise to conceal his long-term aims. He instructed his military staff in June 1940 to draft mild armistice terms with France that would ensure an end to hostilities; but "he let it quietly be known that as a result his demands in the final peace treaty would be that much higher."[1] Three weeks after the invasion of Russia, Hitler told his top aides that the German occupiers should give no hint of their intention to stay permanently in the conquered east. Instead, they should appear to be interested only in the short-term goals of order and security, though in fact they might proceed with "all necessary measures—shooting, resettling, etc."—designed to prepare the future.[2] Following his natural bent to improvise, Hitler assigned to each new occupied territory that temporary status which seemed least likely to interfere with the continued prosecution of the war. Sometimes that status was outright annexation to the Reich; sometimes it was direct administration by German military or civilian officials; sometimes it was indirect control through an apparently autonomous regime. Nazi Europe thus took on a heterogeneous patchwork character; it appeared to be the work of a pure pragmatist rather than a systematic planner.

The outright annexation of territory was relatively rare. Western Poland—the old Polish Corridor—was the most important exception; in 1939 it was converted into two German provinces, renamed the Wartheland and Danzig–West Prussia. Farther south, Polish Silesia was incorporated into German Silesia, and some smaller bits of Polish soil were absorbed into East Prussia. After the western blitz in 1940, Germany reannexed two tiny border areas (Eupen and Malmédy) that had been lost to Belgium by the Treaty of Versailles. In addition, the Grand Duchy of Luxembourg, Alsace, and part of Lorraine were annexed *de facto* though not *de jure*; they were administratively merged with the adjacent German *Gaue* across the Rhine, and subjected to German legislation. When Yugoslavia fell in 1941, two-thirds of Slovenia was annexed, carrying Germany's frontier almost to the Adriatic. The invasion of Russia brought the *de facto* annexation of that segment of Poland (Bialystok province) that the Soviet Union had seized in 1939, and gave Germany a common frontier with the Ukraine. Although Hitler and other German officials indulged in sporadic discussion of further annexations to the Reich, the details were left for postwar decision.

A more common technique during the war years was direct Ger-

---

[1] Walter Warlimont, *Inside Hitler's Headquarters 1939–1945* (London, 1964), p. 102.
[2] I.M.T., *Trials of the Major War Criminals*, XXXVIII, 87.

HIGH TIDE OF NAZI POWER
END OF 1942

----- Farthest German advance, Nov. 1942

Germany as of Sept. 1, 1939

Annexed after outbreak of war

Direct German administration

Indirect German or Italian control

Independent States allied with Germany

EIRE Neutrals

ICELAND

ATLANTIC OCEAN

N. IRE.

EIRE

GREAT BRITAIN

N

NORTH SEA

DENMARK

THE NETHERLANDS

BELGIUM

LUX.

EUPEN-MALMEDY-MORESNET

LORRAINE

ALSACE

GERMANY 1938

SUDETENLAND 1938

PROT. OF BOHEMIA

MORAVIA

BAY OF BISCAY

NOVEMBER 1942

FRANCE

SWITZ.

VICHY FRANCE

(AUSTRIA) 1938

NORWAY

1940

SWEDEN

FINLAND

DECEMBER 1941

SPRING 1942

DANZIG-WEST PRUSSIA

OSTLAND

E. PRUSSIA

(CORRIDOR) 1939

WARTHELAND

BIALYSTOK PROV.

GENERAL GOVERNMENT

POLISH SILESIA

UKRAINE

SLOVAKIA 1939

HUNGARY 1940

BESSARABIA (RUSSIA 1940)

SLOVENIA

BANAT

CROATIA

SERBIA

MONTENEGRO

RUMANIA

1940

NOV. '42

PORTUGAL

SPAIN

Tangier

CORSICA

SARDINIA

BALEARIC IS.

ITALY

ADRIATIC SEA

TO ITALY 1941-3

ALBANIA 1941

BULGARIA

GREECE 1941

TURKEY

MEDITERRANEAN

SEA

MOROCCO

ALGERIA

AFRICA

TUNIS

SICILY

MALTA (BR.)

CRETE (GR.)

FEB. '41

30°

60°

50°

40°

20°

man administration of conquered territories. After the Polish blitz, the rump of Poland which had not been annexed to either Germany or the USSR was baptized the General Government of the Occupied Polish Territories,[3] and was entrusted to a ruthless Nazi bureaucrat named Hans Frank. Hitler at first spoke of returning the General Government to eventual Polish rule; but by the end of 1939 he had decided to make it "the first colonial territory of the German nation."[4] Norway and the Netherlands also came under direct German civilian administration when their sovereigns departed to exile in London. Belgium and the northern and western two-thirds of France received German military administrators; two French *départements* adjoining Belgium were cut off from access to the rest of France, and were placed under the German officials resident in Brussels. The invasion of Russia vastly extended the scope of German direct administration. Two huge Reich Commissariats headed by civilian officials were carved out: the Ostland (the former Baltic states, plus Byelorussia) and the Ukraine. Two additional Reich Commissariats were created on paper, and their commissioners actually appointed: Muscovy (to include the bulk of European Russia north of the Ukraine) and the Caucasus. Neither one became a reality, thanks to the Soviet army's resistance. Nor was either the Ostland or the Ukraine ever turned over completely to its civilian commissioner; large segments remained part of the battle zone, under army control.

The third form of German wartime domination—indirect control—was widely used in western and southern Europe. Here the Germans maintained a more or less fictional appearance of national autonomy, governing either through local Nazi sympathizers or through local notables who were prepared to negotiate or collaborate with the conqueror. Two variant forms of this model had already been tried in Czechoslovakia several months before the war began; in March 1939 the Germans had converted the western half of the country into the so-called protectorate of Bohemia-Moravia, and the eastern half into the compliant satellite state of Slovakia, headed by the Naziphile Catholic priest Father Tiso. A Czech government in Prague possessed some remnants of administrative autonomy (under the watchful eye of the Reich Protector); Slovakia, on the other hand, could claim such attributes of independence as its own army and its own diplomatic

---

[3] The name was shortened in 1940 to "General Government" pure and simple.
[4] S. Piotrowski, *Hans Frank's Diary* (Warsaw, 1961), p. 38.

representatives in pro-Axis capitals. In Norway, the Germans eventually promoted the leading local Nazi Vidkun Quisling to the post of minister-president, in which he enjoyed strictly limited authority in domestic matters. But elsewhere in northern and western Europe they were more chary of working through the local Nazi leaders. In France they preferred to use the widely respected hero of Verdun, Marshal Philippe Pétain—though they were careful to limit Pétain's autonomous action to the southern third of the country. Denmark was given a particularly favored status; although the country was occupied by German forces, the king chose to remain on his throne, and a regular Danish government was allowed to function until 1943. In dismembered Yugoslavia, three puppet regimes of varying types were established. A large new state of Croatia was placed (at least theoretically) under Italian supervision; its *Poglavnik* (leader) was the Croat fascist Ante Pavelić. A small rump Serbian state was entrusted to an old soldier of the Pétain type, General Milan Nedić; and the tiny mountainous region of Montenegro was run (under Italian supervision) by a council of local pro-fascists. In Greece, a collaborationist cabinet that was twice shaken up during the occupation provided a facade for German and Italian control.

All this, of course, provides little indication of Hitler's long-range intentions. Only a final Nazi victory could have provided a sure answer to the question of the Third Reich's future frontiers, and the question of the Reich's postwar relationships with neighboring satellite nations. Probably Hitler himself had not yet decided whether to absorb the Low Countries and eastern France (the old realm of Burgundy) outright, or to convert them into a dependent Flemish state. It is more likely that Bohemia-Moravia and most of ex-Poland were already earmarked for annexation. Elsewhere, the future forms of rule were yet to be determined. Still, some of the Nazis' wartime policies may offer hints of what was in store for the peoples of Europe.

II. COLONIZATION AND GERMANIZATION

One of the commonest words in the Nazi vocabulary was *Lebensraum*—the living space required, according to Hitler, by a vigorous, expanding people such as the Germans. A central purpose of conquest in Europe, therefore, was to provide the master race with land for settlement and resources for exploitation. So long as the war continued, it was of course difficult to draw up precise plans. The Fuehrer had not yet made up his own mind about the exact details of the new order in Europe: which areas would be cleared and colonized, for example, and which non-German elements would be absorbed through a process of Germanization. Some hints of Hitler's intentions do emerge quite clearly, however, from his wartime staff conferences and informal conversations, as well as from the activities of certain planning organizations which he established for the purpose.

The chief responsibility in this realm was assigned, soon after the outbreak of war, to a newly created branch of Heinrich Himmler's SS. A Race and Settlement Office had existed within the SS since 1935, but on October 7, 1939, Hitler added a Reich Commissariat for the Strengthening of Germandom (RKFVD) with Himmler as its head. The purpose of this agency was to plan and carry out the colonization of conquered territory in the east: to clear suitable areas of their Slavic population, and to settle Germans in their place. Initially, the area of settlement was confined to the new provinces of the Warthegau and Danzig–West Prussia (annexed western Poland), from which roughly a million Poles and Jews were forcibly evacuated to that newly created dumping ground, the Government-General. Their property was confiscated and handed over to Himmler's SS bureaucrats for transfer to German settlers. The bulk of the Polish population of the annexed provinces was, however, allowed to remain for the time being, to provide a convenient labor force.

It was easier to expel the Poles than to find the right German colonists to replace them. Hitler was determined to select "only the best, the soundest German blood"; he ordered careful screening with respect to "physical fitness, origin, ethnic-political attitude, and vocational training" in order to create a tough and "pure" pioneer society.[5] A convenient supply was available in the so-called *Volksdeutsche* or "ethnic Germans," who had long ago migrated from Germany itself to various parts of eastern and southern Europe, and who were now to be voluntarily repatriated to strengthen the homeland. About a half-million of these ethnic Germans chose to "come home to the Reich" during the first two years of the war. After careful screening in camps, many of them were resettled in the newly annexed east. By mid-1941, the area had received some 200,000 *Volksdeutsche* (most of whom were placed on farms) and an undetermined number of *Reichsdeutsche* (inhabitants of Germany itself) who mi-

[5] J. B. Schechtman, *European Population Transfers 1939–1945* (New York, 1946), p. 275.

grated voluntarily to the new provinces as officials or businessmen. By 1943, the total number of German migrants in annexed Poland may have approached a million.

With the invasion of Russia in 1941, vast new perspectives opened before the Nazi pioneers. How far would the frontier of German colonization now be pushed, and beyond that frontier, how would the indigenous population be controlled? In March 1941, musing on the future of the east, Hitler had talked in terms of a future Russia divided into several impotent "socialist" states. Three weeks after the invasion began, the Fuehrer still veiled his long-range plans from his closest associates, though he now spoke of the early annexation and Germanization of the former Baltic states and the Crimea. But by January 1942 he was speculating more expansively: "The goal of *Ostpolitik* is in the long run to open up an area of settlement for some hundred million Germans in this territory."[6] This eastward flow was evidently intended to occur over several generations; Hitler spoke at various times of ten or twenty million settlers in the first postwar decade, and brushed aside any clear distinction between areas annexed to the Reich and those merely subject to German military occupation. He obviously viewed the conquered east, as far as the Urals and a little beyond, as one vast living space for the Herrenvolk.

With these vague guidelines, Himmler's SS agencies and Alfred Rosenberg's new Ministry for Occupied Eastern Territories (established shortly after the invasion began) set to work to draft and initiate colonization plans. The Polish General Government was now destined to be annexed to the Reich for settlement by true German stock; the Polish inhabitants would eventually be dumped farther east in Byelorussia, a less attractive and less fertile land. Hans Frank even selected a name for the future German province that would replace the General Government: Vandalengau, to commemorate the earliest carriers of German culture in the east. Parts of the Ostland— the new name for the former Baltic republics—would also be annexed and colonized, though in this region the majority of the indigenous population of Estonians, Letts, and Lithuanians might be retained and Germanized. The old Austrian part of Galicia would also be annexed and resettled—in preparation for which it was merged in 1941 with the General Government.

---

[6] H. Picker, *Hitler's Tischgespräche im Führerhauptquartier 1941-42* (Bonn, 1951), p. 303.

As for the vast bulk of the Soviet Union, Himmler's SS planners in May 1942 came up with a basic document called General Plan East. It called for the gradual German colonization of European Russia by the creation of a network of "frontier marches," where the settlers would be clustered together for purposes of defense and would dominate the chief routes of communication. During the long period of settlement (a process that would continue for several generations), strategically-located military strong points would protect the German-settled areas against native unrest. War veterans would be given priority as colonists, in order to assure a tough breed of fighting pioneers. Some Slavs would be allowed to remain implanted near the German settlements as a source of cheap labor, but none would be permitted to own land or capital. The bulk of the Russians would be driven east of the Urals into Siberia and Central Asia. The threat of pressure from these exiled Slavs would, said Himmler, provide the Germans with a "perpetual eastern military frontier which, forever mobile, will always keep us young."[7]

One curious footnote to the Nazis' plans for Russia was the scheme of annexing the Crimean Peninsula to the Reich, settling it with Germans and linking it to the homeland by a thousand-mile Autobahn. Both Hitler and Rosenberg were obsessed with this plan, and hoped to put it into action before the end of the war. The initial colonists were to be ethnic Germans from Transnistria (a segment of the western Ukraine that Hitler had handed over to the Rumanians in 1941); but for a time Hitler was excited by the idea of resettling the ethnic Germans of the South Tyrol there as well. Compared to the South Tyrol, said Hitler enthusiastically, the Crimea would be "a real land of milk and honey. . . . All they have to do is to sail down just one German waterway, the Danube, and there they are."[8] Reluctantly, however, Hitler had to postpone this tempting realization until the postwar era; and only a handful of German colonists reached the Crimea before Soviet armies reconquered the peninsula.

The story was much the same in all of German-occupied Russia: so long as the war continued, there was neither time nor available manpower to make a serious beginning at settlement. A few scattered colonization experiments were tried in the General Government and in the Zhitomir region in the Ukraine; in the Baltic, too, several thou-

---

[7] I.M.T., *Trials of Major War Criminals*, XXXVIII, 523.
[8] *Hitler's Secret Conversations 1941–1944* (New York, 1961), p. 513.

sand ethnic Germans who had been uprooted from the area in 1939 were brought back to form the nucleus of Germanization. An attempt was also made to comb out ethnic Germans in the Ukraine itself; more than 300,000 were registered, and were given a variety of special privileges in an effort to turn them into loyal frontier settlers. When the great German retreat began in 1943, most of them were evacuated to resettlement camps in the former Polish provinces.

While German plans for the east rested primarily on colonization, the parallel process of Germanization was expected to supplement its effectiveness. By this term, the Nazis did not mean the traditional export of German culture to alien populations. "Our duty in the East," said Himmler in 1942, "is not Germanization in the former sense of the term, that is, imposing German language and laws upon the population, but to ensure that only people of pure German blood inhabit the East."[9] Germanization meant the mass absorption into the Herrenvolk of peoples regarded as racially akin, and the selective absorption of individuals of non-Germanic origin.

In the east, the Baltic peoples (especially the Estonians and Letts), along with such small groups as the Mazurians and the so-called "Water Poles," were considered prime candidates for mass Germanization. In the west, the Scandinavians, Dutch, Flemish, Luxembourgers, Alsatians, and Swiss were viewed either as true Germanic peoples who had lost their sense of racial pride, or as close racial relatives. Nazi plans for all of these areas therefore called for little colonization,[10] but for a thorough purging and re-education of peoples who would then become citizens of the Greater German Reich.

Individual Germanization in non-Germanic areas was a more delicate problem; yet the Nazis tackled it, even among the Slavic *Untermenschen*. In the Czech protectorate and in conquered Poland, Himmler's agents classified certain types as "racially valuable," and sent them to Germany for indoctrination. *Reichsprotektor* Heydrich declared early in 1942 that as many as 40 to 60 percent of the Czech

[9] A. Dallin, *German Rule in Russia 1941–1945* (London, 1957), p. 279.

[10] Colonization on a limited scale did occur in eastern France and the Grand Duchy of Luxembourg. In 1940 the Ostland Company, created to manage expropriated farms in conquered Poland, was given authority over "abandoned or improperly cultivated farms" in eastern France as well. The French owners, many of whom had fled during the Western blitz, were not allowed to return. The Ostland Company took over some nine thousand farms in the *département* of the Ardennes alone, and settled ethnic Germans from the east there. Additional settlement took place after the expulsion of thousands of Lorrainers late in 1940.

nation might be fit for Germanization; the rest would eventually be expelled to the Arctic regions of conquered Russia. Healthy Polish children "of Nordic appearance" were also taken from their families and shipped off for adoption by good German families (particularly those of SS men).[11] A more abortive experiment was Hitler's odd scheme, concocted in 1942, to bring a half-million Ukrainian girls to Germany as domestic servants, with a view to finding them German husbands and absorbing them into the Herrenvolk. Hitler's first visit to the Ukraine had left him entranced with the charm and simple virtues of Ukrainian peasant girls, whose costume and manner evidently recalled to him the girls of his native Austria. But recruitment proved difficult; instead of a half-million volunteers, only about 15,000 ever reached Germany.

III. ECONOMIC EXPLOITATION

Colonization and Germanization were long-term ventures that could be planned but scarcely implemented during the war. The economic reorganization of Europe, on the other hand, might be undertaken at once. Indeed, it seemed essential for the Nazis to speed the building of what they called a *Grossraumwirtschaft* in order to counterbalance the economic strength of the Atlantic powers. Germany's resources alone would obviously not suffice to win a protracted war against a great coalition. The efficient use of conquered Europe's resources might provide the decisive margin.

In principle, the Germans might have chosen to follow either of two alternative paths. The simplest was a policy of smash-and-grab: to strip each conquered country of its raw materials, foodstuffs, and manpower in order to concentrate war production in the Reich and to maintain a high standard of living there. Such a policy presupposed a relatively short war. Or the Germans might have chosen to exploit these same resources on the spot, utilizing the manpower of each subject nation in that nation's factories and on its farms, thus turning the entire continent into an arsenal for German victory. This latter policy would have implied some degree of collaboration with the conquered peoples on grounds of common interests, rather than harsh dictation

---

[11] Some Polish historians claim that the number of children abducted ranged from 100,000 to 200,000. Even the Polish government's figure of 10,000 is considered excessive by an American scholar, R. L. Koehl: *RKFVD: German Resettlement and Population Policy 1939–1945* (Cambridge, Mass., 1957), p. 220.

of the subduer to the subdued. It would have meant, too, a sharing of available resources with the defeated peoples so as to stimulate their will to collaborate and to produce.

Except for a brief interlude in 1943–1944, German officials did not seriously weigh the relative advantages of these two alternatives. At times they tried to combine them in uneasy fashion, but on the whole they strongly preferred the simpler policy of smash-and-grab. There was, to be sure, a considerable amount of talk in 1940 about the mirage of European economic unity under German leadership; and perhaps some German officials meant what they said about the mutual advantages of the postwar New Order. But a better guide to wartime conduct was a policy paper drafted in Berlin four months before the war began. That paper was directed to the new protectorate of Bohemia-Moravia; but it foreshadowed German policy in the other conquered lands.

It is clear that the economic power of the protectorate, and of other territories possibly to be acquired, must of course be completely exhausted for the purposes of the conduct of the war. It is, however, just as clear that these territories cannot obtain any compensation from the economy of Greater Germany for the products which they will have to give us during the war, because their power must be used fully for the war and for supplying the civilian population.[12]

Wartime statements of purpose by Nazi leaders were even more brutally frank. Hermann Goering, whose Four-Year-Plan Office was formally in control of economic policy in the occupied lands, told his occupation officials in 1942: "In the old days, the rule was plunder. Now, outward forms have become more humane. Nevertheless I intend to plunder, and plunder copiously."[13] Himmler in 1943 harangued his SS leaders thus: "How the Russians or the Czechs fare is absolutely immaterial to me. . . . Whether nations live in prosperity or starve to death interests me only insofar as we need them as slaves for our culture, otherwise it is of no interest to me."[14] Hitler himself in 1942 added his aria to the chorus: "The real profiteers of this war are ourselves, and out of it we shall come bursting with fat! We will give back nothing and will take everything we can make use of. And if the

---

[12] I.M.T., *Trials of the Major War Criminals*, XXXII, 395–96.
[13] *Ibid.*, XXXIX, 390–91.
[14] *Ibid.*, XXII, 480.

others protest I don't give a damn."[15] It is true that preachment and practice sometimes diverge; but in this instance, German economic practice largely corresponded to the bombastic pronouncements of Nazi leaders. The techniques varied from place to place, and evolved with time; the goal was everywhere the same.

Exploitation took its starkest form in the conquered east, where Goering ordered the use of "colonial methods." In Poland, there was a sharp contrast between the annexed provinces and the General Government. In the annexed areas, Goering decreed that economic reconstruction and expansion should be pushed forward at once; only those properties owned by the Polish state, by Jews, or by Poles classed as anti-German were confiscated, and were gradually transferred to Germans as owners or "trustees." The Wartheland, largely agrarian in character, was earmarked as the breadbasket of the expanded German Reich. In the General Government, on the other hand, everything was regarded as booty; the Germans stripped it of raw materials, food stocks, and machinery that might be used in the war effort. "Enterprises which are not absolutely essential for the maintenance at a low level of the bare existence of the inhabitants must be transferred to Germany"—so read Goering's directive.[16] Later, when the Germans decided to annex the General Government, the dismantling policy was reversed and a modest industrial buildup was substituted. The purpose, however, was not to benefit the Polish inhabitants but to supply the German armies in the east.

Conquered Soviet territory, except for the Baltic region, received much the same treatment as the General Government, although in this area there were sharp factional disputes among the various Nazi administrative agencies that enjoyed overlapping authority in the east. Because all property in the USSR was state-owned, confiscation was automatic and all-encompassing. The country was to be virtually stripped of its industry, and was to provide the Reich with vast supplies of grain, oil, and minerals. Some of Hitler's advisers urged the abolition of the collective farms as a device to win over the peasantry, but the Fuehrer brushed the idea aside; massive grain production was more important than winning friends. Only in 1942, and then slowly and grudgingly, did he authorize the transformation of the kolkhozy into "communal" farms theoretically owned by the peasants them-

[15] *Hitler's Secret Conversations*, p. 582.
[16] I.M.T., *Trials of the Major War Criminals*, XXXVI, 482.

selves. By that time, the gesture was neither economically nor psychologically effective. The SS meanwhile had undertaken its own land-grabbing policy; by the end of 1942 its economic branch had seized about 1.5 million acres of Soviet soil and was operating what were essentially huge state farms under German managers, with local forced labor.

As the war in the east dragged on, requiring vast quantities of munitions and equipment, Hitler abandoned his anti-industrial policy and authorized the reconstruction of munitions plants in the Don basin. A series of government corporations was set up to operate the various branches of the economy; using state funds, German business firms leased and operated former Soviet enterprises. But rebuilding was slow; months were needed to put the great Dneprostroi power dam back into operation, and local coal production had fallen so low that coal had to be hauled all the way from Upper Silesia. Most Soviet skilled labor, too, had left for the trans-Ural country. The total yield from the once-great industrial basin of the Ukraine lagged at about 10 percent of its former output.

In western Europe, the techniques of economic exploitation appeared less blatant, but were clearly more effective. At the very outset, there was a brief period of pillaging; 250 trainloads of arms and war materials were hauled out of France alone. But the Germans shortly dictated occupation agreements with the conquered countries which gave them legal authority to drain away most of their essential resources. France, Belgium, the Netherlands, and Norway (and later Greece and Yugoslavia as well) were saddled with the cost of supporting an occupation army. The assessments were astronomically inflated; in France, one French official complained, the German exactions would have sufficed to support an occupation force of eighteen million men. From 1940 to 1944, the French paid ten times the actual costs of the military occupation; the same was true of the Low Countries. The excess credit was used by the Germans to buy up available stocks of raw materials, foodstuffs, and finished products for shipment to Germany, thus stripping the defeated countries in technically legal fashion and at no cost to the conqueror. The Germans reaped additional advantage from the monetary exchange rates arbitrarily fixed by Berlin; the effect was to permit German purchases at far below the real value of the goods. Still another device, the establishment of clearing accounts in Berlin, enabled the Germans to buy freely on credit while postponing payment until after the war. The predominantly one-way flow of goods into Germany netted the conquered countries nothing more than paper assets, valueless if Germany should lose the war.

The outright confiscation of property was less common in western and southern Europe than in the east; it was primarily confined to Jewish-owned properties, which were either seized or sequestered for the duration of the war. In various legal and quasi-legal ways, however, the Germans managed to take over ownership or control of many major industrial enterprises. Two large German banks were able, with government aid, to gain control of a number of important investment banks in the conquered countries, and through them to get a grip on their industrial holdings. Direct capital investment sometimes occurred; in other cases, mixed companies were set up (e.g., the French dye trust Francolor, in which I. G. Farbenindustrie acquired 51 percent of the stock, and the Société vinicole de Champagne, which passed under the control of the Mumm family). Virtually all of the extensive French, Belgian, and Dutch holdings in southeastern Europe (e.g., the Bor copper mines in Yugoslavia, and Western shares in Rumanian oil) were taken over by purchase at a price set by the Germans. The threatened alternative was outright confiscation; the former owners therefore indulged in little quibbling. In satellite Rumania— technically an independent ally rather than a conquered victim—the Germans negotiated a ten-year joint plan which they advertised as a model for Europe's long-range future. It reserved to Germany the right to provide capital and technical aid, and opened the way for the creation of jointly-owned corporations, a number of which were founded during the war.

One essential resource available in the defeated countries was manpower. Even before the war broke out in 1939, Germany was beginning to feel the pinch of a labor shortage, particularly in agriculture. Some 300,000 foreign volunteer workers had been recruited in 1938–1939, but more were needed as Germans were called into the armed forces. True, one sizable source of indigenous labor was still untapped: many German women were still in the kitchen rather than in the factory. But the idea of women in industry was abhorrent to Hitler, who preferred to find his recruits elsewhere. Soon after the fall of Poland, the occupation authorities began to ship Polish civilians and prisoners of war to Germany, primarily for farm work. From 1940 onward, the western European countries and Italy (where jobs were hard to find) contributed a flow of volunteer workers. At the end of 1941, almost four million foreigners (civilians and prisoners of war) were employed in Germany. Nearly half of these were Poles, most of whom came from the General Government, where Hans Frank's agents rounded them up by press-gang methods.

By the summer of 1942, the Soviet army's stubborn refusal to collapse made it clear that the period of blitzkrieg was over, and that Germany was committed to a protracted war in which manpower might be the decisive factor. The increasing demands of the armed forces for more soldiers, and the stepped-up armaments program of Albert Speer, imposed desperate measures. Fritz Sauckel, assigned to head a new office of labor allocation, scoured all of occupied Europe for manpower, utilizing every method from persuasion to the most ruthless compulsion. Although Poland by now had been pretty thoroughly stripped, and although few volunteers remained in western Europe, Sauckel's methods at first produced impressive results. During his initial year in office (May 1942–May 1943), he rounded up some 2.1 million foreign workers, raising the 1943 total in Germany to more than 6 million. France and the Low Countries provided a great many, but the largest proportion came from the Soviet Union. Until 1942, the Germans had shown no interest in conscripting labor there; they had even refused to utilize the huge mass of Soviet prisoners of war captured during 1941. An appalling proportion of these prisoners, crowded into totally inadequate camps during the winter of 1941–1942, had died of malnutrition and disease. Eventually, however, racial and ideological distaste could no longer stand in the way of necessity; not only Soviet prisoners but forcibly-conscripted civilian workers from Russia and the Ukraine began to pour into Germany in large numbers. By mid-1943 there were 1.5 million of these so-called *Ostarbeiter* in the Reich. But Sauckel's initial successes of 1942–1943 could not be maintained; during his second year in office, despite intensified effort and pressure, his procurement total fell to just below 1 million. The peak figure of more than 7 million foreign workers—20 percent of Germany's total labor force—was reached in mid-1944, by which time Sauckel's hunting grounds for conscripts had been overrun by the enemy. Another 7 million men and women who remained in their native countries were employed in producing munitions or other goods for the German war effort, or were laboring to build Hitler's Atlantic wall.

Germany's growing manpower difficulties in 1943–1944 contributed to the only significant wartime experiment in building a European rather than a German war economy. Smash-and-grab seemed to have been pushed to its limits; conscript laborers were taking to the hills, and German war production was ceasing to rise. Albert Speer seized his chance to urge an end to Sauckel's labor draft in favor of utilizing local industries and workers to produce on German orders. In France he found a willing listener: Jean Bichelonne, the Vichy Minister of Industrial Production, was a brilliant and ruthless technocrat whose mind worked much like Speer's. Efficiency was a gospel to both men; so was national self-interest. Bichelonne, backed by Laval, saw an opportunity to get more independence from German control by making France the respected industrial partner of Germany; Speer, backed by the German military (which believed that the labor draft had failed), saw a chance to increase munitions output. In September 1943 Speer and Bichelonne reached an accord: the Germans would set a total production program, but would give the French full autonomy to carry it out; they would virtually suspend the conscription of workers for Germany, and would provide other incentives as well. Both Speer and Bichelonne evidently saw these arrangements as the first step toward a long-term goal—a technocratic Europe. But the experiment was brief; Sauckel went straight to the top, and persuaded Hitler in December to order the roundup of a million more French workers in 1944. Hitler lamely observed that "one should . . . try to combine happily both points of view."[17] Instead, he liquidated the sole wartime attempt to abandon smash-and-grab in favor of a European war economy.

The contribution of occupied Europe to Germany's war effort cannot be accurately measured. Immediately after the war ended, an American investigating mission did attempt a rough estimate; it set the foreign contribution at 14 percent of the German gross national product for 1940–1944. Manpower and foodstuffs were most important; thanks to the food supplies bought or seized in both east and west, Germany was able to maintain a scarcely reduced consumption level until the last year of the war. The largest single source of food supply was the Soviet Union, which furnished about nine million tons of grain alone (most of it consumed by the German armed forces in the occupied east). France, though a much smaller nation, furnished

[17] A. S. Milward, "German Economic Policy Towards France," p. 23 (unpublished paper).

almost five million tons of grain, plus important amounts of other items of consumption. In fact, someone has calculated that the Germans drew from the vast bulk of occupied Russia only one-seventh of the supplies obtained, by more sophisticated methods, from France. The Soviets' scorched-earth policy, together with Nazi obtuseness in administering the conquered Ukraine, largely deprived the Germans of an enormous economic asset.

The economic effect of German rule on occupied Europe was, on the other hand, disastrous. Inflation; dangerously-reduced consumption standards; shortages of every essential raw material or product except, perhaps, aspirin; a generalized black market that favored the strong at the expense of the weak, and that broke down respect for orderly processes; potential confusion over the legal ownership of property; potential conflict between those who served the Germans and those who resisted them—all these were costly consequences of Hitler's victories. A few historians have attempted to argue that there were offsetting advantages; that German capital investment and German plans for an integrated European economy showed Berlin's constructive purpose, and foreshadowed a better future for all. Their case may persuade some future generation; it would not find many adherents among those Europeans who saw Hitler's New Order at first hand.

IV. REPRESSION AND LIQUIDATION

Some months after the invasion of the USSR, an obscure Nazi official in the Ukraine inquired plaintively: "If we shoot the Jews, liquidate the war prisoners, starve the major part of the big cities' population, and in the coming year reduce also a part of the peasants through famine there will arise a question: Who is going to produce the economic goods?"[18] This official's query serves as an ironic commentary on the contradictions inherent in German occupation policy: contradictions between economic needs and racial dogmas. It also suggests a curious kind of moral anemia: a dull inability to grasp the enormity of Nazi transgressions against every principle of civilized man.

Poland provided the first test of Nazi intentions. Hitler's design for the Poles at the outset was unclear, probably even in his own mind. He had once written (in 1928) that the Poles could never be Ger-

[18] I. Kamenetsky, *Secret Nazi Plans for Eastern Europe* (New York, 1961), p. 129.

manized, and that that these "racially hostile elements" must be either sealed off (*abkapseln*) from contact with Germans or shipped away somewhere.[19] Through the 1930's, however, he had seemed to exempt the Poles from his strictures against the Slavs, and had even appeared ready to accept Poland as a junior ally. With the defeat of Poland, all pretense was abandoned. The annexed provinces were purged of their entire political and social elite—professional men, large land-owners and businessmen, officials, priests, journalists. Some were jailed, some executed by SS detachments; others (along with the Jews) were forcibly deported to the General Government. In the annexed provinces, all Polish schools and most churches were shut down; Poles were denied the right to enter any profession; the right to marry was denied to Polish males below the age of twenty-eight and females below twenty-five. Low wage ceilings and food rations were set for Polish workers.

Things were not much better in the General Government. All schools above fourth-grade level (except some secondary schools of strictly technical character) were closed. It would be enough, declared Himmler, to provide Polish children with "simple arithmetic up to five hundred at the most; writing of one's name; a doctrine that it is a divine law to obey the Germans and to be honest, industrious and good."[20] Every expression of Polish culture was to be rooted out; theaters, museums, libraries were closed. On the other hand, Poles in the General Government continued to staff the lower echelons of the administration and to exercise the liberal professions; and most churches there remained open. (The priests, declared Hitler in 1940, must assume the duty of keeping the Poles "quiet, stupid and backward.")[21] Despite Germany's increasing need for manpower, sporadic waves of arrests and liquidations destroyed thousands of uncooperative or "racially unfit" Poles. Hans Frank, interviewed by a journalist early in 1940, boasted: "In Prague . . . large red posters were put up announcing that seven Czechs had been shot today. Whereupon I said to myself: If I

---

[19] M. Broszat, *Nationalsozialistische Polenpolitik 1939–1945* (Stuttgart, 1961), p. 21.

[20] Kamenetsky, *Secret Nazi Plans,* p. 106 (quoting an unpublished Nuremberg trial document).

[21] I.M.T., *Trials of the Major War Criminals,* XXXIX, 428. Hitler's attempt to use the Church was, however, purely pragmatic. His goal in the ex-Polish provinces was "to eliminate the church and religion so far as possible and to build here the prototype of a church-free *Weltanschauungsstaat*." M. Broszat, *Verfolgung polnischer Katholischer Geistlicher 1939–1945* (Munich, 1959), p. 86.

wanted to have a poster put up for every seven Poles who were shot, the forest of Poland would not suffice for producing the paper for such posters."[22] After 1941, when the Germans turned to the idea of Germanizing the General Government, high Nazi officials debated at some length the relative virtues of deporting sixteen to twenty million Poles to Siberia or, alternatively, exterminating them. The decision was postponed until after victory. When a German field marshal protested that Nazi methods in Poland made him ashamed of being a German, Hitler responded impatiently: "Wars are not won with methods of the Salvation Army!"[23]

Worse was to come with the invasion of the USSR. "This is a war of extermination," Hitler told his top military advisers in March 1941;[24] and Himmler added, in instructions to his SS officials, that the destruction of thirty million Slavs was a necessary prerequisite for German planning in the east.[25] In May Hitler approved the notorious "Commissar Decree," ordering the immediate execution of captured Soviet political officials. Civilians guilty of hostile conduct were also to be shot; and "the slightest sign of restiveness" among Soviet prisoners of war would call for "ruthless and energetic action." Himmler was authorized to expand his special "action teams" (Einsatzgruppen, already used on a small scale in the Polish campaign) to follow on the heels of the conquering army as extermination squads.

During the early months of the invasion, the Einsatzgruppen worked with deadly efficiency. No official record of their liquidations has survived; but the commander of one of the four units later estimated that his group had accounted for ninety thousand victims during the first year of fighting in Russia. Meanwhile, the ravages of cold and hunger were striking down far greater numbers of Soviet prisoners of war. By the end of 1941, almost four million prisoners had been taken. Adequate facilities were lacking; most of the men were herded into barbed-wire enclosures under the open sky. Before spring came, hundreds of thousands had died of disease or exposure. Thereafter, most of the survivors as well as newly captured prisoners were shipped to work camps in Germany, where conditions were not much better. Of the five million Soviet soldiers captured by the Germans

[22] T. Cyprian and J. Sawicki, *Nazi Rule in Poland* (Warsaw, 1961), p. 100.
[23] Testimony of Dr. Martin Broszat at Frankfurt war crimes trial, *New York Times*, Feb. 29, 1964.
[24] Dallin, *German Rule in Russia*, p. 30.
[25] I.M.T., *Trials of the Major War Criminals*, IV, 482.

during the war, two million died in captivity, and another million were never accounted for. Losses among the three million civilian *Ostarbeiter* deported from the USSR to Germany were in roughly the same proportion, for they were shamefully underfed and over-worked.

Although Germany's pressing need for manpower and the sheer magnitude of the task of handling such masses of men help to explain this gruesome chapter in the history of the war, Nazi racial policy was clearly the decisive factor. With the attack on Russia, the Germans embarked on a savage propaganda campaign designed to justify their conduct in the east. The word *Untermenschen*, heretofore rarely used by the Nazis, now entered the common language; soldiers and civilians alike were deluged with pamphlets and periodicals that purported to demonstrate the subhuman character of the eastern peoples. Carefully-selected photographs of Russian prisoners reinforced this message. That the Nazi leaders believed their own propaganda is clear. The Russians, noted Goebbels in his diary, "are not people, but a conglomeration of animals."[26] And Hitler added, in an order of the day to the armed forces, "This enemy consists not of soldiers but to a large extent only of beasts."[27] Given such convictions, brutality could only be the norm, not the exception.

Nazi racial policy reached its epitome, however, when applied to the Jews. Before the war began, the German leadership had contented itself with the forced emigration and spoliation of the Jews under its rule. Hitler in January 1939 did tell the Reichstag that "if the international Jewish financiers . . . succeed in plunging the nations once more into a world war the result will be . . . the obliteration of the Jewish race in Europe";[28] but this was generally discounted as oratorical hyperbole. After the outbreak of war, the problem in Nazi eyes grew steadily more pressing, and the idea of a permanent "solution" more tempting. Victory in Poland brought between two and three million Jews under German control; victory in the west added a half-million more; the prospect of triumph in Russia would increase the figure by another three million. For a time in 1939–1940 the Nazis evidently planned to use the General Government as a dumping ground for Jews; they set up official ghettoes in the major Polish cities

[26] L. P. Lochner (ed.), *The Goebbels Diaries* (New York, 1948), p. 52.
[27] Dallin, *German Rule in Russia*, pp. 68, 59.
[28] I.M.T., *Trials of the Major War Criminals*, XXXI, 65.

and forced all Polish Jews (plus some others) to take residence there. The fall of France opened the possibility of a larger overseas reservation for all the Jews of Europe; the French colony of Madagascar struck some Nazis as an ideal super-ghetto. Sporadic planning toward this end went on during 1940–1941.

But the euphoria aroused by the invasion of the USSR, and the attractive prospect of a really final solution to Europe's "Jewish problem," impelled the Nazis to throw off all restraint. Late in July 1941, Goering instructed Reinhard Heydrich of the SS to prepare a detailed plan. At an interministerial meeting in the Berlin suburb of Wannsee in January 1942, Heydrich's plan was explained and approved. In practice, it had already gone into operation. Mobile gas vans were in use at Chelmno (in the General Government) from late 1941, and the construction of four large extermination centers (Belzec, Maydanek, Sobibor, and Treblinka, all likewise in the General Government) was under way. A fifth center, Auschwitz (in Silesia) was converted from its former function as an ordinary concentration camp. Equipped with the new Zyklon B gas instead of the earlier carbon monoxide chambers, Auschwitz was to achieve a grim record for efficiency in production-line murder. At its peak, its execution rate was twelve thousand per day. During the next three years, trains of cattle cars from almost every part of Europe hauled their pitiful cargo toward these grim destinations. Within the various ghettoes in cities of east and west, Nazi-appointed Councils of Jewish Elders were forced to select enough victims to fill each successive convoy, until the time came to liquidate the last survivors—the elders themselves. Himmler in a speech in October 1943 urged his SS followers on to greater exertions: not only Jewish men but every Jewish woman and child must be destroyed, he cried, "so that no Jews will remain to take revenge on our sons and grandsons."[29]

The Jews were not the only victims of the extermination camps; many Slavs suffered the same fate, as did thousands of "racial inferiors" and anti-German resisters from other parts of Europe. But the process was slowed somewhat by the rising German need for labor

[29] H. Buchheim et al., Anatomie des SS-Staates (Olten and Freiburg, 1965), II, 447. Reports of the extermination camps began to filter through to the West in 1942. Polish Prime Minister Mikolajczyk provided details in a radio speech in July 1942, and a declaration by the Western Powers in December formally accused the Germans of what was later to be known as genocide. At the time, however, the reports were discounted by most Westerners as mere war propaganda.

after 1942.[30] Special SS units which were in charge of all concentration camps sorted out those arrivals who seemed fit to work, and channeled them toward satellite labor camps appended to the main concentration camps. How many died there from disease, privation, and overwork can never be calculated; only partial records have survived. Probably as many as seven or eight million persons passed through the camps; it is likely that at least two-thirds did not survive, and that of the dead, at least three million were Jews. An additional two million Jews were killed before arrival at the camps. For Europe west of the Soviet border, Hitler's solution for the "Jewish problem" had indeed approached finality; only a million remained alive when the war ended. "We have written a glorious page of our history," boasted Himmler to a group of his SS followers, "but it will never appear on paper."[31] Unluckily for Himmler, his order late in 1944 to dismantle the extermination camps could not be carried out before the arrival of the Soviet armies; while Hitler's last-minute instruction in 1945 to blow up the concentration camps and destroy all their remaining occupants was allegedly frustrated by Himmler himself, under the influence of his therapist, Dr. Felix Kersten.[32]

The enormity of the Nazis' extermination policy tends to overshadow other manifestations of the barbarity that is often stimulated by war. Other totalitarian powers also engaged in ruthless repression, though on a considerably smaller scale. After the fall of Poland, the Soviet occupiers matched the Germans in beheading their newly annexed territory of its native elite. More than a million Poles were forcibly deported to Siberia and Central Asia, from which many of them never returned. The motivation in this case was, however, po-

---

[30] The decision to use concentration camp inmates as slave laborers was taken in the spring of 1942. Prior to that time, "security and education" were described as the major purposes of the camps; henceforth economics took precedence, and many men and women were rounded up for camps simply as laborers and not as political offenders. Oswald Pohl, the SS official in charge of economic enterprises, ordered that "employment [in the camps] must be, in the true meaning of the word, exhaustive. . . . There is no limit to working hours." I.M.T., *Trials of the Major War Criminals*, XXXVIII, 366. Auschwitz, whose functions combined labor and extermination, in 1944 attained a population of 100,000. On the other hand, Belzec, Sobibor, and Treblinka were highly specialized extermination camps without satellite labor camps dependent on them. Their only permanent inmates were small labor gangs who stripped the corpses of clothing and disposed of the bodies. At the other extreme, there were a few "show" camps (notably Theresienstadt) for specially selected Jews who for one reason or another were given protected status.

[31] I.M.T., *Trials of the German War Criminals*, XXIX, 145.

[32] F. Kersten, *The Kersten Memoirs 1940-1945* (London, 1956), p. 277.

litical rather than racial. Some non-Russian minorities within the USSR also suffered. Shortly after the German invasion of Russia, the Soviet government deported eastward some half-million "Volga Germans" who had lived for two centuries north of the Black Sea. Stalin feared that they might make common cause with the invader, and preferred to take no chances.[33] In 1943, the Germans claimed to have found ghastly evidence that the Soviet government had engaged in genocide as well as deportation. They discovered in the Katyn Forest (in former eastern Poland) the mass grave of some twelve thousand officers of the Polish army, who had been taken prisoner by the victorious Russians in 1939. Although Stalin angrily denied Soviet responsibility for this atrocity, circumstantial evidence is strong that the victims were liquidated by Soviet units during their 1941 retreat— perhaps because of misinterpreted orders from Moscow.

It has sometimes been argued that barbarity in wartime is no monopoly of totalitarian states, and that the Second World War provides ample proof of this fact. The Atlantic powers, according to this thesis, committed their own form of genocide by mounting ruthless air attacks on defenseless civilian populations, both in Germany and in the conquered countries. The devastating raid on Dresden early in 1945, and the first atomic attacks on Japanese cities, may be seen from a certain perspective as moral (or immoral) equivalents of the extermination camps. But whether or not this perspective is a valid one, and whether or not all wars bring out the savage strain in all men, one fact seems indisputable: that in the twentieth-century surge toward savagery, the Nazi establishment far outdid all the rest.[34]

V. THE POLITICS OF COLLABORATION

Through all these years of turmoil, a strange collection of puppet politicians, ambitious schemers, fanatical ideologues, and even a few self-sacrificing patriots clung to the appearances of power in the satel-

[33] Many years later (1964), the Volga Germans were legally rehabilitated by decree of the Soviet government, but were not allowed to return to their former homes on the Volga. Several other non-Russian minorities that had been deported during the war were rehabilitated earlier (1956–1957) and invited to return from the Asiatic provinces.

[34] A report by the German Ministry of Justice twenty years after the end of the war calculated that more than 20,000 Nazis had been convicted of war crimes. Of this number, 5026 were convicted by courts of the Western Allies in occupied Germany; 5445 by courts of the German Federal Republic; and about 10,000 by Soviet courts. There were some additional trials and convictions in the various German-occupied countries of western and eastern Europe. *New York Times,* Nov. 13, 1964.

lite and conquered states. It was natural enough that the Germans should wish to ease the task of administering their wartime empire by delegating some responsibility to the local authorities; it was natural, too, that old admirers of the Nazi system should emerge triumphantly, and should be joined by converts to the gospel of success. But the Germans adopted no standard policy line toward these local Nazis or new converts; as in other respects, Hitler preferred to improvise.

Throughout northern and western Europe, the conquered peoples were assured that Hitler intended to respect their national independence and to impose only such occupation controls as were necessary for the conduct of the war. Nowhere in the west did the Germans impose a new government made up of local Nazis, even though there were aspiring candidates everywhere. The nearest approach to such an action was in Norway, where Major Vidkun Quisling proclaimed himself head of government on the first day of the invasion, and won tentative German support. But Quisling's bid was so obviously unpopular among his countrymen that the Germans quickly shelved him in an effort to find other more reputable officials willing to collaborate and to repudiate King Haakon, who had fled to London. Their failure in this enterprise eventually led them in 1942 to fall back on Quisling, who was made Minister-President, and who set out at once to Nazify the country. His Nasjonal Samling movement remained a small sect, however, and was riven by internal conflict; the "moderates" clung to the idea of Norwegian sovereignty, while the extremists preached integration into a Greater German Reich. The Germans' obvious contempt for Quisling, to whom they accorded little autonomy, increased his difficulties. Well before the end of the war, his movement was in rapid disintegration. The Quisling experiment had done little more than to provide a handy label for collaborators everywhere.

A sharply different pattern emerged in Denmark, which the Germans plainly intended to use as a kind of show window to demonstrate how small states could benefit by accepting the new order. King Christian and his cabinet remained in Copenhagen; and since the king was prepared to accept the fact of German occupation in order to soften its impact, the Germans could conveniently preserve the appearance of full Danish independence. The reality, however, was more disagreeable; the Danes were subjected to steady German pressure to align themselves with Nazi aims in Europe. The new Danish foreign minister, Erik Scavenius, eagerly cooperated; Denmark intended, he declared "to collaborate, in the most positive and loyal manner, in the building of this continental Europe directed by Germany."[35] Scavenius brought Denmark into the Anti-Comintern Pact, and was rewarded in 1942 when the Germans forced King Christian to appoint him Prime Minister. But a risky German gamble then backfired. In March 1943 the occupiers permitted parliamentary elections—the only ones held in German-occupied Europe during the war—and the nation overwhelmingly repudiated collaboration. The small Danish Nazi party, headed by a nonentity named Frits Clausen, won only 2 percent of the popular vote. Six months later, strikes and increased sabotage in Copenhagen gave the Germans an excuse to declare martial law, dissolve both the parliament and the cabinet, and resort to direct military rule. King Christian could nevertheless claim, with some justice, that his policy of limited collaboration had protected his people against the full severity of German rule.

In the Netherlands, too, the Nazis' racial doctrine led them to hope that the Dutch might be won over to willing collaboration. For a time that hope seemed justified; Queen Wilhelmina's departure for London angered many citizens, and made them susceptible to German blandishments. A group of leading citizens, declaring their intention to repudiate the errors of the past, promptly organized a new Netherlands Unity party with authoritarian overtones, and set out to make it the backbone of a single-party state; it attracted almost a million members. Some of those members, however, viewed it as a counterweight to Anton Mussert's Dutch Nazi party, and allegedly adopted some quasi-fascist phraseology as camouflage to mislead the Germans. By 1941 German suspicions were aroused, and the party was suppressed.

The Germans had little more enthusiasm for Mussert's Nationaal-Socialistiche Beweging, even though Mussert blatantly aped Hitler. The German Reich Commissioner, Artur von Seyss-Inquart, preferred to run the country directly through high-ranking Dutch civil servants, some of whom found Nazi doctrines attractive. Late in 1942 the persistent Mussert did at last persuade Hitler to proclaim him *Leider* (Fuehrer) of the Netherlands, and to permit the formation of a Dutch Nazi "consultative cabinet." But Mussert's new dignity changed only the appearances; he and his movement played a shadowy role from start to finish. At its peak, it attained a membership of 110,000; it

[35] C. Moret, *L'Allemagne et la réorganisation de l'Europe 1940–1943* (Neuchâtel, 1944), p. 168.

provided more recruits for the Waffen-SS than any other western European nation; and its members, acting as informers, helped to make the purge of Dutch Jews one of the most thorough in Europe.

Belgium's situation was peculiar in the sense that while King Leopold remained in Brussels throughout the occupation, his cabinet escaped to London and functioned as a government-in-exile. Although Leopold described himself as a voluntary prisoner and refused to exercise his royal prerogatives, his popularity at the outset was immense; the Germans found it convenient to use him as a kind of screen, behind which they could rule the country through a direct military administration. As in the Netherlands, many high civil servants kept their posts and carried out German orders. Pro-Nazi groups were strong in Belgium but were sharply divided by the old conflict between Walloons and Flemings. The chief competitors were the Flemish VNV, headed by Staf de Clercq, and the largely Walloon Rexists, led by a flamboyant young agitator named Léon Degrelle. Probably for racial reasons, the occupiers leaned toward the VNV, some of whose members favored outright absorption into the Reich. In 1941, a kind of merger was arranged; the Rexist groups in Flanders adhered to the VNV, in return for which Degrelle was given an organizational monopoly in Wallonia. But both groups were more successful in recruiting for the Waffen-SS than in winning power in occupied Belgium. Degrelle himself went off to the Russian front to serve as an officer in an SS unit. King Leopold's popularity meanwhile suffered a drastic decline; instead of the heroic captive king sharing the travail of his people, he came to be viewed as the self-indulgent sovereign who courted Hitler at Berchtesgaden and who found solace in marriage with a handsome young commoner. Collaboration in Belgium produced only bitter fruits both for its practitioners and for the nation.

In France, collaboration seemed for a time to offer palpable benefits both to Hitler and to the French. Hitler chose to allow the survival of a quasi-sovereign state in the southern third of the country, free of German occupation troops and possessed of its own small army of 100,000 men. Civilian officials named by this Vichy government were also permitted to function in occupied France, though under strict German control. Hitler's apparent generosity was probably motivated by a desire to end the war with France quickly, and to prevent the escape of the French Mediterranean fleet to join the British navy. Some Frenchmen mistakenly assumed that Hitler was demonstrating a special affection for France, a desire to bring France into the new Europe as his favored ally. A few prominent Nazis (notably the German ambassador in Paris, Otto Abetz) favored such a line, and urged it on Hitler during the years that followed. Never did Hitler give it serious consideration. He continued to dislike and distrust the French; he intended to use them, not to make them junior partners.

Whether Marshal Philippe Pétain, who in July 1940 became head of state at Vichy, really believed in collaboration as a long-term policy is a moot point. That he said so from time to time, both publicly and privately, is certain; that he privately disparaged the Germans at times is also clear. His defenders later argued that he had sought only to protect his countrymen against the savage treatment meted out to occupied Poland, and that he had misled the Germans by playing a double game. At the same time, however, he seized the occasion to try to renovate France along corporative lines, and denounced the evils of liberal democracy with genuine fervor.

But Pétain and the men around him at Vichy were not French exponents of National Socialist doctrine. They were, rather, traditionalist and authoritarian in temper; their ideal of a Christian corporative state based on the old social elites resembled the systems of Franco and Salazar rather than those of the new totalitarian theorists. For a time, disciples of Charles Maurras, the aging founder of the right-wing Action Française movement, were strongly influential at Vichy. On the other hand, Pierre Laval, head of the government at Vichy in 1940 and again in 1942–1944, was a lifetime professional politician who had soured on the old parliamentary system and who prided himself on his ability to manipulate the Germans so as to protect French interests. Neither Laval nor Admiral Jean Darlan, who replaced him as head of government in 1941–42, was a pro-Nazi doctrinaire; both men practiced collaboration for pragmatic reasons, and persuaded themselves that they were shielding their countrymen against "Polonization."

To some Frenchmen, the kind of collaboration practiced by Pétain and Laval was halfhearted and futile; they believed that France must volunteer enthusiastically for membership in the new National Socialist Europe. Excluded from high posts at Vichy, they congregated in German-occupied Paris, where they hobnobbed with German officials and directed a steady stream of criticism at Vichy. Some of these men had been Nazi sympathizers before the war; others, like the neo-Socialist Marcel Déat and the ex-Communist Jacques Doriot, were swept along by the tide of Nazi military triumphs. Personal feuds, however, prevented them from cooperating successfully in their attempt to found a single party; and generous German subsidies did not suffice to sell their program either to the men of Vichy or the French people as a whole. It was only in 1944 that they finally gained a partial foothold in the government at Vichy—and by that time, Vichy was more shadow than substance. Meanwhile, in November 1942, the demarcation line between occupied and unoccupied France had been rubbed out; German troops took over the whole country after the Allied landings in North Africa. Pétain's regime preserved the appearances of a sovereign state until 1944, continuing to legislate and to carry on tasks of civil administration; but its debility was obvious. Its incipient corporative-state structure, which differed somewhat from the German and Italian models, collapsed at the liberation; but some of Vichy's social and economic reforms were to survive into the postwar era.

In eastern and southern Europe, the politics of collaboration ranged over an even broader spectrum than in the west. On one extreme were the Poles, all of whose candidates for quisling status (notably Prince Radziwill and Professor Wladislaw Studnicki) were contemptuously rebuffed by Hitler after Poland fell. On the opposite extreme were the new states Slovakia and Croatia, created by German fiat and ruled in totalitarian fashion by local fascist dictators. More commonly, the Germans preferred to adapt their tactics to circumstances, relying on right-wing but not fascist native governments to carry out German orders.

Slovakia, made sovereign by Hitler in March 1939, proved to be a loyal and dependable satellite. Its head of state, Father Josef Tiso, was a clerical corporatist rather than a true Nazi doctrinaire, and was harassed at times by more thoroughgoing Slovak Nazis who kept pushing for power. But Berlin preferred Tiso, and provided him with favored treatment to build up his country's economy. Tiso in turn sent a sizable force to fight in Russia. Croatia, which emerged in 1941, was run by a more thoroughly totalitarian regime headed by the noted terrorist Ante Pavelić, whose Ustaše movement appropriately used as its emblem the initial "U" upon which was superimposed an exploding bomb. Pavelić's men lost no time in justifying their reputation and their symbol. Some two million Serbs who had been included within the boundaries of the inflated Croat state were mercilessly pursued, and thousands were massacred. Although Pavelić was regarded as a protégé of Mussolini, and although Croatia was handed over by Hitler to Italian supervision, the Ustaše quickly grew restless at Italian control. Pavelić agreed to accept an Italian prince, the Duke of Spoleto, as king of Croatia, but the duke prudently postponed his triumphal entry into his new kingdom, and in fact never arrived at all. Some Ustaše leaders began to seek German support as a counterweight to the Italians; and much to Mussolini's irritation, the Germans responded with alacrity. They had gained an economic foothold in the new state even before Mussolini's fall; thereafter, German control was undisguised.

In the so-called protectorate of Bohemia-Moravia, a nominal Czech government and administration were preserved throughout the war. President Hácha, who had bowed to German threats in March 1939, stayed on in office, an abject figure. Premier Eliaš, although pliable, was less fortunate; in 1941 the Germans found that he had maintained *sub rosa* contacts with the Czechoslovak government-in-exile, and executed him. The cabinet of his successor Krejci included not only some genuine Czech Nazis but one Reich German as well. All this was so obviously a facade that one wonders why the Germans found it useful to preserve the appearances of Bohemian self-rule. Certainly few Czechs were misled. Much the same might be said of Greece, partitioned between German and Italian control. A series of Greek prime ministers succeeded one another from 1941 to 1944, persuading themselves (like Laval and others) that they were softening the impact of the occupation, but achieving little to justify their sacrifice. The small rump state of Serbia, headed by General Milan Nedić, was a kind of pale replica of Vichy France. Nedić's well-meaning but simple-minded patriotism was not an effective response to German exactions; and his *idée fixe* of saving Serbia from Tito's Communist partisans left him little time or energy to resist Berlin.

In the three Danubian junior allies of the Axis—Hungary, Rumania, and Bulgaria—Hitler discovered willing collaborators within the old governing elite; there was no need to install local Nazi movements in power, save only at the very end in Hungary. In Rumania, a bitter struggle between the old authoritarian right wing and the fascist Iron Guard headed by Horia Sima (after its founder Corneliu Zelea-Codreanu was murdered in 1938) culminated in a clear victory for the former. Marshal Ion Antonescu, who had been named *Conducator* (Leader) after a palace revolution in 1940, broke with the Iron Guard early in 1941 and drove its leaders into exile. Although

Antonescu was an old-fashioned authoritarian rather than a fascist, Hitler found him an attractive and impressive figure, as Rumanians went; and though he kept Horia Sima on ice in Germany for possible future use, he accepted Antonescu's regime as a loyal partner. The relationship was especially warm during the early phase of the attack on the USSR, in which Antonescu enthusiastically participated. The Rumanians sent thirty divisions to fight in the east—more than any other Axis state except Germany—and provided Hitler with much of his oil supply. But the friendship wore thinner as the fortunes of war turned. By 1943, most of the Rumanian forces were withdrawn from the eastern front, and popular sentiment turned strongly against German exploitation. Toward the end, Antonescu himself was secretly (and unsuccessfully) trying for a separate peace with the Western powers.

Bulgaria in the person of King Boris produced the cagiest of all collaborators. Although Boris permitted German forces to cross his territory in 1941 to get at the Yugoslavs and the Greeks, and although he accepted most of Macedonia as his share of the spoils from the Yugoslav war, he cautiously avoided any further commitment. He found an excuse not to declare war on the Soviet Union in 1941, and sent no troops to fight there. Eventually he joined the Anti-Comintern Pact and dutifully declared war on Britain and the United States, but these were *pro forma* actions. His evasive friendship irritated Hitler, and when Boris died suddenly in 1943 immediately after returning from conversations with Hitler, many Bulgarians suspected foul play. But the Germans were too much occupied elsewhere to concern themselves very actively with Bulgarian affairs; the country limped on under a regency, increasingly restless at its satellite status but unable to find an escape route.

Hungary, so located as to be the gateway for German penetration into southeastern Europe, was peculiarly vulnerable to German influence. Within Hungary's borders lived a large minority of *Volksdeutsche* who might be used as an effective fifth column; and in addition, Hungary boasted one of the largest and most active fascist movements in eastern Europe in Ferenc Szálasi's Arrow Cross organization. For the aging regent, Admiral Nicholas Horthy, collaboration was therefore a necessity even more than a choice. Most of Hitler's demands were met, though with occasional quibbling: German troops attacking Yugoslavia in 1941 were allowed to cross Hungarian soil, and a large

Hu   fight alongside the Germans in Russia.
But   gh mistreated, were not shipped off for
liqu   ly in 1944 Hitler learned of Horthy's
clan   w from the war. In March, the German   ing Hungary to full-scale military oc-
cupa   s arrested and replaced by Szálasi as
head   f power was brief; only four months
later,   drove him across the frontier into
Germ

Prob   isode in collaborationist politics occurred   of the invasion, some high Nazis
hoped   to help administer the conquered
east. T   ed Rosenberg expected to recruit
them a   rity groups: Byelorussians, Ukrainians, th   berg was convinced that separa-
tism cou   in these minority regions, and proposed to   up a series of national committees composed of exiles
in Berlin. A second faction, mainly in the German army, preferred to
look for allies among the Great Russians themselves; it believed that
the promise of relief from Stalin's terrorism would be enough to win
over much of the population. Only four months after the invasion began, exponents of this latter view forwarded to Hitler a proposal for
the creation of a Russian army of liberation and a Russian provisional
government-in-exile.

Hitler's response was brusquely negative. True, before the invasion
he had spoken vaguely of creating several weak socialist states in conquered Russia; but his initial victories encouraged him to substitute a
purely colonialist plan. Rosenberg's separatist scheme he brushed aside
as pure illusion; the futility of trying to appease the Ukrainians had,
he said, been proved in the First World War. As for putting Russians
into uniform and dealing with a Russian exile government, he was
adamantly hostile. Even gestures aimed at winning over the mass of
Soviet citizens—notably the abolition of collective farms—were rejected by Hitler. A more generous policy during the early months of
the eastern war would undoubtedly have induced a considerable share
of the population to collaborate; there is ample evidence that many
villagers, especially in the Ukraine, welcomed the German invaders at
first. That the number would have sufficed to turn the tide of war in
Hitler's favor is, however, pure conjecture. It can only be said that

concessions, when they came, were quite inadequate, and had been more than offset by the brutality of the occupiers.

With the failure of the great 1941 offensive, the idea of trying to find Russian collaborators began to gain new momentum. The armed forces had already begun to utilize, despite Hitler's specific orders, large numbers of Soviet prisoners and civilians who volunteered to work in return for subsistence and protection. By the end of 1941 there were about 200,000 of these so-called *Hilfswillige* or "Hiwis" attached to the German armies; eventually the figure was to reach a half-million. In addition to performing menial tasks, the Hiwis were sometimes formed into companies or battalions for combat or intelligence purposes, especially in the struggle against the partisans. The next step was to put them into German uniform; during 1942, these so-called *Osttruppen* began to appear in increasing number. Most of them were Cossacks, Caucasians, or Central Asians; the common practice was to scatter them out in single battalions attached to German regiments.

These pragmatic arrangements, however, fell far short of collaboration in the true political sense. Certain army elements were still pressing for the creation of a real Russian liberation army and a government-in-exile, with a view to speeding the rate of Soviet desertions if not to laying the foundations for a future Russian collaborationist state. One German expert attached to Rosenberg's ministry suggested ". . . creating a figure similar to that which the French found in General de Gaulle."[36] Someone coined the attractive cliché, "Russians can be beaten only by Russians"; it gained widespread currency during 1942. In Berlin, the army set up an agency to train selected Soviet prisoners as propagandists, but it quickly began to concern itself with political scheming as well.

A potential candidate for the role of "Russian de Gaulle" conveniently turned up in July 1942, when General Andrei Vlasov was captured at Leningrad. Vlasov was shortly persuaded to draft an appeal urging Soviet officers to depose Stalin and seek a separate peace with the Germans; leaflets containing the appeal were dropped in large numbers over the Soviet lines. Emboldened, Vlasov's backers in the German hierarchy now urged that he be named head of a liberation government to be based at Smolensk, and that the *Osttruppen* be grouped together under his command as a liberation army. But they

---

[36] Dallin, *German Rule in Russia*, p. 524.

found no support at the top echelon of either the army or the government: Hitler, Himmler, Keitel, Rosenberg all angrily rejected the idea. "I shall not create any Russian army," declared Hitler in 1943; "that is a phantom of the first order."[37] Through 1943 and most of 1944, Vlasov was kept in a kind of gilded confinement in a Berlin suburb, and trotted out only occasionally for propaganda purposes. Meanwhile, the *Osttruppen,* whose loyalty to the German cause Hitler doubted, were transferred late in 1943 to the western front for use in coastal defense and in combating local resistance groups.

As the eastern war turned strongly against the Nazis, the German leaders finally grew desperate enough to make grudging concessions to Vlasov. Late in 1944 he was permitted to organize a Committee for the Liberation of the Peoples of Russia, and to hold a congress in Prague at which a program for a new federal Russian state was drafted. He was even given command of a liberation army of fifty thousand men, though it was not unleashed to go into action until too late to join in the fighting. The differences between Vlasov and Hitler remained too deep to permit effective collaboration; Vlasov wanted German guarantees for Russia's future, while Hitler wanted mercenary troops and a propaganda weapon to encourage Soviet desertions. Never until the end did Hitler reconcile himself to the idea of restoring a Russian state, even of a puppet variety. Collaboration, whether in eastern or western Europe, was a term that had no appeal to the Fuehrer. Commitments of any sort might tie his hands for the future; and if victorious, he was determined to have his hands completely free.

VI. MYTHOLOGY OF THE NEW EUROPE

"We did not cross our frontiers in order to subdue other peoples in blind madness for conquest. . . . We came as the heralds of a New Order and a new justice." So asserted the editor of a German newspaper late in 1944.[38] Perhaps this editor, through four years of self-intoxication, had come to believe what he wrote. Ever since the great victories of 1939–1940, German publicists had been vigorously and persistently arguing the thesis that their nation was engaged in a great constructive enterprise—a crusade to achieve the unity of Europe; and their view had been echoed by collaborators in the conquered coun-

[37] *Ibid.,* p. 534.
[38] *Pommersche Zeitung,* Sept. 1, 1944. Quoted in A. and V. Toynbee (eds.), *Hitler's Europe* (London, 1954), p. 55.

tries. Conquest, they insisted, was the painful but necessary prelude to reconstruction; Germany's role was not to build a subject empire but to give the word "Europe" a new significance, broader then mere geography.

Talk of the New Order burst forth for the first time in the summer of 1940, after the defeat of France. Initially the stress was on economic interrelationships and advantages; Germany would build a *Grossraumwirtschaft* that would ensure free-flowing trade, would harmonize the complementary economies of industrial and agricultural countries, and would largely free Europe of its old dependence on overseas supplies. Germany's press chief Otto Dietrich, lecturing in Prague in 1941 on "The Spiritual Foundations of the New Europe," declared grandiloquently that the New Order would be based "not on the principle of a privileged position for individual nations, but on the principle of equal chances for all," and promised "a racially constituted but organically combined ordering of the nations."[39] Hitler's admirers throughout western Europe chimed in enthusiastically; this was an ideal to which even former anti-Nazis could rally.[40] Manifestoes like Dietrich's were soon supplemented by even more grandiose demonstrations of intent. Late in 1941, a meeting in Berlin of representatives from all the Anti-Comintern Pact states was hailed as "the first European Congress." The occasion inspired the composition of a new "Song of Europe," which was broadcast throughout the continent; the German press proclaimed the birth of the United States of Europe. The Italian government began pressing strongly for the drafting of a European Charter defining the outlines of the future; Pierre Laval seized the occasion of a meeting with Hitler to observe: "You want to win the war in order to create Europe; why not create Europe in order to win the war?"[41] But Stalingrad and other pressing matters diverted Nazi minds from the building of future utopias; and the European Charter remained stillborn.

Behind this verbal facade lay a quite different reality, far removed from any concept of a community of autonomous nations. The German government itself from time to time put a cautious damper on talk of a New Europe. On the occasion of Molotov's visit to Berlin in

[39] Otto Dietrich, *The Spiritual Foundations of the New Europe* (Berlin, 1941), p. 26.
[40] One example was Francis Delaisi, a well-known left-wing publicist in France; see his *La révolution européenne* (Paris, 1942). Even the left-wing Catholic thinker Emmanuel Mounier believed for a time that fascism might create a truly new Europe.
[41] *Le Monde* (Paris), March 1-2, 1964.

November 1940, for example, the Propaganda Ministry privately reminded the press: "We are fighting primarily not for a New Order in Europe, but for the defense and security of our life interests."[42] When Hitler spoke of Europe, he obviously meant a Greater German Reich to which would be attached various satellites in the west and south and a purely colonial realm in the east. The Slavic and Latin peoples he stubbornly viewed as subjects rather than co-builders of the New Order. In May 1943 Hitler told a group of high Nazis that "the aim of our struggle must be to create a unified Europe," but he then proceeded to offer this curious elaboration of his thought: "All the rubbish of small nations still existing in Europe must be liquidated as fast as possible. . . . The Germans alone can really organize Europe. . . . The Reich will be the master. . . . From there on the way to world domination is practically certain."[43]

True, a preferred status would be granted to the Germanic *Völker*, the racial relatives of the Germans proper. Eventually, these somewhat degenerate Nordics would be merged with the Germans into a single ruling race. But that prospect, as Hitler saw it, lay "a hundred or so years" in the future. "Once the conditions of the race's purity are established, it's of no importance whether a man is a native of one region rather than another—whether he comes from Norway or from Austria."[44] During the interim "hundred or so years," however, Hitler clearly intended that the New Europe should be run by Germans alone, and not by Germanics in the broader sense. Indeed, he even forbade the press to mention plans to settle a considerable number of Dutch farmers in the conquered east, and insisted that German settlers must dominate the newly colonized area.

Some high Nazis—Heinrich Himmler, for example—were more willing than Hitler to broaden the base of the master race without delay. Beginning in 1940, Himmler's recruiting agents sought out Waffen-SS volunteers among the various Germanic *Völker*—Finns, Norwegians, Dutch, Flemings—and later he even tried to comb out some "Nordic" types from the non-Germanic peoples. Hitler remained skeptical about this experiment; more clearly than Himmler, he instinctively recognized the surviving hold of national sentiment even

[42] P. Kluke, "Nationalsozialistiche Europaideologie," *Vierteljahrshefte fuer Zeitgeschichte*, III (1955), 259.
[43] Lochner, *The Goebbels Diaries*, pp. 357, 359.
[44] *Hitler's Secret Conversations*, p. 125.

among the Nazis of the conquered lands. A few Dutch or Norwegian Nazis were ready to see their nations swallowed up in the German Reich; but a large majority, including even such leaders as Quisling and Mussert, aspired to the creation of independent National Socialist states within a European confederation of Germanic *Völker*. Hitler was stubbornly determined not to share leadership with these lesser disciples, in part because he doubted their undiluted loyalty to German leadership, in part because his own sense of German pride made him regard them as inferiors.

For that matter, even Himmler could not shake off the idea of a hierarchical distinction between German *Volk* and Germanic *Völker*. The official SS organ *Das Schwarze Korps* never managed to reconcile the contradiction between Germanic brotherhood and German superiority. Units of Waffen-SS volunteers from Norway, the Netherlands, and Belgian Flanders were given not native but German commanders. Himmler's racism, like Hitler's, was overlaid with a heavy coating of biological nationalism; it flawed his attempt to make the Waffen-SS the embodiment of the new Nordic *Völkerfamilie*.[45]

True, by 1943 it began to seem that SS practice was outrunning SS doctrine. For the first time, the Waffen-SS began to admit volunteers of dubious racial pedigree: Frenchmen, Magyars, Ukrainians, even Turkic peoples and a few Indians. "The SS," proclaimed a recruiting pamphlet issued in Paris, "is being transformed today into one indissoluble community of European youth."[46] By the end of the war, the Waffen-SS had been transmuted from a model of Nordic purity into a motley cross-section of European peoples, with a few Asiatics added for good measure. As the composition of the Waffen-SS changed, the training program for its officers was gradually adapted; it gave steadily greater emphasis to the idea of a New Europe. Out of this development was to grow the postwar myth, propagated by former Waffen-SS officers and by sympathizers like General Heinz Guderian, that the members of the Waffen-SS had been the earliest carriers of the European idea. Unfortunately for exponents of this myth, the broadening tolerance of the SS was the product of harsh necessity rather than evolving theory. Desperate for fighting manpower, the Germans began

[45] Himmler, in a conversation with the rocket expert Walter Dornberger, deplored the failure of many Europeans to recognize Hitler as Europe's champion. "We must bear in mind the greatness of our mission and simply force people to accept their good fortune." Dornberger, *V-2*, p. 192.

[46] *La SS t'appelle* (Paris, 1943), p. 6.

1. Neville Chamberlain greets crowd at Munich, September, 1938. *(Süddeutscher Verlag)*

2. The Munich Conference: Chamberlain, Daladier, Hitler, Mussolini, Ciano. *(U.S. Information Service)*

3. Soviet Foreign Minister Molotov signing the German-Soviet pact, August, 1939; von Ribbentrop and Stalin in background. *(Bibliothek für Zeitgeschichte)*

4. First German troops cross the Polish frontier, September 1, 1939.

5. The western invasion: fleeing Belgians crowd roads while French tanks move toward the front. *(Etablissement Cinématographique des armées françaises)*

6. Hitler rejoicing at the news of France's capitulation. (*Süddeutscher Verlag*)

7. British soldiers on the beach at Dunkirk fire at attacking German planes. (*Fox Photos*)

8. Victory celebration in Berlin: young Nazis strewing flowers on Hitler's path, July, 1940. (*Süddeutscher Verlag*)

9. Marshal Pétain's cabinet at Vichy, July, 1940 (Pierre Laval at Pétain's right). *(Keystone)*

10. German invasion barges in Dunkirk harbor, summer, 1940. *(Imperial War Museum)*

11. David Low cartoon, May 14, 1940: "All behind you, Winston!" (*By permission of the Trustees of Sir David Low*)

12. Churchill touring bombed area in London, September, 1940. *(Fox Photos)*

13. Wreckage in Coventry after German air attack, November, 1940. *(Fox Photos)*

14. Londoners sleeping in tube station during blitz. (*Imperial War Museum*)

15. British wartime art: "Tilbury Shelter Scene" by Henry Moore. (*Tate Gallery*)

16. Churchill and his advisers observing an anti-aircraft demonstration: left to right, Professor Lindemann (later Lord Cherwell), Sir Charles Portal, Sir Dudley Pound, the Prime Minister, General Loch. (*Imperial War Museum*)

17. Hitler meets General Francisco Franco at Hendaye, October, 1940. (*Zentralbild*)

18. Heinrich Himmler (left) and Vidkun Quisling (center) in Berlin. (*Zentralbild*)

19. (*Below*) General Heinz Guderian and his staff a quarter-hour before the invasion of the U.S.S.R., June 22, 1941. (*Zentralbild*)

20. Moscow or the Ukraine? Keitel, Brauchitsch, Warlimont, Hitler and Halder, August, 1941. (*Zeitgeschichtliches Bildarchiv*)

PIECE BY PIECE

21. David Low caricatures one of his favorite targets: Mussolini's Crumbling Empire, March 24, 1941. *(By permission of the Trustees of Sir David Low)*

22. Women isolationists picket the U.S. Congress, 1941.

23. Dimitri Shostakovich in besieged Leningrad composing his *Seventh Symphony*, 1941. *(Soviet Information Office)*

24. Soviet soldiers in the battle of Stalingrad. *(Soviet Information Office)*

25. Soviet wartime art: "Leaving the Natal Soil," by G. Riazhky. (*Soviet Information Office*)

26. Stalingrad after the battle. (*Soviet Information Office*)

27. Generals Henri Giraud and Charles de Gaulle grudgingly shake hands (at Roosevelt's request) during the Casablanca Conference, 1943. *(U.S. Army)*

28. United States troops disembark from a landing craft in Sicily. *(U.S. Army)*

29. American Liberator bombers over the Ploesti oil fields in Rumania. *(U.S. Air Force)*

30. The ruins of Monte Cassino monastery after the battle. *(Imperial War Museum)*

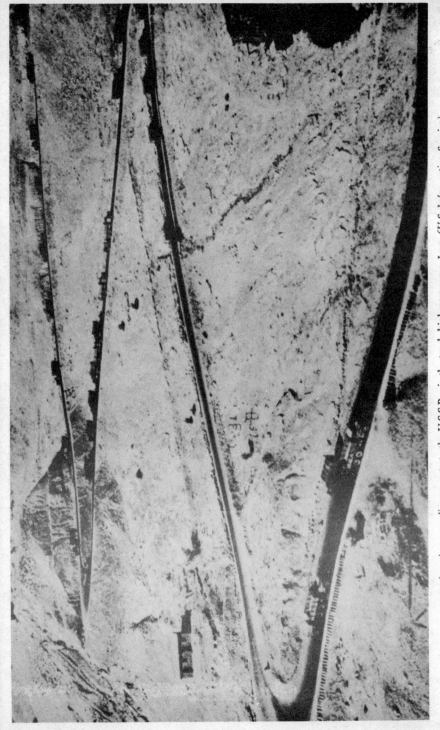

31. American supplies enroute to the U.S.S.R. via the truck highway across Iran. (*U.S. Information Service*)

32. Mussolini arrives in Germany after his liberation from confinement in Italy, 1943. (*Süddeutscher Verlag*)

33. Soviet peasants begin again after the retreat of the German occupation forces. (*Soviet Information Office*)

34. A Yugoslav partisan's cry of defiance before being hanged by his German captors. *(Foto-Tanjug)*

35. Marshal Tito with some of his partisans. *(Foto-Tanjug)*

36. A French maquis unit gathering supplies dropped by parachute. (*Comité d'Histoire de la IIe Guerre Mondiale*)

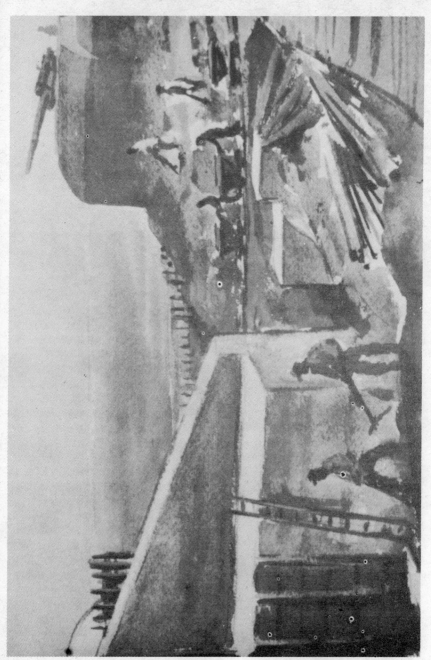

37. German wartime art: "Building Coastal Defenses on the Mediterranean," by Walter Preiss. (*U.S. Army*)

38. The greatest amphibious operation in history: beach in Normandy, June, 1944. (*U.S. Information Service*)

39. A German V-2 weapon (test-launching after the war under British supervision). (*Imperial War Museum*)

40. Martin Bormann and Hermann Goering inspect the scene of the attempt on Hitler's life, July 20, 1944. (*Zeitgeschichtliches Bildarchiv*)

41. United States troops march down the Champs-Elysées in Paris on liberation day, August 25, 1944. (*U.S. Information Service*)

42. Churchill's triumphal return to Paris, November 11, 1944 (between the Prime Minister and General de Gaulle is Georges Bidault, President of the National Resistance Council). *(Süddeutscher Verlag)*

43. The Big Three at Yalta. *(Imperial War Museum)*

44. Hitler greeting teen-age conscripts in Berlin, March, 1945. (*Zeitgeschichtliches Bildarchiv*)

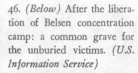

45. Captured women concentration-camp guards. (*Imperial War Museum*)

46. (*Below*) After the liberation of Belsen concentration camp: a common grave for the unburied victims. (*U.S. Information Service*)

47. The toll of war: the ruins of Wesel, 1945. (*U.S. Air Force*)

48. The end of a dictator: Mussolini and his mistress hang upside down at a Milan filling station. *(U.S. Information Service)*

49. The Soviet flag goes up atop the ruined Reichstag building in Berlin. (*Soviet Information Office*)

50. The end in Berlin. *(Zentralbild)*

51. Victory celebration in Red Square: Soviet soldiers with captured German battle flags. *(Soviet Information Office)*

52. The defendants at the Nuremberg war crimes trial. (*Keystone*)

in 1944 to conscript every available subject, not only for the regular army but for the Waffen-SS as well. By the end of the war, most of the members of this one-time elite body were draftees rather than volunteers; and more than half were non-Germans. To the racial purists who deplored this lowering of standards, SS General Gottlob Berger bluntly replied: "For every foreigner who falls, no German mother will have to weep."[47] His phrase summed up in epigrammatic brevity the Nazi conception of the New Europe.

[47] P. Kluke, "Nationalsozialistische Europaideologie," *Vierteljahrshefte fuer Zeitgeschichte,* III (1955), 268.

Chapter Seven

EUROPE'S RESPONSE TO CONQUEST: THE RESISTANCE MOVEMENTS

I. THE UNDERGROUND IN WESTERN EUROPE

RESISTANCE to a conqueror, whether active or passive in nature, is a phenomenon as old as conquest itself. The Napoleonic era produced its resistance movements, notably in Spain; and even Julius Caesar confronted some restless rebels among the subjected Gauls and Britons. But perhaps the phenomenon becomes more generalized in an age when national loyalties have come to overshadow all other loyalties, and when the masses have successfully asserted their right to participate in the conduct of affairs. In any event, the growth of an anti-German underground in every conquered or invaded country was one of the most striking developments of wartime Europe. A Soviet historian has even been inspired to assert that the European resistance movement ". . . was not born of fortuitous and provisional causes, but sprang from the action of irresistible laws of historical evolution."[1] To non-Marxians, this may seem an odd characterization of a movement that contained such a high degree of spontaneity, of individual decision and courage.

Almost everywhere, Hitler's conquest brought him a minority of fanatical or opportunistic collaborators, and a roughly equal minority of active resisters. At the outset, collaborators outnumbered resisters in virtually every country. But as the character of the German occupation grew clearer, and as the prospect of a durable German victory grew more clouded, the proportion was gradually reversed. Midway through the war, the various undergrounds had won the open or tacit support of a large part of the subject population. By 1945, they were in most cases strong enough to move into control of the state machinery after the German defeat. In the process of their growth, however, most resistance movements had developed cracks and fis-

---

[1] E. Boltine, in *European Resistance Movements 1939–1945* [Milan Congress] (Oxford, 1963), p. 9.

sures that revealed the diverse political and social forces at work within them. No other aspect of the Second World War so clearly demonstrated that behind the clashing arms of nations could be heard the thunder of an international civil war.

Everywhere in western Europe, the shock of defeat temporarily stunned the local populations. Apathy, an unreasoning anger at the political leaders who had failed in the crisis, a desperate urge to find a savior—these were the predominant impulses. In Norway and the Netherlands, there was specially bitter resentment toward the sovereigns and their governments who had scuttled off to London, leaving their peoples to face the conqueror alone. The kings of Denmark and Belgium, on the other hand, enjoyed a sudden burst of public affection because they had stayed to share the uncertainties of the occupation. In France, the patriarchal figure of Marshal Pétain provided a substitute for royalty, as he generously offered "the gift of his person" to France. Even before the bulk of the French parliament, convened in Vichy, had turned over full powers to him, the nation as a whole had welcomed him as its savior and defender in time of affliction.

Yet from the very outset, a few lonely voices were raised in dissent; scattered individuals were moved by national pride to strike back somehow at the invader. Clandestine anti-German leaflets, handwritten or typed, began to appear as early as May 1940; and little groups of patriots soon began to be drawn together—usually through the efforts of a single individual cautiously recruiting his close friends—to discuss the possibilities of carrying on the fight or of restoring national morale. The departure of the Norwegian and Dutch sovereigns, once the first shock had worn off, could be seen as gestures of defiance rather than cowardice; both rulers promptly established governments-in-exile in England, and served as rallying-points for physical and moral resistance. So did the Belgian cabinet, which was authorized by King Leopold to go to London even though the king himself remained behind. A dozen leading French politicians left for North Africa intending to set up a center of continuing resistance; but on Pétain's orders, they were headed off at Casablanca and shipped back to France, to be interned there. A substitute quickly appeared: a little-known soldier, General Charles de Gaulle, had flown to London in defiance of orders and on June 18, 1940, issued a radio appeal to his countrymen urging them to carry on the fight.

Britain's surprising failure to collapse in 1940 gradually reawakened some of the hope and confidence the western Europeans needed if they were to re-enter the struggle. Although the German occupation troops sought to be "correct" in their behavior, the exactions of the German authorities were severe enough to inspire growing resentment. The initial enthusiasm for such saviors as King Leopold and Pétain also began to fade after the first few months, both because the saviors failed to accomplish very much and because their conduct toward the Germans struck many citizens as abject. Leopold's visit to Berchtesgaden, where he accepted Hitler's hospitality, shocked many Belgians, even though he had gone there to plead for more generous treatment of occupied Belgium. And Pétain and Laval's much-publicized meeting with Hitler at Montoire in October 1940, which seemed to presage France's entry into the Axis, outraged many Frenchmen.

The British, sensing the rise of discontent in western Europe, naturally set out to encourage it. In July 1940 they had set up what Churchill described as a "ministry of ungentlemanly warfare"—the Special Operations Executive, designed (in Churchill's phrase) "to set Europe ablaze." Its mission was to encourage and, if necessary, initiate subversion and sabotage. At this desperate moment just after the fall of France, British officials exaggerated the possibilities of subversion; the Chiefs of Staff even suggested that Germany might be beaten by a combination of economic pressure, air attacks, and "the creation of widespread revolt in her conquered territories." Before long, however, calmer counsels prevailed, and S.O.E.'s role was seen only as "a valuable contributory factor" in weakening the enemy. From late 1940 onward, S.O.E. sent a growing number of agents into the various western European countries; more than a thousand eventually went to France alone.[2] By mid-1941 the occupied countries were covered by a thin network of resistance groups—some spontaneous, others British-sponsored—devoted to collecting military intelligence, aiding in the escape of refugees and young men who wanted to rejoin the fight, circulating anti-German leaflets and newspapers, and carrying out sabotage assignments.

[2] The activities of S.O.E. led to some tensions and misunderstandings with resistance groups and governments-in-exile, who at times suspected British motives. The Gaullists particularly resented S.O.E.'s practice of recruiting its own agents, and its monopoly of aircraft and supplies used by Gaullist agents. There was also friction between S.O.E. and the largest Norwegian resistance group MILORG over sabotage tactics. For a persuasive statement of the S.O.E.'s case, see the official account by M. R. D. Foot, *SOE in France* (London, 1966), especially pp. 21, 139.

Although the western European underground was initially motivated by injured patriotism, in time it took on an ideological and reformist tone as well. In its broadest sense, this ideology was anti-totalitarian and at the same time collectivist; it aimed to reassert the values of liberal humanism, as modified by twentieth-century democratic socialist and Christian Socialist thought. A growing number of resisters saw the expulsion of the Germans as only one step toward a higher goal—the renovation of the nation's society, economy, and political structure. This reformist temper was weakest in Norway and Denmark, strongest in the Netherlands and France. A leading French underground newspaper chose for its masthead the slogan, "From resistance to revolution." In a curious negative way, resisters and collaborators found themselves arguing the same case: that the defunct prewar systems must be swept away in favor of something fresh and new. But unlike the collaborators, the resisters reasserted the values on which the prewar democratic systems had theoretically rested; they simply insisted that mere hypocritical lip service to those ideals would no longer be tolerated.

This urge toward fundamental reform of the social and political order within a democratic framework was not merely the product of the 1940 disaster. Ideas of the same sort had been advanced during the interwar years, and especially during the depression decade, when small but vigorous reformist groups had proliferated in western Europe. Many of those prewar critics became wartime resisters: they continued to challenge the effectiveness of capitalism, to denounce the time-serving habits of the old politicians, to speak with passion of human rights and human dignity. Now, in the anti-German underground, two rival currents of secular humanism and of Christian democracy showed signs of merging into a single current; Catholics and freethinkers found that they had more in common than they had realized. Most resisters had not been active in prewar politics; the resistance gave them a taste for political action of a renovated kind. They came from every stratum of society, from proletariat to aristocracy; but many of the upper- or middle-class resisters were somewhat alienated types, young men or women who had been mildly or violently in revolt against their society and against their places in it. If the working class provided the infantry of the underground in western Europe, restless members of the old social elites furnished much of the leadership and most of the ideological content.

The western European resistance received its greatest windfall in June 1941, when Hitler's attack on the Soviet Union brought the Communists wholeheartedly into the underground. Hitherto they had maintained an awkwardly neutralist stance, denouncing the German and British "imperialists" with equal fervor, branding de Gaulle and Queen Wilhelmina as tools of the British and scoffing at the prospect that the Americans might soon intervene. A few individual Communists had already joined resistance groups in defiance of the party; now their participation was officially blessed. In addition, the party now created a new underground organization in each Western country—an organization of broad "national front" rather than narrowly Communist character, with an armed guerrilla force as its auxiliary. In numbers, in toughness, in practical underground experience the Communists excelled; their influence in France and Belgium soon outweighed that of any single rival group.

This accession of strength, however, had its corresponding disadvantages. To many non-Communist resisters, it was not clear that the Communists shared the same goals. To be sure, both groups were agreed on undermining German power; but were the Communists planning a different sequence of events after Germany's defeat? In some countries—notably in France—it appeared that the party's attempt to create a national front might be a scheme for giving it a grip on the entire resistance movement, from which it might then catapult into power after victory. Not all non-Communists shared these suspicions; but the party leadership's conduct at times lent support to the skeptics. France was unavoidably the key to Communist hopes in western Europe; the party was strongest there, and from a foothold in Paris its influence could be brought to bear elsewhere. In the end, however, its strength was offset by the growing prestige of Charles de Gaulle, whose Free French movement served as an alternative pole of attraction. De Gaulle had been steadily gaining adherents since 1940, and had won the support of much of the French Empire. By 1943 he was able to transfer his "capital" from London to Algiers, and to establish himself as head of a kind of unofficial government-in-exile. Thanks to S.O.E. support, Gaullist agents in 1943 managed to federate all the major French resistance groups into a single national movement headed by a National Resistance Council and a Military Action Committee; the underground leaders (with varying degrees of enthusiasm) committed themselves to de Gaulle's leadership. From this new position of authority, de Gaulle in 1944 successfully fended off Communist attempts to take over decisive control of the underground guerrilla forces.

The declining fortunes of the Germans from 1943 onward transformed the western European resistance groups into mass movements. The underground press, heretofore small, scattered, and amateur in nature, now developed everywhere into a large-scale operation. In the Netherlands, for example, total circulation of the major papers in late 1943 approached a half-million. Rising hope of a final Allied victory inspired the fainthearted; increasingly savage repression by the Germans produced deepening hatred. Sauckel's forced-labor campaign led thousands of young men to take to the hills in France, Belgium, and Norway, or to hide out with friendly families in the Netherlands. In France, sizable groups of maquisards (guerrillas) in the central and southeastern mountains even fought several small pitched battles with German forces sent to liquidate them. Their military effectiveness, however, was slight compared to that of the part-time saboteurs who cut railway or power lines at night, or the armed units which held their fire for the arrival of the liberating Anglo-American armies.

In Belgium, the Netherlands, and Denmark the terrain largely ruled out guerrilla activities. Resisters there specialized in sabotage and in smuggling out military intelligence to London. The Belgians showed particular skill in this latter art, which they had already learned during the war of 1914. The Danes were especially successful at protecting victims of Nazi persecution. When the Germans in 1943 attempted to round up Denmark's 8000 Jews, all but 570 were hidden or helped to escape to Sweden. The Dutch resistance was slow to develop, but eventually attained a high degree of national solidarity; Mussert's Dutch Nazis were increasingly isolated. Large numbers of labor-service conscripts escaped deportation by hiding out in Dutch homes; the total of such *onderduikers* ("divers") may have reached 300,000 during the last years of the war. The Dutch Jews, on the other hand, were virtually eliminated. In Norway, there was for a time some tension between the largest resistance group (MILORG) and British S.O.E. agents; the latter advocated sabotage, the former hoped to conserve its strength for the moment of liberation. Eventually the two groups worked out an understanding, and accomplished such remarkable coups as the successful 1943 raid on Europe's only heavy-water plant.

By 1944, when the Allied forces landed in Normandy, the western European underground was strong enough to provide impressive support. In France alone, perhaps as many as 200,000 armed and organized resisters were available under centralized command to carry out Allied orders; they seriously hampered German troop movements by rail sabotage, and engaged in guerrilla-type harassment of the enemy. In Belgium, it was the resistance groups that seized intact the invaluable port facilities of Antwerp. In each liberated nation, the underground had worked with its government-in-exile to prepare a staff of administrative officials ready to take over as soon as the Germans departed; in each case, too, a number of resistance leaders were named to cabinet posts. Only in France was there some brief tension between the returning exile government and the domestic underground; here, the Communists had planned that local and regional liberation committees would take over administrative power from the deposed Vichy officials. But de Gaulle was not prepared to bargain; his nominees immediately evicted the liberation committees from the town halls and prefectures, and the Communists grudgingly accepted the accomplished fact. Throughout western Europe, it seemed, the resistance movements had restored national morale and unity, and had ensured a smooth transition to the postwar era.

II. THE UNDERGROUND IN MEDITERRANEAN EUROPE

In the conquered countries of southeastern Europe, the resistance took the form of active guerrilla warfare from the start. Immediately after Yugoslavia's defeat in April 1941, General Draža Mihajlović took refuge in the hills of central Serbia and began to rally a force of Chetniks (the traditional label for outlaw rebels against the Turks). At the same time the secretary-general of the Yugoslav Communist party, Josip Broz, set out to reorganize the activists of his party for underground work, and to form a guerrilla force independent of Mihajlović's. Broz, who adopted the pseudonym Tito, soon managed to carve out a small "liberated zone" in western Serbia, and to attract a following of partisans that included some non-Communists. At first, the two rival movements observed a kind of cautious neutrality toward each other; Tito and Mihajlović even met several times to discuss common action. But before the end of 1941, the talks degenerated into violence. Mihajlović was a monarchist committed to the idea of Serb domination in Yugoslavia; Tito was a Croat and a Marxist who advocated a federal state and drastic social-economic change. Furthermore, the Chetniks were inclined to build their strength toward concentrated use when the time of liberation approached, while the partisans wanted immediate action to harass the German and Italian occupation forces.

Until late 1943, Mihajlović seemed to enjoy a clear edge over Tito. The Yugoslav government-in-exile made him Minister of National Defense and commander-in-chief of all resistance forces (including Tito's partisans); he was widely acclaimed as the most heroic guerrilla leader in conquered Europe. The British government assigned liaison officers to his headquarters, and promised to send arms when it could spare them; the Soviet government advised Tito to accept Mihajlović as national leader. Tito meanwhile was clinging stubbornly to his independence of action, and by his guerrilla tactics was needling the Germans and Italians into sizable counter-insurgent campaigns. In 1942, and again in 1943, his army was driven far back into the mountains of Montenegro; Tito lost half his force of 20,000 men, and barely avoided the encirclement of the remainder.

At that low point in partisan fortunes came a miraculous windfall; the capitulation of Italy to the Allied forces left a vacuum in Italian-occupied Yugoslavia, and Tito moved immediately to fill it. Most of Croatia and the Dalmatian coast fell to his men, along with large supplies of Italian arms; partisan strength rapidly grew until it reached 250,000 men. Parallel with these gains went a shift in the attitude of the Allied powers toward the Yugoslav resistance. British liaison agents, who in 1943 were sent to Tito's headquarters as well as to Mihajlović's, reported that the partisans were far more effective than the Chetniks in fighting the Germans, and that some Chetnik officers had actually been in clandestine touch with the Germans and Italians to carry out joint operations against Tito. Late in 1943, the British cut off their support to Mihajlović and, along with the Americans, began to supply Tito's forces instead. Soviet aid to Tito, curiously enough, did not begin until several months later; it was both grudging in nature and meager in quantity.[3] During the early months of 1944, if we are to believe Yugoslav historians, the partisans were strong enough to tie down some fifteen German divisions—a feat unparalleled by any other resistance movement in Europe. At any rate, the liberation of

[3] Ironically, Britain's decision to aid Tito seems to have reinforced Stalin's suspicions of Tito. Cf. F. W. Deakin in *European Resistance Movements* [Milan], p. 113.

Yugoslav territory in the summer and autumn of 1944 was accomplished not by an invading Allied army, but for the most part by the Yugoslavs themselves.

The course of the Greek resistance bore some resemblance to that of Yugoslavia, though its outcome was strikingly different. Six months after the country was overrun in April 1941, two rival underground movements emerged in the rugged mountain country of the north: The National Liberation Front (E.A.M.), dominated by the Communists, and the National Greek Democratic Union (E.D.E.S.), headed by a right-wing colonel named Napoleon Zervas. A scattering of lesser groups also sprang up in Athens and elsewhere, but failed to attain much significance. As in Yugoslavia, British liaison missions were sent in early to help conduct sabotage and to provide intelligence to London. Here too they sought to encourage coordinated action between the rival groups, but found no way to bridge their ideological differences. Armed clashes, in which the larger E.A.M. forces were usually the aggressors, occurred sporadically through 1943 and 1944. This internal civil war diverted the underground from its fight against the Germans, and led many Greeks to shun the resistance.

The Communists might have been strong enough to destroy their rivals had it not been for the vigorous support accorded to Zervas by the British. Churchill's government had been prepared to risk the communizing of Yugoslavia; it was unwilling to see Greece subjected to the same fate. Thanks to British pressure and British aid, the uneasy balance survived the liberation of Greece in August-September 1944, and was continued in the first post-liberation government. But when the new government attempted to disarm the resistance groups (as de Gaulle was successfully doing in France), the Communists balked and shortly attempted to seize power in Athens. Civil war was the outcome—a civil war whose result was decided by British armed intervention on the side of the non-Communist forces. The remnants of the Communist bands were driven back into the northern mountains, where they vainly waited for Soviet aid to help them renew the fight. Thus in Greece, the net effect of the resistance experience had been to increase the nation's disunity rather than to create a patriotic consensus.

The Italian resistance pattern had its own peculiar complications, deriving from the fact that until September 1943 Italy was not a conquered nation but a member of the conquering Axis. Resistance prior to that date, therefore, had to be motivated by ideological factors—by anti-Fascism or anti-capitalism—rather than by outraged patriotism. Such a resistance movement had indeed existed in Italy ever since Mussolini turned totalitarian in 1925, and it continued during the early war years; but its strength was limited both by the prewar exile of most leading oppositionists and by the unwillingness of many anti-Fascist Italians to turn against their government in time of war. The building of an underground was hampered too by the paradoxical position of the Communists during the years of Stalin's pact with Hitler.

Freed from that contradiction after June 1941, the Italian Communists could contribute their experience and energy to creating an active underground. They sponsored a series of strikes in the Turin region during the autumn and winter of 1942–1943—the first such evidence of mass opposition in an Axis country. Meanwhile there were signs of renewed activity among non-Communists as well. A group of left-leaning democratic intellectuals formed a clandestine Action party in January 1943, and two months later the Christian Democratic party was resuscitated after an interlude of almost twenty years. The Communists, in line with their broad national-front tactics of the period, took the initiative in trying to create a united underground combining these and other groups; but the attempt broke down over such practical issues as the future of the monarchy. Underground newspapers began to appear in large numbers from 1942 onward, and found willing readers in a population that resented the increasing domination of the Germans.

The overthrow of Mussolini in July 1943 was not, however, the work of the resistance; it was a palace revolution engineered by dissident Fascists and lieutenants of the king. But once the new Badoglio government had signed an armistice with the Allies, the way was open for vigorous resistance action. Most of Italy (from Naples to the Alps) was immediately taken over by a German occupation force; and a puppet neo-Fascist republic headed by Mussolini was shortly established in the north. Ideology and patriotism now merged; the anti-Fascists could engage in guerrilla warfare to liberate their country, and any Italian could in good conscience join the fight. In central and northern Italy, partisan bands took to the hills and began to harass the Germans, anticipating a rapid Allied advance from the south to liberate the whole peninsula.

But the Allied advance bogged down; and political conflict continued to plague the resistance. In German-occupied Rome, a clandestine Committee of National Liberation was organized, bringing together the major anti-Fascist groups under the presidency of an aging pre-Mussolini politician named Ivanoe Bonomi. But in Milan, a regional Committee of National Liberation of Upper Italy emerged as a virtually autonomous rival; it was much more heavily weighted to the left, with the Communists in the dominant role. Bonomi's committee somewhat reluctantly designated the Milan committee as its agent in the north; it had little choice in the matter. Meanwhile the Rome committee was sharply divided over its relationship to the king and the Badoglio government, now established in the Allied-occupied south. The dispute was finally resolved in April 1944 when the Communists executed a surprising *volte face*. Party leader Palmiro Togliatti, returning from wartime exile in Moscow, proclaimed his willingness to cooperate with Badoglio and to postpone the question of the monarchy's future until after the war. The various resistance groups now entered the Badoglio cabinet, and a few weeks later forced his withdrawal in favor of Bonomi.

Meanwhile, the intensity of resistance activity in the north was being steadily stepped up. The Milan committee organized a general strike in March 1944 that was probably the largest labor stoppage anywhere in occupied Europe during the war. By summer, the partisan forces in the north numbered more than eighty thousand, and were operating on a scale resembling that of Tito's Yugoslav guerrillas. But autumn came without the arrival of the liberating Allied forces, which had failed to breach the Germans' "Gothic line." On orders from the Allied commander in Italy, the partisans had to suspend operations until the final offensive in the spring. Although they suffered severe losses to German and neo-Fascist raiding parties during the winter, the underground forces participated effectively in the last liberation campaign in 1945, and topped off their performance by capturing Mussolini and his party as they sought to escape. The victorious resistance thus seemed to have restored a degree of unity such as Italians had not known for many years. Its leaders controlled the government, and its conceptions seemed destined to reshape the nation. The situation strongly resembled that in France—except that Italy possessed no equivalent of de Gaulle.

III. THE UNDERGROUND IN EASTERN EUROPE

In the Slavic nations of Eastern Europe, where German rule was harshest and where the Germans' colonialist aims were clearest, one might suppose that active resistance would have been early and almost unanimous. Yet here, too, there were sharp variations from nation to nation, and severe tensions between democratic and Communist resisters. As in Yugoslavia and Greece, the task of creating a unified underground even for the duration of the war was never accomplished in Poland, and only factitiously in Czechoslovakia. In the German-occupied parts of the USSR, the problem was of course quite different.

In the old Czech lands, now the protectorate of Bohemia-Moravia, an embryonic resistance movement existed even before the outbreak of war, and its leaders were in touch with ex-President Beneš in London. The Czech national holiday (October 28, 1939) brought the first public demonstration of anti-German sentiment in occupied Europe; the day ended with clashes between police and demonstrators in Prague, and led to the closing of all Czech universities for the duration of the war. Early in 1940 the underground took organized shape with the creation of a Central Committee of Internal Resistance (UVOD). It provided the Czech government-in-exile with a steady flow of military information, some of it obtained from German army officers hostile to Hitler. After June 1941 the Czech Communists approached UVOD with a proposal for a united front, and shortly announced that such unity had been accomplished. But if an agreement really was reached (a point that remains controversial to this day), cooperation between the two wings of the Czech underground was never wholehearted.

In May 1942, parachuted Czech agents from London assassinated the top SS official in Prague, Reinhold Heydrich. The harsh repression that followed cost UVOD much of its effectiveness. Those members who survived operated henceforth in small clandestine groups without much national direction, and confined themselves mainly to factory slowdowns and individual sabotage. Guerrilla activities were almost impossible, given Bohemia's location and lack of safe mountain hideouts.

The eastern half of former Czechoslovakia had meanwhile become Hitler's model satellite; much of the population actively or passively supported the Tiso regime, which enjoyed relatively favored treatment from the Germans. Yet as the war progressed, Slovakia gradually outpaced the Czech lands as a center of partisan activity. By 1943 both local Communists and Slovak democrats had organized resistance groups, and in the autumn the two factions fused to form the Slovak

National Council, equally weighted between Communists and non-Communists. Outside influence was also brought to bear; Moscow had begun to take an interest in Slovakia's future. Many Slovak troops had been conscripted by the Germans to serve on the Russian front; some of them deserted or were captured, and were trained as agents to be parachuted into their homeland. The first of these agents arrived in 1943, but tensions developed between them and the purely indigenous Communist resisters. Moscow evidently viewed the latter with the same suspicion it was showing toward Tito. In the summer of 1944 more organizers were sent in, Russians as well as Slovaks; they succeeded in rallying some eight thousand partisans in the hill country. In August the Slovak National Council decided to risk a full-scale insurrection without waiting for the arrival of the approaching Soviet armies. The revolt failed; German troops overran the country, and burned sixty villages in retaliation. Appeals to Moscow for aid brought no response. The Slovak Communist partisans, who had utilized the insurrection to conduct their own separate campaign against the Germans, were driven farther back into the hills and suffered serious losses. Those who survived joined the advancing Soviet forces early in 1945 to carry out a complete takeover of the country. In a sense, Slovakia's resistance movement—the element that triumphed, at any rate—was thus imported from the USSR.

In Poland, resistance began early, and reached a level of effectiveness matched by few other countries in occupied Europe. Hitler's policy, to be sure, left the Poles virtually no choice: to resist meant to risk the most savage reprisals, but to submit meant ruthless exploitation and national degradation. To a people as proud and stiff-necked as the Poles, their duty was clear: they gradually organized an elaborate network of institutions that some Poles described as a "secret state."

Shortly after the defeat of 1939, a Polish government-in-exile was established in Paris under the leadership of General Sikorski, and an army-in-exile of eighty thousand men was organized to fight alongside the French. After their second defeat by the Germans in the Battle of France, many of the Polish troops managed to escape to London, while others remained in France and became active in the underground there. The government moved from Paris to London, whence it continued to send directives to the emerging underground in Poland. It was the General Government that became the locus of the "secret state"; the provinces annexed to Germany or to the USSR were too tightly controlled to permit much resistance activity. In the General Government, on the other hand, the lower administrative echelons continued to be staffed by Poles, and these officials became integral parts of the underground. Late in 1940 a variety of small spontaneously-organized groups fused into a united movement which shortly came to be called the Home Army; it operated under orders from the London government-in-exile, and eventually achieved some spectacular successes in railway sabotage and intelligence-gathering. At its peak in 1943–1944, the Home Army came to number about 300,000 men. The Polish underground press also proliferated; more than a thousand clandestine periodicals were circulated, three hundred of them on a regular schedule throughout the entire German occupation. The underground even managed to establish and operate *sub rosa* universities to replace those closed down by the Germans; 2500 students were enrolled, degrees were granted, a number of scholarly works published and clandestinely distributed.

The German attack on the USSR affected resistance movements everywhere, but nowhere so profoundly as in Poland. There, the resistance had been almost as much anti-Soviet as anti-German, for one-third of Poland had been subjected to merciless Soviet rule. An underground had attempted to operate in the Soviet-annexed provinces, but its effectiveness was hampered by the Soviet policy of deporting the Polish elite to Siberian labor camps. Now all was changed; the German attack threw Poles and Russians together in an unaccustomed embrace. In July 1941, diplomatic relations between the USSR and the Polish government-in-exile were restored; the Poles who had been prisoners of war in Russia since 1939 were released to fight alongside the Russians on the eastern front. (Most of these Polish troops, as it turned out, preferred to fight elsewhere; they were eventually evacuated via Iran to the west, and served in the Italian campaign.)

The Polish Communists now joined the active resistance—though as rivals of the Home Army rather than recruits to it. In December 1941 a Union of Polish Patriots, made up of émigré Communists, was established in Moscow under Soviet patronage. It shortly sent agents into Poland to re-establish the almost extinct Communist movement under the new label Polish Workers' party, and to organize its own guerrilla force. These so-called Partisans were far less numerous than the Home Army, but they felt strong enough by 1943 to propose fusion with the latter. The Home Army rejected the offer, fearing a Communist attempt to bore from within. Thereafter, the two forces operated as increasingly hostile rivals.

The tension grew worse after April 1943, when Moscow broke off diplomatic relations with the London Poles. The breach grew out of the Katyn Forest affair; the Poles charged the Soviet regime with the massacre of some twelve thousand Polish army officers who had been captured by the Russians in 1939 and whose bodies were discovered by the Germans in 1943 in a mass grave near their former prison camp. The Kremlin denied the charge, and retaliated by converting the Union of Polish Patriots into a Polish Liberation Committee, which was obviously designed to compete with the London government for postwar control of the country.

As the advancing Soviet armies moved across the old Polish border in 1944, the Home Army was confronted with a difficult dilemma. The Soviet radio issued daily appeals to speed the liberation of Poland by harassing the German defenders. But increased guerrilla action would hasten the arrival of the Soviet armies, which might then brush aside the claims of the London government and put the Polish Liberation Committee in control. Early in August, as the Soviet forces neared Warsaw, the London government-in-exile made its decision: it ordered a full-scale Home Army insurrection in Warsaw to liberate the capital. The political motivation of this decision was clear; the prestige of liberating Warsaw might shape the future. Equally clear was the political motivation of the Soviet government's response. The Home Army, initially successful, soon found itself confronted by four German tank divisions sent in to crush the uprising. The insurgent commander, General Tadeusz Bor-Komorowski, called desperately for Soviet and Allied aid; but the Soviet forces, ten miles away across the river, refused to budge. British and American planes from Italian bases dropped supplies to the beleaguered rebels, but could bring little effective aid unless permitted to land and refuel at Soviet air fields. Such permission was denied by the Soviet government until too late to be of much use. In mid-September, after six weeks of hand-to-hand street fighting, the Soviet armies at last began to move, and occupied a suburb of Warsaw; but there they stopped, despite Bor's appeals. On the sixty-third day after the revolt began, Bor surrendered with the remnant of his forces; he had lost almost half of his forty thousand men. What was left of Warsaw was systematically destroyed by the Germans. The Home Army, badly decimated by this episode, was dissolved early in 1945 by the advancing Russians, and some of its leaders taken to Moscow under arrest. It was a tragic ending for one of the most heroic chapters in the history of the European resistance.

In the occupied portions of the USSR, the role of the underground took on a starker simplicity: its function was to participate in a fight that was not yet lost. Elsewhere in occupied Europe, governments had been driven into exile, and armies had been broken up and disarmed. In the USSR, the government remained established in its capital, and the army continued to defend an unbroken front. After the first few months, therefore, the partisan movement functioned as a loosely integrated part of the nation's total military effort, under orders from the high command. For the most part, too, the Soviet partisan movement was spared the internal political conflict between Communists and non-Communists that split the underground almost everywhere. The principal exception was in the northern and western Ukraine, where scattered bands of anti-Soviet Ukrainian nationalists clashed sporadically with the Soviet partisans. Sometimes the Germans supported these nationalist bands; more often, they found it hard to distinguish one variety of guerrilla fighter from another.

Irregular warfare had been an integral part of the Soviet theory of war since Lenin's day, and the Soviet authorities naturally sought to encourage it at once. Stalin, in his first wartime order of the day addressed to the nation on July 3, 1941, called on all Soviet citizens to engage in partisan action and sabotage wherever possible. In fact, however, Stalin's appeal had little to do with the first phase of guerrilla activity. What happened, rather, was the by-product of the Germans' rapid advance that cut off huge masses of Soviet troops. Hundreds of thousands were herded into German prisoner-of-war compounds; other thousands escaped the net and took to the woods. By no means all of these lost soldiers intended to carry on the fight guerrilla-fashion; most of them simply wanted to avoid capture by hiding out in the forests or in some village. A few, however, had a more considerable stake in the Soviet regime; as army officers or party officials, they belonged to the sub-elite. These were the men who formed the first small bands of partisans in 1941, mainly in the forested country of Byelorussia, the Bryansk region, and the northern Ukraine, which provided adequate cover. By the end of the year about thirty thousand were active, though their lack of arms and experience made them relatively ineffective.

In Moscow, measures to stimulate partisan activity had been

planned even before the war began. In the autumn of 1941 the government set up the first special training camps for guerrilla fighters, and began to send in these specialists by parachute, along with political agents and, somewhat later, trained propagandists. By the summer of 1942 the number of partisans had risen to about 150,000; a year later, it attained 200,000, which was probably the peak figure. The partisans were grouped in bands ranging from three hundred to two thousand in size, and were housed in well-camouflaged dugouts in the woods. Most of them continued to operate in the swamps and forests behind the central German front; the steppe country of the Ukraine was too open to provide cover, and was invaded by roving partisan units only toward the end of the war. Although many partisan recruits were undoubtedly motivated by old-fashioned patriotism, the partisan movement was only in part the product of a spontaneous patriotic rising against the invader. Most of its chiefs were officially assigned to this duty; probably half of the members of the partisan bands were villagers forcibly and unwillingly rounded up for service. The rest were escaped prisoners of war, civilian refugees from the German labor-draft, or individual volunteers.

For the Soviet government, the partisan movement had a double utility. Not only did it hamper German units, and create a sense of insecurity behind the German lines; it could also serve to remind the peasant population in occupied territory that the Soviet regime still existed, and might return some day. This assertion of the Soviet presence was essential in areas where much of the rural population had been deeply alienated by the great collectivization drive of the early thirties, and in those frontier areas farther to the west which had been under Soviet rule only from 1939 to 1941. The partisan units, by using propaganda and by threatening reprisals against village collaborators, could inspire both fear and respect among those citizens whose loyalty to the regime was lukewarm. In the end, the political value of partisan activity seems to have exceeded its military value, though both were considerable. The partisans tied down Axis forces about equivalent to their own strength, and accounted for some thirty-five thousand casualties in enemy ranks; their military contribution was real, but relatively incidental to the accomplishments of the regular Soviet armies. Politically, however, they carried the whole burden of maintaining the Soviet presence over a vast area. In the closing months of the war, too, some partisan units were dispatched across the western frontier into Poland, Rumania, and Slovakia, and helped bolster the weaker Communist partisan forces in those countries.

For the most part, though, the partisans were simply swallowed up during the last year of the war. As the Soviet armies rolled westward across partisan-held areas, the roving bands were absorbed into the larger mass. Most partisans found themselves suddenly converted into uniformed soldiers, subject to the more rigid discipline of the regular armed forces. If their guerrilla experience had given them any taste for independence of thought and action, such tendencies were soon repressed. By May 1945, the partisan forces survived only as partly mythologized history—a history highly useful to the Soviet regime both for its dramatic appeal and for its contribution to the official doctrine that the Soviet masses, rising spontaneously under the guidance of the Communist party, had beaten off the Fascist invader. So an eminent Soviet historian could boast almost twenty years later that the European resistance generally was ". . . a striking expression of the activity of the popular masses, of their direct participation in the historical process . . . ," and could add that of all resistance, "partisan warfare in occupied Soviet territory was the highest and most expressive form. . . ."[4]

IV. THE GERMAN RESISTANCE MOVEMENT

In the occupied countries, the underground was bound together by opposition to an alien invader, and its members could root their activities in the fertile soil of patriotism. A country such as France was, to be sure, a partial exception, since the technically legitimate Pétain government sought to identify patriotism with collaboration in the new Europe. But even in France, resisters could ignore Pétain with a clear conscience, and could regard their action as the finest manifestation of traditional patriotism.

The dilemma of the German resistance was far more serious. In an age of nation-states, any citizen who opposes his government in wartime is likely to feel the pangs of conscience and the threat of repudiation by his countrymen. No matter how tyrannical the regime, no matter how dubious its reasons for embarking on war, the resister confronts the charge of treason in the commonly accepted sense of that term. He may, of course, take a position above national loyalty by asserting his devotion to certain universal ethical principles. He may

[4] Boltine, in *European Resistance Movements* [Milan], pp. 5, 49.

convince himself that his nation's true values have been corrupted by the men in power, and that his goal is to cleanse and restore rather then to sabotage and destroy. Only the rare individual, however, is likely to face the perils and the ambiguities of such a course in wartime.

If the German anti-Nazi resistance movement was small, divided, and generally ineffective during the war years, this moral dilemma undoubtedly goes far to explain the fact. But an equally important factor was the preventive purge of active or potential anti-Nazis that went on before 1939. More than 200,000 Germans were imprisoned or interned during the prewar years, and many others went into voluntary exile. The flow into the concentration camps continued after 1939, though at a slower rate. This preventive action destroyed much of the potential resistance leadership. Furthermore, the Nazi regime's police-state techniques made underground plotting exceptionally hazardous, for no one could be sure whom to trust. An additional handicap was Allied suspicion. Efforts by resistance leaders to make contact with Allied officials were usually viewed skeptically by the latter; the German underground failed to get the kind of aid and encouragement that buoyed up the spirits of resisters elsewhere.[5] All in all, it is perhaps astonishing that active resistance ever developed in wartime Germany.

There was, to be sure, no guerrilla activity, and very little distribution of underground propaganda on a mass scale. The German resistance took the form of small conspiratorial groups that hoped to rid the country of Hitler by a sudden coup, or groups of intellectuals that looked ahead to a moral and political reform in the post-Hitler era. The idea of a military coup had been discussed even before the war broke out; during the Munich crisis in 1938, a few anti-Nazis grouped around General Ludwig Beck had tried to win British support for such a scheme. But Prime Minister Chamberlain had been dubious about the genuineness of the plot, and Beck had failed to persuade the key German generals to cooperate. During the "twilight war" period in 1939–1940, Beck and his associates tried again, this time attempting to use the good offices of Pope Pius XII. The conspirators hoped that the Vatican might persuade the British and French to keep their ar-

---

[5] Even after the attempt on Hitler's life on July 20, 1944, and the vicious purge that followed, Winston Churchill had only this to say: "The highest personalities in the German Reich are murdering one another, or trying to. . . ." Great Britain, *Parliamentary Debates* (Commons), CDII (Aug. 2, 1944), 1487.

mies inactive during the projected military coup. Although the Pope apparently passed on the message with his blessing, the scheme once again came to nothing; Beck was unable to line up enough military support. Hitler's smashing triumph in the west in 1940 put an end to talk of a coup for the next two years.

Small groups of anti-Nazis nevertheless continued to meet and to plan for the future. Count Helmut von Moltke brought together a few friends—mainly aristocratic landowners at first—at his estate in Silesia to discuss their common discontents. These sessions, which began in the summer of 1940, continued at intervals, and new participants of widely varied sorts were drawn in: Socialists, a trade-union leader, a Jesuit priest, high-ranking Protestant laymen. This so-called Kreisau circle foreswore the use of violence to rid the country of the Nazis, but concentrated on "filling the moral and spiritual vacuum" that would follow Germany's eventual defeat. At the University of Munich, a tiny group of intensely idealistic students recruited by Hans and Sophie Scholl adopted the label "White Rose," and began in 1942 to distribute anti-Nazi leaflets. In Berlin, a Communist espionage apparatus popularly called the Rote Kapelle had been operating since 1935, with agents inside many government offices and large munitions plants. Headed by a left-wing activist of good family, Harro Schulze-Boysen, it sent valuable military intelligence to Moscow, published (in six languages) a clandestine periodical addressed to foreign workers in Germany, and eventually began to plan the large-scale sabotage of arms factories. All of these groups, however, ran afoul of the Gestapo. The Rote Kapelle was broken up in 1942, and more than a hundred participants executed. The White Rose group followed in 1943; and Count von Moltke, organizer of the Kreisau circle, was arrested early in 1944.

Meanwhile, Hitler's failure to win a quick victory in Russia had renewed the hopes of the military conspirators. The Beck group attracted some valuable new converts, though few of them at the top echelons of the army. General Henning von Tresckow, a long-time anti-Nazi who became a staff officer on the eastern front, had begun in 1941 to plan an attempt on Hitler's life, but no good occasion arose. Colonel Claus von Stauffenberg, a wounded war hero, joined the plotters in 1942. Carl Goerdeler, former mayor of Leipzig, had been associated with the Beck group from the start, and was expected to become chancellor in the new post-Nazi regime. General Hans Oster, number-two man in the Abwehr (army intelligence branch), provided the conspirators with valuable cover. There were links between this group and the Kreisau circle, even though the latter refused to associate itself formally with plans for violence.

The Stalingrad disaster early in 1943 gave the resistance leaders a new sense of urgency. Several attempts to assassinate Hitler during 1943 went awry for one or another reason. Efforts to get in touch with the British in hope of arranging a rapid peace with the Western powers were cold-shouldered in London. At last, on July 20, 1944, the conspirators made their most dramatic gesture. A bomb deposited by Colonel von Stauffenberg at Hitler's staff conference on the eastern front exploded as planned; but it inflicted only slight injuries on the Fuehrer. When the plotters attempted to seize control of Berlin, they were promptly arrested. The roundup that followed decimated the resistance movement and left it void of leadership during the last months of the war. Seven thousand were arrested after the July 20 incident, and almost five thousand executed; the hangings and shootings continued until the final weeks before the German collapse.

One curious appendage to the German resistance movement operated not on German but on Soviet soil. Soon after the Battle of Stalingrad, Soviet authorities organized a National Committee for Free Germany, made up of émigré Communists who had long lived in Russia and of soldiers recruited from prisoner-of-war camps. Control was in the hands of the émigrés: Wilhelm Pieck, Walther Ulbricht, Erich Weinert. An auxiliary organization was soon added: the League of German Officers, headed by the captured General von Seydlitz, and eventually including Marshal von Paulus, ex-commander at Stalingrad. Both groups aimed their propaganda appeals at the retreating German armies and at the German home front; the troops were urged to desert, the army command to overthrow Hitler in order to save Germany from total disaster. The League of German Officers obviously hoped that an army coup d'état might save Germany from a profound social upheaval—a goal that must have been quite unattractive to their Soviet sponsors. In any case, their propaganda produced no discernible effect on German army or home-front morale. During the last months of the war, the Soviet authorities switched to a policy of screening out likely candidates for intensive indoctrination, with a view to using them in occupied Germany after the war. But the Soviets carefully refrained from converting the Committee for Free Germany into a government-in-exile, in contrast to their procedure in the case of the Poles.

It is doubtless true that the German resistance had virtually no effect on the course or outcome of the war. Someone has remarked, rather cynically, that its sole practical consequence was to permit Hitler to complete the destruction of the old Prussian military caste. A more controversial issue is the moral and spiritual impact of the resistance on postwar Germany. Some of the leading resistance figures saw this as their central purpose: to do penance for the nation's misdeeds, and to reassert a set of humanist values by which the new generation might steer. There can be no doubt that many anti-Nazi martyrs were admirable figures whose courage and principles would be ornaments to any nation. Men like Moltke, Tresckow, Leber, Delp, Scholl, Stauffenberg, and Bonhoeffer embodied the finest heritage of Western culture, and honestly sought to arrive at a doctrine and to shape a system that would blend the best qualities of liberal-conservatism, Christianity, and socialism. Yet some of their critics have charged them with grave shortcomings. The German resistance, these critics allege, was predominantly aristocratic and conservative in composition and outlook; its goal was the restoration of something like pre-1914 Germany. It suffered, too, from nationalist pride and lack of realism: witness Goerdeler's proposal that the new Germany be allowed to restore its 1914 eastern boundary at Poland's expense, and to keep both Austria and the Sudeten Czech territories absorbed in 1938. Within the resistance too (say the critics) there was a faction of "easterners" whose goal was to seek an accommodation with the Soviet Union, and to build the new Germany on a foundation of national Bolshevism.

Some of this criticism appears exaggerated or distorted. There were, for example, few "easterners"; and the resistance was more than a mere collection of conservatives disillusioned at Hitler's coarseness. Yet the German resistance did differ markedly in its composition and general outlook from the resistance norm in occupied Europe. By necessity it was much smaller; perhaps by necessity also it was more elitist in spirit, more suspicious of the masses, more doubtful about the practicability of political democracy. Its members were inclined to see Nazism not as an antiparliamentary political system but as a moral and political illness affecting the whole Western world. In Germany an atomized, secularized society had succumbed to demagogic dictatorship, as might happen to mass societies anywhere; the German masses had been corrupted, and could be saved only by an elite which would restore morality. Their dominant mood strongly resembled that of the German conservatives during the 1920's, when the source of the evil had been not Nazism but liberal democracy. Some of them then had hoped to turn the rootless mass into an organic *Volk*; some had even, for a time, seen this as Hitler's mission. Disillusioned by that experiment, they were not prepared to look to the masses as active allies in restoring sanity and balance to the nation. More then anywhere else in Europe, the German resistance looked to an elitist, decentralized regime with deep Christian roots. Only thus, they believed, could a mass society be prevented from slipping once again into some kind of totalitarian abyss.

Chapter Eight

THE RESURGENCE OF ALLIED POWER

FOR a full twelve months after the fall of France, the United Kingdom stood alone in Europe against Nazi power, supported only by the members of the British Commonwealth and Empire, and by the moral backing of the governments-in-exile. For another six months thereafter, Britain and the Soviet Union shared the impact of Hitler's onslaught. Only then, at the end of 1941, were the armies and the resources of the most powerful extra-European nation thrown into the struggle. The entry of the United States into the war, long anticipated by the British government and people, was bound to alter the scope and probable outcome of the war. Europe's destiny, for so many centuries shaped in peace and war by the Europeans themselves, became in considerable degree dependent on decisions made across the Atlantic.

To be sure, American aid to Britain had long preceded the Pearl Harbor attack that ended United States neutrality. President Roosevelt's inclination to oppose Axis aggression, by force if necessary, had been made clear well before the war broke out, and a substantial minority of American opinion supported him in this respect. But an even more vocal "isolationist" element vigorously opposed any entangling commitments, and at least until France fell, most Americans clung to a neutral stance. During the first year of the war, congressional legislation forebade American ships to enter European waters, and required warring nations to pay cash for any purchases in the United States. This "cash-and-carry" provision lasted until March 1941, but both American opinion and governmental policy had begun to evolve well before that date. France's defeat stiffened the determination of the hard-line isolationists, but swung a great many neutralists into the interventionist camp. Roosevelt was able, in the summer of 1940, to transfer fifty overage destroyers to Britain in exchange for long-term leases on naval bases in Newfoundland, Bermuda, and the Caribbean, and sold Britain large quantities of surplus rifles, light artillery weapons, and ammunition to replace the equipment lost at Dunkirk. By the end of 1940, traditional neutrality was being infringed in a number of ways: e.g., through the training of British pilots at American airfields, and repairs to British warships in American ports.

Meanwhile, British orders for new ships, aircraft, and military equipment were seriously straining British financial resources. By the end of 1940 the bill for these orders already exceeded the total debt incurred by Britain in the United States during the First World War. It was clear that London could not continue to finance purchases at such a rate, even if the British were to liquidate all their overseas assets and empty their vaults of gold.[1] Some of these overseas assets *were* sold; but rather than drive the British over the edge of bankruptcy, Roosevelt sponsored a solution in the form of Lend-Lease. This measure, which became law in March 1941, ended the period of cash-and-carry and ensured that the United States would really become, as Roosevelt phrased it, the arsenal of democracy. Nevertheless, British direct purchases continued to outweigh Lend-Lease deliveries during the rest of 1941, mainly because Britain urgently needed certain items which the cumbersome machinery of Lend-Lease would have delayed. But from 1942 onward, Lend-Lease was to become the channel through which a huge share of American war production flowed—to Britain, to the Commonwealth countries, and to the Soviet Union.

Despite British purchases and Lend-Lease, the buildup of American war industry before Pearl Harbor (December 1941) was relatively slow. The conversion of peacetime plants did not suffice; British orders required the expansion of existing industrial facilities or the building of entirely new plants. British authorities faced a difficult problem of priorities in placing orders: should they concentrate on items that could be produced quickly, or should they stimulate the expansion of those American enterprises that would gradually speed the mobilization of America's own power, and thus prepare the United States for more rapid and effective participation in the war? Since American intervention was still uncertain, the second policy represented something of a gamble. The British in the end adopted a kind of compromise

[1] British Ambassador Lord Lothian, returning from a brief stay in England late in 1940, was reported to have told a group of American journalists: "Well, boys, Britain's broke. It's your money we want." Lord Casey, *Personal Experience, 1939–1946* (New York, 1963), p. 43.

plan, designed to combine both purposes. In the long run, the British stimulus to American industrial expansion was to have a significant effect on the speed of the Allied buildup. Yet the early stages of growth were not very impressive; until early 1942, Britain continued to outpace the United States in munitions output.

The Soviet Union's enforced entry into the war in June 1941 gave the British new hope for the long-run future, and sharply eased Britain's strategic problems. At the same time, however, it added grave new problems of transport and supply. Much of the American-built equipment destined for the British armed forces, together with much of Britain's own production, had to be diverted at once to the USSR. Aircraft, tanks, machine tools, and certain key raw materials formed the bulk of the shipments at first; and during the first year of the Russian war it was Britain rather than the United States that was the number-one supplier. Here again, Lend-Lease was of crucial importance in averting payments problems; and by mid-1942 the Americans bypassed the British in shipments to the USSR.

Even before Pearl Harbor, the British and Americans had begun to work out joint machinery for more effective planning of war production. Somewhat extralegally, officials of the two countries moved toward a pooling of their resources and toward coordination of raw materials purchasing and allocation. With equal secrecy, staff officers had been meeting since early in 1941 to engage in anticipatory strategic planning. No American commitments of entry into the war were given; but it was agreed that if the United States should be compelled to enter, the Anglo-American forces would make Europe rather than the Pacific the initial major theater of war. A kind of common-law alliance was thus in process of creation.

Pearl Harbor opened the way for the rapid development of this rudimentary machinery of cooperation. Only two weeks later, Churchill flew to Washington to join Roosevelt in setting up a joint strategy-making body—the Combined Chiefs of Staff—and three joint allocation boards for munitions, shipping, and raw materials. During 1942, similar boards were added for food and for production and resources. No Supreme War Council was established; the unhappy experiences of the First World War and of the twilight war period were fresh in mind. Both Churchill and Roosevelt, in any case, preferred a more flexible and informal arrangement for top-level decision-making.

During the weeks just before Pearl Harbor, the British purchasing mission in Washington had been campaigning for what it called a victory program, designed to stretch American industry in unprecedented fashion. The proposal rested on a starkly factual balance sheet of output, resources, and needs of the British Commonwealth and the United States. The Pearl Harbor attack shocked the American government into more active interest in these British statistics; early in January 1942, President Roosevelt announced a set of production targets that closely resembled the needs set forth in the victory program. The goal for aircraft was set at 60,000 in 1942, and twice that in 1943. Tanks would rise from 45,000 in 1942 to 75,000 in 1943; new merchant shipping (which had totaled only 1 million tons in 1941) would leap to 8 million and then to 10 million tons. In time, the program was to be fulfilled, and more; over the next four years, American industrial production would virtually double, and the great bulk of the output would be funneled to military use. In addition, whole new industries would be created from scratch: synthetic rubber, and the production of fissionable material for atomic explosives. Meanwhile a vast expansion of the American armed forces was under way; eventually it was to put more than fifteen million men and women into uniform. Thanks to this huge accession of manpower and supplies, the prospects of the anti-Axis alliance suddenly grew far brighter.

II. DEFENSIVE WARFARE ON THE SEA: THE SUBMARINE MENACE

If massive production was one essential key to victory, safe delivery of the goods produced was equally essential. Never before in the history of warfare had logistics posed so many or such complex problems. The sheer quantity of munitions, foodstuffs, and troops to be transported was overwhelming; the distances involved were forbidding. New routes had to be devised by sea, air, and land, since Axis power denied many of the standard routes to the Allies. The jungles and deserts of Africa suddenly became a gateway to the Mediterranean theater of war; Murmansk and Archangel emerged once again as frequent entries in the logs of merchant ships; a railway line across the Iranian plateau was taken over and modernized to provide southern access to the Soviet Union. But while all these enterprises dramatically demonstrated the gradual buildup of Western power, the decisive factor was the threat posed by Germany's submarine fleet. It alone was potentially able to disrupt deliveries and large-scale troop movements, perhaps to the point of counterbalancing the Allied advantage in resources.

Hitler's failure to create a powerful U-boat force during the prewar years has sometimes been offered as evidence that he anticipated no general war at all—or at least no war against the British. Others have argued that it suggests his lack of concern and of understanding with respect to sea warfare. Both cases have some merit. Until the spring of 1939, Hitler probably did hope to avoid a war with Britain, or at least to postpone it for another five years. In January 1939 he approved Admiral Raeder's Z-plan for the gradual creation of a large balanced fleet by 1944–1945: a fleet large enough to challenge Britain's ocean predominance. The unexpected outbreak of war forced the abandonment of the Z-plan, and a gradual shift of emphasis to the building of U-boats alone.

When the war began, the Germans possessed only 56 submarines—almost exactly the number in the British fleet (and likewise in the French fleet).[2] Raeder pressed hard for a rapid buildup, but was frustrated by Hitler's evasive response. Not until July 1940, when it became plain that Britain intended to go on fighting, did the Fuehrer finally authorize a building program of some twenty-five U-boats a month. But even before the results of this decision began to show up in 1941, the small German force was beginning to pose a grave threat to Britain's survival. The capture of Norway and of France provided valuable new bases from which the U-boats could operate into the Atlantic. In addition, Italy's entry into the war reinforced Axis strength with another 115 submarines, which could presumably dominate the Mediterranean. To confront this threat, Britain's sea supremacy seemed critically inadequate. Only 181 British destroyers were available for convoy duty, as compared to 339 during the submarine crisis of 1917. The fleet as a whole was stretched thin by the extent of Britain's worldwide commitments, and by the need to guard against an invasion. Both the Mediterranean and the Channel were closed for a time to merchant shipping, so that vessels had to take longer and more exposed routes. For all these reasons, sinkings rose at an alarming rate. From June 1940 to December 1941, the British lost more than a third of their merchant tonnage; and only 30 percent of these losses were replaced from British shipyards.

[2] The number of submarines operational at any given time is considerably lower than the total number in a nation's fleet. Total rather than operational figures are used here.

A temporary windfall enabled the British to keep going through 1941: namely, the acquisition of many Dutch, Norwegian, Greek, French, and Danish ships after the conquest of those countries. Shipping agreements with the various governments-in-exile permitted Britain to charter these vessels (totaling some three million deadweight tons) for the duration of the war.[3] But even with this added tonnage, the British were hard pressed. It was clear that only an enormous expansion of American shipyards could ensure the delivery of essential munitions, raw materials, and foodstuffs after the end of 1941. Throughout that year, a British shipping mission in Washington worked to encourage an American buildup. Even before the United States entered the war, a vastly increased target of eight million deadweight tons had been set for 1942—a figure high enough, along with British and Canadian production, to match the current rate of losses.

Two developments, however, gravely worsened the shipping situation: Hitler's attack on the Soviet Union, and Japan's attack on Pearl Harbor. The pressing need to supply the Russians via the fastest route —by sea to Murmansk—offered the U-boats tempting new targets. The Murmansk run was relatively safe during the dark winter months, but it became the most hazardous route of all as soon as round-the-clock daylight returned. Several convoys in the summer of 1942 were virtually wiped out by U-boat packs and aircraft based in Norway; on one voyage, 22 of 33 ships went down. Meanwhile, Pearl Harbor had altered the whole character of the war, particularly on the sea. The losses suffered at Honolulu forced the Americans to transfer part of their Atlantic fleet to the Pacific, thus thinning out the number of escort vessels available. The U-boats, which had heretofore confined their action to the eastern half of the Atlantic, could now hunt in the western half as well. Furthermore, a large proportion of the new Liberty ships that had begun to come off the American ways in September 1941 now had to be assigned to Pacific duty. Besides, Raeder's building program was producing impressive results; the number of U-boats rose to 249 in January 1942, and reached 393 a year later. The Allies lost 4.5 million tons of shipping during the first half of 1942 (70 percent of it to submarines); the losses rose even higher during the second half of the year, and continued at this same rate through the first quarter of 1943.

---

[3] For an account of the complications involved in the transfer of these ships, see C. B. A. Behrens, *Merchant Shipping and the Demands of War* (London, 1955), pp. 91–103.

There seemed some reason to fear that the Allied war effort might be near the breaking point, should the Battle of the Atlantic continue to favor the Germans. The Admiralty pleaded for a diversion of Bomber Command's strength to new targets: the German submarine pens along the Norwegian and French coasts. The R.A.F. reluctantly complied, but the results were disappointing; the concrete pens were too tough to be breached. In Berlin, a clash between Hitler and Admiral Raeder led in February 1943 to the latter's replacement by Admiral Doenitz, a fanatical exponent of U-boat warfare. With Hitler's approval, Doenitz threw all the resources of the German navy into a final grand effort to break the sea link between Britain and the United States. During the first twenty days in March, kills reached an all-time high: the Allies lost ninety-seven ships totaling more than a half-million tons. Admiralty officials seriously asked themselves whether the convoy system had lost the battle to the U-boats.

Only in retrospect does it appear that the danger of defeat in the Atlantic was not quite so grave. By mid-1942, American shipyards had begun to build faster than the Germans could sink, so that the size of the Allied merchant fleet once more began to grow. By the end of the year, new construction of oil tankers also exceeded losses. But in addition, the British and Americans were gradually developing new tactics and devices designed to offset the advantage enjoyed by the U-boats. Long-range aircraft (notably Liberator bombers) were at last arriving in sufficient numbers to patrol almost the entire Atlantic sea-lane. The first escort carriers, known as "baby flat-tops," were put into use for Atlantic convoy protection. Regular convoy escorts were reinforced by the use of newly organized "support groups"—clusters of a dozen vessels specialized in hunting down submarines. And the new microwave radar for locating U-boats began to be installed in Allied search planes: radar that, unlike the old longer-wave models, gave the Germans no warning of the approach of a plane. Thanks to this combination of factors, Allied shipping losses in April were cut in two. In May, the tables were dramatically turned: the Germans lost an unprecedented forty-one U-boats, almost a third of their total at sea. Doenitz abruptly broke off the battle of the North Atlantic and called his remaining submarines into port. Some months later, he was to attempt to renew the Atlantic campaign, but without much success. With startling suddenness, the Allies had won clear mastery of the seas. The way was open to the invasion of the Continent.

III. THE AIR OFFENSIVE: STRATEGIC BOMBING

"The Navy can lose us the war," wrote Winston Churchill in September 1940, "but only the Air Force can win it."[4] At that dark stage of the battle, the bomber must indeed have seemed the only possible weapon that would enable Britain someday to take the offensive against the enemy. Later on, when massive Soviet and American land armies became available, a more orthodox kind of onslaught could be envisaged. But even then, bomber attacks would continue to be viewed by the Western Allies as an essential technique for breaking German power. The strategic bombing offensive, which lasted for almost five full years, has been described as "probably the most continuous and grueling operation of war ever carried out."[5] The measure of its contribution to the final defeat of the Axis has, however, been a subject of bitter dispute.

The history of warfare provided no precedent for this kind of campaign. During the First World War, a few German air raiders had dropped bombs on London, but they had caused more irritation than damage, and had inspired angry arguments over the legitimacy of this new weapon. Between the wars, some military theorists had strongly urged the primacy of the bomber in future wars; the Italian air general Giulio Douhet had won particular notoriety by his advocacy of mass terror-bombing to break the morale of civilian populations. In Europe, only the British had taken the new doctrine very seriously. Throughout the interwar years, the Royal Air Force remained committed to the idea of strategic bombing as the proper technique to reinforce the effects of Britain's traditional weapon, the economic blockade. True, British planners were hampered by nagging moral doubts about the legitimacy of mass bombing—doubts that persisted in certain circles well into the Second World War. By the mid-thirties, they were also growing concerned at the prospect that the new German air force might use this technique against London and Paris with even more devastating effect, since the Western capitals offered more vulnerable targets than did the more dispersed German cities.

The R.A.F. nevertheless clung to its offensive principle, contending that the best way to avert destructive German air attacks would be

---

[4] J. R. M. Butler, *Grand Strategy* (London, 1964), III, 523.
[5] C. Webster and N. Frankland, *The Strategic Air Offensive against Germany, 1939–1945* (London, 1961), I, 144.

to possess a powerful deterrent force and, if necessary, to strike first. In 1936–1937 the Air Ministry worked out plans for a fleet of heavy four-motored bombers superior to those of any rival. Bomber Command was to be built up to a total of ninety squadrons (1442 aircraft) by about 1942. The cabinet, however, sharply pruned this proposal for financial reasons, and shifted the main emphasis to fighter planes, which could be built more quickly and more cheaply. After Munich, which starkly revealed Britain's offensive and defensive weakness in the air, an even higher priority was given to fighters. This decision was to prove of crucial importance during the Battle of Britain (though it might have been futile without the simultaneous development of radar). It meant, however, further delays in building up the new heavy-bomber fleet. Britain entered the war with only 33 operational squadrons rather than the 90 requested in 1937, and half of those were obsolescent. Bomber Command, with the strong concurrence of the French, therefore avoided offensive action against Germany as long as possible, on the theory that attacks would provoke massive retaliation by the Germans. Indeed, almost seven months went by before the R.A.F. ventured its first strike against a German land target—a strike that was even then hardly more than a gesture.

Fortunately for the British, the Germans were even more unprepared to engage in strategic bombing. Although their bomber force was the best in Europe both in numbers and in quality, the Germans had designed the *Luftwaffe* for quite another purpose—as a tactical arm to accompany an advancing land army. They had trained no crews and devised no plans for mass attacks either on cities or on selected targets. Thus neither side, during the first year of the war, was capable of dealing a very effective blow at the enemy via the air. The fall of France, however, gave the Germans a unique opportunity to try such a blow in 1940–1941. The capture of French and Belgian bases enabled the *Luftwaffe's* medium and light bombers to cross the Channel with fighter-plane protection all the way to their targets. But the opportunity was fumbled; British fighter planes managed to retain command of the air in daylight, while night bombing proved to be relatively inaccurate and ineffective with the equipment the Germans then possessed. The night-bombing blitz during the winter of 1940–1941 did do extensive damage, but it was for the most part indiscriminate damage that failed to slow British production or injure British morale in any serious way. Indeed, its principal effect may have been to stiffen British morale, and to encourage British determination to retaliate in kind. In the spring of 1941, the German air blitz was suspended while the *Luftwaffe's* attention was shifted eastward to support the invasion of the Soviet Union. It was never to be renewed in any consistent way.

Meanwhile, the British had been groping toward a strategic bombing policy of their own. During the Battle of France they had carried out a few raids on strategic German targets such as oil plants and railway communication centers; and in August 1940 they had struck at Berlin in retaliation for German bombs dropped—probably unintentionally—on central London. Daylight raids, however, soon proved to be far too costly, since the British bombers could neither evade nor fend off German fighters. Just as the *Luftwaffe* over Britain had been forced to turn to night attacks, so Bomber Command by the autumn of 1940 switched its activities to the hours of darkness.

Eventually, this decision was bound to dictate a fundamental change in the whole strategic bombing offensive. Heretofore, the British had put their faith in precision bombing: attacks on targets selected for their peculiar importance to the German war effort. "Indiscriminate" or "terror" bombing, designed to break enemy morale, was widely viewed as immoral. After the experience of the German blitz in 1940–1941, it also seemed to be ineffective. The Chiefs of Staff in January 1941 concluded, "Our own experience indicates the local and transient effects of concentrated attacks on centres of population." Bomber Command was therefore ordered to take as its "sole primary aim" the destruction of Germany's synthetic oil plants. Unfortunately, the primitive state of navigational instruments made precision bombing at night virtually impossible—especially over Germany, where weather conditions were usually unfavorable. Unless new navigational devices could be developed quickly, the shift to night bombing would sooner or later force the abandonment of precision bombing in favor of a search for larger targets.

Some British officials (Churchill among them) had been doubtful about precision bombing from the start. They were moved in part by skepticism about the feasibility of finding and hitting small, scattered targets, and in part by a conviction that the morale of Germans, unlike that of Englishmen, would disintegrate under heavy bombing. "All the evidence," reported the Ministry of Information, "goes to prove that the Germans, for all their present confidence and cockiness will not stand a quarter of the bombing that the British have shown they can take."[6] In some quarters, too, there was an angry desire to give the Germans some of the same bitter medicine they had administered to Warsaw, Rotterdam, and Coventry. One member of Parliament wrote to the Secretary of State for Air: "I am Cromwellian—I believe in 'slaying in the name of the Lord' because I do not believe you will ever bring home to the civil population of Germany the horrors of war until they have become tasted in this way."[7] Midway through 1941, therefore, the Chiefs of Staff abandoned oil in favor of morale as Germany's most vulnerable weakness; Bomber Command was ordered to strike at towns rather than individual plants, and aircraft production was speeded by giving bombers first priority in the production schedule. This decision to adopt a policy of "area bombing" (the new name for what had once been called "indiscriminate bombing") was reinforced by further evidence that seemed to prove the futility of precision bombing. In August 1941, a study of photographs taken during bombing raids concluded that only about one-fifth of the attacking bombers had been getting within a radius of five miles of their intended targets. With such damning evidence at hand, there was little prospect that the advocates of precision bombing would ever recover the initiative, though they kept trying.

It was not only precision bombing, however, that was under severe criticism at the turn of the year 1941–1942; the whole strategic air offensive against Germany seemed threatened. Complaints converged from various quarters. Some critics stressed the fact that eighteen months of bombing had apparently produced little effect on either German war production or German morale; perhaps, then, the whole enterprise was futile and wasteful. Others contended that the anti-submarine campaign was of far more crucial importance, and that Bomber Command should be ordered to shift its targets to the sea war. Still others believed that with the entry of the USSR and the United States into the war, a totally different strategy for crushing the enemy ought to be devised. Doubts about strategic bombing, which had already been voiced for some time within the government, now began to come into the open.

The issue was sharply debated by the War Cabinet's Defense Committee in April 1942, when Churchill's scientific adviser Lord Cherwell

---

[6] Webster and Frankland, *Strategic Air Offensive*, I, 169.
[7] *Ibid.*, III, 115.

presented a forceful memorandum urging the continuation and rapid expansion of area bombing. Cherwell calculated that a stepped-up effort would permit Bomber Command to turn one-third of the German population "out of house and home" within fifteen months. This "de-housing" campaign, aimed at the fifty-eight largest German cities, would, as Cherwell saw it, "break the spirit of the people"; for the demolition of homes would be the hardest of all trials to bear. Cherwell's estimate required that bomber construction continue to receive top production priority, in order to turn out ten thousand bombers during the next fifteen months.[8]

Cherwell's critics in the Defense Committee hammered hard at the reliability of his calculations. Sir Henry Tizard judged them five times too optimistic, and argued that the area bombing scheme could not be decisive unless carried out on a scale far beyond Britain's capacity. Tizard urged the virtual suspension of the strategic bombing offensive in favor of increased air attacks on the U-boats and their bases. Later experience was to show that Tizard's predictions of bombing effectiveness were considerably more accurate than Cherwell's; yet it was the latter's policy that prevailed, in somewhat modified form. Churchill inclined toward the Cherwell position; and it was even more stubbornly held by the new head of Bomber Command, Sir Arthur Harris, who referred contemptuously to the advocates of precision bombing as "panacea-mongers." During 1942, Harris offered what seemed to be evidence that the strategic air offensive might after all produce some impressive results. In May and June, he mounted three spectacular thousand-bomber raids on Cologne, Essen, and Bremen, which quieted the doubts of many critics even though the effects of the raids were debatable. The bombers were aided too by new navigational aids then coming into use: "Gee" in March 1942, "Oboe" in December, "H2S" in January 1943. And at least one effective new tactical device was adopted in August: the creation of Pathfinder Force, a specialized group of flyers assigned to mark out targets for the massed bombers that followed.

It was in 1942, too, that the first of the new Lancaster heavy bombers, designed far back in 1936, came into operational use; they far surpassed the older British aircraft in speed, range, and bomb weight carried. American bombers ordered in 1940 were also beginning to arrive in considerable numbers, though deliveries lagged behind Brit-

[8] Butler, *Grand Strategy*, III, 526.

ish hopes. The American builders had run into unexpected production difficulties; and in addition, the new needs of both the Soviet and the American air forces drained off many of the planes promised to Britain. Although the Americans flew a few raids beginning in August, it was not until January 1943 that the United States Air Force was ready to throw its full weight into the offensive. But the Americans, unlike the British, were stubbornly committed to daylight precision bombing as the only sensible policy; area bombing they considered a waste of essential resources, inspired more by a desire for vengeance than by any rational calculation. Through 1943, the two Allied air forces thus alternated over Germany by day and by night, operating as rivals rather than as coordinated units in a combined offensive.

The impact of Britain's night bombing was undoubtedly the more spectacular. Its climax came at Hamburg in July-August 1943; one week of fire raids destroyed a large part of the city, drove a million residents to seek refuge outside the urban area, and killed two-thirds as many people as did all German air raids over Britain during the entire war. A series of attacks on Berlin later in the year caused proportionately less damage, but still left enormous areas of wreckage in their wake. Yet despite all this, German morale refused to collapse, and German armaments production continued to rise. The expectations of the proponents of area bombing, when subjected to the hard test of reality, proved seriously faulty. Their mistake did not stem from exaggerated estimates of the damage that could be inflicted by air attacks; it resulted, rather, from an erroneous view of the German character and from a mistaken idea of the nature of the German economy. The British had assumed that economy to be taut and over-strained when the war began; instead, it had contained a remarkable degree of slack which could be taken up as the demands of war intensified. Under Albert Speer's guidance, German industrialists and workers were therefore able to keep pace with the British and American air raiders.

If the British night bombers produced spectacular but somewhat disillusioning results, the American daytime offensive for a time seemed threatened by total disaster. The heavily armed American planes, flying in close formation for better protection, proved unable to fend off the German day fighters. Losses rose dangerously, until they reached a climax in October 1943 during a series of massive raids on the ball-bearing plants at Schweinfurt. In six days, the United

States lost 148 bombers—far too heavy a sacrifice for the Air Force to bear. Daylight bombing had to be suspended for several months thereafter. To the British advocates of area bombing, this was conclusive proof that they had chosen the right path; they urged that American air power now be thrown into the night onslaught against German cities. But the Eighth Air Force was neither equipped nor trained for such a conversion; and in any case the Americans remained convinced that the British were on the wrong track. Therefore, they doggedly sought another way out of the impasse. What they needed was a long-range fighter plane that could accompany the bombers to German targets and could overpower German fighters over German soil. Early in 1944, the solution was found in the form of the P–51 Mustang, a rebuilt version of an earlier plane that had failed to perform effectively. When the day raids were resumed in February 1944, the balance shifted sharply against the Germans. American losses fell to bearable levels, while the German fighters were gradually driven from the skies. By May 1944, the daylight bombers could once again begin to concentrate on Germany's oil supply, this time with devastating effectiveness; and the British soon coordinated at least part of their night attacks with this daytime offensive. Together, they produced a German gasoline famine that virtually grounded the *Luftwaffe* during the last year of the war. The Western powers' complete command of the air over Germany, won at last by mid-1944, opened the way to the most devastating phase of the air offensive: the round-the-clock combination of precision and area bombing that ceased only with the German surrender.

Yet no aspect of the Second World War has remained more controversial than the contribution of strategic bombing to the ultimate victory. After the war, Sir Henry Tizard publicly denounced the whole enterprise as a misguided failure that had hurt Britain more than Germany. According to Tizard, Britain's investment of manpower and resources in the bombing campaign exceeded the amount of damage done to the enemy. Worse still, said Tizard, this wasted manpower and these resources might have been used for other more productive purposes: the battle against the U-boats, for example, or the more rapid building of landing craft, so desperately needed in both Europe and the Pacific. Postwar studies suggest that until the very last months of the war, German armaments production continued to rise rather than decline, and that efforts to strangle Germany by destroying such key items as ball-bearing plants were glaring failures. In 1943, bomb-ing reduced Germany's total production by only about 9 percent, and in 1944 by 17 percent; and less than half of this reduction was in armaments.

Still, the strategic bombing offensive cannot be written off quite so easily. The raids on oil facilities in May-June 1944 helped clear the skies of German planes during and after the Normandy landings, thus ensuring the success of the great cross-Channel operation. The attacks on rocket-launching bases reduced the effectiveness of the V-weapon campaign in 1944. Furthermore, the strategic bombers accomplished a long series of indirect results that would be hard to measure, but that were no less important for all that. From 1942 onward, a large segment of Germany's manpower and resources had to be diverted to the unending task of reconstruction of bombed factories and public utilities. Perhaps a million and a half workers were engaged in this task by mid-1944, and many of these were urgently-needed skilled workers. In addition, the bombing campaign forced the *Luftwaffe* to keep the bulk of its strength in Germany for defense, thus limiting German air power on the Russian front and weakening the Wehr-macht's effectiveness there. It also drove the Germans to concentrate increasingly on building fighter planes at the expense of bombers; fighter production rose fivefold from 1942 to 1944, while bomber pro-duction was cut in two. Any resumption of a bombing blitz over England, except by the new V-weapons, was thus averted; the Anglo-American buildup for a Channel crossing could proceed uninterrupted.

Mass bombing, then, undoubtedly hampered the German war effort in much more than a marginal way. What it failed to do was to de-stroy civilian morale—to break the German people's will to work and to endure. In Albert Speer's postwar judgment, "The powers of re-sistance of the German people were underestimated and no account was taken of the fatalistic frame of mind which a civil population finally acquires after numerous air raids."[9] No doubt the British, after their own experience with the civilian response to mass bomb-ing in 1940–1941, ought to have anticipated the effect on the Germans as well. They were misled by a conviction that German morale, for one reason or another, was more vulnerable than that of Englishmen. Probably, too, they underestimated the effectiveness of the civil de-fense techniques devised by the Germans during the early years of

[9] Webster and Frankland, *Strategic Air Offensive*, IV, 383.

the war—techniques that permitted the rapid restoration of public utilities and the evacuation of many city-dwellers to rural areas. Even after the Germans lost control of the air over their own territory in mid-1944, so that the Anglo-American bombers could devastate the country almost at will, there were few signs of serious deterioration of German morale.

The strategic bombing offensive, in the end, made a major contribution to Germany's defeat. Yet in retrospect, it might have contributed even more if its planners had not put such stubborn faith in the vulnerability of German morale. In the final analysis, as Speer was to testify, it was precision bombing that hurt the Germans most. "The American attacks," he declared, "which followed a definite system of assault on industrial targets, were by far the most dangerous. It was in fact these attacks which caused the breakdown of the German armaments industry."[10]

IV. THE LAND OFFENSIVE: FIRST TURN OF THE VISE

In the air, Germany abandoned the initiative in mid-1941, and fell back onto the defensive for the rest of the war. On the sea, Allied shipping construction began to outpace losses in October 1942, and six months later the U-boat was transmuted from hunter into quarry. On land, the turning point came in November 1942, through a series of events whose cumulative impact is more easily seen in retrospect. On November 1–2, General Montgomery's British tank forces broke through the German-Italian front at El Alamein in Egypt, and began the advance that was soon to clear the Axis forces out of the eastern Mediterranean. On November 8, an Anglo-American armada of 650 ships brought an army swarming ashore into Morocco and Algeria, thus inaugurating the first land campaign in the west since the fall of France two and a half years earlier. On November 19, Soviet forces began the counterattack that four days later pinched off the corridor west of Stalingrad, isolating the German Sixth Army and foreshadowing Hitler's gravest military disaster. From November 1942 onward, the ring steadily closed on the Axis.

El Alamein represented the last in a series of sharp turnabouts in the Libyan campaign. Since 1940, British and Axis armored forces had alternated in driving one another some five hundred miles either eastward or westward through the coastal desert. In May-June 1942 the

[10] *Ibid.*

Axis had achieved its greatest success: Rommel's troops surged all the way into Egypt, and were barely checked sixty miles short of Alexandria. The exhausted armies needed a breathing space to recover and await supplies and reinforcements. Although Rommel seemed to enjoy the advantage, the reverse was in fact true. His supply lines now ran a thousand miles through the desert, and the Axis ships that brought men and equipment across the Mediterranean were scourged by British aircraft and submarines from Malta, Gibraltar, and Alexandria. During the summer and autumn months, about a third of Rommel's supply vessels were sunk. Meanwhile the British and Commonwealth troops in Egypt were receiving heavy reinforcements of men and tanks, until by October their strength was double that of the Axis forces. A change in command also put new spirit into the British soldiers; Generals Alexander and Montgomery seemed likely to be a match for Rommel in dash and imagination. The battle was joined on October 23, and only after a week of bitter fighting were the British able to break through Rommel's "devil's gardens"—a defensive strip sowed with a half-million mines. The Axis rout this time was complete; the retreat was not to stop short of capitulation in Tunis six months later. Churchill, elated, was tempted to order that the bells of victory be rung all over Britain, but on second thought resisted the impulse. In the minds of Britons El Alamein was to become, nevertheless, the most glamorous memory of the Second World War. "Before Alamein," Churchill later remarked, "we never had a victory. After Alamein we never had a defeat."

The landings in Morocco and Algeria a week after El Alamein had been agreed upon only after long and sometimes bitter discussions between the British and American governments. Beginning in July 1941, Stalin repeatedly appealed for some kind of diversionary action in the west; and these appeals became more pressing after the United States entered the war. Both the British and the Americans—but particularly the latter—were sensitive to the Soviet demands; from February 1942 they began to study ways to relieve some of the terrible pressure on the Soviet armies. The Americans were strongly inclined toward a cross-Channel operation at the earliest possible moment, on the ground that this would draw off part of the Wehrmacht from Russia. General George Marshall visited London in April and urged a relatively small-scale Channel crossing no later than September, with a full-scale invasion to follow in 1943.

The British, however, were most reluctant to chance such an operation until the prospect of success was strong. Most British military men argued that no more than six divisions could be put ashore in France with the landing craft then available, and that this force would almost certainly be driven back into the sea by the superior German army (thirty-three divisions) stationed in western Europe. Such a disaster, they insisted, would cause a long postponement of the full-scale landings projected for 1943. Prime Minister Churchill fully shared these fears, and furthermore had his own ideas about strategic planning for the assault on Germany. From the moment the United States entered the war, Churchill had begun to shape up a two-pronged operation: one prong to strike at northern Norway, the other at Vichy-controlled North Africa. Not even his own military advisers were fully agreed on this scheme; many of them preferred to defer any kind of action until 1943, and to run the risk of a Soviet collapse in the interval.

The Russians, meanwhile, were increasingly restless at these Western delays in opening a second front. Foreign Minister Molotov was sent to London and Washington in May to argue the Soviet case, and to demand action in 1942 that would draw off forty German divisions. Churchill listened sympathetically, but would not bind himself to any promises. Roosevelt saw the situation as more urgent, since a Soviet collapse would permit the entire Wehrmacht to be transferred to the west, and would make any kind of Western landings hazardous if not impossible. Roosevelt therefore encouraged Molotov to believe that some kind of second front would be established before the year was out. But the subsequent negotiations between Washington and London produced only deadlock. The Americans argued that a six-division landing in France might manage to hold a beachhead until the larger operation in 1943, and that even if it were to fail, such a "sacrifice" attack was necessary to prove the Western Allies' good intentions toward the USSR. The British replied that a six-division landing would draw no German troops away from Russia, since the German forces in France were strong enough to drive off the invaders without reinforcements. In July, Roosevelt sent one last American mission to London in an effort to persuade the British; but the attempt failed. Most of the top American military planners now favored scrapping the whole strategic plan worked out at the Washington conference in December 1941; they recommended that the bulk of American power be shifted to the Pacific, where Japan's expansionist drive had been checked (in Guadalcanal) but not yet broken.

American and Japanese naval strength remained precariously balanced in the South Pacific; Roosevelt's naval advisers argued that a Pacific-first policy would decide the issue, and that Europe should be left to await the defeat of Japan.

Such a decision, if taken, would have altered the whole course of the war in Europe. It was overruled by Roosevelt who, even though the American hope for an early Channel crossing had been frustrated, was determined to engage the enemy somewhere during 1942. Churchill's idea of a North African operation had caught his fancy from the start; they had already discussed it at the Washington conference in December 1941; and now that the more direct route to Berlin was temporarily blocked, the President viewed it as the next-best thing. A decision was quickly reached, therefore, to plan a surprise descent on Morocco and Algeria in the autumn. About 100,000 men would be landed on the first day, with American troops constituting the bulk of the assault wave, on the theory that they might be less vigorously resisted by the Vichy-French defenders. De Gaulle's Free French forces were to be given no share in the operation, since American intelligence reports held that the Gaullists would not be welcomed by the French North Africans. Indeed, for reasons of security, de Gaulle was not even informed of the impending invasion. As for Stalin, whose irritation at Western inaction had been growing steadily through the summer, the prospect of a North African operation brought at least some solace. Churchill himself brought the news to Moscow in August, and used his great powers of persuasion to convince Stalin that this would be a genuine second front, not merely a minor diversion. In the conversation, Churchill produced one of his most celebrated metaphors: he sketched a crocodile, and spoke of plans to attack its soft belly while at the same time (across the Channel) striking at its hard snout. Stalin, intrigued and at least partly mollified, responded with a surprisingly un-Marxian phrase: "May God prosper this undertaking."

Late in October, the expedition was launched from ports in Britain and the United States. The Germans, who mistakenly believed its destination to be Dakar, grouped their submarines south of the Azores, so that the invading fleet went almost undetected. The troops went ashore in Morocco and Algeria before dawn on November 8, hoping that resistance by the Vichy-French forces would be slight or non-existent. Instead, there was bitter fighting at some points, and casualties were heavy. To avert continued bloodshed, General Eisenhower, commander-in-chief of the expedition, sent an agent to negotiate with Admiral Jean Darlan, the highest-ranking Vichy official in North Africa. Darlan happened to be visiting Algiers on personal business, and was caught by surprise in the invasion. At first, in accordance with Pétain's instructions, he ordered vigorous resistance to the Anglo-American forces; but by November 10, after complex and somewhat obscure negotiations, he agreed to order a cease-fire, which was obeyed. In return, Eisenhower accepted an accord by which Darlan assumed "responsibility for French interests in Africa."

The repercussions of the North African landings were far-reaching. Although Marshal Pétain publicly repudiated Darlan's action, the German army on November 11 crossed the French demarcation line and occupied all of southern France. Two weeks later the Germans attempted, in a sudden coup, to pounce on the French fleet at anchor in Toulon harbor. Admiral Laborde forestalled them by scuttling most of his ships; but Hitler preferred this outcome to the escape of the Toulon fleet to North Africa, which he had feared might be imminent. With Pétain's consent, German troops were rushed to Tunisia beginning on November 9; they joined forces with Rommel's troops withdrawing from Libya, and garrisoned the border before Eisenhower could add Tunisia to his conquests. Meanwhile, the "Darlan deal" produced a furious reaction in both Britain and the United States. Critics branded it an egregious new example of appeasement, since Darlan's record of subservience to the Germans had been notorious. Furthermore, it embittered relationships among the various rival French groups. De Gaulle in London was already outraged at having been kept in ignorance of the North African landings; now this Allied preference for a Vichyite redoubled his fury. Complicating matters still further was the presence of General Henri Giraud, a war hero who had escaped from a German prison and who had been brought to North Africa by the Americans to serve as a potential rallying-point for all Frenchmen. This imbroglio was partially cleared up in December 1942 when a young resistance activist assassinated Darlan; but the rivalry between Giraud and de Gaulle continued unresolved. Eventually, in June 1943, a kind of proto-government was set up in Algiers under the joint chairmanship of the two generals. This French Committee of National Liberation rapidly became de Gaulle's instrument; by the end of 1943, the politically unsophisticated Giraud had been levered out of the co-chairmanship and, indeed, out of the Committee entirely.

Meanwhile, the Allied forces had turned to the problem of evicting the Axis from its last North African stronghold in Tunisia. In March 1943, a double series of blows were struck from Algeria (British, American, and French forces) and from Libya (Montgomery's desert army). Six weeks of bloody fighting were needed to roll back the Axis lines and to force the final surrender in May. A quarter-million prisoners were taken, the majority of them Italian. North Africa was clear at last of Axis troops; and southern Italy lay within easy bombing distance. But the fighting had consumed far more time, supplies, and men than most of its planners had anticipated; and the buildup in southern England of an invasion force to attack the Continent had been seriously slowed. The cross-Channel operation, toward which the Allies had been pointing for many months, was the principal victim of the North African campaign.

The third panel in the November triptych of Allied resurgence bears the name of Stalingrad. During the summer of 1942, Hitler's armies in the Ukraine had been hammering steadily forward toward their objective in the Caucasus. Their advance, while the northern battle lines remained almost stationary, pushed out a steadily lengthening southern salient whose left flank was dangerously exposed. It soon became clear that the city of Stalingrad on the lower Volga was the key to the security of the German thrust. As a center of industrial production and communications, its importance to Soviet defense was crucial; among other things, its loss would cut the direct rail and water routes from the Caucasian oil fields to Moscow. Late in July, Hitler ordered part of his southern armies to strike toward Stalingrad while the second part would continue its drive into the Caucasus. This risky division of German strength to "chase two hares at once" (as Stalin put it) drew strong protests from the army chief of staff, General Halder, but to no avail.

For a time, it had seemed that Hitler's gamble would once again pay off. Stalingrad was weakly garrisoned, and there were signs of demoralization and even panic in the Soviet armies of the south. Early in August the southern prong of the German forces captured the first of the Caucasian oil fields; two weeks later, the other prong reached the Volga, and by mid-September the German Sixth Army had penetrated the city of Stalingrad itself. Hitler, sure of victory in the south, had already transferred some units from the Caucasus army to Leningrad, which he proposed to take in a spectacular autumn attack. He ignored general staff warnings of a desperate Soviet buildup of men and equipment on the lower Volga, and of rising Soviet tank production that may have reached 2000 per month at this stage (compared to Germany's 350 per month). His confidence did not seem misplaced; Stalingrad appeared to be doomed.

But Hitler had underestimated his enemy. The battered Soviet forces within the city dug in for a fight to the death, aided by artillery support from across the mile-wide Volga and by reinforcements and equipment ferried across the river at night. While they held on, large Soviet striking forces were gradually massed to the north and south of the city, menacing the flanks of the Sixth Army's salient that were guarded by Rumanian, Hungarian, and Italian troops. By November, they outnumbered the Axis forces confronting them, and had an almost two-to-one advantage in tanks and artillery. The alarmed German commanders in the area urged that Stalingrad be evacuated and the troops pulled back to a stronger winter line; but Hitler ordered them to stand fast. Worse still, the North African landings led him to weaken his air strength on the Russian front by transferring several hundred aircraft to bolster the defense of Tunisia.

On November 19 and 20, the Soviet armies attacked to the north and south of Stalingrad. On the twenty-second the pincers closed, trapping 330,000 Axis troops in the Stalingrad pocket. General von Paulus of the Sixth Army pleaded for permission to break his way out, but Hitler preferred to risk the loss of the entire force rather than the loss of face involved in retreat. "I won't go back from the Volga!" he shouted at his military advisers. A desperate attempt to relieve the encircled troops failed when a tank column striking from the south was turned back by the Red army. For ten weeks the grim struggle raged in the shattered city—the Germans supplied by a wholly inadequate airlift, the Soviets devising ingenious techniques to get supplies across the Volga, both armies tormented by sub-freezing weather and heavy snowstorms. By the turn of the year, the river was frozen over, so that Soviet heavy artillery could be brought across. At last, on February 2, von Paulus defied Hitler's fury by surrendering the broken remnant of his army: just over 100,000 men. The battle had cost the Axis a half-million men dead, wounded, or captured. It meant the frustration of Hitler's designs in the east, and foreshadowed the total collapse of his empire.

Chapter Nine

THE DISLOCATION OF THE NAZI EMPIRE

I. THE END OF THE AXIS

EVEN before the Axis surrender in Tunisia, there were clear signs of crumbling morale in Italy. The nation had entered the war without enthusiasm, and despite Mussolini's attempts to whip up a crusading spirit, thirty months of strain and sacrifice had steadily undermined the Italian will to fight. Besides, the test of war had glaringly revealed the inefficiency and corruption of the Fascist regime. Manpower losses in North Africa and in the Ukraine had been heavy; "the core of the Italian army," reported the German military attaché, "has been destroyed." Shortages of essential war materials, fuel, and foodstuffs were severe, and Italians resented what they viewed as Germany's willful refusal to provide for the country's wartime needs. They resented, too, the scarcely veiled contempt shown by many Germans, and the apparent tendency of German military commanders to regard Italian troops as second-rate auxiliaries who could be sacrificed to protect German elite forces. The myth of Italy's "parallel war" had long since evaporated; even in the Mediterranean theater, decisions were obviously made in Berlin. By 1943 there were rumors in high places that Marshal Goering might declare himself *Reichsprotektor* of Italy, thus stripping away the sham of Axis partnership. Nor were there any successes to offset these sources of discontent. None of Mussolini's declared war aims had been attained; on the contrary, the entire Italian empire in Africa had been lost, and the Mediterranean, far from becoming *mare nostrum,* seemed on the way to being an Anglo-American lake.

Mussolini himself nevertheless clung desperately to his alliance with Hitler, in spite of occasional bursts of resentment at Hitler's arbitrary and condescending conduct. His decision to enter the war in 1940, and his incautious public pronouncements since then, had trapped him in a policy which he must surely have begun to regret. Retreat, however, was impossible for him, and so he sought to reinvigorate the ailing Fascist regime by a drastic shake-up of his government. In February 1943 he demoted some of the most prominent defeatists such as Dino Grandi and his own son-in-law Count Galeazzo Ciano, and publicly asserted his intention to mobilize a million additional men during 1943. Already, however, he had begun to urge Hitler to cut his losses in Russia by seeking a separate peace with Stalin or, short of that, by digging in behind a shorter and more defensive "Eastern wall." Mussolini's desire to liquidate the Russian adventure was shared by most top Fascists, and by many highly-placed Nazis as well. They argued that Axis strength could then be shifted to the Mediterranean and to western Europe, where a stalemate might still stave off defeat. But Mussolini's suggestions were brushed aside by Hitler, who refused to abandon his anti-Soviet crusade and kept asserting his confidence that one more great blow would bring Russia's collapse.

The Western Allies, meanwhile, had begun to plan their strategy for 1943. The battle for Tunisia, much longer and more costly than they had anticipated, had destroyed the last hope of mounting a major Channel crossing before 1944. The American military planners, who had predicted just this consequence of the North African landings, could take pride in their foresight, but still expressed sharp regret at the delay. During an Anglo-American strategy conference in May, the Americans continued to press for a single-minded buildup toward the cross-Channel operation, but in the end gave way to British arguments for a quick blow at the staggering Italians. A Mediterranean crossing, the British contended, would not only knock Italy out of the war, but would clear the entire Mediterranean for Allied shipping, and would provide air bases in southern Italy from which to strike at the Rumanian oil fields and at south German targets. The fall of Italy, they believed, might also bring Spain and Turkey into the war on the Allied side, or would at least render them more susceptible to Allied pressure. In the end, Sicily was chosen as the logical point of attack.

Although the island was heavily garrisoned by Italian forces and two German divisions, the operation proved an easy success. Within a few days after the initial landings on July 9–10, the Allied invaders were pushing inland from solid beachheads. Desperate Italian appeals for German reinforcements (especially of aircraft) were evaded; Hitler preferred to write off Sicily, and to dig into a more easily defended position farther up the Italian peninsula. Hitler's decision marked the beginning of the end for Mussolini. For several months already, King Victor Emmanuel and certain disaffected Fascist leaders had been cautiously seeking ways to dislodge the Duce and to detach Italy from the German alliance. They were offered an opening when Mussolini reluctantly decided to summon a meeting of the Fascist Grand Council on July 24. Party officials loyal to Mussolini had urged this course, on the theory that the atrophied Grand Council might, if revived, bolster the sagging regime and intensify the war effort. Instead, the meeting demonstrated the disintegration of the Fascist elite. After a ten-hour discussion, the Council voted a resolution calling on the king to assume all of his constitutional powers, including personal command of the armed forces. The next day, Victor Emmanuel overcame his long hesitation; he brusquely dismissed Mussolini and replaced him with Marshal Pietro Badoglio, hero of the Ethiopian conquest. The fallen Duce was immediately jailed by the military police.

Although Badoglio publicly proclaimed his fidelity to the Axis, his purpose was to find a way of escape from Hitler's domination—if possible by switching sides. That task was seriously complicated, however, by the Western Allies' official policy of "unconditional surrender," as announced by President Roosevelt at the Casablanca conference in January 1943. Roosevelt's pronouncement, which had won Churchill's somewhat lukewarm support, had been designed both to reassure the Soviet leadership and to quiet Western critics of the socalled "Darlan deal." These critics, and Stalin as well, suspected that the Western powers might settle for a compromise peace engineered by dissident Fascists and Nazis seeking to save their regimes from destruction. Roosevelt may have been motivated also by his recollection of 1918, when the Germans had been accorded armistice terms that permitted them subsequently to raise a cry of double-cross.

Badoglio's private appeal for face-saving terms met an intransigent reception in Washington, which insisted that his surrender must be unconditional, but held out the prospect that the Allies would help him protect Rome against occupation by the Germans. Early in September, Badoglio and the king agreed to an armistice on Allied terms, relying on the hope that the Western powers would show themselves generous in practice. Their hope was not misplaced; on September 30 the British and Americans (with Soviet concurrence) "took note" of the cooperative attitude of the new Italian government, and promoted it to the status of active co-belligerent against Germany. Thus only six weeks after the overthrow of Fascism, Italy had been transmuted from junior partner in the Axis into junior partner in the anti-Hitler coalition. Unconditional surrender had proved, in this case at least, to be a highly flexible concept.

The symbolic effect of the destruction of the Axis could not fail to be considerable. Not only had the Western Allies won a toehold in "Fortress Europe" itself, but the myth of totalitarian invincibility had been exploded. Indeed, since Mussolini had been the pioneer of Fascism, his fall was particularly resounding. But the conversion of Italy from enemy into ally did not mean the end of German control in the peninsula. On the contrary: Hitler had immediately begun to send reinforcements into Italy after Mussolini's fall, and to plan swift action in case of a "betrayal" by Badoglio. When the armistice was announced on September 8, the Germans promptly disarmed most of the Italian troops, seized Rome, and took over all but the southern tip of the peninsula. The king and Badoglio barely escaped capture, and made their way to Brindisi in the south. By November, German divisions in Italy outnumbered those of the allies by twenty-five to eleven.

Even before the signature of the Italian armistice, the first Allied troops had crossed from conquered Sicily onto the toe of Italy. They were reinforced by a larger American amphibious force that landed in the gulf of Salerno on September 9. After overcoming sharp initial resistance from the Germans, the Americans began to fight their way up the western coast of the peninsula, while the British thrust up the east coast. Naples fell on October 1, and the Allied troops pushed northward toward Rome. In December, however, Generals Eisenhower and Montgomery were called to England, along with some of the Allied troops in Italy, to begin final preparations for the Channel crossing scheduled for 1944. The remaining Allied forces under Generals Alexander and Clark ran up against Marshal Kesselring's German troops, which had dug into strong positions along the Garigliano and Rapido rivers, overlooked by the ancient Benedictine abbey of Monte Cassino.

Late in January 1944, in an effort to outflank the Germans, an Allied force was ferried by sea to Anzio, thirty miles south of Rome. For a brief moment, the road to Rome lay open to the attackers; but the advantage of surprise was lost when the Allied commander chose to consolidate his beachhead rather than thrust inland at once. Kesselring therefore had time to build up his defenses and to launch a counterblow that threatened for a time to drive the Anglo-Americans into the sea.

Churchill later recalled his disappointment in a characteristic phrase: "I had hoped that we were hurling a wildcat onto the shore, but all we had got was a stranded whale."[1] While the Allies held on grimly at Anzio, the Germans were resisting just as stubbornly along the Garigliano. In February, after a full month of bitter struggle, the Allies decided that they could no longer spare Monte Cassino which, they believed, was being used by the German command as an observation post. But the destruction of the abbey proved fruitless; German resistance slackened not one bit. The attack was suspended in mid-February; heavy rains had turned the rivers into torrents, and the battlefield into a scarred landscape of water-filled shell holes across which tanks could no longer make their way. Not until May could the campaign be resumed; Monte Cassino was at last outflanked and fell to the Allies. At the same time, the troops in the Anzio beachhead broke out of their trap, and the reunited forces entered Rome on June 4.

This long and bloody Italian campaign—still only half-finished when Rome fell—bred controversy both at the time and in later retrospect. One fact is clear: the Allied strategists who planned the invasion had never intended to use Italy as the gateway to Fortress Europe. Their principal aims had been to knock Italy out of the war, to conquer airfields from which to launch bombing raids, and to keep as many German divisions as possible pinned down during the scheduled cross-Channel operation in 1944. The British also hoped to use Italy as a base from which to launch diversionary operations into the Balkans and the eastern Mediterranean—operations that the German strategists feared and expected. The Americans, however, stubbornly rejected such schemes as likely to divert essential forces from the cross-Channel buildup. Throughout 1944, therefore, the outnumbered Allied armies in Italy continued to blast away at the Germans' powerful defenses. The tempting prospect of amphibious landings in the north, which might have cut off the peninsula at the Po Valley and thus isolated Marshal Kesselring's forces, could not be undertaken due to a shortage of landing craft, desperately needed at the Channel and in the Pacific. Rome did not fall until two days before the Channel crossing; Kesselring's so-called "Gothic line" (just south of the Po Valley) was not broken until April 1945. Thus almost two full years elapsed between the initial Allied landings in Sicily and the liberation of northern Italy from German control. The price paid in blood and in

[1] Churchill, *Second World War*, V, 488.

property damage was heavy; and to a lesser degree, inter-Allied harmony also suffered. The slow advance northward fed Soviet suspicions that the Western Allies were using the Italian campaign as a sham second front in order to postpone opening a real one. It may be that the yield from the Italian venture failed to justify the cost. Yet the yield cannot be overlooked: twenty-five German divisions pinned down in Italy, plus about the same number retained in the Balkans to guard against a possible thrust across the Adriatic.

During the long months of rugged fighting in Italy, a shadowy neo-Fascist regime had been resurrected by Hitler, with Mussolini as its formal head. The fallen Duce, after his arrest in July 1943, had been kept in confinement for six weeks before being dramatically rescued from his mountain prison by a band of paratroopers sent by Hitler. He was promptly named head of a new Italian Social Republic, with its seat of government at Salò on Lake Garda. A number of Mussolini's old henchmen rallied to his cause and were given high posts in the regime; they professed to be committed to a purer and more vigorous version of Fascism, dedicated to the interests of the common man. In reality, the Salò regime was no more than a rickety facade; behind its posturings, the German occupation forces controlled northern Italy and carried on the fight against the spreading resistance movement. The Italian Social Republic was merely a propaganda device mounted by Hitler in an effort to conceal the disintegration of his European fortress; it left behind, when it collapsed, nothing more than a myth of "people's Fascism" perpetuated by those Salò officials who survived.

II. THE END OF EMPIRE IN THE EAST

Hitler's defeat at Stalingrad early in 1943 can be seen in retrospect as the psychological if not the military turning point of the struggle in Russia, and perhaps of the war as a whole. At the time, however, its significance was not quite so clear. The enormous strain of that gigantic battle had been felt by the victors as well as the vanquished, and it seemed possible that the Soviet armies would be too exhausted to launch their own offensive. Besides, the German front was still deep within Russia: Leningrad remained a city almost surrounded and besieged, Kiev and Kharkov were in German hands, the Crimea and even part of the Caucasus were still occupied. To roll back the German front for a thousand miles, as far as the 1941 frontier of the Soviet state, would be an enormous enterprise.

The Soviet forces sought nevertheless to follow up their Stalingrad victory without delay. The Stalingrad army moved down the Don toward the Black Sea, threatening to cut off some 400,000 German troops in the Caucasus. At the last moment Hitler uncharacteristically authorized a retreat through the narrow Rostov corridor, thus averting another major disaster. The Russians then struck westward in the Ukraine, and drove all the way to Kharkov, whose capture was triumphantly announced. But the Germans promptly turned the tables by a counterblow that recaptured Kharkov, and a three-month stalemate followed. By July 1943, both sides had built up enough strength to strike again. The Germans took the initiative in a violent blow at Kursk—their third and last summer offensive on Soviet soil. Within a week the Soviet forces had blunted their attack, and began to push the retreating Germans westward in a long, almost unbroken advance that was not to end until Berlin fell in April 1945. Never in history had there been a sustained campaign of such length, or involving such enormous masses of men and equipment. Although Soviet casualties since 1941 had been far higher than those of the Germans, the Red army received a steady flow of reinforcements from the vast Soviet population, while the German manpower pool was drying up. Weapons and supplies were also reaching the Soviet forces in sufficient quantity now—in part thanks to American and British shipments, but for the most part from the newly opened industrial areas beyond the Urals. For every new tank received by Hitler's army, the Red troops were now receiving three; and among them were the first of the so-called Stalin tanks, the most effective heavy model produced during the war.

By the end of 1943, two-thirds of the Soviet territory occupied by the Germans had been liberated, and the Russians were approaching the borders of their eastern European neighbors. Well before now, Germany's satellite nations had lost their enthusiasm for the war, and had begun to seek ways to escape. Peace feelers had been cautiously put out through agents in various neutral capitals, and some of the Balkan leaders had even hoped for a time that Mussolini might take the lead in getting them out of the war. News of the Allied landings in Normandy on June 6, 1944, and the subsequent Allied breakout from their bridgehead in July, intensified the desperate attempt to throw off German control in eastern Europe. The Finns, who had been unsuccessfully attempting to negotiate with Moscow since February, finally restored Marshal Mannerheim to power on August 1, and inaugurated talks that led to a Soviet-Finnish armistice on September 19. The Polish Home Army on August 4 began the uprising in Warsaw that was to drag on for two full months before it was finally crushed by the Germans. Three months later, the shattered ruins of Warsaw fell to the advancing Russians, and by the end of January 1945 the Soviet army stood on German soil, only forty miles east of Berlin.

Meanwhile, late in August 1944, the southern units of the Red army had begun to roll into the Balkans. Rumania and Bulgaria were overrun by early September. With Tito's prior consent, Soviet units entered Yugoslavia, where they found that Tito's guerrillas had already managed to clear most of the country of the Germans. Only the taking of Belgrade required some help from Soviet tanks. At this point, however, the triumphant Soviet advance up the Danube Valley was suddenly checked. On October 15, the Germans arrested the Hungarian regent, Admiral Horthy, on the quite correct suspicion that he had been attempting to negotiate his country's way out of the conflict. Hungary was Germany's last buffer on the southeast, and Hitler was determined not to give it up easily; nor was he willing to lose the use of the Hungarian army that had fought with considerable distinction throughout the eastern campaign. German armored divisions were sent to occupy Budapest, and the city seemed destined to become a Stalingrad in reverse, if Hitler could repeat the Russian exploit. The Soviet advance stalled when it struck this obstacle, and remained stalled throughout most of the winter. But as Soviet forces massed for the kill in eastern Germany and in the suburbs of Budapest, it was clear that vengeance for 1941 was not far off.

III. THE NORMANDY INVASION

Everywhere the Germans and their remaining allies were on the defensive. In the Pacific, the bloody six-month struggle for Guadalcanal had ended almost simultaneously with the Soviet victory at Stalingrad; for the first time, the Japanese were dislodged from a conquered territory. By the spring of 1943, the Americans were strong enough in the South Pacific to switch to the offensive—an offensive of a novel sort, since it involved a succession of amphibious assaults on heavily defended islands, many of which were bypassed in the process and left for later mopping-up operations. This process of leapfrogging or "island-hopping" moved the Americans 1300 miles closer to Tokyo by mid-1944. During these same months, the British and Americans had opened a new front in the jungles of northern Burma, where they hoped to reopen the Burma Road over which supplies could be sent to their Chinese allies. Progress there was slow and exhausting, but by the summer of 1944 the attackers were beginning to wear down the Japanese resistance.

But the central focus of Allied attention continued to be western Europe. The long-awaited Channel crossing, delayed by the North African expedition and by British fears of a premature gamble, came at last on June 6, 1944. At the Teheran Conference in November 1943, the three major Allies had finally agreed on the date and character of the operation. The thrust into northern France would be supported by a secondary action directed against the southern French coast; Stalin promised to launch a simultaneous offensive in the east to tie down German forces that might otherwise be transferred to France. Churchill alone still expressed some reservations at Teheran, arguing for an expedition into the eastern Mediterranean that might bring Turkey into the war, and suggesting that a drive from the head of the Adriatic through the Ljubljana gap toward Vienna might be preferable to a landing in southern France. Stalin wrongly suspected that Churchill was once again trying to postpone the Channel crossing; in fact, Churchill's persistent interest in the Mediterranean theater probably stemmed from the fact that it was the only war zone where British forces predominated and might still score some glorious victories. Churchill's views were overborne by Roosevelt and Stalin, both of whom were determined to see the Western armies come to grips with the bulk of the German forces at the earliest possible moment.

The buildup for the Channel crossing had been under way since 1942. It was an undertaking of colossal proportions: no amphibious operation on this scale had ever been tried in the history of warfare. Two hundred thousand men, with all their vehicles and equipment, had to be landed during the first forty-eight hours on beaches heavily defended by mines and concrete bunkers. The initial spearhead had to be reinforced during the days that followed with a steady flow of men and matériel, building up to a total of 640,000 men at the end of eleven days. In the absence of port facilities for unloading all this cargo, two floating "Mulberry harbors" had to be prefabricated and towed across the Channel to provide safe anchorage. Ways had to be devised to conceal the concentration of huge troop formations and landing craft along the southern coast of England, in order to mislead enemy intelligence. Naval and air attacks had to be carefully coordinated with the troop sailings in order to soften up the German defenses. Most unpredictable of all, weather conditions over the Channel had to be calculated in advance, for an untimely storm might disrupt the entire operation.

The Allied planners had long debated the proper site of the landings. At first, they had taken for granted that the logical location would be the area between Le Havre and Boulogne, where the Channel was narrowest and the coastline least rugged. But the ill-fated Dieppe raid in August 1942 inspired some rethinking, and by the summer of 1943 the planners decided that the coast near Caen in Normandy was the only feasible site for a large operation. Although the water passage was three times longer, it seemed likely that a surprise could more easily be achieved there—especially if feints toward the narrows of the Channel could be made to look real. Four beaches spaced along a coastline of fifty miles were pinpointed for the initial landings. Beginning in March, the British and American strategic air forces were ordered to shift part of their effort from German industry to the transportation system of northern France. From mid-May, roads and railways were under such heavy attack that German military commanders in the area found it difficult even to meet for staff conferences to concert their plans. The *Luftwaffe* could provide little protection, for the shortage of aviation gasoline and of trained pilots left its large fighter force earthbound. On D-day, German airmen were able to fly only about five hundred sorties compared to three thousand flown by the American air force alone.

The Germans, meanwhile, had been bracing themselves for the invasion that was sure to come; but they were sharply divided as to the best plan of defense. Some commanders, like Marshal Rommel, forcefully argued that the Allied troops must be turned back on the beaches; once beachheads were established, they believed, the invaders could not possibly be dislodged. Rommel's experience in North Africa had given him a healthy respect for Allied material strength, if not for Allied strategic genius. The commander-in-chief in France, Marshal von Rundstedt, on the other hand, insisted that if the Anglo-Americans managed to gain precarious beachheads, they could then be overwhelmed by tank forces that would drive them back into the sea. Such a disaster, he believed, would shatter Allied morale and might change the course of the war. Rundstedt's scheme required that the bulk of the German armored forces be held in reserve, to be thrown into the battle only when the Allies had made their commitment beyond hope of withdrawal. Furthermore, holding back the German tanks would prevent their being wasted against a decoy landing that might precede the real thing. Hitler, who retained direct control of the armored reserves, opted for this latter tactic. He was also determined to keep his tanks so located that they might move either toward Boulogne or toward the Normandy beaches. Unlike most of his military advisers, however, he sensed that Normandy rather than Boulogne was the most likely point of attack.

Although unexpected bad weather interfered with the Allied timetable and came near forcing a month's postponement, the Normandy operation in the end went off almost on schedule and without major hitches. By evening on June 6, five seaborne and three airborne divisions were ashore. During the first week, the four beachheads were joined and pushed inland, against stubborn but inadequate German defenses. Hitler still suspected that this might be only a large-scale diversion, and refused at first to send either reinforcements or tanks to the scene. When it became clear that Normandy was the real battlefield, the armor began to arrive—too late. The Germans managed to keep the Allied forces hemmed in for more than a month; but late in July, the breakout occurred. American forces drove to the west and south, clearing Brittany and much of Normandy; then swung eastward, accompanied by the British and Canadians who had been held up near Caen. By the end of August, the retreating Germans had crossed the Seine, and Paris had been liberated by the French resistance movement, supported by American and Free French units.

Meanwhile, on August 15, the supplementary landing in southern France had been effected. The invaders this time included the First French Army, which had been chafing to participate in the liberation of the homeland. They met only slight resistance as they mounted the valley of the Rhône toward Lyon, and then swung eastward toward the German frontier. There, in September, they joined forces with the Normandy invaders, whose advanced units had been racing eastward in pursuit of the retreating Germans. For a time, Allied intelligence thought that German resistance might crumble, and that the war might end in 1944. But even now, under this relentless pounding on both eastern and western fronts, reinforced by newly intensified bombing of the Reich from the air, the Germans doggedly held on. Their stubbornness finally earned them a breathing spell. The American spearheads had moved too fast for their supply units; by September, a shortage of gasoline checked their headlong advance toward the Rhine. Meanwhile, in the Danube Valley, the German defenders of Budapest had dug in for a siege; and in East Prussia, German forces braced to defend the soil of the Old Reich against the Soviet attackers.

In the west, a brief but sharp controversy now erupted within the Allied command. General Bernard Montgomery, Britain's most charismatic battlefield hero, argued that Germany could be knocked out in 1944 if struck a powerful blow without delay. He urged that all the Anglo-American mechanized forces be placed under his command in Belgium for a strike across the Rhine, past the Ruhr Valley, and thence toward Berlin. General Eisenhower, who was more doubtful that Germany was on the verge of collapse and who was concerned about the problem of supply, opted instead for a more cautious broadfront strategy. In mid-September, however, he authorized Montgomery to try the first stage of his plan: an attempt to seize several key bridges across the lower Rhine in the Netherlands, and thus to outflank the northern end of Germany's Siegfried Line. Disaster followed. Airborne troops dropped at Arnhem on September 17 met unexpectedly stiff resistance, and the coup failed. The episode confirmed Eisenhower's faith in the broad-front strategy, and led to a pause of several months while Allied forces and supplies were built up for the spring campaign.

IV. THE END OF THE THIRD REICH

The Germans, confronted by overwhelming power on their western and eastern borders and by a threatened Russian breakthrough in the Danube Valley, faced a situation that to any rational man was hopeless. Some of Hitler's advisers had been trying to persuade the Fuehrer to divide his enemies by seeking a separate peace with the Western Allies who, they thought, might then join the Germans in resisting the advance of Soviet power. A few even favored transferring all German forces to the eastern front and leaving Germany's western frontier wide open to Allied entry. Another faction favored a quite opposite policy: an attempt to resurrect the German-Soviet pact of 1939, in the hope that Moscow might consent to halt its armies at the old German frontier. But the hour was far too late for either scheme

to succeed—if, indeed, either one could ever have been made operative. As for Hitler, he wasted no thought on either proposal—perhaps
because he recognized their chimerical nature, more likely because his
decisions, since the assassination attempt of July 20, were increasingly irrational. He insisted on no retreat in either east or west, and
refused to bolster either front at the expense of the other. Instead, he
drafted adolescent boys and combed out industry to form new divisions, and talked of miraculous salvation through new weapons or
through enemy weakness or division. But the time for effective new
weapons was past. The V-2 bases in the Netherlands would shortly be
captured by the Allies; the schnorkel submarine device had been designed too late; and the Messerschmidt jet plane, which came into
operational use in September 1944, could not by itself turn the tide.

Hitler's only effective move during the last winter of the war was
to reinforce the defenses of Budapest, thus temporarily checking the
Soviet threat from the southeast. A more dubious decision was his
order to carry out a sudden surprise attack on the western front. In
December, a powerful tank-led German force struck in the Ardennes
Forest region with a view to splitting the Allied front and driving
straight through to Antwerp, the great supply port for the Western
buildup. The offensive achieved only limited success; although it startled
and temporarily unnerved the overconfident Western troops, it fell far
short of destroying their morale as Hitler had hoped. Ten days sufficed to
check the Germans' advance; they had fruitlessly sacrificed more than
100,000 men and six hundred tanks desperately needed to slow the impending Allied invasion.

In February 1945, Eisenhower's forces began to crunch ahead all
along the line from Strasbourg to the North Sea. At about the same
time, Budapest fell at last to Soviet forces, for whom the road to Vienna
now lay open. In the north, the Red army began methodically to
destroy the long German salient stretching along the Baltic coast to
East Prussia, after which it would be free to strike toward Berlin. It
was the Western armies that moved most rapidly; the Rhine was
crossed early in March, and the Ruhr Valley was shortly cut off from
the rest of Germany. The speed of the advance forced Eisenhower
to consider plans for a junction with the Soviet forces moving westward. If no meeting-place were arranged, there might be accidental
clashes between the victors, as in Poland between the Germans and
Russians in September 1939. On March 28, Eisenhower wired his

plans to the Allied military mission in Moscow, asking that Stalin be informed. The Western commander declared his intention to liquidate the Ruhr pocket during April, and then to strike eastward into central Germany for a junction with the Soviet armies in the Leipzig-Dresden area, a hundred miles south of Berlin. His aim was to split the German defenses in two, and to be prepared to swing south if, as Allied intelligence predicted, the Germans attempted to withdraw into a heavily fortified "national redoubt" in the mountains of the south.

The British, who had not been consulted about this plan, were astonished and outraged at Eisenhower's action. They had argued all along that top priority should go to the capture of Berlin, both to end German resistance and to forestall the Russians for political and psychological reasons. But Eisenhower, backed by Marshall in Washington, stood firm; he would make Berlin a major objective, he declared, only if he were informed by his superiors that in this case political must outweigh military considerations. Stalin meanwhile had received Eisenhower's message, and indulging his customary suspicions had concluded that his western allies were trying to trick him. Eisenhower's real purpose, he decided, was to win the race to Berlin. Summoning Marshals Zhukov and Konev, Stalin ordered them to mount an attack on April 16, but at the same time sent a disarming message to Eisenhower declaring his approval of Western plans and his own intention not to attack until the second half of May. "Berlin," he declared, "has lost its former strategic importance."[2] Churchill, profoundly skeptical of Stalin's sincerity, redoubled his efforts to persuade Eisenhower to drive for Berlin; it was, he declared, "highly important that we should shake hands with the Russians as far to the east as possible." His plea failed; when American spearheads reached the Elbe river in mid-April, they were ordered to stop and await the arrival of the Russians.[3]

Thirty-five miles east of Berlin, Zhukov and Konev were meanwhile preparing their own all-Soviet race for the capital. On the morning of April 16, 1.5 million Soviet troops supported by enormous masses of artillery and tanks launched the final attack. The German defenders were outnumbered by at least two to one, and probably more; the city itself was garrisoned only by a hastily trained army of teen-age and overage recruits. Confronted by disaster, the Nazi estab-

---

[2] C. Ryan, *The Last Battle* (New York, 1966), pp. 215, 243–52.

[3] Similar restraint by Eisenhower in Czechoslovakia permitted Soviet troops to take Prague early in May. Here again, Churchill had urgently favored a race for the city.

lishment now at last began to disintegrate; there was a rush of party and government officials to escape to the south or the west. Hitler in March had ordered a scorched-earth policy—the destruction of every military and industrial installation that might be useful, "at once or in the future," to the enemy. His subordinates, led by Albert Speer, had dared at last to ignore a Fuehrer order, and had quietly sabotaged the scorched-earth scheme. In mid-April several ranking Nazis—among them Ribbentrop, Himmler, and Goering—had undertaken on their own to make contact with the Western Allies in hope of ending the slaughter and perhaps saving something of the Nazi system from the wreckage. Some of Hitler's closest intimates urged him to leave Berlin for an Alpine refuge, whence he might continue to direct resistance or might even escape abroad. Instead, Hitler stubbornly remained in the ruins of his chancellery, and methodically prepared his own exit. On April 29, he was shaken by the news of Himmler's "treason," and of Mussolini's execution by a partisan band as the Duce sought to escape into Switzerland. The next day, with Soviet troops only a few blocks away, Hitler dictated his last testament, naming Joseph Goebbels Reichschancellor and Admiral Karl Doenitz "president of the Reich." After a hasty marriage ceremony that bound him to his long-time companion, Eva Braun, Hitler left orders that his body be burned to avoid capture by the Russians, and shot himself. Doenitz, astonished at his sudden elevation to the top post in a disintegrating regime, tried for a separate armistice with the Western Allies, but was rebuffed. On May 7, therefore, in a dusty schoolhouse at Reims, Doenitz's representative accepted the Allied terms—unconditional surrender on all fronts. At midnight on the eighth of May, the European phase of the Second World War came to an end.[4]

[4] Soviet accounts place V-E day on May 9, when a formal ratification of the surrender terms was arranged, at Soviet insistence, in Berlin.

Chapter Ten

PREPARATION OF THE POSTWAR ERA

I. THE SHAPING OF ALLIED WAR AIMS

IN A simpler age than ours, peacemaking could be largely separated from war-making, and could be postponed until after the day of victory. In the twentieth century, on the other hand, war and its aftermath have come to interpenetrate in complex fashion. The combatants' hopes and fears about the future tend to shape the military and diplomatic conduct of the war; and conversely, the conduct of the war unavoidably influences that future. In the quest for allies, long-term commitments are made; and within each warring nation, minds are conditioned and emotions aroused by the tensions of a long-protracted struggle. Even the choice of battlefields and landing sites may influence the nature of the postwar settlement, since the presence of an occupation army may weigh heavily on the fate of a region.

But the central factor affecting the formulation of war aims in a coalition war is likely to be the conflict of national purposes within the victorious coalition. The simple fact that Britain, the USSR, and the United States entered the Second World War at different times and for different reasons demonstrates their divergent views of the nature of the war and the goals to be sought after victory. Unlike the British, neither the Russians nor the Americans had seen the defense of Poland in 1939 as adequate justification for embarking on a major war. Deeper still was the cleavage between the Soviet view of the Second World War and the view largely shared by the British and Americans. To the Soviet leadership, the war that began in 1939 had been a struggle among the capitalist states for power and spoils. But superimposed upon this conflict was a second and quite different war, beginning in 1941: a war of the "freedom-loving peoples" against unprovoked aggression. In this second war, as Soviet leaders saw it, the "freedom-lovers" were able to profit by the division within the capitalist world, and thus to utilize the power of one segment of that world against its own interests. To the Western powers, on the other hand, the conflict that began in 1939 was a single coherent struggle of

204

steadily-broadening scope—a struggle to avert world domination by three totalitarian or authoritarian regimes that challenged the basic values of the liberal-democratic age. Given the depth of these differences within the anti-Axis coalition, it was patently impossible for Anglo-American and Soviet leaders to deal with each other in a spirit of real mutual trust. Indeed, the roots of their mutual distrust can probably be traced back for a full generation, to the events of the First World War. One might argue that the war of 1939–1945 was superimposed upon an older and more enduring conflict within the Western world—a kind of international civil war that dated from 1917, and that was only partially and temporarily submerged when the Russians and the Anglo-Saxons were thrown together. Once the common enemy showed signs of weakening, that more profound conflict was sure to re-emerge.

During the early years of the struggle, the Western belligerents spent little energy reflecting on the distant question of war aims. Until 1940, British and French thinking rested on empty illusions about Germany's vulnerability to a long blockade; there would be plenty of time, it seemed, to work out plans for a postwar Europe. After France fell, the British were so desperately concerned with averting disaster that postwar planning would have been an unthinkable luxury. At best, they could try to attract allies by offering promises of postwar advantage. Such an effort directed at the Soviet Union in 1940 proved to be a miserable failure. The unorthodox Labour politician Sir Stafford Cripps, who was believed to be *persona grata* in Moscow, was named ambassador to the USSR, and dangled before Stalin the prospect of unopposed Soviet influence in the postwar Balkans. Stalin scorned the suggestion (and passed on word of it to Hitler). Perhaps Stalin's cold reception of the proposal indicated that he had no such ambitions in the Balkans; more probably it reflected his low estimate of Britain's ability to deliver the goods. At the time, it must have seemed a realistic judgment, given Britain's isolation and weakness.

An even more crucial necessity, as British leaders saw it, was the task of reinforcing American sympathy for the British cause and hastening, if possible, American entry into the war. To that end, Churchill was eager to show the Americans that his conception of the postwar world harmonized with theirs. In August 1941, Churchill and Roosevelt met off the Newfoundland coast to discuss their common goals. The resultant Atlantic Charter, based on a British draft, provoked memories of Woodrow Wilson's Fourteen Points during an earlier war: it was marked by the same tone of high idealism, and confined itself to general principles. The Charter bound its signers to make no postwar territorial changes contrary to the wishes of the inhabitants of such territories. It promised that forms of government would be freely chosen by each people, and that some kind of international security system would be established. A general framework for postwar planning was thus provided; there remained the more delicate task of applying principles to specific problems.

Shortly before this Atlantic conference, Hitler's attack on the Soviet Union had altered all perspectives. Churchill at once offered to send all possible aid that could be spared by Britain, and told his private secretary, when the latter remonstrated mildly: "If Hitler invaded Hell, I would at least make a favorable reference to the Devil in the House of Commons."[1] The Americans a few weeks later added their promise to provide "all practicable economic assistance." But Churchill failed in his attempt to extract a *quid pro quo*: a pledge by Stalin that after the common victory, the prewar boundary between Poland and the USSR would be restored. True, the Soviet government did announce in September that it adhered to the principles of the Atlantic Charter— but only with reservations to cover "the circumstances, needs, and historic peculiarities of particular countries." Furthermore, Stalin privately expressed some skepticism about the real war aims of the Anglo-Saxon powers, as distinct from the fine phrases of the Charter. Churchill therefore sent Foreign Minister Anthony Eden to Moscow in December 1941 for an initial discussion of war aims.

During the talks that followed, Stalin offered the first clear hint of his intentions. The British, he insisted, must agree to Soviet retention of all territory acquired during the period of the German-Soviet pact, and in addition must authorize Soviet acquisition of air bases in Rumania and air and naval bases in Finland. Stalin offered in return to approve whatever security arrangements the British might make for postwar bases in France, the Low Countries, Norway and Denmark. Eden, who had gone to Moscow planning to talk about such matters as the disarmament of postwar Germany and the creation of federal bonds linking the weaker European states, was taken aback by Stalin's

---

[1] Eighteen months later, Stalin was likewise to invoke Satan in approving the Americans' agreement with Darlan: "Military diplomacy should know how to use for the war aims not only the Darlans but the devil and his grandmother." A. J. Rieber, *Stalin and the French Communist Party 1941–1947* (New York, 1962), p. 19.

Realpolitiker line, and after consultation with Churchill, politely refused to make such territorial commitments. Stalin nevertheless continued to insist during the weeks that followed. In March 1942 Churchill reluctantly decided to accept Stalin's demands, partly in order to secure the Anglo-Soviet treaty of alliance he was seeking, and partly to strengthen the Soviet leaders' resolution to resist the impending German offensive of 1942. Roosevelt, however, firmly rejected what one of his advisers bluntly called a "Baltic Munich"; and he stood firm even after a personal visit by Soviet Foreign Minister Molotov to Washington. The President sought to divert Molotov by focusing attention on military preparations for a second front, and by sketching out his general plans for a postwar peace-keeping system that would associate the Soviet Union with Britain and the United States as a full partner. In May 1942, impelled perhaps by bad news of German victories in southern Russia, Stalin finally settled for what he could get: an Anglo-Soviet treaty of alliance without precise commitments on postwar frontiers. It was clear, however, that the question of eastern European boundaries was only postponed.

Within the Grand Alliance, the immediate issue of a second front necessarily pushed postwar planning aside. For the hard-pressed Soviet armies in 1942, a military diversion was of absolutely crucial importance; for the Americans, the sensible procedure was to win the war first, and then to tackle such postwar problems as boundaries. Yet whatever the Americans might prefer, postwar issues kept creeping forward to complicate the angry debate over the second front. Such was increasingly the case after the Battle of Stalingrad, when the Soviet leaders could at last raise their eyes above the immediate struggle for survival and could begin to plan the offensive that would carry them into the heart of Europe.

Five weeks after Stalingrad, Eden went to Washington for the first general Anglo-American discussion of postwar plans. Staffs of political and economic experts had been at work in the Foreign Office and the Department of State for some time, but their studies of various territorial and organizational problems were still in the preliminary stage. Nevertheless, both London and Washington thought it wise to compare notes without delay. Although no Soviet representative participated, the Soviet presence brooded over the conversations. Both the British and the Americans took for granted that the USSR would continue to demand retention of most if not all of the territory acquired between 1939 and 1941: the Baltic states, eastern Poland, Bessarabia, and a strip of Finnish soil. These demands they were generally prepared to accept for reasons of *force majeure*, though only on condition that Poland's losses in the east should not be excessive, and that these losses be balanced by Polish annexations in East Prussia and Silesia. At this stage, neither the British nor the Americans anticipated any serious territorial disputes in the Danube Valley or the Balkans, nor did they expect that the Soviet Union would try to dominate southeastern Europe.

Germany's future was discussed at Washington for the first time, though in a highly tentative way. Both powers, it was clear, were thinking in terms of a partitioned Germany, but their ideas on the subject had not yet crystallized. There was more extended discussion of tht future peace-keeping organization, and of the need to establish strategic bases throughout the world under its control. Roosevelt was inclined to favor a four-power directorate, in which the Americans and British would share with the Soviet Union and China the task of policing the world. Eden was more reticent on this point, for the British had been thinking of a world organization subdivided into regional bodies (such as a council of Europe), and of encouraging several federal groupings of the Continental European states.

Some of these smaller states had themselves been exploring the prospect of postwar federal ties. In London, the Czechoslovak and Polish governments-in-exile had discussed such an idea, even though the Czechs had not forgotten how the prewar Polish regime had joined Hitler in despoiling their territory. But the Soviet attitude toward all such federal schemes in either eastern or western Europe was coldly hostile. Stalin viewed them as devices by which the Western enemies of the Communist state would attempt to create a new *cordon sanitaire* along the USSR's borders, and would seek to convert western Europe into a chain of Anglo-American satellites. Indeed, there were signs by 1943 that the Soviet government would regard any Western-oriented regime along its frontier, whether federated with neighboring states or not, as an intolerable threat to Soviet security. Moscow's brusque rupture of diplomatic relations with the Polish government-in-exile in April 1943, and the establishment of a potential rival government of Polish exiles in Moscow, portended serious East-West tension over the future of eastern Europe.

Edouard Beneš, president of the Czechoslovak government-in-exile, nevertheless hoped that through his good offices this growing tension might be relaxed. Beneš's experience during the Munich crisis had left him favorably disposed toward Moscow, but somewhat disillusioned about his Western allies. His goal was a treaty with the USSR that would ensure the postwar stabilization of central Europe by guaranteeing Czechoslovakia's independence and territorial integrity, and that would restore the pre-Munich frontiers. Such a treaty, Beneš believed, might reduce the suspicion between the Atlantic powers and the Soviet Union by demonstrating Moscow's unselfish intentions. The British, however, objected strongly on the ground that none of the great powers ought to make separate wartime agreements with any individual small power. Such agreements, they held, would lead to competitive bargaining among the great powers, and would endanger their postwar collaboration. At the very least, the British argued, the pact ought to be a three-way affair that would include Poland as well. Beneš did his best to persuade Moscow to broaden the treaty in this fashion, but Stalin stubbornly refused to deal with the London Poles, and had no interest in encouraging a Polish-Czechoslovak rapprochement that might become the nucleus of an east European federation. After a deadlock of many months, the British reluctantly retreated, and a Soviet-Czechoslovak treaty was signed in December 1943. The USSR pledged itself not to interfere in Czechoslovak internal affairs, and to support the restoration of the pre-Munich frontiers. Stalin's promises, if taken at face value, seemed to prove his honorable intentions toward at least one country of east-central Europe. But the pact also constituted a roadblock against the emergence of a strong federation of the smaller powers in that part of the Continent. Whether Stalin's intentions at that stage were purely defensive in spirit, keyed to the idea of Soviet security alone, remained unclear to his Western partners. Likewise, viewed through the eyes of the Moscow leadership, British and American intentions doubtless seemed unclear. The Kremlin had not forgotten the *cordon sanitaire* era just after the First World War. Thus mutual suspicion continued to shadow the postwar planning of the three great powers as the liberation of the Continent drew near.

II. PLANNING FOR THE LIBERATION ERA

By the late summer of 1943, the postwar era was beginning to seem, for the first time, tantalizingly close. The Soviet armies were driving westward in a sustained advance that appeared likely to reach the old Soviet border within a few months. In Italy, Mussolini had fallen, and the Western Allies were negotiating surrender terms with the Badoglio government. Severe tensions were developing within Hitler's empire in southeastern Europe: Hungarian and Rumanian emissaries were seeking contact with the Western governments in an effort to arrange a separate peace, while in Yugoslavia and Greece the Communist and anti-Communist resistance groups were feuding and occasionally fighting each other. Polish-Soviet relations remained in a state of crisis, with neither side willing to give an inch. Soviet leaders continued to voice sporadic suspicions that the Western powers might betray them by negotiating a separate peace with the Germans; Western leaders feared that it was Stalin who might be tempted to withdraw from the war when his armies reached the old Soviet frontier, leaving the British and Americans to confront the Germans and Japanese alone.

Even in western Europe, the prospect of liberation posed some uncertainties. Charles de Gaulle plainly intended to assume immediate control in France as soon as the Germans were expelled; but his ambitions were threatened by the American government's coolness toward him personally and by Roosevelt's insistence that Frenchmen must be allowed free choice of their own future leadership. Despite British support of de Gaulle, the Americans pushed ahead with plans for a period of Allied military government in France during the immediate post-liberation period. In the other occupied nations of northwestern Europe, however, formal civil affairs agreements for the early transfer of administrative authority were amicably worked out between the Western powers and the various governments-in-exile.

The British even more than the Americans had now begun to look ahead to the liberation period, and to fret about the prospect that this final stage of the war might prejudice and even dictate the course of events in postwar Europe. If the nascent conflicts in eastern and southeastern Europe could not be damped down, they might escalate into a period of chaos there that would offer tempting possibilities of aggrandizement to the Soviet Union. Even if such chaos could be averted, the presence of invading armies would enable the dominant power to dictate its own solutions unless the Allies could reach prior agreement as to occupation zones and policies. Not only eastern Europe but Germany itself constituted a potential danger zone.

Until mid-1943, there had been only sporadic mention of such matters in inter-Allied talks. In July, the British government proposed that the three major Allies establish a "European commission" to concert plans for the liberation period and even beyond. The Americans, with some reservations, concurred. Stalin meanwhile seized upon the idea with enthusiasm, and sought to alter it to fit his purposes. The liberation period, he pointed out, had already begun; southern Italy was in Allied hands. It was time for the creation of a "military-political commission," for the Soviet leadership could no longer tolerate the conduct of its Western allies; they had been treating the USSR "just as a passive third observer." Stalin was obviously determined to get a major voice in the control of liberated Italy; he demanded that the new inter-Allied commission be based in Sicily, and that it be vested with broad powers in both the military and the political spheres.

The time had clearly arrived for high-level discussions. In October 1943, the American, British, and Soviet foreign ministers met for the first time in Moscow to examine both immediate issues and tentative plans for the liberation era. Stalin's demand for a voice in Italian affairs appeared to be met by the creation of an Advisory Council for Italy, with French as well as Soviet membership. In fact, however, this Council amounted to little more than a facade; real supervisory control in Italy was assigned to an Anglo-American Control Commission. The precedent thus established was to echo loudly some months later. "Having excluded Russia from any but nominal participation in Italian affairs, the Western Powers prepared the way for their own exclusion from any but a marginal share in the affairs of Eastern Europe."[2]

Other post-liberation problems, too, came before the foreign ministers at Moscow. A three-power European Advisory Commission, based in London, was set up to make studies and recommendations concerning the liberation period. Anthony Eden once again argued the British case for encouraging postwar confederations among the smaller states of Europe, and urged also that the powers adopt a self-denying ordinance against the creation of spheres of influence in Europe. But Molotov pushed aside both proposals. The idea of confederations, he declared, was "premature and even harmful," while talk of spheres of influence was ridiculous if it was supposed to apply to Soviet ambitions. In the end, both proposals were watered down into a much more general four-power declaration (China being the fourth signer). It bound the signatories to forgo the use of their armies in liberated or conquered countries for self-seeking purposes; to set up a general international organization as soon as possible; to consult together on

[2] W. H. McNeill, *America, Britain, and Russia: Their Cooperation and Conflict* (London, 1953), p. 309.

international problems pending the creation of that body; and to act jointly in receiving any enemy surrender. The foreign ministers carefully avoided the sensitive issue of eastern European boundaries, and confined themselves to generalities on the treatment of conquered Germany. Such matters were scheduled to be discussed at an even higher level during the first summit conference scheduled for Teheran in November.

The mood of harmony that pervaded the Moscow conference left all the participants with a new sense of hope; and that optimistic spirit seemed to be justified by the success of the Teheran Conference. For the first time, Churchill, Roosevelt, and Stalin met for a direct exchange of views, and discussed their differences in relatively amicable fashion. True, there were occasional sharp clashes, especially between Churchill and Stalin; but the session undoubtedly marked the high point of wartime cooperation among the three major allies. Stalin's long-standing irritation at the delay in opening a western front was allayed by a firm Anglo-American promise to mount a Channel crossing in the spring of 1944. Stalin in turn indicated his intention to join the struggle against Japan once Germany had been crushed. With these immediate issues cleared away, postwar problems could be approached in a less rancorous spirit.

Of all these problems, the most explosive was the fate of Poland. Stalin again bluntly asserted his determination to retain the 1941 frontier, and to absorb parts of East Prussia and Finland as well. Both Churchill and Roosevelt were now reluctantly prepared to consider these demands, on condition that Poland be compensated by the annexation of extensive German territories to the north and west. It was important, said Churchill, that the nations bearing responsibility for governing the postwar world should be satisfied nations; and one of these nations would of course be the Soviet Union. The Big Three arrived, therefore, at general agreement on a policy of "moving Poland westward"—probably as far as the Oder River. The precise location of the future Soviet-Polish boundary, however, produced considerable confusion. Stalin, in demanding the restoration of the 1941 frontier, showed a tendency to call it the Curzon Line.[3] Eden demonstrated that the 1941 frontier and the Curzon Line did not coincide exactly, and that the Soviet negotiators were actually demanding considerably

---

[3] The so-called Curzon Line, defined in a note signed by British Foreign Secretary Lord Curzon in 1920, represented an attempt to establish an approximate ethnographic frontier between Poland and Russia.

more than the Curzon Line. Stalin eventually agreed to settle for the Curzon Line, on condition that the Lvov region fall on the Soviet side of the border.

With respect to the fate of defeated Germany, there were somewhat sharper differences. Roosevelt and Stalin shared the view that Germany must be dismembered as insurance against future aggressive tendencies. Although Churchill concurred in principle, he preferred to stress the need to separate "militaristic" Prussia from the rest of Germany, and he proposed to merge the southern German states with Austria and Hungary in what he described as "a broad, peaceful, cowlike confederation." This scheme aroused Stalin's strong objections; all Germans were alike, he asserted, and any confederation that contained Germans would be used as a vehicle for revived German military power. Furthermore, he undoubtedly suspected Britain's motives in continually advancing the idea of small-state confederations. In the end, the problem of German dismemberment was handed over to the new European Advisory Committee for study and recommendation.

Although the Teheran Conference adjourned in an amicable and buoyant mood, there were some participants who nursed serious doubts. Churchill, despite his conviction that the USSR must be a satisfied state, feared that the effect of Soviet policy might be to "pulverize" Europe into a congeries of unhappy, divided, dependent states, clients of the rival great powers. This view was shared by at least one American participant, Charles E. Bohlen, who in a brief but cogent memorandum summed up his opinion of Soviet aims as revealed at Teheran:

Germany is to be broken up and kept broken up. The states of eastern, southeastern, and central Europe will not be permitted to group themselves into any federations or association. France is to be stripped of her colonies and strategic bases beyond her borders and will not be permitted to maintain any appreciable military establishment. Poland and Italy will remain approximately their present territorial size, but it is doubtful if either will be permitted to maintain any appreciable armed force. The result would be that the Soviet Union would be the only important military and political force on the continent of Europe. The rest of Europe would be reduced to military and political impotence.[4]

Indeed, the new note of harmony that had prevailed at Moscow and Teheran soon gave way to dissonance once more. The tentative decision of the Big Three to "move Poland westward" outraged the Pol-

[4] U.S. Department of State, *Foreign Relations of the United States: Conferences at Cairo and Tehran* (Washington, 1961), p. 846.

ish government-in-exile; and Churchill's repeated efforts to bring the Poles around ran into stubborn resistance. Churchill sought to persuade them that ". . . by taking over and holding firmly the present German territories up to the Oder, [the Poles] will be rendering a service to Europe as a whole by making the basis of a friendly policy towards Russia and close association with Czechoslovakia."[5] His argument was coldly received by the Poles, who were willing to annex German territory but who declared they had no authority to give up an inch of Polish soil. No doubt they recognized, too, one hidden consequence of the Teheran plan. It would almost certainly throw Poland and the Soviet Union together as bulwarks against German resurgence, and would thus strip Poland of its future freedom to maneuver between Germany and Russia. Nevertheless, by strenuous effort Churchill finally browbeat the reluctant Poles into accepting the Teheran plan, provided that some face-saving concessions be made to alter the eastern frontier line in Poland's favor. But these concessions Moscow brusquely refused to make. Once more the situation was deadlocked, and the future clouded.

Meanwhile, the Soviet authorities had begun to suspect the Anglo-Americans of nefarious designs in western Europe as well. In February 1944, the Soviet ambassador in Washington reported an alleged American scheme to create a bloc of puppet states to the west of Germany. Probably he had picked up rumors of a proposal advanced by the Belgian foreign minister, Paul-Henri Spaak, with the support of the Belgian, Dutch, and Norwegian governments-in-exile. Spaak advocated the formation of a postwar bloc that would include all of western Europe from Norway to the Iberian Peninsula. But Foreign Minister Anthony Eden had promptly squelched Spaak. It would be dangerous, Eden said, to organize either a western or an eastern European bloc, since one bloc would lead to another, and the two rivals would eventually begin to bid against each other for German support. Spaak vainly argued that the process was already under way in eastern Europe, where a Soviet-dominated bloc was in fact being built. Eden, aware of strong Soviet and American antagonisms to the idea of blocs, continued to evade the proposal throughout 1944, and to reassure Moscow that Soviet suspicions were groundless.[6]

---

[5] Churchill, *Second World War*, V, 450–51.

[6] Another advocate of a postwar "strategic and economic federation" of western Europe was Charles de Gaulle, whose plan would have included only France, the Low Countries,

In southern and southeastern Europe, too, the advance of the Allied armies brought new sources of discord. In Italy, where the Western powers had frustrated Soviet desires for an equal voice, the Soviet government sought to augment its influence by abruptly announcing an exchange of diplomatic representatives with the new Badoglio government. American and British protests were ignored; in the end, the Western powers had to swallow the *fait accompli*. In Yugoslavia, Moscow began to show a more active interest in Marshal Tito by sending an important mission to his headquarters, while in Greece, the Communist branch of the underground organized a Committee of National Liberation designed to compete with the Greek government-in-exile. Churchill in May 1944 asked himself whether it was not time for a frank confrontation on ". . . the brute issues between us and the Soviet Government. . . . Broadly speaking, the issue is, Are we going to acquiesce in the Communisation of the Balkans and perhaps of Italy?"[7] On reflection, however, Churchill avoided such a confrontation and sought instead to work out some sort of accommodation. In Yugoslavia the British abandoned Mihajlović in favor of Tito, and persuaded King Peter to replace the pro-Mihajlović men in his government-in-exile. They urged the new prime minister, Ivan Šubašić, to begin negotiations with Tito looking toward a combined government. Likewise in Greece, the British managed to persuade King George to admit several left-wing politicians to his exiled cabinet. In both cases, the Soviet government made no attempt to interfere.

These developments encouraged the British to believe that Moscow might be receptive to a broader and more formal *modus vivendi*: a geographical division of authority in southeastern Europe during the liberation period. In May 1944, Eden casually suggested to the Soviet ambassador that it might be convenient if Britain were to "take the lead in policy" with respect to liberated Greece, while the Soviets might do the same in Rumania. Moscow responded favorably to this suggestion, but inquired about the American attitude. The British therefore proceeded to sound out Washington, arguing that the proposed agreement would be binding only until the peace settlement, and that it would not prejudice the latter. But the Americans, sensing a concealed sphere-of-influence scheme, demurred. Roosevelt declared

the Rhineland (detached from Germany), and possibly Great Britain. C. de Gaulle, *Mémoires de guerre* (Paris, 1956), II, 618.

   [7] Churchill, *Second World War*, V, 72–73.

a preference for "consultative machinery to dispel misunderstanding and restrain the tendency towards the development of exclusive spheres."[8] Churchill did his best to overcome these American doubts. "No fate," he declared, "could be worse for any country than to be subjected in these times to decisions reached by triangular or quadrangular telegraphing. . . . Action is paralyzed if everybody is to consult everybody else about everything before it is taken. . . ."[9] Although Roosevelt reluctantly consented to a three months' trial of the British scheme, the American doubts were so obvious that the Russians chose to drop the matter.

Meanwhile, the British had begun to press strongly for a change in Western military plans that would, they contended, carry the Western armies into the Danube Valley in the late summer of 1944. Existing plans called for an Allied landing in southern France to support the Channel crossing scheduled for June. Immediately after the Channel operation was launched, Churchill and his generals began to argue vigorously for cancellation of the landing in southern France in favor of a substitute drive from the head of the Adriatic through the Ljubljana gap into the Hungarian plain. They contended that the southern French operation would be hazardous and wasteful, whereas their Adriatic scheme would disrupt Germany's defense plans throughout southeastern Europe and would force Hitler to divert troops from northern France. Their proposal had political overtones, for if successfully implemented, it might have brought Anglo-American forces into the central Danube Valley before the advancing Soviet troops could reach that point. But these implications of the scheme were seen mainly in the later retrospect of the Cold War; at the time, the British argued their case on strictly military grounds, and the Americans rejected it on the same grounds. The Americans expected the southern France landings to be quick and effective (which proved to be the case); and they believed that the British underestimated the risks of a drive through the Ljubljana gap. These American negatives were undoubtedly well based; but the consequence was to leave the Danube Valley as an undammed channel up which the Soviet armies could eventually flood all the way to Vienna and beyond.

Those Soviet forces had remained poised at the Rumanian frontier throughout the spring and early summer of 1944, while the main

---

[8] L. Woodward, *British Foreign Policy During the Second World War* (London, 1961), p. 293.

[9] Churchill, *Second World War*, VI, 75.

Soviet thrust into Poland and East Prussia was under way. In August they went into action, and burst across into Rumania. King Michael, who had been trying for some time to jettison his pro-Axis premier, Marshal Antonescu, and to get out of the war, now succeeded at last in a palace coup and appealed for an armistice. More than two weeks went by, however, before such an armistice was finally signed; and during those two weeks, the Soviet armies overran almost the entire country. American and British efforts to influence the armistice terms, and to acquire a significant voice in the tripartite Control Commission for Rumania, were brushed aside by Soviet officials, who argued that they were simply following the precedent set by the Western powers in Italy. The parallel, though not exact, was close enough to be both plausible and painful. One obvious difference was the fact that the Soviet-dictated armistice terms were not confined to strictly military provisions; they were designed to redraw the boundaries of Rumania in anticipation of the eventual peace settlement. The Rumanians committed themselves to return Bessarabia and northern Bukovina to the USSR, in return for which they would recover all or part of Transylvania from Hungary.

The Soviet government's determination to shape the future of Rumania without reference to the opinions of the Western Allies was now clear. That it intended to play the same role in Bulgaria soon became equally plain. The Bulgarians had managed to avoid declaring war on the USSR, and had sent no troops to the Soviet front. In September 1944, in a desperate attempt to escape catastrophe, the Bulgarians installed a new cabinet and opened armistice negotiations with the British and Americans. But before these negotiations could be concluded, the USSR suddenly declared war on Bulgaria, and Soviet troops poured across the frontier. This four-day war transformed the situation; in Sofia, a left-wing coalition seized power, and the Soviet authorities elbowed their way into control of the armistice proceedings. Despite some sharp recriminations by the Western powers, the USSR demanded and secured terms roughly like those that had been forced on Rumania.

With the path now open into Yugoslavia, Hungary, and Greece, it began to seem that the Soviet armed forces would fix an unshakable grip on all of southeastern Europe. Churchill, who had been fretting over this prospect for several months, was now more convinced than ever that an agreement on great-power responsibilities during the liberation period must be sought without delay. Roosevelt, who was in the midst of his re-election campaign, declared his inability to consider the question until after November, so Churchill decided to go to Moscow alone in quest of an agreement. On his arrival early in October 1944, Churchill immediately confronted Stalin with a practical proposal. He later recalled the episode in this fashion:

> The moment was apt for business, so I said, "Let us settle about our affairs in the Balkans. Your armies are in Rumania and Bulgaria. We have interests, missions, and agents there. Don't let us get at cross-purposes in small ways. So far as Britain and Russia are concerned, how would it do for you to have ninety per cent predominance in Rumania, for us to have ninety per cent of the say in Greece, and go fifty-fifty about Yugoslavia?" While this was being translated I wrote out on a half-sheet of paper:

Rumania	
Russia	90%
The others	10%
Greece	
Great Britain	90%
(in accord with	
U.S.A.)	
Russia	10%
Yugoslavia	50–50%
Hungary	50–50%
Bulgaria	
Russia	75%
The others	25%

> I pushed this across to Stalin, who had by then heard the translation. There was a slight pause. Then he took his blue pencil and made a large check upon it, and passed it back to us. It was all settled in no more time than it takes to set down.[10]

This remarkable bit of off-the-cuff diplomacy was, however, clouded by two uncertainties: could such an informal agreement, with its somewhat ambiguous percentages, be translated into working reality? And could the absent member of the Big Three, the United States, be persuaded to approve? During the weeks that followed, both questions seemed to receive at least a tentatively affirmative answer. Roosevelt, informed of the Moscow agreement by Churchill and by Ambassador

[10] Churchill, *Second World War*, VI, 227. Some subsequent haggling followed over these percentages, which were finally revised to 80-20 for Bulgaria and Hungary. Woodward, *British Foreign Policy*, p. 308.

Averell Harriman (who had sat in as an observer at the talks), responded cordially though somewhat noncommittally. And there were at least some encouraging signs that Moscow took the agreement seriously and intended to respect it. The ticklish question of how to manage "50–50" control of Yugoslavia did not have to be faced, since Tito's forces assumed the main task of liberating Yugoslavia.

Even the intractable Polish situation seemed at last to be on the way to possible solution, thanks to the Churchill-Stalin meeting. Churchill, in the midst of the Moscow talks, had summoned the leaders of the Polish government-in-exile to the Soviet capital, and had devoted his best effort to working out a compromise on frontiers and on the nature of the post-liberation government of Poland. Until almost the very end of the conference, the task had seemed hopeless. It was scarcely a propitious moment to seek Polish-Soviet harmony; the bitter memory of the recent Warsaw uprising, and the USSR's unwillingness or inability to save the beleaguered city from destruction, loomed up in all minds. Polish Prime Minister Mikolajczyk was willing to consider broadening his government-in-exile, but not in such fashion as to give the Soviet-sponsored Polish Committee of National Liberation a controlling voice. As for the Soviet-Polish frontier, he flatly refused to accept Stalin's demand for the Curzon Line, even if Poland were to be compensated in the west at Germany's expense. Stalin's position was equally harsh and stubborn, and the talks seemed totally deadlocked. Yet at the very end, there was a slight thaw in the frigid atmosphere. Mikolajczyk reluctantly agreed to try to persuade his London colleagues to accept the Curzon Line, and promised to form a government that would be friendly though not subservient to the Russians. Stalin, in more jovial mood, seemed for the first time inclined to restrain the ambitions of his Polish Communist protégés. This ray of light, together with the agreement on apportioning responsibilities in southeastern Europe, sent Churchill home in much more sanguine mood. "Our relations with the Soviet Union," he told the House of Commons in a burst of enthusiasm, "were never more close, intimate and cordial than they are at the present time."[11]

III. CRACKS IN THE GREAT COALITION

The cautious optimism inspired by the Moscow conference, and encouraged by certain events of the weeks that followed, was to be of

[11] Great Britain, *Parliamentary Debates (Commons)*, CLIV (Oct. 27, 1944), p. 491.

short duration. Even before the next summit conference at Yalta in February 1945, Churchill was privately expressing to Roosevelt his growing disenchantment. "This may well be a fateful Conference," he wrote, "coming at a moment when the Great Allies are so divided and the shadow of the war lengthens out before us. At the present time I think the end of this war may well prove to be more disappointing than was the last."[12]

The reasons for this darkening mood, just at the moment when ultimate triumph in Europe was coming clearly into view, are not hard to discover. For one thing, the tentative beginnings of agreement on the Polish question broke down almost immediately after the Moscow conference. Within a month, the Soviet government and the London Poles were again exchanging bitter charges of bad faith and devious intentions. Prime Minister Mikolajczyk, frustrated in his effort to work out a compromise, resigned in November; his successor was more stubbornly determined to give no ground in the struggle with the USSR. Early in January 1945, Moscow promoted its Polish National Committee to the status of a provisional government, thus bringing an open breach that the British and Americans had desperately tried to avert.

Somewhat less intense, but adding to the general tension, were the continuing sources of irritation throughout southeastern Europe. In Rumania and Bulgaria, the Soviet occupation authorities ruled in arbitrary fashion, ignoring the British and American members of the control commissions, and tolerating or encouraging the agitation and intrigues of the local Communists. It was still not clear whether the Soviet goal was to turn these countries into outright satellites, but some Western observers on the spot now believed this to be the case. In Yugoslavia, too, the situation was beginning to cause concern. British pressure helped to bring about, in December 1944, an agreement between Tito and Ivan Šubašić, prime minister of the government-in-exile, for the merger of their two governments. It committed the two signers to hold free elections within three months after total liberation of the country, and to delay the return of the king until the nation had spoken on its future regime. But the projected merger was to be a highly unequal one: twenty-five of Tito's men to three of Šubašić's. The British, believing this to be the best they could get, persuaded the reluctant King Peter to approve. They can scarcely have been very

[12] Churchill, *Second World War*, VI, 341.

optimistic, however, about the prospects for Western-style democracy in Yugoslavia. In Hungary, the imminent fall of Budapest to Soviet arms was producing sharp conflict over the wording of the armistice terms and the machinery for inter-Allied control there. The Western powers were determined to avoid the trap into which they had fallen in Rumania and Bulgaria; they demanded genuine equality on the Hungarian control commission. But once again the Soviet authorities were adamant. Molotov put the situation quite baldly: "It was not necessary for the Soviet Union to conclude an armistice with Hungary since the Red Army was practically the master of that country. It could do what it wished."[13] London and Washington were offered a harsh but simple choice: to let the USSR control occupied Hungary, or to challenge Soviet pretensions by force.

Counterbalancing all these irritants, of course, was the Soviet Union's effective cooperation in the military sphere during the winter months of 1944–1945, and Stalin's hands-off policy in Greece during the bloody civil conflict that erupted there in December and January. When it seemed that the Greek Communists might succeed in their attempt to overthrow the non-Communist government, British occupation forces actively intervened to tip the balance. No hostile word or action came from Moscow. Perhaps the Soviet armies were too busy elsewhere to interfere; more probably, Stalin was respecting his agreement with Churchill, which had placed Greece under British control during the liberation period. No doubt the Western leaders would have understood Stalin better if they had been privileged to hear his confidences to Tito during the latter's visit to Moscow in April 1945: "This war [declared Stalin] is not as in the past; whoever occupies a territory also imposes on it his own social system. Everyone imposes his own system as far as his army can reach. It cannot be otherwise."[14]

But the Western Allies could only guess at what was really in the minds of their Soviet counterparts. It was in a mixed mood of skepti-

[13] H. Feis, *Churchill, Roosevelt, Stalin* (Princeton, 1957), p. 548.

[14] M. Djilas, *Conversations with Stalin* (New York, 1962), p. 114. During an earlier visit in June 1944, Djilas was told by Stalin: "Perhaps you think that just because we are the allies of the English we have forgotten who they are and who Churchill is. They find nothing sweeter than to trick their allies. . . . And Churchill? Churchill is the kind who, if you don't watch him, will slip a kopeck out of your pocket. . . . And Roosevelt? Roosevelt is not like that. He dips in his hand only for bigger coins. But Churchill? Churchill—even for a kopeck." Djilas, p. 73.

cism, irritation, and cautious hope that Roosevelt and Churchill flew to Yalta in February 1945 for the second of the wartime summit conferences. Churchill, despite his rising pessimism, still insisted that "the only hope for the world is the agreement of the three Great Powers. If they quarrel, our children are undone."[15] Roosevelt shared this view, and held to his faith that a durable understanding was still possible.

At Yalta, the central concern had shifted from winning the war to shaping the postwar era. With Allied armies on German soil in both east and west, decisions on the future of Germany could no longer be postponed. The Big Three, on the basis of proposals worked out by the European Advisory Commission, agreed on the assignment of occupation zones; and despite Stalin's reluctance, assigned a zone to the French as well. Much more difficult were the problems of reparations and limits on German industrial power. Only four months earlier, at the Quebec conference, Churchill and Roosevelt had tentatively adopted the so-called Morgenthau Plan, which proposed to turn Germany into an essentially agrarian society. But by the time Yalta convened, cooler heads had prevailed in London and Washington, and the Western powers favored a less drastic de-industrialization policy. Stalin, on the other hand, still insisted on a severe settlement, designed not so much to punish the Germans for past crimes as to secure reparations for damage done and to erect safeguards against future German aggression. Stalin proposed reparations in kind (machinery, raw materials, etc.) to a value of twenty billion dollars, with half of the total to be assigned to the USSR. Both the British and the Americans considered such a figure unrealistic, on the ground that it would force outside suppliers to feed and support an indigent Germany. The conference finally assigned the problem to a three-power reparations commission for further study.

Stalin also raised the issue of the partition of postwar Germany—an issue that had been discussed somewhat sporadically during the war years. At Teheran in 1943, the Big Three had talked informally of dismemberment, and all had seemed to favor it in one form or another. At Yalta, Stalin pressed for a firm decision, but found both Churchill and Roosevelt somewhat more reluctant now. American State Department and British Foreign Office officials had been opposed to partition all along, and had been urging their case on their respective leaders.

[15] Woodward, *British Foreign Policy*, p. 462.

They doubted that a dismembered Germany would contribute to long-term stability in central Europe, and at least some of them feared that partition would enable the Soviet Union to absorb eastern Germany as a client state.[16] Stalin's insistence at Yalta was blunted by these Anglo-American doubts, and the Big Three finally assigned the problem to still another three-power committee for further study. During the months that followed Yalta, British and American policy hardened against partition, and Stalin himself reluctantly abandoned the idea—perhaps out of fear that the Western powers might outbid him in a contest for influence in Germany. The Soviet propaganda line toward Germany softened during the spring of 1945, and Stalin's victory statement immediately after Germany's surrender explicitly ruled out dismemberment as a Soviet aim.

The persistent issues of eastern Europe also occupied much of the conference time at Yalta. Poland, as usual, was the most intractable of these. A pro-Soviet provisional government headed by Boleslaw Bierut had now been installed in Warsaw, and enjoyed Soviet recognition. Churchill and Roosevelt could hope for nothing better than to achieve a merger between the Bierut regime and the London government-in-exile. After long wrangling, Stalin accepted an ambiguously worded agreement to "reorganize" the Bierut government by adding several ministers from the London group and from the Polish underground. Stalin also assured his Western colleagues that free elections would be held as soon as the war ended—perhaps within a month; but he would not hear of provision for international supervision of these elections. On the vexed question of the Polish-Soviet frontier, the Western powers formally agreed to the Curzon Line, with slight modifications in favor of Poland. But new friction developed over the issue of territorial compensations to Poland in the west. In earlier discussions, the Big Three had talked of placing the Polish-German frontier at the Oder River and its tributary, the eastern Neisse. At Yalta, Stalin insisted on extending the new Poland all the way to the western Neisse, thus incorporating an additional area west of the upper Oder that contained a solidly German population of 2.7 million people. This arrangement, as the Western leaders could not fail to see, would virtually guarantee permanent tension between Poland and Germany,

[16] The British Chiefs of Staff, on the other hand, favored partition on the ground that at least part of Germany might thus be saved for the West if the wartime coalition with the USSR were to break down.

and would be likely to increase Poland's dependence on the Soviet Union. Churchill protested: "It would be a great pity," he declared, "to stuff the Polish goose so full of German food that it died of indigestion."[17] The forcible expulsion of so many millions of Germans from that area, Churchill argued, would cause grave difficulties. In the end, the Western leaders held firm on this issue. Poland, the Big Three agreed, would receive "substantial accessions of territory," but its western frontier would not be defined until the peace conference.

These Yalta decisions on Germany and eastern Europe dealt with a series of *ad hoc* problems, and fitted together into no very coherent pattern. To the American representatives at Yalta, there was need to assert an overarching principle that might check and control selfish ambitions during the crucial post-liberation months, and might serve as a point of reference for settling future disputes. The Americans therefore proposed a Declaration on Liberated Europe, asserting in general terms the ideals to which the major powers had subscribed at various times during the war. The three powers were asked to state their intention to assist the liberated peoples, "during the temporary period of instability" that would follow the end of hostilities, "to solve by democratic means their pressing political and economic problems." The Declaration called for "the earliest possible establishment through free elections of governments responsive to the will of the people," and bound its signatories to consult together on the implementation of these promises. The Declaration was briefly and sketchily discussed toward the end of the conference, and was accepted by Stalin with only minor changes. The American delegates departed with the comforting conviction that a major victory had been achieved. The Soviet government, they believed, had conceded a principle which it would henceforth hesitate to violate in flagrant fashion. Its word had been given to help re-establish free governments by democratic means and through free elections; and it had promised to act through consultation with its allies rather than through arbitrary unilateral measures.

Subsequent events were to reveal the flaw in this American assumption. The Declaration on Liberated Europe, it soon became clear, had rested on a basic misunderstanding. As the Americans saw it, the Declaration could not be reconciled with the spirit of the Churchill-Stalin agreement made at Moscow; its acceptance had therefore swept that earlier agreement into the discard. Spheres of influence and

17 Churchill, *Second World War*, VI, 374.

"90% responsibility" could not be harmonized with the new commitments which Stalin had taken on at Yalta. But the Soviet view of the matter, so far as it can be determined from Soviet words and actions, seems to have been quite different. The Americans, Stalin assumed, wanted the Yalta Declaration simply for purposes of propaganda and window dressing. Its fine phrases, like those of the Atlantic Charter, would be useful for mass consumption at home and in Europe, but were not intended to be taken as a guide for action. If the Americans had intended the Declaration as a substitute for the Moscow agreement—so the Kremlin presumably reasoned—they would have said so in explicit fashion. In fact, the Americans had asserted no such connection between the two documents; therefore the Moscow agreement remained in effect by tacit consent. It is likely that the American negotiators, in their eagerness to win Soviet acceptance, had failed to recognize how serious this difference of interpretation might be. Or perhaps they may have thought that once Stalin had been persuaded to sign, the Western powers could more easily pull him, bit by bit, toward the Western conception of democracy in eastern Europe.

The post-Yalta era was to bring complete frustration of these American hopes; and the arguments that ensued over Soviet violations of the Yalta Declaration served only to increase resentment both in Moscow and in the West. Rumania provided the first test case. Less than two weeks after Yalta, rising agitation in Bucharest led to violent clashes between the police and Communist critics of the rather conservative coalition government. British and American attempts to act through the Control Commission were frustrated by a Soviet refusal to call it into session. Instead, Moscow dispatched Andrei Vishinsky to Bucharest to take things in hand. Vishinsky wasted no time in palaver; he ordered King Michael to name a new cabinet based on "the truly democratic forces of the country," and when matters dragged a bit, gave the king two hours to comply. In the end, it was Vishinsky who hand-picked the new premier, a compliant politician named Petru Groza, and who browbeat the king into appointing a government heavily loaded with "truly democratic" ministers. The Control Commission was ignored throughout; and protests from Washington and London went unheeded. There was little the Western powers could do save to refuse recognition of the Groza government.

The situation in Bulgaria was equally exasperating. There, the coalition cabinet was already dominated by the Communists and was responsive to Moscow's wishes. Again, the Americans and British tried unsuccessfully to get a voice in decision-making, and proposed tripartite agreement on safeguards to ensure fair postwar elections. Moscow's response was chilly; such "foreign interference," it declared, would be offensive to the new Bulgarian leadership. In Hungary, where the Moscow agreement called for "80–20" control, matters were not much better. After Budapest fell on February 13, the Soviet authorities permitted the establishment of a genuine coalition cabinet; but here again the tripartite Control Commission was bypassed by the Soviet commander, and Soviet troops hastened to exact reparations by stripping the country of equipment and foodstuffs. In Yugoslavia, the Tito-Šubašić agreement of 1944 finally produced a merger, in March 1945, between Tito's faction and the government-in-exile; but the new government quickly revealed itself to be a mere facade for Tito's absolute control. A disillusioned Churchill wrote off Tito as "thoroughly unreliable, a communist, and completely under the domination of Moscow."[18]

On the other hand, the course of events in Finland and Czechoslovakia seemed at least slightly more encouraging. The Soviet-Finnish armistice of September 1944 did not even call for a military occupation of the country, and the Finns were allowed to hold genuinely free elections in March 1945. The Czechoslovak situation was more complex. Stalin, in the 1942 treaty of alliance, had promised to keep hands off the country's internal affairs and to respect its pre-Munich frontiers. President Beneš in turn had promised to broaden his government-in-exile to include some of the Czechoslovak Communist leaders who had been living in Moscow in exile. In October 1944 the Red army crossed the old Czechoslovak border and rapidly liberated the easternmost province (variously called Ruthenia, Subcarpathian Russia, or Subcarpathian Ukraine). Communist activists at once staged "elections" of so-called "national committees," much like the Soviets of 1917 Russia; and these committees called for the annexation of the province to the USSR. When Beneš protested, Stalin explained that his government could not forbid the local population "to express their national will," and would therefore have to annex the area.

Beneš, reconciling himself to this loss, left London for Moscow in March 1945 and proceeded to reorganize his government. Although non-Communists remained in the majority, the eight Communist

18 Quoted in J. L. Snell, *Illusion and Necessity* (Boston, 1963), p. 168.

ministers held most of the key posts, and the new premier, Zdeněk Fierlinger, was a dedicated fellow-traveler. Beneš also agreed to legalize the powers of the local and regional "national committees," and to make them the political base upon which liberated Czechoslovakia would be built. All of the old right-wing parties were outlawed on grounds of collaboration; a program of drastic socio-economic reforms, drafted by the Communists, was adopted virtually intact. After making these concessions to Moscow's wishes, Beneš found the road to Prague at last open to him and his coalition government. There seemed to be at least some prospect that Czechoslovakia might re-emerge as an independent state.

But these mildly hopeful signs, if they partially counterbalanced Soviet arbitrariness in southeast Europe, were seriously shadowed by the continuing deadlock over Poland. The Yalta agreement had provided for a reorganization of the Soviet-sponsored Bierut government in Warsaw; but angry controversy followed over the interpretation and implementation of this agreement. To the Western powers, it seemed increasingly plain that Moscow's idea of reorganization was a merger on the lines of the old recipe for horse-and-rabbit stew: one horse and one rabbit. Stalin and Molotov, on the other hand, kept up a steady fire of charges that the British and Americans were scheming to install an anti-Soviet regime in Warsaw, on the very borders of the USSR. By mid-March, the trend of events in eastern Europe led Churchill to write despairingly to Roosevelt of ". . . a great failure and an utter breakdown of what was settled at Yalta."[19] Roosevelt, somewhat less gloomy despite the evidence of deepening hostility, and still inclined to think of himself as a mediator between Churchill and Stalin, kept trying for an accord on Poland; and after Roosevelt's death on April 12, so did his successor, President Truman. The effort was futile; indeed, the tension over Poland only grew worse. In April, ignoring Western protests, Moscow negotiated a treaty of mutual assistance with Bierut's still unreconstructed Polish Provisional Government. Shortly thereafter, the West learned that sixteen top leaders of the anti-Communist Polish underground, tempted out of hiding in Warsaw by a Soviet safe-conduct, had been whisked off to prison in Moscow and held incommunicado for several weeks while the Soviet government professed ignorance of their whereabouts. If any further irritant were needed, it was furnished by Moscow's stubborn insistence

[19] Churchill, *Second World War*, VI, 426.

on fixing the Polish-German boundary at the western Neisse river. As the Russian armies advanced, they promptly turned over administrative control of this territory to the Poles, who began at once to expel the remaining German residents. The Russians clearly intended to confront the future peace conference with a *fait accompli*.

The fate of eastern Europe had thus become the chief focus of conflict within the Grand Alliance. But as the war neared its conclusion, other issues also contributed to the emergent tension and suspicion. The imminence of victory was rapidly stripping away the temporary scaffolding of mutual trust and cooperation that had partially concealed a grimmer reality: the deep-seated mutual suspicion that had marked Soviet-Western relations ever since 1917. One suggestive episode was an abortive German effort, early in 1945, to arrange a surrender of the German forces in northern Italy. In February, an SS general named Karl Wolff approached the British and Americans with a proposal to try to negotiate such a surrender. The Western powers agreed to arrange exploratory talks in Switzerland, and so informed Moscow. A long and angry dispute ensued between Stalin and the Americans. Stalin demanded full Soviet participation in these talks from the outset; the Americans demurred, on the ground that Soviet forces were not engaged on the Italian front, and because they privately suspected a Soviet intention to delay the negotiations until victory had been won on the eastern front. By April, Stalin was bluntly accusing his western allies of negotiating with the Germans behind his back, and of permitting the transfer of several German divisions from Italy to the eastern front. Although Stalin's charges of bad faith were unfounded, he was doubtless convinced of their validity.

This rising suspicion was fed by the fact that in April German resistance in the west began to crumble, while the German armies in the east continued to put up a stubborn last-ditch fight. The Soviet leaders concluded that the Germans were seeking, or had already secured, an accommodation with the Western powers in order to present a common front to the advancing Soviet forces. That some high Nazis hoped for such a switch in policy is clear enough; but they received not the slightest encouragement from the British and Americans. Unconditional surrender, addressed to all three of the major Allies, remained the staunch demand of the Western leaders; and it was on those terms that an armistice was eventually signed on May 7.

While Moscow nursed its false fears of a Western "double-cross," Western leaders were growing steadily more disillusioned about Soviet intentions in central as well as eastern Europe, and about the prospect of continuing the wartime alliance into the postwar era. Churchill in particular had lost his optimism, and had concluded by March 1945 that the only barrier to another great war would be to deploy the vast military strength of the United States and Britain against the onrush of Soviet power. With firm support from his diplomatic and military advisers, Churchill now began to advocate a policy of confrontation. The Western armies, he urged, should push forward at full speed as far as their momentum would allow; and on meeting the Soviet armies, should stand fast at that line until Moscow would accept a satisfactory agreement on the character of postwar Europe. This was a plan that embodied some risk of a clash between the Western and Soviet armies. It implied, too, that Anglo-American military strength might have to remain committed to central Europe for years to come. At the time, none of the top American leaders were willing to face that prospect. Eisenhower remained convinced that his decisions should rest on military considerations alone, unalloyed by political factors. He therefore continued his plan for a broad-front advance, designed to achieve a junction with the Soviet armies in central Germany along the Elbe River, and to permit a secondary thrust southward toward the Danube to grapple with possible last-ditch German resistance in some kind of Alpine redoubt. Truman gave Eisenhower firm support against the rising British pressure to race the Russians to Berlin and Prague. The Americans, though disturbed at the morbid suspicions and abrasive conduct of the Soviet government, still clung to the hope that patience and restraint might yet avert an open clash within the Grand Alliance. Churchill's policy of confrontation, they feared, would destroy the last chance for negotiated settlement in Europe, and would also deprive the Americans of Soviet aid in the final phase of the war against Japan. Besides, confrontation would probably be futile, since it would only ensure that the USSR would fasten its unilateral grip on much of Germany, Czechoslovakia, and Austria as well as on eastern Europe. And the implication of the Churchill policy—that American troops might have to remain in strength in the heart of Europe for an indefinite period—was too shocking for American leaders to absorb. Late in April, therefore, Eisenhower ordered the Western forces to hold at the Elbe, and pulled back such small units as had pushed beyond it toward Berlin and

Prague. Soviet troops fought their way into the center of Berlin on May 2, and entered Prague a week later. Meanwhile, on May 7, General Alfred Jodl had signed an act of unconditional surrender to both the Western and the Soviet governments. The end of the war in Europe was officially proclaimed by the British and Americans on May 8; Stalin delayed his victory proclamation until May 9, in order to permit a formal ratification ceremony in Berlin.

IV. FROM WARTIME ALLIANCE TO COLD WAR

Although the war in Europe was over, a cloud of uncertainty still hung over the conquered heart of the Continent, and over the fate of the wartime coalition as well. The victors had not yet reconciled their differences over the treatment of conquered Germany; in Austria, the triumphant Russians had set up a provisional government despite Anglo-American protests; and at the head of the Adriatic there was a serious threat of conflict as Tito's partisan forces moved in to seize control of Italian territory around Trieste. The atmosphere was chilled too by an American presidential order on May 8 abruptly suspending further Lend-Lease deliveries to the European Allies. This action, required by a literal interpretation of the terms of the Lend-Lease Act, threatened to be equally injurious to the British and the Russians; but it was the Russians who viewed it most resentfully. They took it to be a gesture of hostility, a weapon designed to force Soviet compliance in postwar negotiations and to slow the pace of Soviet reconstruction. Whatever may have been Washington's motives, the episode added a new source of conflict at a crucial moment.[20]

The problems of Austria and Trieste, however, proved to be manageable ones. In Vienna, which had been captured by Soviet forces on April 13, the Soviet authorities had sponsored the establishment of an Austrian provisional government under the Socialist Karl Renner. This unilateral action irritated the Americans and British, who refused to recognize Renner and demanded that Western missions be allowed to come to Vienna at once to survey the situation. The Russians evaded this request until mid-May, when Allied representatives were at last allowed to fly into the city. All three powers shortly recognized the Renner government, and (along with the French) arrived at a satis-

[20] Gar Alperovitz, in *Atomic Diplomacy: Hiroshima and Potsdam* (New York, 1965), pp. 35–39, demonstrates that at least some of Truman's advisers were set on what he calls a "showdown strategy," and viewed the Lend-Lease cutoff as a weapon to that end.

factory division of Austria into four occupation zones. In the Trieste area, Tito's men occupied most of the province of Venezia Giulia and were about to take over the city itself when British Commonwealth troops were landed to forestall them. Truman, despite British urging, had been reluctant to challenge the Yugoslavs: "I wish," he told Churchill, "to avoid having American forces used to fight Yugoslav forces or being used in combat in the Balkan political arena."[21] In the end the presence of the British troops kept Trieste out of Tito's hands, although most of the city's hinterland remained permanently under Yugoslav control.

There remained the central problem of conquered Germany. True, dismemberment had evaporated as an issue on May 9, when Stalin's victory proclamation said bluntly that "the Soviet Union . . . does not intend either to dismember or to destroy Germany." Only the French continued to push their demand that the Rhineland, the Ruhr Valley, and Westphalia be separated, politically as well as economically, from the rest of Germany. Yet as partition disappeared as a long-range policy objective, it threatened to re-emerge as a more immediate and practical reality. The four occupation zones defined at Yalta were, according to the agreement, to be administered under a common set of rules applied by a four-power control council. But the victors were still at odds about the nature of those rules. Unless agreement could be reached, the occupation zones would be rapidly transmuted into rigidly separate states, clients of either their eastern or their western neighbors. A new summit conference was clearly necessary, if anything were to be salvaged of wartime hopes for a stable central Europe.

That conference, delayed for some weeks by Truman's reluctance, finally convened at Potsdam in mid-July.[22] Roosevelt's absence meant a change in the tone of top-level discussions, even though Truman relied for the most part on the same advisers who had served his predecessor. Midway through the conference, an even more startling change brought Clement Attlee to Potsdam in place of Churchill, whose party went down to a resounding defeat in the British parliamentary elections. Lone survivor of the wartime Big Three, Stalin's figure domi-

---

[21] J. C. Grew, *Turbulent Era* (Boston, 1952), II, 1477.

[22] Alperovitz, in *Atomic Diplomacy*, contends that Truman postponed the conference until after the first atomic-bomb tests, so that he might use the bomb as a diplomatic weapon in negotiating with Stalin. It seems probable that Secretary of War Stimson and Secretary of State Byrnes did advocate that strategy; it is less certain that Truman accepted it.

nated the scene at Potsdam. But if the men were new, it was the same old issues that engaged their attention: Poland, southeastern Europe, the treatment of Germany.

Shortly before Potsdam, a new step toward breaking the Polish deadlock had been taken. Roosevelt's long-time confidant Harry Hopkins, sent on a special mission to Moscow by Truman, managed to get negotiations started again. Late in June, the two hostile factions of Polish leaders met in Moscow and worked out an agreement for reorganization of the Polish government. Six pro-Western Poles were added, including Mikolajczyk as deputy prime minister. This concession sufficed to bring recognition of the reorganized government by the Western powers. But two stubborn issues remained: a guarantee of free elections in Poland, and the location of the Polish-German frontier. On the election issue, nothing the Western delegates could do would budge Stalin or Bierut; the very suggestion of outside observers at the elections was termed a slight to Poland's national honor. Indeed, Bierut went so far as to assure an astonished Churchill that the Polish elections "would probably be more 'democratic' than those in Great Britain."[23] The best that could be attained was a grudging promise that the elections would be scheduled early in 1946. Stalin proved equally immovable on the question of the Polish-German frontier. The Poles were solidly in control as far as the western Neisse river, and the Western powers could find no way to break their grip. After lengthy wrangling, they agreed to leave the area between the upper Oder and the western Neisse under Polish administration pending a peace treaty, but insisted that final disposition of the area must await that treaty. The Bierut who returned to Warsaw must have been a jubilant man.

The Western powers were equally frustrated in their attempts to reverse the trend of events in southeastern Europe. They reminded Stalin of the oft-violated Yalta Declaration on Liberated Europe, and insisted that he agree to supervised elections in Rumania, Bulgaria, and Hungary. They complained too that Tito had violated the promises contained in the Tito-Šubašić agreement—that instead of restoring democratic liberties, he had shackled the press and established a police state in Yugoslavia. Stalin bluntly rejected these accusations, and declared himself "hurt" by such charges. He had no intention of "Sovietizing" the countries of southeastern Europe, he declared; elections there would be free for all non-fascist parties. It was only in

[23] Woodward, *British Foreign Policy*, p. 544.

Greece, he asserted, that democracy was being flouted and promises broken. Terrorism against democratic elements was rampant there, and the Greek government was threatening to attack its peaceful neighbors. But behind this verbal smoke screen, Stalin's real concerns were not hard to detect. Indeed, Stalin himself put it with brutal frankness during a private conversation: ". . . any freely elected government [in eastern Europe] would be anti-Soviet and that we cannot permit."[24]

The German problem was almost as intractable. The powers did officially bury the idea of partition by agreeing to treat Germany (within its 1937 frontiers) as a single unit; and they did arrive at partial agreement on reparations. The Russians were authorized to continue to remove "surplus" industrial equipment in their occupation zone, and were promised 15 percent of the surplus equipment in the British and American zones. An additional 10 percent in the western zones would go to the Russians in exchange for food and coal from the Soviet zone. But Potsdam brought no meeting of minds on a total reparation figure, or on a clear definition of "surplus" as applied to industrial dismantling. The effect of Potsdam was to ensure that *de facto* partition would be Germany's fate.

Churchill, in one of his last personal exchanges with Stalin in April 1945, had written prophetically:

There is not much comfort in looking into a future where you and the countries you dominate, plus the Communist Parties in many other States, are all drawn up on one side, and those who rally to the English-speaking nations and their associates or Dominions are on the other. It is quite obvious that their quarrel would tear the world to pieces and that all of us leading men on either side who had anything to do with that would be shamed before history.[25]

As the first two atomic bombs in history brought an end to Japanese resistance only a few days after the Potsdam Conference adjourned, the statesmen of the warring powers had ample reason to reflect on Churchill's words. The accidental coalition forged by Hitler had endured long enough to destroy its creator, but now its *raison d'être* had disappeared. Imperceptibly, without any real interlude of peace, Europe and the world moved from hot to cold war. The so-called postwar era had begun.

[24] P. E. Mosely, *The Kremlin and World Politics* (New York, 1960), p. 214.
[25] Churchill, *Second World War*, VI, 497.

Chapter Eleven

THE IMPACT OF TOTAL WAR

I. THE WAR AS REVOLUTION

EVERY modern war, someone has said, is also a revolution. It could hardly be otherwise; the stress and strain of total and protracted conflict unavoidably works profound changes in men and institutions. Some might argue that for the most part, these changes represent no drastic shift in direction, but only a speeding up of trends already under way in the prewar years. Yet even when existing processes are merely hastened, the unsettling impact may produce results equal to those of major revolutions. Neither the boatman nor the historian can afford to ignore "the difference in character and consequence between a gentle current and a cataract."[1]

At the outset, no European could possibly foresee the depth and breadth of the war's impact on his life and on the lives of his successors. True, there were a few hopeful doctrinaires like the Russian refugee Victor Serge who rejoiced at this "war of social transformation" which would introduce an era of controlled and planned economies. There were the Axis leaders, too, for whom the war would be a constructive cataclysm bulldozing away the debris of "decadent" Europe and opening the way for a totally new age. And in the West, there were those who spoke in panicky or apocalyptic fashion about the imminent end of civilization.

But it was the fall of France that shocked many western Europeans into the first dim realization that the Europe they had known had little chance of surviving Hitler's war. Some of them—notably the collaborationists in the defeated countries—saw a German victory as inevitable now, and concluded that they must adapt to whatever revolutionary changes Hitler might dictate. But even those Westerners who refused to capitulate were shaken into a new awareness. Charles de Gaulle in 1940 described the war as "the greatest revolution the world has ever known." The British too, jolted out of their lethargy, began to express

---

[1] Hancock and Gowing, *British War Economy*, p. 555.

not only a new resoluteness but also a clearer realization that the basic values of Western culture were at stake. Churchill, who now became their official spokesman, had insisted from the outset on this broader and deeper nature of the struggle. "This is not a question of fighting for Danzig or for Poland," he had told the House of Commons in September 1939. "We are fighting to save the whole world from the pestilence of Nazi tyranny and in defense of all that is most sacred to man. . . . It is a war, viewed in its inherent quality, to establish, on impregnable rocks, the rights of the individual, and it is a war to establish and revive the stature of man."[2] But along with this British determination to defend traditional values, there emerged in 1940 a new consciousness that traditional ways and structures could never be restored *in toto*. The venerable and conservative *Times* of London, in a lead article just after Dunkirk, issued a call for a redefinition of values to fit the twentieth century. The day of narrow, clashing nationalisms was over, said the *Times*; and so was the day of "rugged individualism which excludes social organization and economic planning. . . . The new order cannot be based on the preservation of privilege, whether the privilege be that of a country, of a class, or of an individual."[3]

This urge for renovation, for building a new and better Europe on the ruins of the old, grew over the years into a persistent theme not only in Britain but also in the German-occupied countries. Resistance movements, governments-in-exile, and individual citizens sought sustenance and comfort by lifting their eyes to the future, and drafting plans for new institutions and refurbished ideals. Indeed, one hardheaded British official complained in 1944 that "the time and energy and thought which we are all giving to the Brave New World is wildly disproportionate to what is being given to the Cruel Real World."[4] But while cynics might scoff at this kind of wartime theorizing, the genuineness of the wartime urge for change can scarcely be doubted. And the expectations built up by this mood of revolutionary reform could not fail to operate as a powerful force in postwar Europe.

Yet the changes for which men consciously thirst and work and die are not the only ones produced by a great war. More profound and

[2] Great Britain, *Parliamentary Debates: Commons*, CCCLI (Sept. 3, 1939), 297.

[3] *Times* (London), July 1, 1940.

[4] Hancock and Gowing, *British War Economy*, p. 542.

more sweeping, perhaps, are those that are unintended and even unforeseen. Mass warfare in the industrial age possesses its own powerful impetus, twisting and distorting the political and social institutions of the peoples caught up in the whirlwind. Peacetime limits on the powers of government give way to an increased centralization of authority, which narrows the individual's role and rights. Furthermore, deep beneath the surface of men's consciousness lie attitudes and impulses that may be altered, often in incalculable ways, by the strain of protracted war. Thus the Second World War seems to have initiated or reinforced trends toward a mood of lawlessness, toward a confusion and corruption of values, toward a decline in man's belief in a rational universe. The mechanization of warfare brought a concurrent deterioration in the methods of waging war: the old restraints (feeble enough at best) began to lose their force in an era of long-range weapons and air bombardment. The battlefield, no longer limited and defined, was everywhere; it was occupied by civilians and soldiers alike. Chance alone seemed to determine not only who gained and lost status and security, but even who died and who survived. Old beliefs in causality tended to dissolve before these evidences of chaos; there was a growing sense that irrational forces rule man's fate. No scientist, no historian has yet discovered a technique for measuring the enduring after effects of war; but no thoughtful man can doubt their severity or their persistence.

II. THE IMPACT ON POLITICAL STRUCTURES

"No protracted war," Tocqueville once wrote, "can fail to endanger the freedom of a democratic country. . . . War does not always give over democratic communities to military government, but it must invariably and immeasurably increase the powers of civil government; it must almost compulsorily concentrate the direction of all men and the management of all things in the hands of the administration. If it does not lead to despotism by sudden violence, it prepares men for it more gently by their habits. All those who seek to destroy the liberties of a democratic nation ought to know that war is the surest and the shortest means to accomplish it."[5]

Tocqueville's dictum, appropriate enough in his own day, is even more applicable in the twentieth century. When nations must mobilize their total resources for a long struggle, the normal tensions between

[5] Alexis de Tocqueville, *Democracy in America* (New York, 1945), II, 284.

authority and liberty are intensified, and the trend toward dictatorship affects even the most democratic of nations. Where parliaments survive, their usual functions are sharply restricted; decision-making becomes increasingly concentrated in the hands of a small executive group, or even in those of one man.

Such had been the experience of the European nations during the First World War; such was even more clearly the case during the Second. In the totalitarian states, of course, this process had already taken place before 1939; the German, Italian, and Soviet political systems were, in a sense, on a war footing even in peacetime, and needed little adaptation when war came. The democratic states, on the other hand, had to grope their way toward some kind of workable compromise. Thanks to the experience of the 1914 war, they were able to convert more rapidly and more efficiently this time. Both the British and the French parliaments had anticipated such an emergency, and had laid plans before 1939 for vesting their governments with emergency powers. These special arrangements were promptly voted into effect in September 1939: Neville Chamberlain was authorized to set up a small War Cabinet, while Premier Daladier was partially freed from parliamentary control by an extensive grant of wartime decree powers.

The period of the twilight war demonstrated, however, that even more centralization of control was needed—not merely to match that of the totalitarian enemy, but simply to ensure the most effective use of national power. The problem was particularly grave in France, where political divisions and personal rivalries in the cabinet hamstrung the government's activity. When Paul Reynaud replaced Daladier as premier in March 1940, his efforts to act with more vigor and dispatch were frustrated by internal dissension that threatened to wreck the cabinet if he moved too brusquely. Reynaud dared not even replace his army commander, General Maurice Gamelin, in whom the new premier lacked confidence. The failings of the French political system in the crisis weeks of 1940 appalled even many sound republicans, and paved the way for Marshal Pétain and Pierre Laval to substitute a frankly authoritarian system after France's defeat. It also enabled Charles de Gaulle to establish his Free French movement on essentially autocratic lines. Although de Gaulle eventually made some grudging concessions to the idea of democratic controls, these limitations remained more theoretical than real during the war years. Only a strong regime, de Gaulle argued, could speak out effectively for

France's right to great-power status in the postwar world. Thus both Pétainist and Gaullist Frenchmen were given a taste of authoritarian rule for the first time in several generations. Some of them were to find that taste attractive; others grew increasingly restive, and looked forward to the restoration of a more responsive peacetime democracy.

In Great Britain, the tank-trap called the English Channel provided enough respite to allow a strengthening of political authority after France fell. The change was partly one of personal style: Winston Churchill was a far more forceful and assertive leader than Chamberlain. It was partly a natural reaction to the intensification of the war; any British prime minister after May 1940 would have had to take a bolder lead. But the Churchill era brought some important structural changes as well. Churchill combined with the prime ministership the newly created post of minister of defense, thus absorbing direct control of all three branches of the armed services, and becoming in effect both supreme commander and head of government. The War Cabinet was reduced in size from nine to five members (though it later expanded again). An Emergency Powers Act, adopted by Parliament after a single day's debate, gave the government "practically unlimited authority over all British citizens and their property."[6]

The sweeping character of Churchill's personal authority was almost unprecedented in a modern democracy. He was confronted by no powerful rival: neither a civilian minister of defense, nor a single "economic czar," nor a military chief of staff speaking for the armed forces as a whole. He operated through his small War Cabinet (which rarely if ever challenged him) and through a four-member Chiefs of Staff Committee (C.O.S.) representing the three branches of the armed services. As the war went on, the War Cabinet was gradually stripped of any role in the formulation of strategy, and found itself confined to matters of foreign and economic policy. An extensive network of some sixty War Cabinet committees handled much of the routine work of wartime government. Meanwhile the authority of the C.O.S. rapidly expanded, until it shared with Churchill the real direction of the war. The unprecedented concentration of power in the hands of Churchill and the C.O.S. led to sporadic protest in press and Parliament, especially at times when the fortunes of war were low. The goal of most of the critics was to strip Churchill of strategic di-

[6] A. J. P. Taylor, *English History 1914–1945* (London, 1965), p. 479.

rection of the war by substituting a supreme military commander for the C.O.S. Such a change would have reduced Churchill's role to that of official rhetorician and morale-builder, leaving the supreme commander to run the war. But these pressures were resisted to the end; and the Churchill-C.O.S. combination (despite sporadic tensions and even sharp clashes) developed an effectiveness that won the admiration of the Germans as well as of Britain's allies. Its achievements reconciled Parliament to a sharply reduced though not insignificant wartime role as occasional critic and outlet for popular irritations.

Britain's wartime system of government meshed smoothly with that of the United States when the latter became an ally in 1941. The Americans promptly set up a new committee called the Joint Chiefs of Staff (J.C.S.) on the model of the British C.O.S., and Anglo-American coordination was provided through a Combined Chiefs of Staff Committee composed of the J.C.S. and the C.O.S. From 1942 onward, this body became the vital center of Anglo-American military planning and operations. Many of the usual problems of coalition warfare were thus avoided from the outset. But it was not the machinery alone that made the system work smoothly. The personal relationship between Churchill and Roosevelt was of crucial importance, along with the fact that the coalition operated as a real partnership of equals throughout most of the war. Britain's two-year advantage over the United States in military buildup and experience counterbalanced the enormous American preponderance in manpower and resources. Toward the end, however, that preponderance was seriously undermining the equality of the partnership, and was forcing the British into reluctant acceptance of joint responsibility for certain decisions that ran against their better judgment. Perhaps another year or two of war might have threatened the harmony of the coalition. Victory in 1945 averted that danger, and gave both the British and the Americans the right to boast that few coalitions in history had worked so well.

In the Axis states and the Soviet Union, the war brought fewer problems of political adaptation, since authority there was already highly concentrated. Yet there remained one vital area of uncertainty: the wartime relationship between the political leaders and the professional soldiers. The tradition of military predominance in time of war was especially strong in Germany, where during the First World War there had emerged a kind of dictatorship of the high command. No such tradition existed in Italy or Russia; yet there, too, it seemed that the conditions of war might offer the soldiers a chance to demand a major share in shaping policy.

Such an increase in army influence did occur in the Soviet Union— though certainly not by Stalin's choice. At the outset, Stalin lost no time in formalizing the absolute power which he already possessed *de facto*. The direction of the war was vested in a new five-man State Defense Committee under Stalin's chairmanship; and a few weeks later Stalin named himself both commissar for defense and commander-in-chief of the armed forces. He was also a member (along with Molotov) of the new supreme military headquarters called the Stavka—the nearest Soviet equivalent to the British C.O.S. To ensure party control over the armed forces, a decree in July re-established the authority of the party's watchdogs, the political commissars, who would henceforth share command of each military unit. The Kremlin clearly remained suspicious of the loyalty of its military cadres, even after the drastic purge of 1937–1938.

But the demands of war were to force a gradual softening of Stalin's grip. The initial defeats suffered in 1941 seem to have had a chastening effect, for they revealed the disastrous consequences of the purge. The incapacity of Stalin's political generals—many of them old comrades of civil war days—threatened the survival of the Soviet regime. Beginning in the autumn of 1941, a quiet "purge by battle" was carried out; new commanders were chosen not for their political reliability but by the sole criterion of ability demonstrated in the field. Meanwhile the authority of the Stavka slowly but steadily expanded. Its representatives functioned as a kind of mobile C.O.S. as they were dispatched to key battle areas (e.g., Stalingrad) to supervise operations. True, Stalin at no time relinquished his right to the final word in strategic matters. He showed an obsessive concern for minutiae, and at times he interfered with, harassed, and browbeat his generals in rather startling fashion.[7] Yet by the time of Stalingrad, the relationship between Stalin and his high command seems to have evolved into something not vastly different from that between Churchill and the C.O.S. Despite occasional friction, the strategic and operational direction of the war in the Soviet Union had become a cooperative enterprise, in which the soldiers had an effective voice. As a symbol of this new relationship, Stalin in October 1942 freed his commanders from the galling control

---

[7] E.g., see Marshal Georgi Zhukov in *Voenno-Istoricheskii Zhurnal*, No. 10 (1966), pp. 75–76.

of the political commissars. "Out of its subordination, the army marched into equality with the Party."[8]

This growth of reasonably confident collaboration within the USSR was never extended to cover general inter-Allied direction of the war. Neither the Western powers nor the USSR was interested in broadening the Anglo-American Combined Chiefs of Staff Committee to include Soviet representatives. Late in 1943, the Americans did suggest the creation of a four-power United Chiefs of Staff Committee to exist alongside the Combined Chiefs of Staff and to function "when necessity arose." The proposal was dropped when the British pointed out that the new body might try to claim superiority over the C.C.S. Some months later, in July 1944, the Soviet authorities suggested the creation of a tripartite military committee in Moscow to coordinate matters of military importance. The Western powers, after some discussion, agreed on condition that the tripartite committee be merely advisory to the C.C.S. and the Soviet general staff. No Soviet response came; and the war ended without any formal coordinating machinery. Stalin preferred, on the whole, to fight his own "parallel war." Perhaps it was just as well. A broadening of the Anglo-American command machinery might have seriously hampered or destroyed its effectiveness; probably the C.C.S. functioned well because it included only two well-suited partners. For somewhat similar reasons, it was probably fortunate that the great powers excluded the smaller associated powers from the direction of the war. Coalition wars are undoubtedly the most difficult kind to fight. If a broadly inclusive supreme allied council had been organized to discuss and shape the strategic conduct of the war, the enterprise might have degenerated into constant bickering and fatal delays. Happily, most representatives of the smaller allies accepted their uncomfortable role in good spirit, and rested their confidence in the good faith of the Anglo-Americans.

It was Adolf Hitler who faced the greatest test of the totalitarian leader's ability to dominate his army in wartime. There, the army's sense of pride and independence was deeply rooted, and the public was conditioned to expect military control once the guns began to speak. In the circumstances, Hitler's total triumph over the soldiers was impressive, but also costly. His monopoly of power equaled that of Stalin, and increased as the war moved on. Hitler developed no equivalent of the British War Cabinet or the Soviet State Defense Com-

[8] J. Erickson, *The Soviet High Command* (London, 1962), p. 667.

mittee. A Ministerial Council for National Defense, set up at the outbreak of the conflict, withered away after December 1939; as for the Reich cabinet, it never met during the war.

Nor did the Germans develop any equivalent of the British C.O.S. In February 1938, Hitler had dismissed the minister of defense without appointing a successor, and had personally assumed command over the armed forces as a whole. He had simultaneously created a new High Command of the Armed Forces (*Oberkommando der Wehrmacht*, or OKW) which appeared to be the nucleus of a unified command system destined to coordinate the army, navy, and air force. But the demarcation of roles was not clear-cut, and it became increasingly confused during the course of the war. The OKW, which might have developed into an agency even more powerful and effective than the British C.O.S., shriveled into little more than Hitler's military working staff, destined not to help plan overall strategy but to translate the Fuehrer's inspirations into the form of operational orders and to transmit them to the three service commands (or even over the heads of those commands to an individual commander at the front). The OKW chiefs, Field Marshal Wilhelm Keitel and General Alfred Jodl, preened themselves on their absolute loyalty to Hitler and slavishly followed his orders. The army's high command (OKH), though restive and bitter at this high-handed and capricious treatment, had no effective spokesman in Hitler's immediate entourage, and found no other way to bring its potential influence to bear. Meanwhile, much to the army's irritation, the commanders-in-chief of the *Luftwaffe* (Goering) and of the navy (Raeder and Doenitz) enjoyed direct personal access to the Fuehrer. From December 1941 Hitler made things still worse by naming himself commander-in-chief of the army as well as supreme commander of the armed forces; he thus took over complete charge of army operations, issuing detailed as well as general instructions. In 1942 he even assumed active command of an army group in the Caucasus while remaining in his headquarters more than a thousand miles away. Compounding the confusion was the fact that OKH was given operational control of the war in Russia, while OKW was in charge on all the other fronts. Since Hitler laid down the law to both agencies, there could be no ultimate rivalry; but the arrangement was awkward and inefficient. No wonder some high-ranking soldiers in Germany envied the smooth-working and simple command organization developed by their enemies in the west.

Hitler's solution for the problems of conducting a coalition war was no more effective. The German and Italian high commands were not linked by any equivalent of the Anglo-American Combined Chiefs of Staff; military consultations occurred sporadically, at the irregular summit conferences between the two dictators. Mussolini's desire to fight his own "parallel war" was matched by Hitler's determination to give the Italians no voice in his strategical planning. Mussolini, whose direct personal control of Italian strategy and operations was as complete as Hitler's in Germany, found himself increasingly dependent on his German ally for war matériel and military support. The Italian fiasco in Greece, and the dispatch of General Rommel to Libya, reduced the idea of a "parallel war" to a mere facade for German domination of the Mediterranean theater. The effect was increasing ill-will between the Axis partners. Hitler's relations with the Japanese were even more tenuous; machinery for military coordination was totally lacking.

In the management and the strategic direction of the war, the Atlantic democracies and the Soviet Union clearly outdid the Axis powers in effectively adapting their systems to the demands of the epoch. The presumed superiority of dictatorship in time of crisis was belied by the course of events; constitutional systems proved flexible enough to borrow such authoritarian techniques as were necessary for survival and victory. One result of that success was to bolster the confidence of many Europeans in free government—a confidence that had been widely shaken during the interwar years. But it also inspired a disturbing fear that in an age of chronic crisis, the distinction between wartime and peacetime conditions might become increasingly blurred, and that the traditional balance between authority and liberty, sharply shifted by the demands of the Second World War, might suffer a permanent change.

III. THE SOCIAL IMPACT

Wars leave their mark not only on political structures, but on every aspect of human organization. Indeed, their effects on social structures may be even deeper and more durable. On the other hand, measuring those effects is clearly more difficult; for societies are complex things, and the changes that occur may reveal themselves only gradually, well after the last shot is fired.

One obvious effect of total mobilization is a certain militarizing of

society, at least for the duration of the war. The long strain calls
for intensified social discipline: a greater regimentation of the citizen's
life, a more hierarchical set of relationships, a partial replacement of
civilian by military values. The altered demands of war also bring
sharp changes in mores and in social values; new kinds of achievement
are highly honored and yield fame and status, while others are pushed
into the background. The normal channels of social mobility are
twisted or blocked as by an earthquake, and new channels are suddenly wrenched open for heretofore obscure citizens. A reordering of
social relationships inevitably follows—sometimes in the direction of
greater leveling, sometimes in the direction of increased inequalities.
As a rule, the chief social benefits of modern war have gone to the
professional soldier at the expense of those who practice the peacetime arts. Midway through the First World War, the German officer
Wilhelm Groener rather smugly remarked: "The uniform counts more
among us now than the black coat of the civilian, and the cry for
dictatorship by the military is raised on every side."[9] Early in the
Second World War, an American social scientist somberly predicted
that the conflict would produce a world of "garrison states" in which
the "specialists in violence" would fix a durable grip on societies everywhere.[10]

Some of the foregoing changes did occur in Europe during the Second World War—though with particular nuances from one society to
another, and with some rather surprising aberrations. One notable fact
was that while the usual militarizing of society did occur in the broad
sense of that term, it failed to put the military into the saddle anywhere, and in one case even reduced the political and social authority
enjoyed by the armed forces. That case was Germany. During the war
of 1914–1918, the German military had fixed its grip on almost every
aspect of domestic life, from political decision-making to industrial
production, food rationing, labor policy, the control of public information, and censorship. After 1939, the armed forces found themselves
excluded from all such functions, and even from such responsibilities
as the raising and training of reserves. Just as Hitler himself increasingly monopolized the strategic and even the operational conduct of
the war, so the various agencies of the Nazi party absorbed all do-

[9] Quoted in G. A. Craig, "The Impact of the German Military on the Political and Social
Life of Germany during World War II," *Rapports du XIIe Congrès International des Sciences
Historiques* (Vienna, 1965), IV, 297.

[10] H. J. Lasswell, "The Garrison State," *American Journal of Sociology*, XLVI (1941),
455–68.

mestic administrative tasks—police and security, manpower allocation, psychological mobilization and indoctrination. "The Fuehrer," wrote Goebbels in 1943, "is totally opposed to the Wehrmacht engaging in tasks that are not germane to it. . . . The Wehrmacht is to limit itself to conducting the war in a military sense and to leave everything else to civilians."[11] If the conflict further increased Germany's "garrison state" qualities, it did so at the expense and not to the advantage of the professional soldier. The traditional prestige of the German officer corps, and its assumption of a dominant role in past wars, worked against the army at a time when the nation's new political elite jealously refused to share authority with any potential rival.

In the Soviet Union, on the other hand, the war did bring a carefully controlled shift in status and authority to the advantage of the military. The vast influx of Soviet citizens into the armed forces after 1941, and the Kremlin's increased dependence on the generals' courage and loyalty, assured the soldiers of greater deference and higher status. But although honors and praise were dealt out generously, the officer corps was given no expanded role outside the sphere of military operations; the tasks of social control and of adapting Soviet society to wartime needs were exclusively reserved to the political elite. Even though the bloodiest fighting and the greatest destruction of the war occurred on the Russian front, the war's effects on the Soviet political system and social structure were probably slighter than in any other participating country. For unlike the Western democracies, the Soviet Union had already become a garrison state before the war; and unlike Germany, the Soviet Union did not have to face the postwar social upheaval caused by defeat.

One would expect the war to have had a far greater impact on the liberal societies of the West, where the transition from peace to war was bound to be more unsettling. Such was indeed the case; yet the changes were not always the ones that might have been predicted. The apparent shift toward a garrison state in Great Britain (the only western European nation to endure the long strain of protracted war as an independent belligerent) brought increased status and authority to the military, but not at the expense of civilian officialdom or of the civilian population as a whole. Survival and victory depended on the united effort of the British people, whether in or out of uniform; total mobilization put everyone onto the front lines. Episodes like the Battle of Britain were peculiarly important in eroding the differences be-

<hr/>

[11] Lochner, *The Goebbels Diaries*, pp. 540–41.

tween civilians and soldiers. And when the war effort depended as much on the production and delivery of goods as on battlefield heroics, special privileges for men in uniform would have been difficult to justify.

The war brought, too, a drastic process of leveling, a kind of flattening of the social pyramid. British leadership had no choice but to practice what someone has called "demostrategy"; it implied an intensified state concern for the health and morale of the whole population. From the early months of the war, the government ordered a marked broadening of social services provided to all citizens, regardless of class or military status. The emergency evacuation of millions of women and children from Greater London suddenly brought to light a number of social deficiencies of which few Britons had been consciously aware. It was clear that the nation's hospital facilities were desperately inadequate, and that hundreds of thousands of urban refugee children had in the past been inadequately fed, clothed, and cared for. The government introduced a whole series of emergency welfare measures; but more important still, the conditions of war stimulated a nationwide mood of reform. From this mood emerged the welfare-state concept in its modern form. So great was its appeal that when Sir William Beveridge issued his famous report in 1943, outlining a postwar plan for universal social security, the bulky and austere document became an overnight best seller; queues of citizens stood before bookstores to get their copies.

Wartime government controls contributed, too, to the leveling process. Critical shortages of consumer goods after 1940 forced an austerity standard for all; and changing mores reinforced government regulation to impose a growing uniformity in standards of living, of dress, and of public conduct generally. Long years of war required rigorous social discipline, and such discipline was made more bearable when it was shared by everyone. Yet along with the flattening of the social pyramid, there occurred a marked increase in social mobility. New opportunities were opened to many men and women whose roles had been humble or obscure in peacetime. The rise of the scientists was perhaps the most striking example. Only a few years before the war, a British cabinet minister had remarked condescendingly, "What I like about scientists is that they are a team, so that one need not know their names."[12] Suddenly, in the war years, the names of certain scien-

[12] Earl of Birkenhead, *The Professor and the Prime Minister* (Boston, 1962), p. 198.

tists came to be almost as well known among the cognoscenti as those of generals and ministers. On a broader scale, the rise of women in social status was equally notable. The increase in the number of British women employed in industry, government, and the armed forces exceeded that of any other warring country; it profoundly altered the role and the self-image of British women. The new technological aspect of the war also had its effect (in Britain as elsewhere) in pushing forward men of technical and managerial talent, both in the government and in the armed services. Sir John Anderson, a highly skilled career civil servant without experience as a politician, held important cabinet posts throughout the war, and in 1945 was even nominated by Churchill to succeed to the prime ministership in case Churchill and Eden were killed en route to Yalta. Likewise, the new-style armed forces enabled the military managers to assert a right to equality with charismatic battlefield leaders.

Perhaps the most drastic immediate impact of the war on social structures occurred in the German-occupied countries of the Continent. Defeat and occupation radically transformed the dominant value-systems and the relationships among social groups. Some previously favored elements suddenly found themselves transformed into outsiders, threatened by physical destruction as well as social ruin. Others found the channels of upward mobility suddenly opened wide to those who were opportunistically inclined. In areas like Poland and occupied Russia, the conquerors consciously endeavored to liquidate the whole intellectual and professional elite, and to substitute an imported German ruling class. In western Europe, favors often went to men who had been disgruntled misfits or frustrated failures in their pre-war societies. But the deeper social effects in the occupied countries were aftereffects, to be felt during the postwar years. For the nucleus of a new elite gradually emerged from the various resistance movements; its members were catapulted after 1944 into positions of political, economic, and social prominence to which only a few of them could have aspired without the upheaval of the war. Nowhere were they to attain a monopoly of postwar power or status; many would be shunted back into obscurity after a few months or years of fleeting notoriety. But the long-range effect was to produce a kind of circulation of the elites, out of which would come an amalgam of old-established and newly-arrived elements in roles of authority and status.

In the defeated Axis nations, too, the social effects of the war were

mainly aftereffects; but the impact was no less profound for being delayed. Germany and Italy had already undergone a partial social revolution during the prewar years—a revolution that had brought the new
Fascist or Nazi party elite into uneasy partnership with those elements of the older elites that chose to collaborate. In Germany, a
radical wing of the Nazi movement had favored a much more sweeping social revolution that would liquidate most of the older elite and
would culminate in a thoroughly totalitarian system. This impulse was
strongest within the SS, some of whose leaders talked of creating an
"SS-state" in which all the key positions would be monopolized by
members of that elite formation. The war did bring an impressive
growth in the size and influence of the SS, but at the same time
forced postponement of its leaders' ambitions. So long as the fighting
lasted, they concentrated their energies on the task of creating and
consolidating a German empire in the east, while deferring their domestic goals for implementation after victory was won.

But the social revolution that eventually followed Germany's defeat
was to be of a quite different sort. The destruction of much of the
Nazi elite, the temporary disgrace of those powerful elements that had
collaborated with Hitler, and the massive influx of a huge uprooted
refugee population from the east were to produce a kind of social disintegration out of which a largely new social order would eventually
emerge. The refugees (mostly from Protestant regions) were scattered in camps throughout the western zones of occupied Germany,
and many eventually settled in what had been solidly Catholic areas.
The effect was a somewhat greater religious and social "homogeniza-
tion" of the western zones. On the other hand, the permanent division
of Germany that split off the heavily Protestant eastern part led to a
sharp increase of Catholic influence in the segment that eventually
came to be governed from Bonn.

Still more profound were the social changes that emerged from the
massive physical destruction of the country, and from the disastrous
blows suffered by the old ruling elites. The rebuilding of the German
economy opened the way to the creation, for the first time in German
history, of a thoroughly capitalist system in place of the old uneasy
mixture of industrial capitalism and quasi-feudal traditionalism. The
industrial-managerial group rapidly emerged as the unchallenged
upper stratum of society, able to assert its individualistic, competitive
values as those of the new Germany. Greater social mobility, a per-

sonal success ideology, and a somewhat exaggerated materialism seemed on the way to replacing the more rigid and status-ridden order of the past. What kind of amalgam would eventually emerge remained somewhat uncertain, but it was clear enough that the war had opened the way to a quite unintended kind of social revolution in Germany.

IV. THE PSYCHOLOGICAL IMPACT

That modern war strains and disrupts the political, social, and economic fabric of a highly organized continent is too obvious to be doubted. Its effects on the psychological fabric are much more controversial. Common sense and experience testify that an individual may be traumatized by a shattering personal experience; and certainly millions of individual Europeans suffered some kind of traumatic experience during the Second World War. But whether whole societies may be traumatized by a collectively experienced catastrophe is more open to debate. Those who believe that communities of men possess a kind of collective mind or psychological fabric will be more likely to seek out and to accept evidence of the generalized impact of disaster. Yet even those who are skeptical of the idea of "socially-shared psychopathology" will recognize that the long strain and the terrifying climaxes of modern war must leave their mark on tens of thousands of survivors.

Such evidence as emerged from the Second World War relates not to entire populations but to special groups: members of the armed forces, children separated from their families, prisoners of war, civilians subjected to heavy bombing raids, and concentration camp inmates. The data, though extensive, is spotty, and rarely permits confident generalization. Only the Americans and the British compiled information and made studies of psychological responses during the war itself; as for the data from Germany, most of it was gathered immediately after the war by American teams, or was contributed by survivors of the concentration camps. Probably the surest conclusions are those that concern the short- and long-range effects of mass bombing.

The approach of war had inspired panicky fears in Britain and France about the anticipated consequences of air attacks. The British Air Ministry estimated that air-raid casualties during the early weeks of war would run into the millions, and would produce widespread neurosis and panic. Indeed, a committee of psychiatrists had predicted in 1938 that psychological casualties might exceed physical injuries by a ratio of three to one, so that the former might approach three or four million cases during the first six months. When war was declared, therefore, more than three million women and children were hastily evacuated from Greater London to the country districts or to smaller towns. When the expected air raids failed to materialize, the majority of the refugees found their own way back to London. By the time the German blitz of 1940–1941 began, the initial panic had passed. This time there was no organized evacuation; many Londoners preferred the risks of bombing to the dislocation and tensions of life as unwelcome guests in a crowded rural or small-town home. In fact, there is fairly persuasive evidence that children suffered more severely from the psychological effects of separation from their families than from the rigors of the air raids.

The impact of the bombing, when it came at last, seemed to belie the fears and predictions of the experts. There was no mass hysteria, no social disruption inspired by panic or shock. The nearest approach to spontaneous mass action or "civil disobedience" was the occupation of London subway stations by thousands of citizens who lacked air-raid shelters. Civil defense officials worked tirelessly and efficiently to care for the injured, to clear street obstructions, and to restore disrupted public utilities. There was no increase in the number of mental disorders reported; the number of suicides and of arrests for drunkenness or disorderly conduct actually decreased during the war years. On the other hand, cases diagnosed as "temporary traumatic neurosis" were frequent in heavily-bombed areas, and increased absenteeism from work on grounds of illness often followed an air attack. There was also a rise in the incidence of such psychosomatic disorders as peptic ulcers in bombed areas.

Fortunately for the British, the air blitz tapered off after about ten months, and there was a long respite before the period of V–1 and V–2 attacks in 1944. No doubt this interlude reduced the nervous strain in British cities, and helped to keep the number of psychological casualties low. Meanwhile, the Germans were beginning to confront a steadily intensifying barrage of air raids both more severe and more protracted than anything the British—or any other people heretofore—had known. Here, too, the experience seemed to prove the remarkable capacity of human beings to bear up under unprecedented strain and terror. As in England, there was neither mass panic nor social disruption (save in a few instances when the municipal authorities failed to respond effectively to emergency conditions following an air raid). Even in the massive Hamburg raids, which laid waste half the city and left 48 percent of the population homeless, the effect was widespread shock rather than mass hysteria or economic breakdown. Berlin, which underwent the longest period of almost uninterrupted raids (eighteen months) and which by 1945 was reduced largely to rubble, continued to function as an organized community until the very end. In Germany as in England there seems to have been no increase in the number of mental disorders. But here, too, the number of ulcer cases rose in bombed areas, and work absenteeism was more common after raids. Signs of tension and strain were general; the German authorities finally had to abandon the use of air-raid sirens to warn against isolated attacks, in an effort to reduce fatigue caused by unnecessary alarm.

The remarkable resilience of both the English and the Germans when subjected to intense air warfare blasted the prewar myth about the devastating effects of terror bombing; but perhaps it tended to create a new myth in place of the old. It was easy to conclude, during and after the war, that mass bombing had been a relatively ineffective weapon, and that its psychological effect had actually been to improve the morale of an attacked population, to intensify its will to resist. Such a conclusion can be neither affirmed nor denied on the basis of the evidence from the Second World War. Even though mass hysteria did not occur, there was widespread shock that amounted to temporary traumatic neurosis, and that produced a kind of numb indifference rather than a heightened determination to fight and win. As for the long-range consequences of these temporary psychological disorders, the evidence is scanty. One British study of mental cases carried out in 1948 showed only 3 percent of this sample to be clearly connected with air-raid experience during the war. It is quite possible, however, that hidden damage of a deeper sort went undetected.

The psychological impact of the war on members of the armed forces is difficult to assess, since only the British and the Americans kept detailed statistics. British psychiatric casualties seem to have averaged about 10 percent of total battle casualties; but this average concealed a wide variation, ranging from 2 to 30 percent, depending on the particular conditions and the duration of a given battle. Long periods of severe strain produced serious effects. For example, in the garrison at Malta, under intense air bombardment in 1942–1943, more than one man in four eventually showed some kind of pathological response. In 1940, a ship loaded with exhausted and demoralized British troops who had fought in the French campaign was sunk near Bordeaux, and the soldiers dumped into a sea coated with flaming oil; every man who was rescued suffered severe psychological aftereffects. Many of the Dunkirk survivors reached home in a state of total neurotic collapse, "suffering from acute hysteria, reactive depression, functional loss of memory or of the use of their limbs, and a variety of other psychiatric symptoms. . . ."[13]

During the First World War, all such disorders had been lumped under the misleading label "shell shock," and it was assumed that such men were either weaklings or cowards. At best, they had been given a spell of rest and then sent back to the front lines, where they often broke down completely, and became incurable casualties. This mistake was corrected in the Second World War by improved understanding and better methods of treatment. Both the British and the Americans soon learned that it was essential to treat acute hysteria cases as quickly as possible, before the abnormal behavior patterns had time to become stabilized in the nervous system. They learned, too, that to send "cured" neurotics back into action was almost always futile, and that a transfer or a discharge was the only alternative to permanent damage. They learned, finally, that not only weaklings were susceptible to psychological battle disorders; that "practically everyone has his neurotic breaking point if the stresses are severe enough."[14] The advance of psychiatric knowledge had at least one clearly favorable result: it sharply reduced the number of permanent psychological casualties in the British and American armed forces, as compared to the record of 1914–1918.[15]

---

[13] William Sargant, "Psychiatry and War," *Atlantic Monthly*, CCXIX (1967), p. 102.

[14] Sargant, "Psychiatry and War," p. 106; *cf.* R. H. Ahrenfeldt, *Psychiatry in the British Army during the Second World War* (New York, 1958), p. 256.

[15] Churchill, however, viewed the work of psychiatrists with a jaundiced eye. "I am sure it would be sensible [he wrote in 1942] to restrict as much as possible the work of these gentlemen, who are capable of doing an immense amount of harm with what may very easily degenerate into charlatanry. . . . There are no doubt easily recognizable cases which may benefit from treatment of this kind, but it is very wrong to disturb large numbers of healthy, normal men and women by asking the kind of odd questions in which the psychiatrists specialise. There are quite enough hangers-on and camp-followers already" (Churchill, *Second World War*, IV, 918).

German and Soviet leaders shared Churchill's prejudices in even greater measure. The German armed forces used psychologists to administer tests to officer candidates, but abandoned even this practice in 1942. No information is available on the incidence of war-induced neuroses or psychoses in Germany or the USSR.

No experience of strain and terror during the Second World War exceeded that of the men and women confined in German concentration camps. Inadequate food, brutal treatment, harsh labor assignments, constant uncertainty about the future seem to have produced radical personality changes in many inmates. The program of calculated terror used by the SS guards was evidently designed to strip the prisoner of all human traits, to destroy his self-respect, to "depersonalize" him. The effect of the treatment varied widely: regression toward infantile traits was perhaps the commonest result, while others managed some sort of adaptation in order to survive. In most cases, the central concern after the first few weeks came to be self-preservation; all other values faded before this urge to live, no matter what the cost. Some long-time prisoners even came to model themselves after the SS guards, and to ape their conduct and values. Only a few managed to cling, despite the inhuman conditions in the camp, to those altruistic traits that mark normal human conduct. The enduring effects of the concentration camp experience were to be demonstrated after the war by the frequency of psychological disorders among former inmates. Chronic anxiety and panic were frequent, while certain mental and physical diseases that occurred ten or twenty years later have been diagnosed as the result of brain injury caused by malnutrition and prolonged, intense fear experienced during the concentration camp years.

The full breadth and depth of the war's psychological impact on the peoples of Europe will, of course, never be measured. At least one psychiatrist, on returning to the Continent in 1945, contended that almost every inhabitant of occupied Europe showed some traits that might be described as neurotic or even psychotic. Others spoke of a new set of impenetrable "psychological boundaries" that would henceforth separate those with sharply differing sets of wartime experiences. Still others spoke with a touch of awe of the unexpected power of adaptation shown by ordinary human beings in time of crisis. On the surface, Europe after the end of the war seemed to return quite rapidly to a kind of normalcy, and its citizens a decade later no longer appeared to be haunted by the terrible memory of their wartime experiences. Yet who is to say whether deeper lesions may not have persisted, marring and distorting the psyche of the "normal" European who survived the conflict? "Perhaps," suggests Richard M. Titmuss, "more lasting harm was wrought to the minds and to the hearts of men, women and children than to their bodies. The disturbances to family life, the separation of mothers and fathers from their children, of husbands from their wives, of pupils from their schools, of people from their recreation, of society from the pursuits of peace—perhaps all of these indignities of war have left wounds which will take time to heal and infinite patience to understand."[16] Thucydides remarked long ago that ". . . war, which takes away the comfortable provision of daily life, is a hard master and tends to assimilate men's characters to their conditions." It may be that characters warped by the experience of protracted total war will never quite return to their former shape, and that from these warped qualities may emerge the neuroses of the next generation.

V. THE IMPACT ON INTELLECTUAL AND CULTURAL LIFE

Epochs of war are rarely times of creativity in the realm of the spirit. Men's thoughts and energies tend to be swallowed up by the harsh demands of the struggle; it absorbs or annihilates most intellectual activities. Yet even in such times, the life of the mind goes on, though at reduced intensity; some individuals find occasion to reflect and to create, if only as a way to retain their sanity. And in a more practical sphere, governments often find advantage in encouraging the arts in wartime, although this encouragement is likely to be inspired by such instrumental motives as to maintain morale or to convey a desired message to the masses.

Almost every government that was caught up in the war gave some attention to stimulating the arts. In Germany and the Soviet Union, which already enjoyed managed cultures, the enterprise was particularly orthodox and utilitarian. Joseph Goebbels, whose authority as minister of people's enlightenment encompassed cultural life, insisted that the outbreak of war should alter nothing—that because of Germany's cultural pre-eminence through the ages, "the muses should not be silenced as elsewhere by the clash of arms." Besides, for Goebbels the arts were no mere pastime for peace, but "a sharp spiritual weapon for war."[17] Theaters remained open in surprising number until the very last phase of the war; glossy art magazines continued to appear, despite restrictions on paper and manpower. National Socialist art, literature, and drama continued to be custom-built to reinforce party doctrine; its purpose was to inculcate a sense of massiveness and power,

[16] R. M. Titmuss, *Problems of Social Policy* (London, 1950), p. 538.
[17] H. Heiber, *Joseph Goebbels* (Berlin, 1952), p. 299.

of group unity and passionate self-righteousness. Spontaneity and originality were the most obvious casualties, but they had already succumbed in 1933.

One of Germany's few wartime innovations in culture was the establishment in 1941 of a staff of uniformed war artists destined to immortalize on canvas the nation's victorious campaigns. Eventually this staff grew to include eighty painters, who spent three-month tours of duty at the front and produced an enormous mass of "combat art." Hitler hailed their work as proof that direct personal experience far outweighed the results of cloistered study under the uninspired "daubers" of the art academies. "This war," he declared with more enthusiasm than accuracy, "is stimulating the artistic sense much more than the last war."[18] Hitler was less concerned with uncovering new talent, however, than with planning the Supermuseum of German Art which he intended to build in Linz after the victory. His brief last will, found in the ruins of Berlin in 1945, contained a plaintive appeal that this project be carried to completion by his successors. Instead, only the Volkswagen factory lived on as a monument to the Fuehrer's creative genius.

Of all the arts, it was the cinema that lent itself most effectively to the cultural policy of the Nazi state at war. Goebbels' interest in the film as a propaganda device led him to sponsor not only a remarkable series of war documentaries recording each successive campaign, but also a number of enormously costly pseudohistorical pageants designed to justify the German war effort and, toward the end, to bolster the nation's flagging morale. The first and probably the most successful of these was Veit Harlan's *Der Jud Süss*, a virulently anti-Semitic epic. *Ohm Krüger*, a tale of the Boer War, was designed to stir up hatred of the devious and oppressive English, inventors of the concentration camp. Biographical films of Frederick the Great and Bismarck, inflated to superhuman stature, provided examples of German leadership and military success. Toward the end of the war, Goebbels pinned his fading hopes of victory on the film entitled *Kolberg*: an account of a small East Prussian city under French siege in 1807, stubbornly holding out against overwhelming odds until the last-minute arrival of a relieving army. *Kolberg* was given a gala double premiere on January 30, 1945: one showing in half-ruined Berlin, the other in the French town of La Rochelle, where a small German force had been cut off by the Allied advance.

[18] *Hitler's Secret Conversations*, p. 507.

In the Soviet Union, literature and the arts were likewise expected to play major roles as auxiliary weapons in the war. "What is of paramount importance today," asserted the official organ of Soviet writers and artists, ". . . is the *activizing* function of art which possesses the invaluable faculty of inspiring men to fight."[19] The goal, it added, was not military literature but militant literature. Soviet writers responded with an enormous outpouring of novels, plays, poetry, and journalistic pieces that only occasionally rose above aesthetic mediocrity but that struck a responsive chord in a nation fighting for survival. With few exceptions, writers found their subject matter in episodes of the current war—especially variations on the theme of the common man caught up in the conflict and transfigured, somewhat to his own surprise, into a hero. Historical studies glorifying Russia's past also began to appear; in Leningrad under siege, a new 500,000-copy edition of *War and Peace* was published in an effort to bolster morale. Most of the literature of the time strongly reflected the powerful wave of national consciousness, of love for the Russian motherland, that was inspired by the war. Konstantin Simonov's semi-journalistic novels and plays and simple, highly emotional poetry made him the most widely read author of the war years, though Alexey Surkov rivaled his popularity as a poet, and Vassily Grossman, Alexander Korneichuk, and Leonid Leonov were equally successful playwrights. Ilya Ehrenburg, best known of the literary journalists, devoted his facile talents to essays filled with the most virulent hatred of the Germans. "Two eyes for an eye," "a pool of blood for a drop of blood," were typical of Ehrenburg's passionate cries for vengeance upon those "gray-green slugs," the invaders of Russia. The cinema, a field in which the USSR had already pioneered before the war, was also mobilized in the service of morale. The most notable masterpieces of the war years were undoubtedly Sergei Eisenstein's last films, *Alexander Nevsky* (completed just before the invasion) and *Ivan the Terrible*, a monumental pageant glorifying that controversial tsar from Russia's dark past. Even the composers were swept along by the flood tide of wartime emotion. Dimitri Shostakovich's enormously popular Seventh ("Leningrad") Symphony, composed during the siege of the city in 1941, echoed the mood and even the events of the time.

In German-occupied Europe and in Fascist Italy, the arts profited

[19] Quoted in G. Struve, *Soviet Russian Literature 1917–1950* (Norman, Okla., 1951), p. 300.

little from government sponsorship—with the possible exception of the cinema, which experienced a kind of renaissance almost everywhere. Opportunities for diversion were rare in wartime Europe; the cinema provided almost the only easy escape from the reality and drudgery of daily existence. Everywhere, theaters were crowded and attendance steadily rose. Since the Continent was cut off from American and British films, new fields were opened to European producers. Mussolini moved at once to take advantage of the opportunity; in 1941 and 1942, Italy produced more films than any other European country. Their quality was generally mediocre; but the rapid expansion of the industry eventually opened the way to a new younger generation of directors—notably Roberto Rossellini and Vittorio de Sica—who took the first steps toward the neo-realistic style that was to put its mark on postwar Italian films.

In France, an even more remarkable wave of new talent appeared, and was matched by successful experimentation by some of the established directors. Goebbels, who was determined to assert Germany's dominance in the entire European film industry, was sufficiently concerned at this burst of French creativity to take countermeasures. He set up a German-owned film company in Paris, and planned gradually to tempt the most talented French actors to work for the new firm or for Berlin producers. One of the most brilliantly executed wartime films, H. G. Clouzot's *Le Corbeau* (a characterological study of a small French town), was produced by the German-owned company. Most of the outstanding French films, however, were made by independent French directors and firms who owed nothing to either German or Vichy sponsorship; and almost none were devoted to wartime themes. Notable among them were Jean Delannoy's *L'Eternel Retour*, Jacques Becker's *Goupi-Mains-Rouges*, and Marcel Carné's *Les Visiteurs du Soir* and *Les Enfants du Paradis*.

Of all governmental efforts to stimulate the wartime arts, those in Great Britain may have produced the most remarkable and lasting changes. The outbreak of war temporarily disrupted British cultural life; most places of entertainment were closed by the blackout, and a great many professional musicians and actors found themselves out of work. The Board of Education and a small private foundation stepped in with funds to tide them over the emergency, and to keep alive some amateur musical groups as well. Out of this accidental beginning was to grow the state-supported Council for the Encouragement of Music and the Arts, chaired after 1942 by no less a figure than John Maynard Keynes, and endowed with a government subsidy that grew larger in each wartime year. Instead of expiring in 1945, the CEMA was to live on into peacetime under a new name—the first long-term experiment (except in totalitarian states) in subsidizing the arts.

During the war years, the CEMA sponsored a broad and varied program of dramatic, musical, and artistic entertainment. Concerts and plays were staged by both professional and amateur groups in dozens of British cities, as well as in armaments factories and in bombed-out areas (where, for morale purposes, an orchestra was often dispatched immediately after the all-clear signal). The National Gallery, left vacant when its collections were stored for safekeeping, was taken over for daily concerts at noon, under the guidance of the gallery director Sir Kenneth Clark and the noted pianist Dame Myra Hess. The CEMA also subsidized a group of "war artists"—among them men of the caliber of Henry Moore, who spent a year or more sketching scenes in bomb shelters and munitions plants. The theater continued to function in lively fashion, and the British cinema, like that of the Continent, underwent a kind of rejuvenation. Indeed, some British historians have argued that the war actually increased the tempo of intellectual and cultural activity in Britain. This may have been true in a quantitative sense, as well as in the sense that there was a certain democratizing of culture as good music, art, and theater were made easily available to all. It would be more difficult to contend that the war brought an outburst of creativity. Neither public sponsorship nor private inspiration managed to produce any outstanding works of literature, of music, or of art in wartime Britain. Wartime novels and poetry lacked the sentimental and heroic rhetoric of the literature of 1914–1918; their dominant note, rather, was low-keyed restraint. The most representative novels were those of J. B. Priestley—though Evelyn Waugh's sardonic trilogy written just after the war probably came closer to catching the mood of wartime Britain. Perhaps A. J. P. Taylor is right in suggesting that to the British the Second World War was not a profound spiritual experience, and that a prosaic war, accepted by all and fought in businesslike fashion as a job that must be done, is not likely to produce general intellectual ferment. At most, the war stimulated British artists, writers, and composers to reflect the new mood of national pride and unity, and to seek inspiration in the native British tradition rather than in Continental models.

But the real impact of any war on intellectual and cultural life is not revealed in the somewhat artificial and manipulative efforts of governments to stimulate artistic expression. It must be sought elsewhere, in the moods and attitudes of thoughtful and creative men whose view of themselves and of the world is altered by the experience. Such effects are not easy to detect while the war continues; they are more likely to reveal themselves in the postwar years, when a chastened older generation and a restless, questioning new generation are suddenly freed from the stresses of the conflict, yet find that its burdens still weigh upon their spirits. Only the tentative beginnings of such postwar manifestations belong in a book whose chronological limits are the war years.

The war struck Europe at a time of low resistance to infection by intellectual doubt and despair. For two generations, the dominant values and beliefs of the post-Enlightenment era had been under attack; old certainties had been dissolving without being replaced by positive new values and convictions. The interwar years had been most strongly marked by this mood of cultural despair—a mood from which fascist movements (especially in Germany) had profited greatly. True, the decade of the 1930's had brought some signs of a resurgent humanism, an attempt to reassert Enlightenment values against the anti-rationalists and the cultural pessimists. Many European intellectuals, writers, and artists turned back toward social and political commitment in these years of economic breakdown and rising barbarism. And the outbreak of war seemed for a moment to strengthen this resurgence, for a war against Hitler could be seen as a crusade for humane values against the new savagery.

Hitler's triumphant course from 1939 to 1941 came as a profound shock to many thoughtful Europeans, for it seemed to suggest that the enemies of the Enlightenment tradition, the spokesmen for the mood of cultural despair, had been right all along. The deepest impact was felt in the countries overrun by the Nazis; in Britain and the Soviet Union, on the other hand, the fight for survival left little time for the luxury of introspection. On the occupied Continent, however, men were forced to re-examine all that they had believed, and to seek new explanations. A few took the easy way out: they accepted the Nazi *Weltanschauung* as the spirit of the new age, and rivaled Hitler in proclaiming its merits. The largest group of intellectual converts (some of whom had already become fascist sympathizers before the war) was to be found in France: writers like Robert Brasillach, Pierre

Drieu la Rochelle, Abel Bonnard, Alphonse de Chateaubriant, and (in more ambiguous fashion) Louis-Ferdinand Céline. Others, like the German essayist Ernst Jünger and the French satirist Marcel Aymé, sought refuge in ironic detachment or sheer escapism. But there were still others who continued to grope in the gloom for another exit. It was here, in the conquered countries (and to a lesser degree in Germany as well, when the early victories gave way to exhausting deadlock), that the war really did become a profound spiritual experience; and it was here that some faint signs of intellectual renewal made their appearance.

For some of these lonely spirits, reflecting in solitude or communing in small groups, the crisis of Europe and of the West seemed to derive from the abandonment of what was true and good in the Enlightenment tradition. Decades of derogatory or fearful talk about the rise of the mass-man, they believed, had devalued the worth of the individual and the concept of basic human rights. The rising tide of anti-rationalism had submerged the less dramatic fact that even the mass-man retains a spark of rationality. Because the world sometimes seems to lack system and sense, too many Europeans had concluded that it could not be subjected to man's purposes through the use of science and reason. The goal, then, must be to reassert a kind of traditional humanism with a strongly socialist cast, concerned less for the techniques of social change than for its human goals. In both western and eastern Europe, flickering signs of this new mood could be seen emerging, principally among heirs of the positivist tradition and among younger Marxians. Its most widely read literary expression was Vercors's *Silence de la mer*, published underground in France in 1942.

A second current of renewal was rooted in Christian belief. For several decades the various Churches had seemed to be losing their effectiveness in grappling with modern problems, and their influence had been in serious decline. When neither Protestants nor Catholics offered strong resistance to Hitler's new paganism, and when part of the hierarchy readily collaborated with the Nazi conqueror, it began to seem that the Churches must have reached an advanced state of moral decay. Yet the challenge was now severe enough to produce a healthy reaction. In France, Italy, and the Low Countries, small groups of Catholic laymen, supported by a considerable number of parish priests and regular clergy as well as a few members of the hierarchy, embarked not only on active resistance but also on an attempt to re-examine the Christian's role in the modern world. In

France Emmanuel Mounier, a young lay Catholic who in the prewar decade had developed the doctrine he called personalism, began to emerge as *spiritus rector* of the young Christian democrats. Mounier challenged both the "established disorder" of bourgeois democracy and the introspective advocates of cultural despair; he talked of "rediscovering man-as-a-social-being," of the need for "community" and *engagement*, or commitment to a cause. In Germany, a few hardy Protestant pastors (of whom Dietrich Bonhoeffer was to become best known) struck out on the even more dangerous and difficult path of moral resistance to their own government at war. Bonhoeffer's *Letters from Prison*, written prior to his execution by the Nazis early in 1945, argued that even though men must learn to live as though God were dead, they must not lose their determination to bear witness to the values of Christian humanism. In his cell, he remarked, he had discovered "religion-less Christianity"—a faith that could survive without the apparatus of the Church. Only the familiar Christian virtues could gird men to confront the darkness of the secular world that men had made.

Still a third current of resurgent humanism may have been even more representative of the mood induced by the war. Loosely and popularly labeled existentialism, it grew directly out of the prewar *Kulturpessimismus* that had driven some intellectuals to fascism and others to nihilism. The existentialists, for whom neither Marxian nor Christian doctrine offered a comforting set of certainties, found themselves adrift in what they saw as an absurd world, a world without meaning, beyond man's comprehension or control. Jean-Paul Sartre, their most talented and influential spokesman, had provided literary expression to their somber outlook in his prewar novel *La nausée* (1938), which offered only the meager consolations of artistic creativity as a palliative for total despair. Albert Camus reflected this same grim mood in his prewar writings, including his first novel *L'étranger*, completed just before the fall of France (though not published until 1942).

The irrational horror of total war could not fail to enrich the soil for the existentialists' seed. It assured them of a vastly broadened postwar audience, conditioned to accept the idea of an absurd and incomprehensible world. Yet that same experience of war somehow affected the leading spokesmen of existentialism, and pulled them back into at least the edges of the older humanistic current. Sartre during the war years moved toward Mounier's concept of *engagement*, seen as the obligation of the thoughtful man to assert his own freedom, to give his life meaning by dedicating himself to action for the cause of humanity. His play *Les Mouches*, staged in German-occupied Paris in 1943, hinted at the direction of his thought, though its full development was to come only after the war. As for Camus, who always rejected the existentialist label, his wartime transition was still more rapid and profound. A moralist in the old European tradition, an old-fashioned liberal humanist born after his time, Camus found himself reverting to a belief in certain fundamental values even in a world of absurdity. As early as 1941, his private notebooks show him seeking a way to rally "the community of men" against absurdity, against despair; "a pessimist with respect to the human condition," he mused, "I am an optimist with respect to man." Already he had completed his essay *Le mythe de Sisyphe*, an assertion of man's invincible courage and self-reliance; he was about to become an active participant in the anti-German underground; and he was reflecting on the ideas that would shape his postwar novel *La Peste*, whose powerful evocation of men's varying responses to evil was to stir the sensibilities of a whole new generation whose formative years had been those of the war.

Whether these three currents of resurgent humanism could merge successfully into one, and whether their combined force would be great enough to carry postwar Europe toward recovery and renewal, was beyond any European's powers of divination in 1945. For the hope they offered was clouded by the signs of political and ideological conflict among the victors, and by the awareness of many European intellectuals that war—particularly a war like that of 1939–1945—is not likely to condition men's minds and spirits for the practice of the humane values. Perhaps that awareness underlay the musings of the still obscure French Jesuit Pierre Teilhard de Chardin, as he viewed the scene from his enforced exile in distant China:

At the root of the greatest disturbance on which the nations have embarked today, I distinguish the signs of a change in the human age. Like it or not, the age of the "lukewarm pluralisms" finally has passed. Either, then, a single people will succeed in destroying or absorbing the others or else the peoples will join in a common soul in order to become more human. Unless I deceive myself, that is the dilemma set by the present crisis. In the collision of events, may the passion to unite be lighted in us and become more ardent each day as it faces the passion to destroy. . . .[20]

[20] M. Picón-Salas, *The Ignoble Savages* (New York, 1965), pp. 166–67.

On May 8, 1945, the fragmentary remnant of Hitler's Germany surrendered. Many years earlier, in anticipation of war, Hitler had remarked privately: "We may be destroyed, but if we are, we shall
drag a world with us—a world in flames."[21] Joseph Goebbels had also
warned grimly that in case of defeat, the Nazis would know how to
slam the door behind them and not be forgotten for centuries.[22] Some
Europeans like Léon Blum sensed uneasily that Goebbels might be
right, and that the Nazis' downfall might even conceal a deeper victory. "I tremble [wrote Blum] at the thought that you are already
conquerors in this sense: you have breathed such terror all about
that to master you, to prevent the return of your fury, we shall see
no other way of fashioning the world save in your image, your laws,
the law of Force."[23]

Hitler had embarked on the war with the aim of remaking Europe
according to some new design—a design to be fashioned by the Germans alone, and to endure for a thousand years. He is said to have
prophesied, however, that "if Germany does not win this war, it
will not be won by Britain or France but by the non-European powers." Perhaps, behind his self-confidence and bluster, there lurked a
dim realization of the truth: that his attempt to consolidate Europe
under German control might not be countenanced by the non-European peoples. Perhaps he sensed that the men and the resources of
overseas continents might come pouring into the European theater
of war, and that the outcome then might be to end the brief epoch of
European dominance of the world—a dominance already threatened
by the rise of newer nations overseas.

Six years of war more destructive than any in human history could
scarcely fail to speed the downward spiral of European power and influence. The human and material losses alone seemed almost irre-
placeable. The dead in Europe approximated 30 million—a toll half
again as great as that of the First World War.[24] The Soviet Union alone
probably lost some 16 million citizens; central and western Europe,
over 15 million. Poland's casualty rate—15 percent of the total population—exceeded that of any other nation. The Polish dead (in majority

[21] H. Rauschning, *The Voice of Destruction* (New York, 1940), p. 5.
[22] H. Arendt, *The Origins of Totalitarianism* (New York, 1958), p. 332.
[23] L. Blum, *L'Oeuvre de Léon Blum* (Paris, 1955), V, 514.
[24] There are no generally accepted casualty figures, official or unofficial, for either of
the world wars. Civilian casualties are particularly controversial.

Jews) totalled 5.8 million; Germany lost 4.5 million, Yugoslavia 1.5 million, France 600,000, Rumania 460,000, Hungary 430,000, Czechoslovakia 415,000, Italy 410,000, the United Kingdom almost 400,000, the Netherlands 210,000. Never before had civilians so widely shared with soldiers the bloody risks of war: almost half of Europe's dead were civilians, as compared to one-twentieth in the First World War. Europe's prewar Jewish population had been reduced from 9.2 million to 3.8 million; and only about 1 million of these survivors lived west of the Russian frontier. Accompanying the carnage was an uprooting of populations of unprecedented scope in Europe's history. Between 1939 and 1947, sixteen million Europeans were permanently transplanted from their homelands to other parts of the continent. Eleven million of these were Germans who fled or were driven out of eastern Europe in 1945–1946. This massive German retreat from the east seemed to mean the end of an epoch, of a sporadic *Drang nach Osten* that had begun in the Middle Ages. It transformed the ethnographic map of eastern Europe.

The destruction of physical property was also unprecedented in scope. In the Soviet Union, seventeen hundred cities and towns and seventy thousand villages had been devastated; so were 70 percent of the industrial installations and 60 percent of the transportation facilities in the invaded areas. In Berlin, 75 percent of the houses were destroyed or severely damaged; someone estimated that to clear the city's rubble would require the use of ten fifty-car freight trains per day for sixteen years. In some cities (e.g., Düsseldorf), 95 percent of the homes were uninhabitable. In France and the Low Countries as well as in Germany, most waterways and harbors were blocked, most bridges destroyed, much of the railway system temporarily unusable. In England, whole sections of central London and of other industrial cities had been laid waste by incendiary bombs. Almost everywhere on the Continent, industrial and agricultural production was down by more than half; food, clothing, and consumer necessities were in desperately short supply; circuits of trade had been almost totally disrupted. Except for a few oases like Sweden and Switzerland, Europe seemed destined to be, at least for some years, a vast dilapidated slum and poorhouse.

Europe's financial plight was equally dismaying. Although the British had managed to finance almost half of their war effort on a pay-as-you-fight basis, Britain in 1945 had the dubious distinction of being the world's largest debtor nation. The European allies were technically liable to pay for American Lend-Lease supplies worth $30 billion, of which $13.5 billion had gone to the British and $9 billion to the USSR. Britain was also heavily in debt to the dominions and other members of the sterling bloc. France, whose currency had been virtually ruined by German occupation exactions, owed less under Lend-Lease, but desperately needed continued outside help to avert financial disaster; the same was true of the Netherlands and Italy. The Germans, who had maintained a fictitious financial stability during the war and had counted on victory to bail them out, lay prostrate with a public debt that had increased almost tenfold since 1939, and with a currency inflated sevenfold.

Europe's dismal state seemed even more grave when contrasted with the unprecedented wealth and power of the triumphant United States. American battlefield casualties (300,000 dead) had been relatively small in absolute figures, and seemed even slighter when calculated on a per capita basis. American industry, far from being ravaged by the war, had grown in hothouse fashion; the index of industrial production rose from 100 to 196 during the war years, while the gross national product increased from $91 billion to $166 billion. The American share of the world's merchant marine, which in 1939 had stood at 17 percent compared to Europe's 63 percent, now exceeded that of all the European nations combined.

This shattered Europe was confronted not only by a transatlantic rival of overwhelming power, but also by a restless and newly assertive Africa and Asia, no longer willing to accept a role of colonial subjection. The war had undermined the moral influence as well as the economic and military power of the European states. Japan's early victories had shattered the old image of Western invincibility, and had encouraged other Asiatic peoples to agitate for change. The Americans, preaching the gospel of anti-colonialism, had contributed to this new mood. Some of the colonial peoples—the Indians, the Congolese, the inhabitants of French Africa—had made important contributions in manpower or resources to the Allied victory, and felt justified in presenting their bill for payment. For the exhausted Europeans, colonial empires might still appear to be a base upon which to rebuild their status as world powers; but this appearance was shadowed by the threat that the cost of holding empires might soon outweigh the benefits.

Thus the end of the conflict in Europe, viewed through the wild and sometimes hysterical jubilation of V-E day, could not fail to leave most Europeans sobered and gloomy. If the war had been fought to preserve a workable balance of power in Europe, there was some reason to doubt that the goal had been achieved; for the advance of Soviet control almost to the heart of the Continent might eventually prove as disruptive as Germany's conquest of eastern Europe. If, on the other hand, the war had been fought to preserve the values of Western culture against destruction by a brutal tyranny, there was some reason to wonder whether those values could survive so harrowing an experience, and could harness the passions aroused by the struggle.

For some Europeans, escape seemed the only way out; they looked to the chance of emigrating to some relatively unscathed part of the overseas world, where they might make a new start. For others, the consolations of faith offered a stronger appeal; there was a significant reawakening of interest in religion. A far more striking phenomenon, however, was the temporary decline of nationalist sentiment in favor of some kind of supranational ideal. The intense nationalistic fervor normally stimulated by any war was in this case partially counterbalanced by the sense that in Europe the sovereign nation-state had seen its day, and could survive only if merged into a larger entity, massive enough to exert some influence in an altered world. During the latter months of the war, some tentative explorations into the federal idea were inaugurated, mainly by private citizens, but also by governments. In London, the Belgian, Dutch, and Luxembourg governments-in-exile even managed to work out plans for a postwar economic union, which emerged after 1945 as Benelux. But the future of these hopes on the morrow of victory remained opaque, for alongside them could be seen signs of a vigorously assertive nationalism, embodied for example in de Gaulle's followers in France and in the victorious British who had stood fast for so long against the tempest.

Europeans in May 1945 could not anticipate what the postwar years would bring. There was no precedent for the state to which they had been reduced by the most savage and destructive war in Europe's history. They could hope that Soviet power in eastern Europe would be exercised with restraint, and would gradually be relaxed in order to restore a reasonably stable European balance. They could hope that the United States, made wise by the record of error after another great war, would this time show a generous and sympathetic understanding of Europe's needs, and would use its power and wealth to constructive ends. They could hope that the vanquished Germans, beaten to their knees and temporarily outlawed from European society, would eventually emerge chastened and "Europeanized" in outlook, rather than humiliated and filled with a paranoid urge for revenge. Of these hopes, some were to be fulfilled in large measure; others would long remain clouded by uncertainty. But even the most optimistic Europeans in 1945 could not foresee the speed and vigor of economic recovery and expansion that would quickly heal the physical scars of war, that would convert most of the continent from potential slum and poorhouse into a society of unprecedented affluence and renewed self-confidence. Perhaps men are always inclined to underestimate the resilience of the human race, its stubborn capacity to scramble back from the pit into which it has been cast by its own follies. Perhaps those observers who in 1945 had talked gloomily of "the end of Europe" had overlooked the possibility of a new beginning.

BIBLIOGRAPHICAL ESSAY

PUBLISHED OR MICROFILMED SOURCE MATERIALS

Although no European government has yet opened its archives to scholars, the defeat of Germany provided historians with an almost unprecedented windfall of official documents from that country. The bulk of the German Foreign Office archives was captured by the victors, along with an enormous collection of Wehrmacht files and Nazi party records. Most of these materials were subsequently returned to the German government, but only after the most important items had been microfilmed and, in some cases, published. For the Foreign Office records, Vol. III of George O. Kent's *A Catalog of Files and Microfilms of the German Foreign Ministry Archives 1920–1945* (The Hague, 1966) covers the war years. For the documents stored in United States Army warehouses at Alexandria, Virginia (primarily Wehrmacht records, but including files of many other German government agencies as well), the American Historical Association's Commission for the Study of War Documents has prepared a series of more than thirty mimeographed "Guides to German Records." Other captured German files are in the Imperial War Museum in London, and in Moscow.

Extensive selections from the German Foreign Office files have been published by a committee of American, British, and French scholars under the title *Documents on German Foreign Policy 1918–1945* (Washington, D.C., 1949–1964). Volumes VIII–XIII of Series D cover the early war years 1939–1941; the project will eventually be completed by the German government.

Another major collection of published records emerged from the various Allied trials of war criminals conducted at Nuremberg during the early postwar years. The largest of these collections (which contains only about one-tenth of the documentation presented as evidence) is International Military Tribunal, *Trial of the Major War Criminals*, 42 vols. (Nuremberg, 1949). A brief selection in English translation was published by the United States Chief of Counsel for Prosecution of Axis Criminality, *Nazi Conspiracy and Aggression*, 10 vols. (Washington, D.C., 1946–1948). Some twenty volumes of selected documents and testimony from subsequent trials have also been issued by the British or the American government. Individual scholars (mainly German) have edited a number of valuable military and personal records: e.g., Percy Ernst Schramm *et al.*, *Kriegstagebuch des*

Oberkommandos der Wehrmacht, 4 vols. in 7 (Frankfurt 1961–1965); H.-A. Jacobsen, *Halders Kriegstagebuch*, 3 vols. (Stuttgart, 1962–1964); Walther Hubatsch, *Hitlers Weisungen für die Kriegführung 1939–1945* (Frankfurt, 1962); H. Heiber, *Hitlers Lagebesprechung: die Protokollfragmente seiner militärischen Konferenzen 1942–1945* (Stuttgart, 1962); Felix Gilbert, *Hitler Directs His War* (New York, 1950); Henry Picker, *Hitlers Tischgespräche im Führerhauptquartier, 1941–42* (Bonn, 1951); H. R. Trevor-Roper, *Hitler's Table Talk 1941–1944*, tr. from the German (London, 1953); François Genoux, *The Testament of Adolf Hitler*, tr. from the French (London, 1961); Max Domarus, *Hitler: Reden und Proklamationen*, Vol. II, 1939–1945 (Würzburg, 1963).

The victorious powers have been more selective in publishing their own wartime records. Italy's Commissione per la pubblicazione dei documenti diplomatici has made a start: the ninth series of its vast project *I documenti diplomatici italiani* (Rome, 1952–) will cover the years 1939–1943. Five volumes in this series have already appeared. For the United States, the Department of State's annual volumes *Foreign Relations of the United States* have reached the year 1945; one or two volumes for each wartime year deal with European affairs. There is also a stout volume of American documents on each of the major wartime conferences, including Yalta and Potsdam. The French government has published the principal documents of the Wiesbaden Commission charged with enforcing the Franco-German armistice terms: P. Caron and P. Cézard (eds.), *La délégation française auprès de la Commission allemande d'armistice*, 5 vols. (Paris, 1947–1959). The Soviet Union has issued four volumes of selected materials: two of these contain the personal correspondence exchanged between Stalin, Churchill, and Roosevelt (*Correspondence between the Chairman of the Council of Ministers of the USSR and the Presidents of the USA and the Prime Ministers of Great Britain*, 2 vols. [Moscow, 1957]), while the other two are concerned with Soviet-French and Soviet-Czechoslovak relations (*Sovetsko-Frantsuskie Otnosheniia vo Vremia Velikoi Otechestvennoi Voiny 1941–1945* [Moscow, 1959], and *Sovetsko-chekhoslovatskie Otnosheniia vo Vremia Velikoi Otechestvennoi Voiny 1941–1945* [Moscow, 1960]). There are also some published materials from the Belgian and the Hungarian foreign ministry files: C. de Visscher and F. Vanlangenhove (eds.), *Documents diplomatiques belges, 1920–1940*, Vol. V, 1938–1940 (Brussels, 1967); Lajos Kerekes (ed.), *Allianz Hitler-Horthy-Mussolini: Dokumente zur ungarischen Aussenpolitik* (Budapest, 1966); L. Zsigmond (ed.), *Magyarország Külpolitikája a II világháboru kitörésénak idöszakaban 1939–1940* (Budapest, 1962). The General Sikorski Historical Institute in London has issued one volume from the archives of the Polish government-in-exile: *Documents on Polish-Soviet Relations 1939–1945* (London, 1961). The Papacy has recently undertaken an important series from the Vatican archives, three volumes of which have appeared: *Le Saint-Siège et la guerre en Europe: mars 1939–août 1940* (Vatican City, 1965); *Lettres de Pie XII aux Evèques allemands, 1939–1944* (Vatican City, 1966); *Le Saint-Siège et la situation religieuse en Pologne et les pays baltiques, 1939–1945* (Vatican City, 1967).

Immediately after the war, several governments instituted parliamentary commissions of inquiry into the events of the war years, and published the testimony together with selected documents: e.g., France, Assemblée Nationale, *Commission d'enquête parlementaire sur les événements en France de 1939 à 1945,* 10 vols. (Paris, 1951–1952). There are similar publications for the Netherlands (18 vols.) and Denmark (10 vols. to date). For Yugoslavia, there is a bulky official collection of documentary materials on resistance activities: *Zbornik Dokumenata i Podataka o Narodnoosobodilackorn ratu Jugoslo-Jenskih naroda,* 17 vols. (Belgrade, 1949–1960). The French government has published a documentary study of war damage and losses: France, Président du Conseil, *Dommages subis par la France et l'union française du fait de la guerre et de l'occupation ennemie,* 9 vols. (Paris, 1950). The United States government, immediately after Germany's capitulation, dispatched teams of experts to examine the effects of the strategic bombing campaign. Their reports, much broader in scope than the title would suggest, were published in 316 volumes: *United States Strategic Bombing Survey* (Washington, 1946–1947).

PERIODICALS

The most useful periodicals for the war period are the *Revue d'Histoire de la Deuxième Guerre Mondiale* (Paris, 1949–) and the *Vierteljahrshefte für Zeitgeschichte* (Stuttgart, 1953–). Both contain specialized articles and detailed bibliographies; the French quarterly also carries valuable book reviews and focuses entire issues on particular topics. Useful Soviet periodicals are *Voprosy Istorii, Novaia i Noveishaia Istoriia,* and *Voenno-Istoricheskii Zhurnal.* An international review dealing with the European underground movements, *Cahiers Internationaux de la Résistance,* appeared briefly in Vienna (also published in German); an Italian periodical is *Il Movimento di Liberazione in Italia* (Milan, 1949–).

GENERAL ACCOUNTS

Most general surveys of the war focus primarily or entirely on its military aspects. Three exceptions that attempt a broader synthesis are Arnold and Veronica Toynbee (eds.), *Hitler's Europe* (London, 1954); André Latreille, *La seconde guerre mondiale* (Paris, 1966); and Raymond Cartier, *La seconde guerre mondiale,* 2 vols. (Paris, 1966–1967). Louis L. Snyder's *The War: A Concise History 1939–1945* (New York, 1960) is a readable account; Roberto Battaglia's *La seconda guerra mondiale* (Rome, 1961) offers a left-wing

Italian view; H. G. Dahms' *Geschichte des zweiten Weltkriegs* (Tübingen, 1965) is probably the best German survey. H.-A. Jacobsen's *1939-1945: der zweite Weltkrieg*, 3d ed. (Darmstadt, 1960), contains a meticulous chronology and a collection of documents. Leo Stern's *Der zweite Weltkrieg*, 2d ed. (Berlin, 1960), provides an East German view. Most of the general Soviet histories (whose viewpoint is conveniently summarized in Matthew Gallagher, *The Soviet History of World War II: Myths, Memories, and Realities* (New York, 1963), have been outdated by the publication of the USSR's official history of the war: Institut Marksizma-Leninizma, *Istoriia Velikoi Otechestvennoi Voiny Sovetskogo Soiuza*, revised ed., 6 vols. (Moscow, 1963-1965). Special mention must be made of Winston Churchill's remarkable memoir-history *The Second World War*, 6 vols. (Boston, 1948-1953). Although one critic likens it to "a one-way telephone conversation," it remains the most readable account of the period. Many of the volumes in the British official history of the war are also invaluable.

IMMEDIATE BACKGROUND

Raymond J. Sontag's forthcoming volume in this series will provide an up-to-date analysis of the origins of the war. Arnold and Veronica Toynbee *et al., The Eve of War, 1939* (London, 1958) is a careful and perceptive account. Elizabeth Wiskemann's *Europe of the Dictators 1919-1945* (London, 1966) is particularly well informed on central European developments. A. J. P. Taylor's *Origins of the Second World War* (London, 1961) offers a stimulating but controversial revisionist view; Taylor sees the outbreak of war as the product of blunders by both sides. Even more controversial are David L. Hoggan's two monographs, *Der erzwungene Krieg*, 5th ed. (Tübingen, 1964), and *Frankreichs Widerstand gegen den zweiten Weltkrieg* (Tübingen, 1963). Hoggan attempts to shift the burden of responsibility from Hitler to such Western statesmen as Halifax, Daladier, and Roosevelt. Two effective statements of the more orthodox position are Walther Hofer, *War Premeditated 1939* (London, 1955) and E. M. Robertson, *Hitler's Pre-War Policy and Military Plans 1933-1939* (London, 1963). There are some excellent chapters in G. A. Craig and Felix Gilbert, *The Diplomats, 1919-1939* (Princeton, 1953). William R. Rock's *Appeasement on Trial* (New York, 1966) re-examines Chamberlain's policy in 1939 and stresses the effect of public opinion in blocking a renewal of appeasement. Robert J. O'Neill's *The German Army and the Nazi Party, 1933-1939* (London, 1966) shows how Hitler manipulated the Reichswehr; so does John W. Wheeler-Bennett's *The Nemesis of Power* (New York, 1954). Robin Higham's *Armed Forces in Peacetime: Britain 1918-1940* (Hamden, Conn., 1962) and *The Military Intellectuals in Britain 1918-1939* (New Brunswick, N.J., 1966) analyze the shortcomings of Britain's military establishment. John Erickson's *The Soviet High Command: a Military-*

Political History 1918–1941 (London, 1962) is an extraordinarily well-informed and perceptive study.

THE PROBLEM OF HITLER'S WAR AIMS

In addition to the works listed above, the following studies are useful: Ludwig Dehio, *Gleichgewicht oder Hegemonie* (Krefeld, 1948); L. Gruchmann, *Nationalsozialistische Grossraumordnung* (Stuttgart, 1962); Paul Kluke, "Nationalsozialistische Europaideologie," *Vierteljahrshefte für Zeitgeschichte*, III (1955), 240–75; Horst Kühne, *Faschistische Kolonialideologie und zweiter Weltkrieg* (Berlin, 1962), an east German version; Günter Moltmann, "Weltherrschaftsideen Hitlers," in Otto Bruner and Dietrich Gerhard (eds.), *Europa und Übersee* (Hamburg, 1961); Wolfe W. Schmokel, *Dream of Empire: German Colonialism, 1919–1945* (New Haven, 1964); Alton Frye, *Nazi Germany and the American Hemisphere* (New Haven, 1967). A wartime view of Hitler's plans for a new Europe may be found in Claude Moret's *L'Allemagne et la réorganisation de l'Europe* (Neuchâtel, 1944).

MILITARY ASPECTS: GENERAL

Two good up-to-date surveys are Basil Collier, *The Second World War* (New York, 1967), and Peter Young, *World War 1939–1945, a Short History* (London, 1966). Older German overviews are Walter Görlitz, *Der zweite Weltkrieg*, 2 vols. (Stuttgart, 1951–1952), and Kurt von Tippelskirch, *Geschichte des zweiten Weltkriegs* (Bonn, 1954). Soviet works include B. S. Telpuchowski, *Die Sowjetische Geschichte des Grossen Vaterländischen Krieges*, tr. from the Russian (Frankfurt, 1961); G. A. Deborin, *Vtoraia Mirovaia Voina* (Moscow, 1958); and S. P. Platonow *et al., Vtoraia Mirovaia Voina* (Moscow, 1958). Special mention should be made of the remarkable six-volume series in the British official history entitled *Grand Strategy* (London, 1964–) by J. R. M. Butler, J. M. A. Gwyer, and John Ehrman.

Other studies of general scope: H.-A. Jacobsen and Jürgen Rohwer (eds.), *Decisive Battles of World War II: the German View*, tr. from the German (London, 1966); Hanson W. Baldwin, *Battles Lost and Won: Great Campaigns of World War II* (New York, 1966); Seymour Freidin and William Richardson, *The Fatal Decisions* (New York, 1956); Gert Buchheit, *Hitler der Feldherr* (Rastatt, 1958); Percy Ernst Schramm, *Hitler als militärischer Führer* (Frankfurt, 1962); Andreas Hillgruber, *Hitlers Strategie: Politik und Kriegführung 1940–1941* (Frankfurt, 1965); F. H. Hinsley, *Hitler's Strategy* (Cambridge, 1951); H.-A. Jacobsen, *Deutsche Kriegführung 1939–1945* (Hanover, 1961); F. W. von Mellenthin, *Panzer Battles 1939–1945*, tr. from the German (London, 1955); R. T. Paget, *Manstein, His Campaigns and His Trial* (London, 1951); Günther Blumentritt, *Von Rundstedt, the Soldier and the Man*, tr. from the German (London, 1952); C. N. Bradley, *On Their Shoulders: British Generalship in the Lean Years, 1939–1942* (London, 1964); Francis de Guingaud, *Generals at War* (London, 1964); Trumbull Higgins, *Winston Churchill and the Second Front 1940–1943* (New York, 1957), anti-Churchill; Forrest M. Pogue, *The Supreme Command* (Washington, D.C., 1959); Martin Blumenson *et al.*, *Command Decisions* (Washington, 1960); Maurice Matloff and E. M. Snell, *Strategic Planning for Coalition Warfare*, 2 vols., (Washington, D.C., 1953–1959); Eddy Bauer, *La guerre des blindés* (Paris, 1962).

The list of memoirs by Western, German, and Soviet generals is a long one, and their usefulness varies widely. From the British side there are Marshal Bernard Montgomery, *Memoirs* (London, 1958); Earl Alexander, *The Alexander Memoirs* (London, 1962); Lord Ismay, *The Memoirs of General the Lord Ismay* (London, 1960); Roderick Macleod and Denis Kelly (eds.), *Time Unguarded: the Ironside Diaries 1937–1940* (New York, 1962); Francis de Guingaud, *Operation Victory* (New York, 1947); Arthur Bryant, *The Turn of the Tide* (London, 1957) and *Triumph in the West* (London, 1959)—two volumes based on the reminiscences and papers of Lord Alanbrooke. The American contributions include Dwight D. Eisenhower, *Crusade in Europe* (Garden City, 1948); Omar N. Bradley, *A Soldier's Story* (New York, 1951); Mark Clark, *Calculated Risk* (New York, 1950). The Germans have been most prolific of all: Franz Halder, *Hitler as War Lord*, tr. from the German (London, 1950); Adolf Heusinger, *Befehl im Widerstreit* (Tübingen, 1950); Wilhelm Keitel, *The Memoirs of Field-Marshal Keitel*, tr. from the German (New York, 1965); Marshal Kesselring, *Soldat bis zum letzten Tag* (Bonn, 1953); Erich von Manstein, *Verlorene Siege* (Bonn, 1955); Lothar Rendulic, *Gekämpft, Gesiegt, Geschlagen* (Heidelberg, 1952); Frido von Senger und Etterlin, *Neither Fear nor Hope*, tr. from the German (London, 1963); Walter Warlimont, *Inside Hitler's Headquarters*, tr. from the German (London, 1964); Siegfried Westphal, *Heer in Fesseln* (Bonn, 1950); Helmuth Greiner, *Die oberste Wehrmachtführung, 1939–1943* (Wiesbaden, 1951); Heinz Guderian, *Panzer Leader*, tr. from the German (London, 1952). French contributions include Maurice Gamelin's *Servir*, 3 vols. (Paris, 1946–1947); Maxime Weygand's *Mémoires*, 3 vols. (Paris, 1950–1957); Alphonse Juin's *Mémoires*, 2 vols. (Paris, 1959); and Jean de Lattre de Tassigny's *Histoire de la première armée française* (Paris, 1949). The memoirs of Soviet generals, which are concerned exclusively with the war on the eastern front, are listed below under the heading THE WAR IN RUSSIA.

POLISH CAMPAIGN

Robert Jars, *La campagne de Pologne* (Paris, 1949) is still useful, though Robert M. Kennedy's *The German Campaign in Poland* (Washington, D.C.,

1956) is more detailed. The Polish government-in-exile's account (with summaries in English) is *Polskie Siły Zbrojne w drugiej wojnie światowej*, 2 vols. (London, 1951–1959). Basil Spiru's *September 1939* (Berlin, 1959) offers the East German view. Dominik Wegierski's *September 1939* (London, 1940) is a personal account by a young Pole.

NORWEGIAN CAMPAIGN

Two excellent British accounts of the operations are T. K. Derry, *The Campaign in Norway* (London, 1952), and J. L. Moulton, *The Norwegian Campaign of 1940* (London, 1966). Walther Hubatsch, *"Weserübung": die deutsche Besetzung von Dänemark und Norwegen 1940*, 2d ed. (Berlin, 1960), is a detailed examination of German planning and operations; Carl-Axel Gemzell, in *Raeder, Hitler und Skandinavien* (Lund, 1965), stresses Admiral Raeder's role in persuading Hitler to act in order to secure submarine bases for an Atlantic offensive.

WESTERN CAMPAIGN

H.-A. Jacobsen's *Fall Gelb* (Wiesbaden, 1957) and the same author's *Dokumente zur Vorgeschichte des Westfeldzugs* (Göttingen, 1956) and *Dokumente zum Westfeldzug* (Göttingen, 1960) contain the most detailed and thorough account of German preparations. The most recent French reassessment is General Beaufre's *Le drame de 1940* (Paris, 1965). Earlier French studies include Pierre Lyet, *La bataille de France* (Paris, 1947); Adolphe Goutard, *1940: la guerre des occasions perdues* (Paris, 1956); General Conquet, *L'énigme des blindés, 1932–1940* (Paris, 1956); and Jacques Bénoist-Mechin, *Sixty Days that Shook the World*, tr. from the French (London, 1963). The official British version is Major L. B. Ellis, *The War in France and Flanders (1939–1940)* (London, 1953). Telford Taylor's *The March of Conquest* (New York, 1958), is absorbing and well documented. The memoirs of a German intelligence officer, Ulrich Liss, are enlightening: *Westfront 1939/40* (Neckargemünd, 1959); so are those of General Edward Spears, Churchill's personal emissary to France during the crisis: *Assignment to Catastrophe*, 2 vols. (London, 1954). The Soviet view may be found in A. M. Nekrich, *Voina kotoruiu nazvali "strannoi"* (Moscow, 1961); and V. P. Smirnov, *"Strannaia voina" i porazhenie Frantsii* (Moscow, 1963).

BATTLE OF BRITAIN

Telford Taylor's *The Breaking Wave* (New York, 1967) is the most recent reassessment, based on study of the German sources. Good British accounts are Ronald Wheatley, *Operation Sea Lion* (Oxford, 1958); Edward Bishop, *The Battle of Britain* (London, 1960); and Duncan Grinnel-Milne, *The Silent Victory* (London, 1958). From the German side we have Karl Klee, *Das*

Unternehmen "Seelöwe" (Göttingen, 1958) and Walter Ansel, *Hitler Confronts England*, tr. from the German (Durham, N.C., 1961). Drew Middleton's *The Sky Suspended* (London, 1960) is a dramatic reconstruction by an American journalist; Marcel Jullian, *The Battle of Britain*, tr. from the French (New York, 1967), offers a French view. Constantine FitzGibbon's *The Blitz* (London, 1957) carries the story through the winter of 1940–1941. There are several excellent accounts of the air battle: notably Basil Collier's *The Defense of the United Kingdom* (London, 1957) and *The Battle of Britain* (London, 1962); and Derek Wood and Derek Dempster's *The Narrow Margin* (London, 1961).

MEDITERRANEAN AND NORTH AFRICAN CAMPAIGNS

Four of the six projected volumes in the British official history have been published: I. S. O. Playfair, C. J. C. Molony *et al.*, *The Mediterranean and the Middle East* (London, 1954–1966). Romeo Bernotti's *Storia della guerra nel Mediterraneo 1940–1943*, 2d ed., (Rome, 1960) stresses naval operations. Two useful studies of the airborne conquest of Crete are John Hall Spencer, *Battle for Crete* (London, 1962), and J. M. G. Stewart, *The Struggle for Crete* (London, 1967). Mario Cervi's *Storia della guerra di Grecia*, 2d ed. (Milan, 1965), is a frank and fair-minded account of Mussolini's Greek misadventure. The battles in North Africa have been refought almost as vigorously as in the original actuality. Most of the generals involved have told their own stories. R. W. Thompson severely criticizes Montgomery's role in *The Montgomery Legend* (London, 1967); the rival Rommel legend is admiringly cultivated in B. H. Liddell Hart (ed.), *The Rommel Papers*, tr. from the German (London, 1953). Two good German studies are Paul Carell's *The Foxes of the Desert*, tr. from the German (New York, 1961), and H. G. von Esebeck's *Afrikanische Schicksaljahre* (Wiesbaden, 1956); a British view may be found in Correlli Barnett's *The Desert Generals* (London, 1960) and *The Battle of Alamein* (New York, 1964). George Howe's *Northwest Africa: Seizing the Initiative* (Washington, D.C., 1957) is a volume in the United States Army's official history; less favorable to the Americans is General Louis Koeltz's *Une campagne que nous avons gagnée (Tunisie 1942–1943)* (Paris, 1959).

THE WAR IN RUSSIA

The titanic struggle on Soviet soil has given rise to an enormous literature, with German and Soviet authors leading the way. General accounts of the eastern campaign include (in addition to the six-volume official Soviet history); Paul Carell, *Hitler's War on Russia*, tr. from the German (London, 1964); Alan Clark, *Barbarossa* (London, 1965), which in general defends Hitler's strategic leadership against his generals' criticism; Trumbull Higgins, *Hitler*

and Russia (New York, 1966); George E. Blau, *The German Campaign in
Russia* (Washington, D.C., 1955); Michel Garder, *Une guerre pas comme les
autres* (Paris, 1962); P. E. Schramm, *Deutschland-Russland 1941–1945* (Han-
over, 1960); I. M. Shliapin *et al., Kommunisticheskaia Partiia v Period Velikoi
Otechestvennoi Voiny* (Moscow, 1958); F. D. Vorob'ev and V. M. Kravtsov,
Otechestvennaia Voina Sovetskogo Soiuza 1941–1945 (Moscow, 1961).

Recently, a number of leading Soviet commanders have begun to publish
personal accounts of the war years. Marshal Andrei I. Eremenko has contributed four books: *Na Zapadnom Napravlenii* (Moscow, 1959), on the first
phase of the war; *Protiv Falsifikatsii Istorii Vtoroi Mirovoi Voiny*, 2d ed.
(Moscow, 1959), an attack on certain German military memorialists; *Stalingrad* (Moscow, 1961); and *V nachale voiny* (Moscow, 1964). Marshal Vasili
I. Chuikov's memoirs are in two volumes: *The Beginning of the Road*, tr.
from the Russian (London, 1963), and *The Battle for Stalingrad*, tr. from
the Russian (New York, 1964). Marshal Ivan S. Konev recalls the last phase
of the war in his *Sorok Piatyi* (Moscow, 1966), while General Nikolai K.
Popel' focuses on the early period in *V Tiazhkujiu Poru* (Moscow, 1959) and
Tanki Povernuli na Zapad (Moscow, 1960). Portions of Marshal Georgi
Zhukov's recollections have appeared in the periodical *Voenno-Istoricheskii
Zhurnal* for 1966. Marshal Konstantin K. Rokossovsky has edited a collabora-
tive account of the Battle of Stalingrad: *Velikaia Pobeda na Volge* (Moscow,
1965). On the German side, there are Marshal Friedrich von Paulus' account
of *Stalingrad*, tr. from the German (Paris, 1961); the memoirs of Warlimont,
Guderian, von Manstein, and Heusinger (listed earlier); and a series of
essays edited by A. Philippi and F. Heim, *Der Feldzug gegen Sowjetrussland*
(Stuttgart, 1962).

From the long list of memoirs or diaries by lesser officers, common soldiers,
or journalists, here are a few representative examples: Hans Dibold, *Arzt in
Stalingrad*, 2d ed. (Salzburg, 1954); Edwin E. Dwinger, *Die verlorenen
Söhne* (Munich, 1956); Erich Kern, *Das goldene Feld* (Munich, 1957);
Karl Maron, *Von Charkow bis Berlin* (Berlin, 1960); H. Pabst, *The Outer-
most Frontier*, tr. from the German (London, 1957); Erich Weinert, *Memento
Stalingrad*, 2d ed. (Berlin, 1960); Pietro Giuffrida, *L'A.R.M.I.R.* (Rome,
1953); P. Mus'iakov, *Sevastopol'skie Dni 1941–1943* (Simferopol, 1963); Kurt
Schiebold, *Opfergang in Rumänien* (Tübingen, 1952). Among the memoirs
of non-German volunteers in the "European crusade" against Bolshevism are
those of the Belgian Léon Degrelle, *Die verlorene Legion* (Stuttgart, 1952);
and the Dane Sven Hassel, *The Legion of the Damned*, tr. from the Danish
(London, 1957).

Among the individual battles and campaigns in the east, Stalingrad has
drawn most attention. Walter Görlitz's biography of the German commander,
Von Paulus and Stalingrad, tr. from the German (London, 1963), is a controversial but important defense of its subject. Heinz Schröter's *Stalingrad*

"biz zur letzten patrone" (Osnabrück, 1952) is the work of a German war correspondent who in 1943 was assigned the task of writing an official history of the battle, but whose manuscript was suppressed by Goebbels. Other German accounts are Heinrich Gerlach, *The Forsaken Army*, tr. from the German (New York, 1959); V. Rohden, *Die Luftwaffe ringt um Stalingrad* (Wiesbaden, 1952); and Joachim Wieder, *Stalingrad und die Verantwortung des Soldaten* (Munich, 1962). The best of the Soviet accounts is A. M. Samsonov's *Stalingradskaia bitva* (Moscow, 1960); a good British study is Ronald Seth's *Stalingrad, Point of Return* (London, 1959).

On the siege of Leningrad, there are several excellent works: A. V. Karasev's *Leningradtsy v Gody Blokady 1941–1943* (Moscow, 1959); Dmitri V. Pavlov's *Leningrad 1941: the Blockade*, tr. from the Russian (Chicago, 1966); Leon Gouré's *The Siege of Leningrad* (Stanford, 1962); V. P. Sviridov *et al., Bitva za Leningrad 1941–1944* (Leningrad, 1962). On the battle of Moscow in 1941–1942: A. M. Samsonov, *Velikaia Bitva pod Moskvoi* (Moscow, 1956); Ronald Seth, *Operation Barbarossa, the Battle for Moscow* (London, 1964); *Razgrom Nemetsko-Fashistkikh Voisk pod Moskvoi* (Moscow, 1964). On the battle of Kursk: I. Marken, *Die Kursken Schlacht*, tr. from the Russian (Berlin, 1960). On the Crimean operations: Andreas Hillgruber, *Die Räumung der Krim 1944* (Berlin, 1959). On the Caucasus: A. S. Sawjalow and T. J. Kaljadin, *Die Schlacht um den Kaukasus*, tr. from the Russian (Berlin, 1959). On the ill-fated Vlasov army: Edwin E. Dwinger, *General Wlassow: eine Tragödie unserer Zeit* (Frankfort, 1951); George Fischer, *Soviet Opposition to Stalin* (Cambridge, Mass., 1952); Alexander Dallin, *German Rule in Russia 1941–1945* (London, 1957). On the last months of the struggle in the east: Cornelius Ryan, *The Last Battle* (London, 1966); John Toland, *The Last Hundred Days* (New York, 1966); Jürgen Thorwald, *Es begann an der Weichsel* (Stuttgart, 1950) and *Das Ende an der Elbe* (Stuttgart, 1950), combined in shortened English translation as *Flight in the Winter* (New York, 1951).

THE CAMPAIGN IN ITALY

Good overall surveys are Eric Linklater, *The Campaign in Italy* (London, 1951); Robert Jars, *La campagne d'Italie 1943–1945* (Paris, 1954); and W. G. F. Jackson, *The Battle for Italy* (New York, 1967). Specialized studies include Martin Blumenson, *Anzio* (Philadelphia, 1963); Wynford Vaughan-Thomas, *Anzio* (New York, 1961); Charles Connell, *Monte Cassino* (London, 1963); Fred Majdalany, *The Battle of Cassino* (Boston, 1957); Rudolf Böhmler, *Monte Cassino* (Darmstadt, 1955); Douglas Orgill, *The Gothic Line* (London, 1967). Also useful are the memoirs of General Alexander, Marshal Kesselring, General Frido von Senger und Etterlin, and General L. K. Truscott (*Command Missions* [New York, 1954]).

Several volumes in the American and British official histories of the war provide excellent coverage of the final campaigns in the west: Gordon A. Harrison, *Cross-Channel Attack* (Washington, D.C., 1951); Martin Blumenson, *Breakout and Pursuit* (Washington, D.C., 1962); Charles B. MacDonald, *The Siegfried Line* (Washington, D.C., 1963); Forrest W. Pogue, *The Supreme Command* (Washington, D.C., 1959); L. R. Ellis, *Victory in the West: the Battle of Normandy* (London, 1963). In addition to the memoirs cited earlier, these are relevant: Hans Speidel, *Invasion 1944*, tr. from the German (Chicago, 1950); and Dietrich von Choltitz, *Un soldat parmi les soldats*, tr. from the German (Avignon, 1964). Good secondary studies include Cornelius Ryan, *The Longest Day* (New York, 1957); John Frayn Turner, *Invasion '44* (New York, 1959); S. L. A. Marshall, *Night Drop* (Boston, 1962); Eversley Belfield and E. Essame, *The Battle of Normandy* (London, 1965); Friedrich Ruge, *Rommel face au débarquement 1944*, tr. from the German (Paris, 1960); Paul Carell, *Sie kommen!*, 2d ed. (Oldenburg, 1960); Friedrich Hayn, *Die Invasion* (Heidelberg, 1954); B. M. Kulis, *Vtoriyij Front* (Moscow, 1960); Admiral Lemonnier, *Les cent jours de la bataille de Normandie* (Paris, 1961); Jacques Mordal, *La bataille de France* (Paris, 1964); Cornelius Bauer, *The Battle of Arnhem*, tr. from the German (London, 1966); John Toland, *Battle: the Story of the Bulge* (New York, 1959); Charles B. MacDonald, *The Battle of the Huertgen Forest* (Philadelphia, 1963); S. L. A. Marshall, *Bastogne* (Washington, D.C., 1946); Jacques Nobécourt, *Hitler's Last Throw*, tr. from the French (London, 1965); Hans Dollinger (ed.), *Die letzten hundert Tage* (Munich, 1965); Andrew Tully, *Berlin: Story of the Battle* (New York, 1963); R. W. Thompson, *The Price of Victory* (London, 1960).

WAR IN THE AIR

The Allied strategic bombing campaign, the most controversial aspect of the air war, is the subject of a superb official history by Sir Charles Webster and Noble Frankland: *The Strategic Air Offensive Against Germany 1939–1945*, 4 vols. (London, 1961). Frankland has summarized his own conclusions in a brief essay, *The Bombing Offensive Against Germany* (London, 1965). A briefer and more popular official history is D. Richards and H. S. Saundby, *Royal Air Force 1939–1945*, 3 vols. (London, 1953–1954). The official American account is by Wesley F. Craven and James L. Cate: *The Army Air Forces in World War II*, 7 vols. (Chicago, 1948–1958). The *Luftwaffe*'s record is examined (tr. from the German, if title in English) in Karl Bartz's *Swastika in the Air* (London, 1956); Werner Baumbach's *Broken Swastika* (London, 1960); Georg W. Feuchter's *Geschichte des Luftkrieges* (Bonn, 1954); Adolf Galland, *The First and the Last* (London, 1955); Ernst Heinkel's *Stürmisches*

Leben (Stuttgart, 1953); Karlheinz Keus and H.-J. Nowarra, *Die deutschen Flugzeuge 1933–1945* (Munich, 1961); Hans Rudel, *Stuka Pilot* (New York, 1958); Theo Weber, *Die Luftschlacht um England* (Frauenfeld, 1956). Little has appeared on the Soviet air force; Robert A. Kilmarx's *History of the Soviet Air Force* (London, 1962) is therefore useful. An Italian viewpoint may be found in Rodolfo Gentile's *Storia delle operazioni aeree nella seconda guerra mondiale* (Rome, 1953); a French angle in Pierre Barjot's *Histoire de la guerre aéro-navale* (Paris, 1961). Andrew Boyle's *Trenchard* (London, 1962) portrays the prewar organizer of the R.A.F. Sir Arthur Harris, in *Bomber Command* (London, 1947), defends his wartime advocacy of saturation bombing; so does Harris' former deputy, Sir Robert Saundby, in *Air Bombardment: the Story of Its Development* (New York, 1961). The latest contribution is Lord Tedder's personal account, *With Prejudice* (London, 1967). Books on the air Battle of Britain are listed above under that heading. Other special studies include Basil Collier's *The Battle of the V-Bomb* (London, 1964), and David Irving's *The Destruction of Dresden* (London, 1963). The impact of the bombing campaign in Germany is assessed in Erich Hampe's *Der zivile Luftschutz im zweiten Weltkrieg* (Frankfurt, 1963), and in Hans Rumpf's *The Bombing of Germany*, tr. from the German (London, 1963).

WAR ON THE SEA

The British official history, Captain S. W. Roskill's *The War at Sea, 1939–1945*, 3 vols. in 4 (London, 1954–1961), is the most valuable single study. For the German navy, there are the memoirs of the top wartime commanders, Erich Raeder, *My Life*, tr. from the German (Annapolis, 1960); and Karl Doenitz, *Memoirs*, tr. from the German (London, 1959). A multivolume official history of the Italian navy's role is underway: *La marina italiana nella seconda guerra mondiale*, 12 vols. to date (Rome, 1957–). Romeo Bernotti has published a three-volume *La guerra sui mari nel conflitto mondiale* (Livorno, 1947–1950); a shorter account is M. A. Bragadin's *The Italian Navy in World War II*, tr. from the Italian (Annapolis, 1957). For the role of the French fleet, there are several studies: Admiral Paul Auphan and Jacques Mordal, *The French Navy in World War II*, tr. from the French (Annapolis, 1959); Admiral Raymond de Belot, *La marine française pendant la campagne 1939–1940* (Paris, 1954); and Jacques Mordal, *La marine française à l'épreuve* (Paris, 1956). On Soviet naval campaigns, see A. G. Golovko, *With the Red Fleet*, tr. from the Russian (London, 1965); I. D. Kirin, *Chernomorskii Flot v Bitve za Kavkaz* (Moscow, 1958); and N. P. V'iunenko, *Chernomorskii Flot v Velikoi Otechestvennoi Voine* (Moscow, 1957). Portions of Admiral N. G. Kuznetsov's memoirs, entitled "Pered Voinoi," appeared in the periodical *Oktiabr* in 1965.

Studies of special topics include C. B. A. Behrens, *Merchant Shipping and the Demands of War* (London, 1955); Raymond de Belot, *La guerre aéronavale dans l'Atlantique* (Paris, 1950) and *La Méditerranée et le destin de l'Europe* (Paris, 1961); David Divine, *The Nine Days of Dunkirk* (New York, 1959); General Bernard Fergusson, *The Watery Maze: The Story of Combined Operations* (London, 1961); and David Woodward, *The Secret Raiders: the Story of the German Armed Merchant Raiders* (New York, 1955).

ESPIONAGE AND INTELLIGENCE OPERATIONS

Two general studies of German intelligence activities are Wilhelm Hoettl [Walter Hagen], *The Secret Front*, tr. from the German (London, 1953); and Paul Leverkuehn, *German Military Intelligence*, tr. from the German (London, 1954). Louis De Jong, in *The German Fifth Column in the Second World War*, tr. from the Dutch (Chicago, 1956), demonstrates that the fifth column was largely a myth. Walter Schellenberg, in *The Schellenberg Memoirs*, tr. from the German (London, 1956), reveals some of the secrets of Himmler's police. On the Abwehr, see Oscar Reile, *Geheime Westfront: die Abwehr 1935–1945* (Munich, 1962); and Rainus Longhardt-Söntgen, *Partisanen, Spione und Banditen: Abwehrtätigkeit in Oberitalien 1943–1945* (Neckargemünd, 1961); also Enno Stephan, *Geheimauftrag Irland: Deutsche Agenten im irischen Untergrundkampf 1939–1945* (Oldenburg, 1962). On Soviet intelligence: David J. Dallin, *Soviet Espionage* (New Haven, 1955); Otto Heilbrunn, *The Soviet Secret Services* (London, 1956); Pierre Accoce and Pierre Quet, *La guerre a été gagnée en Suisse* (Paris, 1966); and W. F. Flicke, *Agenten funken nach Moskau* (Kreuzlingen, 1954). On Italian intelligence: General Cesare Amè, *Guerra segreta in Italia, 1940–1943* (Rome, 1954). On Western intelligence activities: Jacques Bergier, *Agents secrets contre armes secrètes* (Paris, 1955); Peter Churchill, *Of Their Own Choice* (London, 1952); Allen Dulles, *The Secret Surrender* (New York, 1966); George Martelli, *Agent Extraordinary* (London, 1960). See also RESISTANCE MOVEMENTS, below.

CIVIL-MILITARY RELATIONS IN WARTIME

On the general problem, there are some useful chapters in Harry L. Coles (ed.), *Total War and Cold War* (Columbus, Ohio, 1952), and in Samuel P. Huntington (ed.), *Changing Patterns of Military Politics* (New York, 1962). There are suggestive ideas in Samuel P. Huntington, *The Soldier and the State: the Theory and Politics of Civil-Military Relations* (Cambridge, Mass., 1957), and Stanislaw Andrzejewski, *Military Organization and Society* (New York, 1955). Good general surveys with brief sections on the Second World War are Richard A. Preston *et al., Men in Arms* (London, 1963), and Theodore Ropp, *War in the Modern World* (Durham, N.C., 1959). Harold J. Lasswell's essay "The Garrison State," in the *American Journal of Sociology*, XLVI

(1941), 455–68, reflected the excessive fears of many liberals that free societies could not survive a modern war. On civil-military relations in wartime Britain, the British official history of the Second World War is invaluable—notably Vols. V and VI of the series entitled *Grand Strategy*, by John Ehrman (London, 1950–1956). There is a good chapter in Franklyn A. Johnson's *Defense by Committee* (New York, 1961); see also Sir John Kennedy, *The Business of War* (London, 1957), and Vice-Marshal E. J. Kingston-McCloughry, *The Direction of War* (London, 1955). On Germany: Wilhelm Ritter von Schramm, *Staatskunst und Bewaffnete Macht* (Munich, 1957); Gordon A. Craig, "The Impact of the German Military on the Political and Social Life of Germany during World War II, *Rapports du XIIe Congrès International des Sciences Historiques* (Vienna, 1965), IV, pp. 297–302; and the memoirs of numerous German military men, notably Walter Warlimont. On the Soviet Union, the fundamental work is John Erickson's *The Soviet High Command* (listed earlier).

ECONOMIC ASPECTS OF THE WAR YEARS

The economic history of the war years is, when compared to the military side, a badly underdeveloped field. It is also badly unbalanced, for most of the notable monographs deal with the British war economy. Several volumes in the British official history of the war are invaluable, notably the overall survey by W. K. Hancock and M. M. Gowing, *British War Economy* (London, 1951); R. J. Hammond's three volumes on *Food* (London, 1951–1962); Peggy Inman's *Labor in the Munitions Industries* (London, 1957); H. M. D. Parker's *Manpower* (London, 1957); M. M. Postan's *British War Production* (London, 1951); and H. D. Hall and C. C. Wrigley, *Studies of Overseas Supply* (London, 1956). Non-official studies include Ernest J. Carter, *Railways in Wartime* (London, 1964); J. P. Martin, *Les finances publiques britanniques 1939–1955* (Paris, 1956); and D. N. Chester (ed.), *Lessons of the British War Economy* (Cambridge, 1951).

The great mass of German economic documentation has only begun to be exploited, notably by Alan S. Milward in his first-rate study *The German Economy at War* (London, 1965). My account draws heavily on Milward's work. Supplementing the Milward volume is Berenice A. Carroll's *Design for Total War* (The Hague, 1968). Burton H. Klein's *Germany's Economic Preparations for War* (Cambridge, Mass., 1959) was a pioneering analysis which first exploded the legend that Hitler had armed Germany to the teeth during the 1930's. Prior to the publication of these monographs, historians were largely dependent on the findings of the United States Strategic Bombing Survey, which first pointed up the mismanagement of German war production. More specialized works on Germany include Wolfgang Birkenfeld, *Der Synthetische Treibstoff 1933–1945* (Göttingen, 1964); René Erbe, *Die nationalsozialistische Wirtschaftspolitik 1933–1939 im Lichte der Modernen Theorie* (Zürich, 1958); Fritz Federau, *Der zweite Weltkrieg; seine Finanzierung in Deutschland* (Tübingen, 1962); Wolfram Fischer, *Die Wirtschaftspolitik Deutschlands 1918–1945* (Lüneburg, 1961); Enno Georg, *Die Wirtschaftslichen Unternehmungen der SS* (Stuttgart, 1963); Edward L. Homze, *Foreign Labor in Nazi Germany* (Princeton, N.J., 1967); Rolf Karlbom, "Sweden's Iron Ore Exports to Germany, 1943–1944," *Scandinavian Economic History Review*, XIII (1965), 65–73; Alan S. Milward, "Could Sweden Have Stopped the War?," unpublished essay refuting Karlbom's thesis; W. Kumpf, *Die Organisation Todt im Kriege* (Oldenburg, 1953); André Piettre, *L'économie allemande contemporaine 1945–1952* (Paris, 1953). The study of Germany's economic policies in occupied Europe is still in its infancy. For the existing literature on the subject, see below under *German Occupation Policies.*

The Soviet Union's economic war effort has been a high-priority subject for Soviet historians in the past decade. Two good general accounts are I. E. Chadaev, *Ekonomika SSSR v Period Velikoi Otechestvennoi Voiny* (Moscow, 1965), and Grigorii S. Kravchenko, *Voennaia Ekonomika SSSR* (Moscow, 1963). They replace the older essay of N. A. Voznesenskii, *The Economy of the USSR during World War II,* tr. from the Russian (Washington, D.C., 1948).

On labor's role there is A. V. Mitrofanova's *Rabochii Klass Sovetskogo Soiuza v Pervyi Period Velikoi Otechestvennoi Voiny* (Moscow, 1960), and G. G. Morekhina's *Rabochii Klass-Frontu; Podvig Rabochego Klassa SSSR v Gody Velikoi Otechestvennoi Voiny* (Moscow, 1962). On the rural sector: I. V. Arutiunian, *Sovetskoe Krest'ianstvo v Gody Velikoi Otechestvennoi Voiny* (Moscow, 1963). All of these subjects are also treated in the official Soviet history of the war and in G. I. Shigalin, *Narodnoe Khozialistvo SSSR v Period Velikoi Otechestvennoi Voiny* (Moscow, 1960). Harry Schwartz, *Russia's Soviet Economy,* 2d ed. (New York, 1954), contains a convenient summary of the war years.

The best study of economic warfare is W. N. Medlicott, *The Economic Blockade,* 2 vols. (London, 1952–1959); an American account is D. L. Gordon and Royden Dangerfield, *The Hidden Weapon* (New York, 1947). There are few good works on the economic role of the neutral countries; but see the official Swiss account, *L'économie de guerre en Suisse (1939–1945)* (Berne, 1951), and Gunnar Hägglof's *Svensk Krigshandelspolitik under andra Världskriget* (Stockholm, 1958). On the economic consequences of the war: Jean Chardonnet, *Les conséquences économiques de la guerre 1939–1946* (Paris, 1947), more statistical than imaginative; G. D. N. Worswick and P. H. Ady (eds.), *The British Economy 1945–1950* (Oxford, 1952)—notably the chapter by P. J. D. Wiles; G. Frumkin, *Population Changes in Europe since 1939* (New York, 1951); Eugene M. Kulischer, *Europe on the Move:*

War and Population Changes 1917–1947 (New York, 1948); Joseph B. Schechtman, *European Population Transfers 1939–1945* (New York, 1946).

SCIENCE AND TECHNOLOGY

General studies of the role of scientists in the Second World War are mainly focused on the British scene. Ronald W. Clark's *The Rise of the Boffins* (London, 1962) is lively and well informed. The wartime controversy between Tizard and Lord Cherwell has been carried on into the postwar years by a whole series of writers, most of whom demonstrate a personal loyalty to one or the other protagonist: C. P. Snow, *Science and Government* (Cambridge, Mass., 1961); Earl of Birkenhead, *The Prof in Two Worlds* (London, 1961); P. M. S. Blackett, "Tizard and the Science of War," *Nature,* CLXXXV (1960), 647–53; Ronald W. Clark, *Tizard* (London, 1965), which uses Tizard's personal papers for the first time; Sir Roy Harrod, *The Prof: a Personal Memoir of Lord Cherwell* (London, 1959).

The development of radar is treated in some of the works listed above, as well as in Robert M. Page's *The Origins of Radar* (Garden City, 1962); Sir Robert Watson-Watt's *Three Steps to Victory* (London, 1958); and Dudley Saward's *The Bomber's Eye* (London, 1959). On rocket development, Walter Dornberger's *V-2*, tr. from the German (New York, 1954), and David Irving's *The Mare's Nest* (London, 1964) are particularly enlightening; see also Eric Burgess, *Guided Weapons* (New York, 1957); Martin Caidin, *Red Star in Space* (n.p., 1963); Sir Philip Joubert de la Ferté, *Rocket* (New York, 1957); Asher Lee (ed.), *The Soviet Air and Rocket Forces* (New York, 1959); James McGovern, *Crossbow and Overcast* (London, 1965). On the introduction of operational research: J. G. Crowther and R. Whiddington, *Science at War* (London, 1947), and Great Britain, Air Ministry, *The Origins and Development of Operational Research in the Royal Air Force* (London, 1963). On the role of European scientists in developing the atomic bomb, there are two excellent works: Margaret Gowing, *Britain and Atomic Energy, 1939–1945* (London, 1964), to which my account is heavily indebted; and Ronald W. Clark, *The Birth of the Bomb* (London, 1961). The obscure story of German atomic research during the war has at last been clarified in David Irving's *The Virus House* (London, 1967); the American role is recounted in General Leslie R. Grove's *Now It Can Be Told* (New York, 1963). On the development of jet aircraft: Sir Frank Whittle, *Jet: the Story of a Pioneer* (London, 1953). On tank development: Richard M. Ogorkiewicz, *Armor: a History of Mechanized Forces* (New York, 1960). On scientific gadgetry generally: Rudolf Lusar, *German Secret Weapons of the Second World War*, tr. from the German (London, 1960); Leslie E. Simon, *German Research in World War II* (New York, 1947); M. M. Postan *et al., Design and Development of Weapons* (London, 1964); Gerald Pawle, *The Secret War 1939–1945* (London, 1956).

On wartime medical research, there are two excellent volumes in the British official history of the war: V. Zachary Cope (ed.), *Medicine and Pathology* (London, 1952), and F. H. K. Green (ed.), *Medical Research* (London, 1953). A curious sidelight is provided in Lionel Tushnet's *The Uses of Adversity* (New York, 1966), which recounts studies of the effects of starvation carried out by doctors in the Warsaw ghetto. Dutch wartime research is surveyed in I. Boerema (ed.), *Medische ervaringen in Nederland tidjens de bezetting, 1940–1945* (Gröningen, 1947).

Although the effort to control men's minds attained a new peak of intensity in 1939–1945, the literature on the subject is generally disappointing. Postwar efforts to assess the effectiveness of wartime techniques have not been very convincing; one is thrown back on the subjective judgments of the participants.

General studies of propaganda warfare, with some material on the Second World War, include: Maurice Mégret, *La guerre psychologique* (Paris, 1963); Terence H. Qualter, *Propaganda and Psychological Warfare* (New York, 1962); Lindley Fraser, *Propaganda* (London, 1957). Two works edited by Daniel Lerner are focused more directly on the period 1939–1945: *Sykewar: Psychological Warfare against Germany* (New York, 1949) and *Propaganda in War and Crisis* (New York, 1951).

Among the more specialized studies, one stands out as particularly thorough and illuminating: Ernest K. Bramsted's *Goebbels and National Socialist Propaganda, 1925–1945* (East Lansing, Mich., 1965). Also useful are Z. A. B. Zeman, *Nazi Propaganda* (London, 1964); Jeremy Bennett, *British Broadcasting and the Danish Resistance Movement* (Cambridge, England, 1966); W. A. Boelcke (ed.), *Kriegspropaganda 1939–1941; geheime Ministerkonferenzen im Reichspropagandaministerium* (Stuttgart, 1966); Alexander L. George, *Propaganda Analysis* (Evanston, 1959); Walter Hagemann, *Publizistik im Dritten Reich* (Hamburg, 1948); Ernest Kriss and Hans Speier, *German Radio Propaganda* (London, 1944); Leo J. Margolin, *Paper Bullets: a Brief Story of Psychological Warfare in World War II* (New York, 1946); Maurice Mégret, "Les origines de la propagande de guerre française," *Revue d'Histoire de la Deuxième Guerre Mondiale*, No. 41, pp. 3–28; M. P. Skirdo, *Moral'nyi Faktor v Velikoi Otechestvennoi Voine* (Moscow, 1959); Hasso von Wedel, *Die Propagandatruppen der Deutschen Wehrmacht* (Neckargemünd, 1962); Bernhard Wittek, *Der britische Ätherkrieg gegen das Dritte Reich* (Münster, 1962). Two recent doctoral dissertations, still unpublished, are based on extensive research in the German records: Jay W. Baird, "German Home Propaganda, 1941–1945, and the Russian Front" (Columbia University, 1966), and Jeffrey R. Willis, "The Wehrmacht Propaganda Branch" (University of Virginia, 1964).

Of the memoirs written by former psychological warriors, probably the most enlightening are those of the ex-head of the PWE, Robert Bruce Lock-hart: *Comes the Reckoning* (London, 1947). Sefton Delmer's *Black Boomerang* (London, 1961) is a breezy defense of "black" and "gray" propaganda opera-tions. John Baker White's *The Big Lie* (London, 1955) is popularized but well informed. Other reminiscences include Hugh Dalton, *The Fateful Years* (London, 1957); Hans Fritsche, *Hier spricht Hans Fritsche* (Zürich, 1948); Erich Weinert, *Memento Stalingrad*, 2d ed. (Berlin, 1960), on Soviet propa-ganda activities on the Stalingrad front; Günther Weisenborn, *Memorial* (Berlin, 1946).

PSYCHOLOGICAL IMPACT OF THE WAR

Attempts to assess the general psychological impact of the war's long strain and intense terror have been rare and largely unsatisfactory. The Dutch psychiatrist A. M. Meerloo (who spent some time in a concentration camp) essayed such an overall judgment in his *Total War and the Human Mind* (New York, 1945) and *Aftermath to Peace* (New York, 1946). Somewhat more effective are studies focused on particular groups of victims. The Strategic Bombing Survey pioneered in its volume entitled *The Effects of Strategic Bombing on German Morale* (Washington, D.C., 1946). Fred C. Iklé's *The Social Impact of Bomb Destruction* (Norman, Okla., 1958) is a useful survey and *mise-au-point*. Irving L. Janis, *Air War and Emotional Stress* (New York, 1951), is the work of a British psychologist. Friedrich Panse's *Angst und Schreck* (Stuttgart, 1952) is based on interviews. M. G. Vroom's *Shrik, Angst en Vrees* (Den Helder, 1942) was an on-the-spot analysis of reactions to bombing in a small Dutch city.

There are three revealing studies of the psychological effects of the con-centration camp experience: Bruno Bettelheim, *The Informed Heart: Auton-omy in a Mass Age* (Glencoe, Ill., 1960); Elie A. Cohen, *Human Behavior in the Concentration Camp*, tr. from the Dutch (New York, 1953); Charles Richet and Antonin Mans, *Pathologie de la déportation* (Paris, 1956). The authors—doctors or psychiatrists—all spent some time as camp prisoners.

The best accounts of the use of psychiatric techniques among the fighting forces are Robert H. Ahrenfeldt's *Psychiatry in the British Army in the Second World War* (New York, 1958), and William Sargant's "Psychiatry and War," *Atlantic Monthly*, CCXIX (1967), 102–09. Little has been pub-lished on the use of psychiatry (or lack of it) in Germany or the Soviet Union; but see P. M. Fitts, "German Applied Psychology during World War II," *American Psychologist*, I (1946).

GERMAN OCCUPATION POLICIES

There is no satisfactory general study of German policies in occupied Europe, though an American scholar, Norman Rich, is at work on such a project, while Alan S. Milward is studying Nazi economic policy in France.

Two preliminary surveys are Maxime Mourin, *Le drame des états satellites de l'Axe, de 1939 à 1945* (Paris, 1957), and Enzo Collotti (ed.), *L'occupazione nazista in Europa* (Rome, 1964). German agricultural policies throughout the Continent are examined in Karl Brandt *et al., Management of Agriculture and Food in the German Occupied and Other Areas of Fortress Europe* (Stanford, 1953). Some wartime publications attempted to set forth German purposes in their New Europe: e.g., H. Backe, *Um die Nahrungsfreiheit Europas* (Leipzig, 1942); Karl Richard Ganzer, *Das Reich als europäische Ordnungsmacht* (Hamburg, 1941); and Claude Moret, *L'Allemagne et la réorganisation de l'Europe* (listed above). The Institut für Besatzungsfragen at Tübingen University has issued (in mimeographed form) a series of specialized studies concerning particular aspects of Nazi occupation policy in either eastern or western Europe; some examples are listed below. These highly controversial studies rest primarily on the texts of Nazi decrees rather than on an analysis of the spirit and conduct of Nazi policy, and conclude that German occupation policy was constructive rather than exploitative.

For the occupation in eastern Europe, two remarkable studies stand out: Alexander Dallin's *German Rule in Russia 1941–1945* (listed earlier), and Martin Broszat's *Nationalsozialistische Polenpolitik, 1939–1945* (Stuttgart, 1961). Both are based on exhaustive study of the German records, and are indispensable. Broszat's volume may be supplemented by the same author's *Nationalsozialistische Polenpolitik: Gutachten* (Frankfurt, 1963) and *Verfolgung polnischer katholischer Geistlicher 1939–1945* (Munich, 1959). There is an excellent monograph on Nazi resettlement policy by Robert L. Koehl: *RKFDV: German Resettlement and Population Policy 1939–1945* (Cambridge, Mass., 1957). Other studies include Gerald Reitlinger, *The House Built on Sand* (London, 1960); Ihor Kamenetsky, *Hitler's Occupation of the Ukraine* (Milwaukee, 1956) and *Secret Nazi Plans for Eastern Europe* (New York, 1961); Tadeusz Cyprian and Jerzy Sawicki, *Nazi Rule in Poland, 1939–1945,* tr. from the Polish (Warsaw, 1961); Czeslaw Madajczyk, *Generalna Gubernia w planach hitlerowskich* (Warsaw, 1961); Werner Markert (ed.), *Osteuropa Handbuch: Polen* (Cologne, 1959); Stanislaw Piotrowski, *Hans Frank's Diary* (Warsaw, 1961), an analysis of Frank's conduct as head of the General Government; K. M. Pospieszalski, "Le statut du peuple polonais sous l'occupation allemande," *Revue d'Histoire de la Deuxième Guerre Mondiale*, No. 40 (1960), pp. 1–20; Jürgen Thorwald, *Wen sie verderben wollen* (Stuttgart, 1952). Representative volumes in the Tübingen series are Berthold Gerber, *Staatliche Wirtschaftslenkung in den besetzen und annektierten Ostgebieten* (Tübingen, 1959), and Robert Herzog, *Besatzungsverwaltung in den besetzten Ostgebieten* (Tübingen, 1960). The USSR has published several volumes of documents on Nazi policies in Soviet territory: e.g., *Nemetsko-Fashistskii Okkupatsionnyi Rezhim na Ukraine* (Kiev, 1963); *Orlovskaia Oblast' v Velikoi Otechestvennoi Voine* (Orel, 1960); *Le crime méthodique: documents éclairant la politique de l'Allemagne nazie en territoire soviétique* (Moscow, 1963); *Prestupnye Tseli – Prestupnye Sredstva; Dokumenty* (Moscow, 1963). There are several useful (but often tendentious) memoirs by German occupation officials or collaborators: Karl I. Albrecht, *Sie aber werden die Welt zerstören* (Munich, 1954); Otto Bräutigam, *Überblick über die besetzen Ostgebiete während des zweiten Weltkrieges* (Tübingen, 1954); Hans Frank, *Im Angesicht des Galgens* (Munich, 1953); Alexander Hohenstein, *Warthe-ländisches Tagebuch aus den Jahren 1941/42* (Stuttgart, 1961); Roman Ilnytzkyj, *Deutschland und die Ukraine 1934–1945*, 2 vols. (Munich, 1955–1958). Certain contemporary publications are also suggestive: e.g., Edwin E. Dwinger, *Wiedersehen mit Sowjetrussland* (Jena, 1943), and Alex von Gadolin, *Der Norden, der Ostraum und das neue Europa* (Munich, 1943).

On the occupation in western and southern Europe: E. Jäckel, *Frankreich in Hitlers Europa* (Stuttgart, 1966); Pierre Arnoult, *Les finances de la France et l'occupation allemande* (Paris, 1951); Louis Baudin, *Esquisse de l'économie française sous l'occupation allemande* (Paris, 1945); Eugène Schaeffer, *L'Alsace et la Lorraine 1940–1945* (Paris, 1953); Paul Kluke, "Nationalsozialistische Volkstumpolitik in Elsass-Lothringen, 1940–45," in *Festgabe für Hans Herzfeld* (Berlin, 1958); F. Baudhuin, *L'économie belge sous l'occupation 1940–1944* (Brussels, 1945); J. Willequet, "Les fascismes belges," *Revue d'Histoire de la Deuxième Guerre Mondiale*, No. 66 (April 1967), pp. 85–109; A. H. Paape, "Le mouvement national-socialiste en Hollande," *Revue d'Histoire de la Deuxième Guerre Mondiale*, No. 66 (April 1967), pp. 31–60; I. Schöffer, *Het nationaal-socialistische beeld van de geschiedenis der Neder-landen* (Amsterdam, 1956); Netherlands, Ministry of Economic Affairs, *Organised Robbery* (The Hague, 1949); T. C. Wyller, *Fra okkupasjonsaarenes maktkamp* (Oslo, 1953); Enzo Collotti, *L'amministrazione tedesca dell'Italia occupata, 1943–1945* (Milan, 1963); L. Hory and Martin Broszat, *Der Kroatische Ustascha-Staat 1941–1945* (Stuttgart, 1964); Václav Král (ed.), *Lesson from History: Documents Concerning Nazi Policies . . . in Czecho-slovakia* (Prague, 1961). A special issue of the *Revue d'Histoire de la Deuxième Guerre Mondiale* (No. 54, April 1964) is devoted to aspects of the occupation in France; the first few months have been examined by Günter Geschke in *Die deutsche Frankreichspolitik 1940 von Compiègne bis Montoire* (Frankfurt, 1960). On the Wiesbaden armistice commission, see the memoirs of General Marcel Vernoux: *Wiesbaden, 1940–1944* (Paris, 1954). Contemporary works or memoirs by occupation authorities or "quislings" include Vidkun Quisling, *Die nationale Revolution in Norwegen: Reden* (Oslo, 1944); Max Freiherr du Prel (ed.), *Die Niederlande im Umbruch der Zeiten—Alte und neue Bezie-hungen zum Reich* (Würzburg, 1941); Robert Ernst, *Rechenschaftsbericht eines Elsässer* (Berlin, 1954). Representative volumes in the Tübingen series: Rosemarie Denzel, *Die chemische Industrie Frankreichs unter den deutschen Besetzung* (Tübingen, 1959); Hans Kistenmacher, *Die Auswirkungen der deutschen Besetzung auf die Ernährungswirtschaft Frankreichs* (Tübingen, 1959); Alfred Münz, *Die auswirkungen der deutschen Besetzung auf Währung und Finanzen Frankreichs* (Tübingen, 1957); Manfred Weinmann, *Die Landwirtschaft in Frankreich während des zweiten Weltkriegs* (Tübingen, 1961).

NAZI PERSECUTION OF "RACIAL" AND POLITICAL ENEMIES

This most appalling aspect of the war years has already produced a massive literature. There are two useful bibliographies: Ilse R. Wolf's *Persecution and Resistance under the Nazis* (London, 1960), and Jacob Robinson and Philip Friedman's *Guide to Jewish History under Nazi Impact* (New York, 1960). Of the general studies, the most thorough is Raul Hilberg's *The Destruction of the European Jews* (Chicago, 1961). Other attempts at synthesis are Roger Manvell and Heinrich Fraenkel, *The Incomparable Crime* (New York, 1967); Joseph Billig, *L'Hitlerisme et le système concentrationnaire* (Paris, 1967); Leon Poliakov, *Harvest of Hate*, tr. from the French (Syracuse, N.Y., 1954); Gerald Reitlinger, *The Final Solution* (New York, 1953); Wolfgang Scheffler, *Judenverfolgung im Dritten Reich, 1933–1945* (Berlin, 1960); T. Berenstein *et al.* (eds.), *Faschismus-Getto-Massenmord: Dokumentation über Ausrottung und Widerstand der Juden in Polen* (Berlin, 1961); Randolph L. Braham, *The Destruction of Hungarian Jewry: a Documentary Account*, 2 vols. (New York, 1963); Jewish Historical Museum of Amsterdam, *Documents of the Persecution of Dutch Jewry 1940–1945* (Amsterdam, 1965); Artur Eisenbach, *Hitlerowska politika zaglady Zydow* (Warsaw, 1961); Abram Kajzer, *Za drutami smierci* (Lodz, 1962); Eugen Kogon, *Der SS-Staat*, 5th ed. (Mannheim, 1959), tr. as *The Theory and Practice of Hell* (New York, 1950); Heinz Kuhnrich, *Der KZ-Staat* (Berlin, 1960); Edmond Paris, *Genocide in Satellite Croatia 1941–1945*, 2d ed. (Chicago, 1962); Gerhard Schoenberner, *Der gelbe Stern*, 2d ed. (Hamburg, 1961); Josef Wulf, *Das Dritte Reich und seine Vollstrecker* (Berlin, 1961). Paul Rassinier, *Le mensonge d'Ulysse*, 5th ed. (Paris, 1961), argues the extreme right-wing thesis that the "final solution" was a Communist-invented legend.

Studies focused on individual concentration camps include: H. G. Adler *et al.* (eds.), *Auschwitz: Zeugnisse und Berichte* (Frankfurt, 1962); H. G. Adler, *Theresienstadt 1941–1945*, 2d ed. (Tübingen, 1960), and *Die verheimlichte Wahrheit* (Tübingen, 1958); Marie-Josée Chombart de Lauwe (ed.), *Les françaises à Ravensbrück* (Paris, 1965); Charlotte Delbo, *Le convoi du 24 janvier* (Paris, 1966); Leslie H. Hardman and Cecily Goodman, *The Survivors: the Story of the Belsen Remnant* (London, 1958); Eberhard Kolb, *Bergen-Belsen* (Hanover, 1962); Zdenik Lederer, *Ghetto Theresienstadt*, tr. from the Czech (London, 1953); Jan Sehn, *Le camp de concentration d'Oswiecim-Birkenau*, tr. from the Polish (Warsaw, 1957); Jean-François Steiner, *Treblinka* (Paris, 1966), a semi-fictional reconstruction from oral testimony. The *Revue d'Histoire de la Deuxième Guerre Mondiale* has published a considerable number of articles on the concentration camps.

From the long list of reminiscences by survivors of the camps, only some representative examples can be listed: Anon., *Pamietnik znaleziony w Oswiecimie* (Warsaw, 1962); Marcel Conversy, *Quinze mois à Buchenwald* (Geneva, 1945); Micheline Maurel, *Un camp très ordinaire* (Paris, 1957); Edmond Michelet, *Rue de la Liberté: Dachau 1943–1945* (Paris, 1955); L. H. Nouveau, *Un autre monde: seize mois à Buchenwald* (Paris, 1961); Myklos Nyiszly, *Auschwitz: a Doctor's Eyewitness Account*, tr. from the Hungarian (New York, 1960); Ralph Oppenheimer, *An der Grenze des Lebens: Theresienstadter Tagebuch* (Hamburg, 1962); David Rousset, *The Other Kingdom*, tr. from the French (New York, 1947); Rudolf Vrba and Alan Bostic, *I Cannot Forgive* (London, 1963); Reska Weiss, *Journey Through Hell* (London, 1961); Leon Weliczer Wells, *The Janowska Road* (London, 1966); Krystyna Zywalska, *Przezylam Oswiecim* (Warsaw, 1951). There is a single volume of reminiscences by an ex-jailer: Rudolf Hoess, *Commandant of Auschwitz*, tr. from the German (London, 1959). David Rousset's novel *Les jours de notre mort* (Paris, 1947) is a remarkable fictional evocation of the experience by a former camp inmate. Also notable are the works (already listed) of Bruno Bettelheim and Elie A. Cohen, both written by psychiatrists who had been interned.

Memoirs of life in the Nazi-organized ghettos of Poland are also numerous: Mary Berg, *Le ghetto de Varsovie* (Paris, 1947); Samuel Goldstein, *Cinq années dans le ghetto de Varsovie*, tr. from the Polish (Brussels, 1962); Abraham I. Katsch (ed.), *Scroll of Agony: the Warsaw Diary of Chaim A. Kaplan* (New York, 1965); Jacob Littner, *Erinnerungen aus einem Erdloch* (Munich, 1948); Bernard Mark (ed.), *Im Feuer vergangen* (Berlin, 1960); Bernard Mark, *Der Aufstand im Warschauer Ghetto* (Berlin, 1957); Michel Mazor, *La cité engloutie* (Paris, 1955); David Rabinowitz, *Pamietnik* (Warsaw, 1960); E. Ringelblum, *Notes from the Warsaw Ghetto* (New York, 1958); D. D. Sierakowiak, *Sierakowiaka* (Warsaw, 1960); Josef Wulf, *Lodz: das letzte Ghetto* (Bonn, 1962); Josef Wulf, *Vom Leben, Kampf und Tod in Ghetto Warschau* (Bonn, 1958); Isaac Zuckerman (ed.), *The Fighting Ghettos*, tr. from the Hebrew (Philadelphia, 1962).

Books on the war-crimes trials of 1945–1950 and of the 1960's provide valuable details about the system of Nazi repression: Leo Alexander, *Sociopsychologic Structure of the SS: Psychiatric Report of the Nürnberg Trials* (Chicago, 1958); Raymond Phillips (ed.), *The Belsen Trial* (London, 1949); Karl Heinz Thielke (ed.), *Fall 5: Anklagepläder, ausgew. Dokumente: Urteil des Flickprozesses* (Berlin, 1965); François Bayle, *Croix gammée contre caducée* (Neustadt, 1950), on medical experiments in the camps; A. Mitscherlick and F. Mielke, *The Death Doctors*, tr. from the German (London, 1962); Hannah Arendt, *Eichmann in Jerusalem* (New York, 1963); Robert M. W.

Kempner, *Eichmann und Komplizen* (Zurich, 1961); Leon Poliakov (ed.), *Le procès de Jerusalem* (Paris, 1963); Lord Russell of Liverpool, *The Trial of Adolf Eichmann* (London, 1962); Bernd Naumann, *Auschwitz: a Report of the Proceedings against Robert Karl et al. at Frankfurt*, tr. from the German (London, 1967).

RESISTANCE MOVEMENTS

The exploits of the anti-German underground have given rise to an extensive literature, particularly in the countries of Continental Europe. No doubt it is natural that while American and British historians of the war have concentrated on military and diplomatic aspects, historians of the German-occupied countries have preferred to view the resistance as central, both strategically and morally.

The most convenient general sketch is Henri Michel's brief study *Les mouvements clandestins en Europe (1938–1945)* (Paris, 1961). Two international conferences, at Liège and Milan, brought together specialists from both eastern and western Europe; the papers read there (some of them exceptionally valuable) have been published under a common title, *European Resistance Movements 1939–1945* (Oxford, 1960 and 1963). Other general surveys are Heinz Kuhnrich, *Der Partisanenkrieg in Europa 1939–1945* (Berlin, 1965); Ronald Seth, *The Undaunted* (London, 1956), a journalistic account; and *Die Völker in Widerstandskampf* (Berlin, 1960), produced by a committee of Soviet and East German historians. On the British S.O.E.'s role in encouraging resistance movements, see E. H. Cookridge [Edward Spiro], *Inside SOE, the Story of Special Operations in Western Europe 1940–1945* (London, 1966), and Michael R. D. Foot, *SOE in France* (London, 1966). Foot's is the official British version based on the S.O.E. files.

On the resistance in France, an official Comité d'histoire de la Deuxième Guerre Mondiale has sponsored the publication of a dozen solid studies: notably Henri Michel, *Les courants de pensée de la Résistance* (Paris, 1962); Marie Granet and Henri Michel, *Combat* (Paris, 1957); René Hostache, *Le Conseil National de la Résistance* (Paris, 1958). Henri Noguères *et al.* have begun a four-volume *Histoire de la résistance en France* (Paris, 1967–), of which only the first volume has appeared. Robert Aron's *Histoire de la libération de la France* (Paris, 1959) focuses mainly on the underground; Blake Ehrlich's *The French Resistance* (London, 1966) is a good popular account. The long list of memoirs by ex-resisters includes Auguste Lecoeur, *Le partisan* (Paris, 1963); Christian Pineau, *La simple vérité* (Paris, 1960); Charles Tillon, *Les F.T.P.* (Paris, 1962); and G. Renault, *On m'appelait Rémy* (Paris, 1951). On the Free French movement in exile, Charles de Gaulle's *Mémoires de guerre*, 3 vols. (Paris, 1954–1959) are indispensable, along with Jacques Soustelle's *Envers et contre tout*, 2 vols. (Paris, 1947–1950), and Colonel Passy's [Armand Dewavrin] *Souvenirs*, 3 vols. (Monte Carlo and

Paris, 1947–1951). Robert Mengin, *No Laurels for De Gaulle*, tr. from the French (London, 1967), offers an anti-Gaullist view of the London years. Alban Vistel's *Héritage spirituel de la résistance* (Lyon, 1955) attempts to assess the deeper significance of the episode; Michel Borwicz's Sorbonne thesis *Ecrits de condamnés de mort* (Paris, 1955) portrays the idealism of the movement.

On the underground in the Low Countries and Scandinavia, the literature is less rich, with the single exception of the Netherlands. Werner Warmbrunn's *The Dutch under German Occupation* (Stanford, 1963) is a solid account; L. E. Winkel's *De ondergrondse pers 1940–1945* (The Hague, 1954) is a thorough survey of the press; B. A. Sijes' *De Februari-staking* (The Hague, 1954) focuses on one of the few large popular outbreaks in occupied Europe; Allard Martens and Daphne Dunlop's *The Silent War* (London, 1961) is episodic. For Belgium there is George K. Tanham's unpublished Stanford dissertation, "The Belgian Underground Movement" (1951). David Lampe, *The Savage Canary* (London, 1957), is a good popular account of the Danish resistance; but see also Jørgen Haestrup's *Kontakt med England, 1940–1943* (Copenhagen, 1954) and *Hemmelig Alliance*, 2 vols. Copenhagen, 1959), as well as Jeremy Bennett's book (listed earlier). The best study of the Norwegian underground is Sverre Kjeldstadli, *Hjemmestyrkene* (Oslo, 1959).

For Italy, Charles F. Delzell's *Mussolini's Enemies* (Princeton, 1961) is thorough and balanced. The best and most objective Italian account is Giorgio Bocca, *Storia dell'Italia Partigiana* (Bari, 1966). Most Italian books on the resistance show a leftist bias: e.g., Roberto Battaglia, *The Story of the Italian Resistance*, tr. from the Italian (London, 1958). Other accounts include Mario Bendiscioli, *Antifascismo e resistenza* (Rome, 1964); Giampiero Carocci, *La Resistenza italiana* (Milan, 1963); Ada Gobetti, *Diario Partigiano* (Turin, 1956); Raimondo Luraghi, *Il movimento operaio torinese durante la Resistenza* (Turin, 1958); Pietro Secchia and Filippo Frascati, *La Resistenza e gli alleati* (Milan, 1962); Nuto Revelli, *La guerra dei poveri* (Turin, 1962).

On the various Balkan underground movements, there is a general but somewhat anecdotal account by Costa di Loverdo, *Les maquis rouges des Balkans 1941–1945* (Paris, 1967); see also Theodor Arnold, *Der revolutionäre Krieg* (Pfaffenhofen/Ilm, 1961). For Yugoslavia, Vladimir Dedijer's *Tito Speaks* (London, 1953) is a valuable firsthand account; see also Dedijer's diary *With Tito through the War* (London, 1951). A series of useful articles by K. M. Dincíc appeared in the *Revue d'Histoire de la Deuxième Guerre Mondiale*, Nos. 34 (1959), 38 (1960), and 42 (1961). The Bulgarian story is told in Petŭr Georgiev and Basil Spiru, *Bulgariens Volk im Widerstand 1941–1944*, tr. from the Bulgarian (Berlin, 1962); the Greek phase in André Kedros, *La résistance grècque 1940–1944* (Paris, 1966).

Polish scholars have made the writing of resistance history into a major industry—partly for ideological reasons, partly because the subject matter is so rich. Translations into Western languages include General Tadeusz Bor-Komorovski's own story, *The Secret Army* (London, 1951); S. Korbonski's *Fighting Warsaw* (London, 1956); Waçlaw Zagorski's *Seventy Days: a Diary of the Warsaw Insurrection* (London, 1957); Günter Fraschka's *Aufstand in Warschau* (Rastatt, 1960); H. von Krannhals' *Der Warschauer Aufstand 1944* (Frankfurt, 1962). In Polish, some representative works are Jan Ptasinski, *Z mazowieckich pol-wspomnienia partyzanta* (Warsaw, 1959); G. Zaleski, *Satyra w konspiracji* (Warsaw, 1958); Zygmunt Zaremba, *Wojna i konspiracja* (London, n.d.); L. Ponahajba, *Organizacja i dzialania bojowe Ludowego Wojska Polskiego 1943–1945* (Warsaw, 1958); J. Kirchmayer, *Powstanie Warszawskie* (Warsaw, 1959). For Czechoslovakia, see the official pamphlet by Jiří Doležal and Jan Křen, *Czechoslovakia's Fight* (Prague, 1964); H. Gordon Skilling, "The Czechoslovak Struggle for National Liberation in World War II," *Slavonic and East European Review* (1960); Andrew Elias, "The Slovak Uprising of 1944" (unpublished Columbia University dissertation, 1963); Peter Jilemnicky, *Der Wind dreht sich*, tr. from the Slovak (Berlin, 1951).

The Soviet partisan movement has also been an officially encouraged subject for historians in recent years; the emphasis has been on local studies of individual bands or districts. For Western scholars, far and away the most useful analysis is that of John A. Armstrong *et al.*, *Soviet Partisans in World War II* (Madison, Wis., 1964). My account draws heavily on Armstrong's findings. Other works include Edgar M. Howell, *The Soviet Partisan Movement 1941–1944* (Washington, D.C., 1956); Aleksei F. Fedorov, *The Underground Committee Carries On*, tr. from the Russian (Moscow, 1952); Walter Hawemann, *Achtung, Partisanen! Der Kampf hinter der Ostfront* (Hanover, 1953); Peter Kolmsee, *Der Partisanenkampf in der Sowjetunion* (Berlin, 1963); *Sovetskie partizany: iz istorii partizanskogo dvizeniia v gody Velikoi Otechestvennoi Voiny*, 2d ed. (Moscow, 1963); V. Glukhov, *Narodnyie Mstiteli* (Kaluga, 1962); V. Lyashchenko, *Karaiushchii Gorod* (Moscow, 1962).

The literature on the German underground is both voluminous and controversial. Hans Rothfels' *The German Opposition to Hitler*, 2d ed. (Chicago, 1962), defends the anti-Hitlerite plotters against charges that they were nationalist reactionaries. Gerhard Ritter's *The German Resistance*, tr. from the German (London, 1959), adopts a similar position, and minimizes the role of the left-wing resisters. A contrary argument is advanced by George K. Romoser in his unpublished University of Chicago dissertation (1958), summarized in his article "The Politics of Uncertainty: the German Resistance Movement," *Social Research*, XXXI (1964), 73–93. According to Romoser, the leading German conspirators were strongly elitist and suspicious of the masses; therefore they made no attempt to win popular support, and embodied the neo-conservative mood of pre-Hitler days. Terence Prittie's *Germans Against Hitler*

(London, 1964) is a general survey by an unusually well-informed British journalist. Hermann Graml *et al.*, *Der deutsche Widerstand gegen Hitler* (Cologne, 1966) focuses on ideology. A special issue of the *Revue d'Histoire de la Deuxième Guerre Mondiale*, No. 36 (1959), contains some excellent articles on the German resistance; so does the July 1964 issue of *Vierteljahrshefte für Zeitgeschichte*.

Reminiscences, diaries, or collected writings of former underground activists include Ulrich von Hassell, *The von Hassell Diaries 1938–1944*, tr. from the German (New York, 1947); Fabian von Schlabrendorff, *The Secret War Against Hitler*, tr. from the German (London, 1966); Dietrich Bonhoeffer, *Letters and Papers from Prison*, tr. from the German (London, 1953); Alfred Delp, *Zwischen Welt und Gott* (Frankfurt, 1957). The abortive plot of July 20, 1944, is the subject of numerous works: Maurice Baumont, *La grande conspiration contre Hitler* (Paris, 1963); Dietrich Ehlers, *Technik und Moral einer Verschwörung, 20 Juli 1944* (Frankfurt, 1964); Joachim Kramarz, *Stauffenberg*, tr. from the German (New York, 1967); Karl-Heinrich Peter (ed.), *Spiegelbild einer Verschwörung: der Kaltenbrunner-Bericht an Bormann und Hitler* (Stuttgart, 1961); Hans Royce (ed.), *20 Juli 1944*, 3d ed. (Bonn, 1960); Eberhard Zeller, *Geist der Freiheit* (Munich, 1954). On the army's role: Gert Buchheit, *Soldatentum und Rebellion* (Rastatt, 1961); Wolfgang Foerster, *Generaloberst Ludwig Beck* (Munich, 1953). On Admiral Canaris and resistance in the Abwehr: Karl Heinz Abshagen, *Canaris*, tr. from the German (London, 1956); Ian G. Colvin, *Chief of Intelligence* (London, 1951); Constantine FitzGibbon, *The Shirt of Nessus* (London, 1956); Karl Bartz, *Die Tragödie der deutschen Abwehr* (Salzburg, 1955). On the German Communist underground: A. S. Blank, *Kommunisticheskaia Partiia Germanii v Bor'be Protiv Fashistskoi Diktatury* (Moscow, 1964); W. F. Flicke, *Spionagezentrale Rote Kapelle*, 3d ed. (Munich, 1958). On the non-Communist left: Annedore Leber, *Conscience in Revolt*, tr. from the German (London, 1957); Annedore Leber and Countess Freya von Moltke, *Für und wider* (Berlin, 1961). On the student resistance groups: James Donohoe, *Hitler's Conservative Opponents in Bavaria* (Leiden, 1961); Arno Klonne, *Gegen den Strom* (Hanover, 1958); Ferdinand Oertel, *Jugend in Feuerofen* (Rechlinghausen, 1960). On resistance in the Churches: Friedrich Zipfel, *Kirchenkampf in Deutschland 1933–1945* (Berlin, 1965). On the resistance in Austria: Hermann Mitteracker, *Kampf und Opfer für Österreich* (Vienna, 1963); Otto Molden, *Der Ruf des Gewissens* (Vienna, 1958); Herbert Steiner, *Zum Tode verurteilt: Österreicher gegen Hitler* (Vienna, 1964).

The story of the Free Germany Committee and the League of German Officers, both organized on Soviet soil after Stalingrad, has been told and retold by almost all of the surviving leaders and by a great many followers as well: e.g., Walter Ulbricht, *Zur Geschichte der deutschen Arbeiterbewegung*, Vol. 2 (Berlin, 1952); Wilhelm Pieck, *Reden und Aufsätze*, Vol. 1 (Berlin,

1952); Erich Weinert, *Das Nationalkomitee "Freies Deutschland," 1943–1945* (Berlin, 1957); Heinrich Graf von Einsiedel, *I Joined the Russians,* tr. from the German (New Haven, 1953); Egbert von Frankenberg, *Meine Entscheidung* (Berlin, 1963); F. W. Krummacher, *Ruf zur Entscheidung* (Berlin, 1966); Else and Berndt von Kügelgen, *Die Front war überall,* 2d ed. (Berlin, 1963); Jesko von Puttkamer, *Von Stalingrad zur Volkspolizei* (Wiesbaden, 1951); Luitpold Steidle, *Das Nationalkomitee "Freies Deutschland"* (Burgscheidungen, 1960). The best secondary synthesis of the episode is Bodo Scheurig's *Freies Deutschland* (Munich, 1960), supplemented by the same author's documentary collection *Verrat hinter Stacheldraht?* (Munich, 1966).

WARTIME DIPLOMACY

General surveys of the subject are few. Good, but brief, is John L. Snell's *Illusion and Necessity: The Diplomacy of Global War 1939–1945* (Boston, 1963); Jacques de Launay's *Secret Diplomacy of World War II,* tr. from the French (New York, 1963), is sketchy. V. L. Israelian offers the orthodox Soviet line in his *Diplomaticheskaia Istoria Velikoi Otechestvennoi Voiny* (Moscow, 1959), and *Antigitlerovskaia Koalitsiia* (Moscow, 1964). A Polish version, similar in tone, is Stefan Boratynoki, *Dyplomacja Okresu II Wojny Swiatowej* (Warsaw, 1957).

German-Italian relations have been extensively studied, notably by Elizabeth Wiskemann, *The Rome-Berlin Axis,* 2d ed. (London, 1966); F. W. Deakin, *The Brutal Friendship* (New York, 1962); and Mario Toscano, *Pagine di Storia Diplomatica Contemporanea,* Vol. 2 (Milan, 1963). Vinicio Araldi's *Il Patto d'Acciaio* (Rome, 1961) is the work of an ex-Fascist. Conrad F. Latour has carefully examined the South Tyrol question in his *Südtirol und die Achse Berlin-Rom, 1938–1945* (Stuttgart, 1962). Useful diaries or memoirs include Malcolm Muggeridge (ed.), *Ciano's Diary, 1939–1943* (London, 1947), and *Ciano's Diplomatic Papers* (London, 1948); Filippo Anfuso, *Rom-Berlin in diplomatischem Spiegel* (Munich, 1951); Alberto Mellini Ponce de Leon, *L'Italia entra in guerra* (Bologna, 1963) and *Guerra diplomatica a Salò* (Bologna, 1950); Enno von Rintelen, *Mussolini als Bundesgenosse* (Tübingen, 1951).

On German-Soviet relations during the period of alliance, see especially Gustav Hilger and Alfred G. Meyer, *The Incompatible Allies* (New York, 1953); Gerhard L. Weinberg, *Germany and the Soviet Union 1939–1941* (Leiden, 1954); and Philipp W. Fabry, *Der Hitler-Stalin Pakt 1939–1941* (Darmstadt, 1962). Fabry argues that Soviet duplicity forced Hitler to attack the USSR in 1941. Andreas Hillgruber's *Hitlers Strategie: Politik und Kriegführung 1940–1941* (Frankfurt, 1965) is an exhaustive study of Hitler's alternatives during the crucial year between the fall of France and the invasion of Russia. A. M. Nekrich, in his *1941: 22 iuniia* (Moscow, 1965), argues that Stalin clung to the hope of buying off Hitler until the end, and feared a separate peace between Hitler and the British. Alfred Anderle and Werner Basler (eds.), *Juni 1941: Beitrage zur geschichte des Hitlerfaschisten Überfalls auf die Sowjetunion* (Berlin, 1961), denounce those historians who see Hitler's attack as a preventive war. Peter Kleist's *Zwischen Hitler und Stalin* (Bonn, 1950) is the work of a former Eastern expert on Ribbentrop's staff. Kleist claims to have been approached in Stockholm in 1942–1943 by Soviet agents who were attempting to arrange a separate peace.

On Germany's relations with the smaller European nations and with overseas powers: Andreas Hillgruber (ed.), *Staatsmänner und Diplomaten bei Hitler* (Frankfort, 1966); Andreas Hillgruber, *Hitler, König Carol und Marschall Antonescu* (Wiesbaden, 1954); Hermann Neubacher, *Sonderauftrag Südost 1940–1945: Bericht eines fliegenden Diplomaten* (Göttingen, 1956); Rudolf Rahn, *Ruheloses Leben* (Düsseldorf, 1949); Lajos Kerekes (ed.), *Allianz Hitler-Horthy-Mussolini* (Budapest, 1966), documents from the Horthy papers and the Hungarian foreign ministry; Lothar Krecker, *Deutschland und die Turkei im zweiten Weltkrieg* (Frankfurt, 1964); L. Zsigmond (ed.), *Magyarorszàg Külpolitikája a II világháború kitörésének idöszakaban 1939–1940* (Budapest, 1962); Saul Friedländer, *Hitler and the United States*, tr. from the German (London, 1965); James V. Compton, *The Swastika and the Eagle* (Boston, 1967); Ernst L. Presseisen, *Germany and Japan: a Study in Totalitarian Diplomacy* (The Hague, 1958); Johanna M. Meskill, *Hitler and Japan: the Hollow Alliance* (New York, 1966); Donald S. Detwiler, *Hitler, Franco und Gibraltar* (Wiesbaden, 1962).

Italy's relations with the Western powers and the USSR before 1940 and after 1943 may be studied in these works: Mario Toscano, *Una mancata intesa italo-sovietica nel 1940 e 1941* (Florence, 1953); Raffaele Guariglia, *Ricordi, 1922–1946* (Naples, 1950); André François-Poncet, *Au palais Farnese 1938–1940* (Paris, 1961); R. Bova Scoppa, *Colloqui con due Dittatori* (Rome, 1949); Norman Kogan, *Italy and the Allies* (Cambridge, Mass., 1956).

On Soviet relations with the other European powers: F. D. Volkov, *SSSR-Angliia Nakanune 1929-1945 gg. Anglo-Sovetskie Otosheniia Naka i v Period Vtoroi Mirovoi Voiny* (Moscow, 1964); Alfred J. Rieber, *Stalin and the French Communist Party 1941–1947* (New York, 1962); Milovan Djilas, *Conversations with Stalin*, tr. from the Yugoslav (New York, 1962); Eduard Beneš, *Memoirs*, tr. from the Czech (London, 1954); Josef Korbel, *The Communist Subversion of Czechoslovakia 1938–1948* (Princeton, 1959); Paul E. Zinner, *Communist Strategy and Tactics in Czechoslovakia 1918–1948* (New York, 1963); Eduard Taborsky, "Beneš and Stalin—Moscow, 1943 and 1945," *Journal of Central European Affairs*, XIII (1953), 154–81; Stanislaw Kot, *Conversations with the Kremlin and Despatches from Russia*, tr. from the Polish (London, 1963); Z. Stypulkowski, *Invitation to Moscow* (New York, 1951); S. Kopanski, *Wspomnienia wojenne 1939–1946* (London, 1961).

On British wartime diplomacy, Sir Llewelyn Woodward's *British Foreign Policy During the Second World War* (London, 1961) is essential; it is a careful digest of the materials in the Foreign Office archives. Philip Goodhart's *Fifty Ships that Saved the World* (Garden City, 1965) examines the so-called "destroyer deal" with the United States in 1940. Useful memoirs include the Earl of Avon [Anthony Eden], *The Reckoning* (London, 1965); Alfred Duff Cooper, *Old Men Forget* (London, 1954); Lord Casey, *Personal Experience, 1939–1946* (London, 1962).

For the role of the United States during the period of neutrality, two works by William L. Langer and S. Everett Gleason are indispensable: *The Challenge to Isolation 1937–1940* (New York, 1952) and *The Undeclared War 1940–1941* (New York, 1953). Two good recent reassessments are Robert A. Divine, *The Reluctant Belligerent: American Entry into World War II* (New York, 1965), and Gaddis Smith, *American Diplomacy During the Second World War* (New York, 1965). Anne Armstrong, in *Unconditional Surrender: the Impact of the Casablanca Policy upon World War II* (New Brunswick, N.J., 1961) examines one of Roosevelt's most controversial wartime decisions. The memoirs of Robert Murphy, *Diplomat Among Warriors* (New York, 1964), and of Admiral William Leahy, *I Was There* (New York, 1950), are of some interest; so is Robert Sherwood's *Roosevelt and Hopkins* (New York, 1948), which utilizes the papers of Harry Hopkins.

On the European neutrals and quasi-neutrals, see especially Annette Baker Fox, *The Power of Small States: Diplomacy in World War II* (Chicago, 1959). Other specialized studies are P. E. A. Romeril, *War Diplomacy and the Turkish Republic: a Study in Neutrality 1939–1945* (Leiden, 1963); Dante A. Puzzo, *Spain and the Great Powers, 1936–1941* (New York, 1963); E. N. Dzelepy, *Franco, Hitler et les alliés* (Brussels, 1961); J. Davignon, *Berlin (1936–1940): Souvenirs d'une mission* (Brussels, 1951); Stephen D. Kertesz, *Diplomacy in a Whirlpool: Hungary Between Nazi Germany and Soviet Russia* (South Bend, Ind., 1953); A. I. Puškaš, *Vengriia vo Vtoroi Mirovoi Voine* (Moscow, 1963). An extensive and highly controversial literature has grown up around the part played by the Vatican during the war; it focuses primarily on the alleged failure of Pope Pius to speak out or act effectively on behalf of the Jews and other persecuted peoples. In addition to the three volumes of Vatican documents listed earlier, these works are relevant: Paul Duclos, *Le Vatican et la seconde guerre mondiale* (Paris, 1955); Igino Giordani, *Vita contro morte* (Milan, 1956); Alberto Giovannetti, *Il Vaticano e la guerra (1939–1940)* (Vatican City, 1960); Jeno Levai, *Geheime Reichssache: Papst Pius XII hat nicht geschwiegen* (Cologne, 1966); Maxime Mourin, *Le Vatican et l'U.R.S.S.* (Paris, 1966); Ernesto Rossi, *Il manganello e l'aspersorio*, 2d ed. (Florence, 1958); M. M. Sheinmann, *Der Vatikan im zweiten Weltkrieg*, tr. from the Russian (Berlin, 1954). Norway's attempt to remain neutral in 1939–1940 is described from the Norwegian government archives by Nils Örvik in *Norge i Brennpunktet fra forhistorien til 9 april 1940* (Oslo, 1953). Diplomatic aspects of Finland's "winter war" of 1939–1940 are examined in Douglas Clark, *Three Days to Catastrophe* (London, 1966), and Max Jakobson, *The Diplomacy of the Winter War* (Cambridge, Mass., 1961); see also the memoirs of Hitler's ambassador in Helsinki, Wipert von Blücher: *Gesandter zwischen Diktatur und Demokratie: Erinnerungen* (Wiesbaden, 1951); and those of Vaino Tanner, *The Winter War* (Stanford, 1957). Finland's role throughout the war is recalled in the memoirs of former Finnish ambassador G. A. Gripenberg: *Finland and the Great Powers*, tr. from the Swedish (Lincoln, Neb., 1966). The attempt by Vichy France to preserve a precarious quasi-neutrality has been carefully analyzed in Adrienne Hytier, *Two Years of French Foreign Policy* (Geneva, 1958); on the same subject, see also the curious defense of Pétain by L.-D. Girard in *Montoire: Verdun diplomatique* (Paris, 1948). On de Gaulle's relations with the British and Americans: Arthur L. Funk, *Charles de Gaulle: the Crucial Years* (Norman, Okla., 1959).

On postwar planning and the origins of the cold war: Herbert Feis, *Churchill, Roosevelt, Stalin: the War They Waged and the Peace They Sought* (Princeton, 1957) and *Between War and Peace: the Potsdam Conference* (Princeton, 1961); Martin F. Herz, *Beginnings of the Cold War* (Bloomington, Ind., 1966); Gar Alperovitz, *Atomic Diplomacy* (London, 1966), which attacks the "orthodox" Western interpretation and charges American leadership with responsibility for the cold war; Harley A. Notter, *Postwar Foreign Policy Preparation 1939–1945* (Washington, D.C., 1949), an official documentary account; Philip E. Mosely, *The Kremlin and World Politics* (New York, 1960); Edward J. Rosek, *Allied Wartime Diplomacy: a Pattern in Poland* (New York, 1958), strongly pro-Polish and anti-Soviet, critical of Western "weakness"; Count Edward Raczynski, *In Allied London*, tr. from the Polish (London, 1963); Waclaw Jedrzejewicz (ed.), *Poland in the British Parliament 1939–1945*, 3 vols. (New York, 1946–1962); Piotr S. Wandycz, *Czechoslovak-Polish Confederation and the Great Powers, 1940–1943* (Bloomington, Ind., 1956); Louis J. Halle, *The Cold War as History* (New York, 1967); André Fontaine, *Histoire de la guerre froide*, Vol. I (Paris, 1965); W. T. Kowalski, *ZSSR a granica na odrze i nysie Luzyckiej, 1941–1945* (Warsaw, 1965); V. A. Sekistov, *"Strannaia Voina" v Zapadnoi Evrope i v Bacceine Sredizemnogo Morya, 1939–1943 gg.* (Moscow, 1958), which argues that the Western powers conducted a "phony war" until 1943; Boris Meissner, *Russland, die Westmächte und Deutschland* (Hamburg, 1953).

INTELLECTUAL AND CULTURAL ASPECTS OF THE WAR PERIOD

Any list of books on this aspect of the war is likely to seem a structureless hodgepodge. Historians have not yet reached the point where they are ready to risk assessing the impact of the war on cultural life and intellectual attitudes; even the raw materials for arriving at such an assessment are difficult to assemble. This section will therefore be brief and tentative.

On the literature of the war years, there are two stimulating essays by French critics: Paul Sérant's *Le romantisme fasciste: étude sur l'oeuvre politique de quelques écrivains français* (Paris, 1959), and Pierre-Henri Simon's *L'homme en procès: Malraux-Sartre-Camus-Saint Exupéry*, 2d ed. (Paris, 1965). For the literature of other warring nations, there are no equally sophisticated commentaries, though the relevant chapters of two books on Soviet literature are useful: Marc Slonim, *Soviet Russian Literature: Writers and Problems* (New York, 1964), and Gleb Struve, *Soviet Russian Literature 1917–1950* (Norman, Okla., 1951). For the German scene, Dietrich Strothmann's *Nationalsozialistische Literaturpolitik* (Bonn, 1960) is mainly statistical and juridical, while Josef Wulf's *Literatur und Dichtung im Dritten Reich* is a varied compendium of bits and pieces. There are two good anthologies of British war poetry: Ian Hamilton (ed.), *The Poetry of War 1939–1945* (London, 1965), and Brian Gardner (ed.), *The Terrible Rain: the War Poets 1939–1945* (London, 1966). Charles W. Hoffmann's *Opposition Poetry in Nazi Germany* (Berkeley, 1962) finds that these German writers anticipated the style and mood of the postwar era. There is an interesting monograph by Konrad F. Bieber on *L'Allemagne vue par les écrivains de la Résistance française* (Geneva, 1952).

Little has appeared on the wartime theater or the fine arts, except for Basil Dean's *The Theatre at War* (London, 1956). Reproductions of the works of British war artists were published in a 12-volume series, *War Pictures by British Artists* (Oxford, 1942). There are a few interesting suggestions in Hellmut Lehmann-Haupt, *Art Under a Dictatorship* (New York, 1954), and in Sir Herbert Read's essay "The Situation of Art in Europe at the End of the Second World War," in his *Philosophy of Modern Art* (Cleveland, 1954). On films, the relevant chapters in Georges Sadoul's *Histoire générale du cinéma,* Vol. 6 (Paris, 1954), and René Jeanne and Charles Ford's *Histoire encyclopédique du cinéma* (Paris, 1958) are useful. Worth mention also are Richard Hiepe, *Gewissen und Gestaltung: Deutsche Kunst im Widerstand* (Frankfurt, 1960); David Roxan and Ken Wanstall, *The Rape of Art: the Story of Hitler's Plunder of the Great Masterpieces of Europe* (New York, 1965); and Rose Valland, *Le front de l'art (1939–1945)* (Paris, 1961), on French techniques for limiting Nazi plunder.

On the effort of certain young Catholics in France after 1940 to develop a new elite, set of values, and world view, these items are useful: Gilbert Gadoffre (ed.), *Vers le style du XXᵉ siècle* (Paris, 1945); [Emmanuel Mounier], *Mounier et sa génération: lettres, carnets et inédits* (Paris, 1956); R. Josse, "L'école des cadres d'Uriage 1940–1942," *Revue d'Histoire de la Deuxième Guerre Mondiale*, No. 61 (1966), pp. 49–74; Robert Hervet, *Les chantiers de la jeunesse* (Paris, 1962); Jacques Duquesne, *Les catholiques français sous l'occupation* (Paris, 1966).

Few novels or plays of durable merit were written and published in wartime Europe. Jean-Paul Sartre's play *Les mouches* (1943) was probably an exception; most writers confined themselves to absorbing the impressions that would be crystallized after the war in notable literary works. For the reader who would grasp the mood of the war years, some of these postwar novels are of unique value: for example, Sartre's trilogy called *Les chemins de la liberté;* Albert Camus's *La peste;* Theodor Plievier's battle trilogy entitled, *Moscow, Stalingrad,* and *Berlin;* Konstantin Simonov's *The Living and the Dead* and *Days and Nights;* David Rousset's *Les jours de notre mort* (on the concentration camps); Bruno Werner's *The Slave Ship* (on life in Nazi Berlin); and Evelyn Waugh's satirical trilogy on wartime Britain, *Men at Arms, Officers and Gentlemen,* and *Unconditional Surrender.*

DOMESTIC EVENTS IN THE NATIONS OF EUROPE

Most of the books so far listed are concerned either with Europe as a whole or with some particular aspect of wartime history. There are, in addition, some useful monographs, memoirs, and diaries that focus on a single national state and that are too general in scope to appear under a specialized topical heading. A selection of such works will conclude this bibliography.

On Great Britain, there are three useful though rather breezy popular surveys: E. S. Turner, *The Phoney War on the Home Front* (London, 1961); Lawrence Thompson, *1940: Year of Legend, Year of History* (London, 1966); and Harry Hopkins, *The New Look* (London, 1963). A. J. P. Taylor's *English History 1914–1945* (London, 1965) contains a stimulating section on the war. Valuable biographies include the Earl of Birkenhead, *Life of Lord Halifax* (London, 1965); Alan Bullock, *The Life and Times of Ernest Bevin,* Vol. 2 (London, 1967); John W. Wheeler-Bennett, *John Anderson, Viscount Waverley* (London, 1962). Memoirs: Sir Percy Grigg, *Prejudice and Judgment* (London, 1948); James Leasor, *War at the Top* (London, 1959); Sir George Mallaby, *From My Level* (London, 1965); Gerald Pawle, *The War and Colonel Warden* (London, 1963); Sir John Slessor, *The Central Blue* (London, 1956); Harold Macmillan, *The Blast of War 1939–1945* (London, 1967). Finally, special mention should be made of the various volumes in the Civil Series of the British official history of the war—a series that provides details and insights unmatched for any other warring nation. Outstanding in this series is R. M. Titmuss, *Problems of Social Policy* (London, 1950)—surely one of the finest books yet published on any aspect of the war.

On France, there are several notable studies by Robert Aron, based on extensive use of oral testimony: *Histoire de Vichy (1940–1944)* (Paris, 1954); *Les grands dossiers de l'histoire contemporaine* (Paris, 1962); and the first volume of *Histoire de l'épuration* (Paris, 1967–). Henri Michel's *Vichy: année 40* (Paris, 1966) is excellent; so are Henri Amouroux's *La vie des français sous l'occupation* (Paris, 1961), and Robert O. Paxton's *Parades and Politics at Vichy* (Princeton, 1966), on the Vichy army. Useful biographies include J. R. Tournoux, *Pétain et de Gaulle* (Paris, 1964); Pierre Bourget, *Un certain Philippe Pétain* (Paris, 1966); A. Mallet, *Pierre Laval*, 2 vols. (Paris, 1955); Hubert Cole, *Laval, a Biography* (London, 1963). Almost every prominent ex-Vichy official has written self-justifying memoirs; it would be arbitrary to single out a few for special mention. Additional monographs of interest are: Joseph Billig, *Le commissariat général aux questions juives*, 2 vols. (Paris, 1957); Yves-Maxime Danan, *La vie politique à Alger de 1940 à 1944* (Paris, 1963); Louis Noguères, *La dernière étape, Sigmaringen* (Paris, 1956), on the last weeks of the Vichy regime, and *Le suicide de la flotte française à Toulon* (Paris, 1961); Mme. F. A. Puppo, *Gli armistizi francesi del 1940* (Milan, 1963); Marcel Vigneras, *Rearming the French* (Washington, 1957); Jacques Fauvet, *Histoire du parti communiste français*, Vol. 2 (Paris, 1965).

General monographs on Germany: Martin Broszat, *Der Nationalsozialismus —Weltanschauung, Programm und Wirklichkeit* (Stuttgart, 1960); Emil Franzel, *Das Reich der braunen Jacobiner* (Munich, 1964); Günter Fraschka, *Das letzte aufgebot; vom Sterben der deutschen Jugend* (Rastatt, 1960); Horst Laschitza, *Deutschland und die deutsche Arbeiterbewegung 1939–1945* (Berlin, 1963); Walter Oehme, *Ehrlos für immer* (Berlin, 1962), on the wartime judicial system; H. R. Trevor-Roper, *The Last Days of Hitler* (London, 1947). On the SS: Hans Buchheim *et al.*, *Anatomie des SS-Staates*, 2 vols. (Olten-Freiburg, 1965); Edouard Calic, *Himmler et son empire* (Paris, 1966); E. Neusüss-Hunkel, *Die SS* (Hanover, 1956); George H. Stein, *The Waffen-SS* (Ithaca, N.Y., 1965); Paul Hausser, *Waffen-SS im Einsatz* (Göttingen, 1953); Felix Stein, *Die Armee der Geächteten* (Göttingen, 1963)—the two last books being by former Waffen-SS commanders. On the Churches: Hans Buchheim, *Glaubenskrise im Dritten Reich* (Stuttgart, 1953); H. J. Gamm, *Der braune Kult: das Dritte Reich und seine Ersatz Religion* (Hamburg, 1962); Guenter Lewy, *The Catholic Church and Germany* (New York, 1964); Heinrich Roth, *Katholische Jugend in der NS- Zeit* (Düsseldorf, 1959); Gordon C. Zahn, *German Catholics and Hitler's Wars* (New York, 1962); Friedrich Zipfel, *Kirchenkampf in Deutschland 1933–1945* (Berlin, 1965).

Biographies of German leaders: Achim Besgen, *Der stille Befehl: Medizinalrat Kersten, Himmler, und das Dritte Reich* (Munich, 1960); Hans Bernd Gisevius, *Adolf Hitler* (Munich, 1963); Walter Görlitz, *Adolf Hitler* (Göttingen, 1960); Helmut Heiber, *Adolf Hitler* (London, 1962); Alan Bullock, *Hitler: a Study in Tyranny*, rev. ed. (London, 1962), an absolutely first-class study; Helmut Heiber, *Joseph Goebbels* (Berlin, 1952); Roger Manvell and Heinrich Fraenkel, *Doctor Goebbels: His Life and Death* (London, 1960), and *Heinrich Himmler* (London, 1965); F. C. Schaumburg-Lippe, *Dr. Goebbels: ein Porträt* (Wiesbaden, 1964); Josef Wulf, *Martin Bormann* (Gütersloh, 1962). Diaries: H. G. Seraphim (ed.), *Das politische Tagebuch Alfred Rosenbergs* (Göttingen, 1956); William L. Shirer, *Berlin Diary* (New York, 1941); H. G. von Studnitz, *While Berlin Burns*, tr. from the German (London, 1964); Ursula von Kardorff, *Diary of a Nightmare: Berlin, 1942–1945*, tr. from the German (New York, 1965). Memoirs: Paul Schmidt, *Statist auf diplomatischer Bühne 1923–1945*, 10th ed. (Frankfurt, 1964); Klaus Granzow, *Tagebuch einer Hitlerjugend, 1943–1945* (Bremen, 1965); Theodor Haecker, *Journal in the Night*, tr. from the German (New York, 1950); Fritz Hesse, *Das Spiel um Deutschland* (Munich, 1953); Konstantin Hierl, *Im Dienst für Deutschland 1918–1945* (Heidelberg, 1954); Felix Kersten, *The Kersten Memoirs 1940–1945*, tr. from the German (London, 1956); Peter Kleist, *The European Tragedy*, tr. from the German (Isle of Man, 1965); Melita Maschmann, *Account Rendered*, tr. from the German (New York, 1965); Wilfred von Oven, *Mit Goebbels bis zum Ende*, 2 vols. (Buenos Aires, 1949); Franz von Papen, *Memoirs*, tr. from the German (London, 1952); Wilhelm Prüller, *Diary of a German Soldier*, tr. from the German (London, 1963); Herman Rauschning, *Hitler Speaks* (London, 1940); Ernst von Weizsäcker, *Memoirs*, tr. from the German (Chicago, 1951); A. Zoller, *Hitler Privat* (Düsseldorf, 1949).

On Italy: Emilio Faldella, *L'Italia nella seconda guerra mondiale*, 2d ed. (Bologna, 1960); Ferdinand Siebert, *Italiens Weg in den zweiten Weltkrieg* (Frankfurt, 1962); Giuseppe Gorla, *L'Italia nella seconda guerra mondiale* (Milan, 1959). Biographies: Giorgio Pini and Duilio Susmel, *Mussolini: L'uomo e l'opera*, 2d ed., 4 vols. (Florence, 1957–1958); Sir Ivone Kirkpatrick, *Mussolini, Study of a Demagogue* (London, 1964). Memoirs: Filippo Anfuso, *Da Palazzo Venezia al Lago di Garda, 1936–1945* (Bologna, 1957); Giuseppe Bottai, *Vent'anni e un giorno* (Milan, 1949); Eugen Dollmann, *Roma nazista* (Milan, 1949); Benito Mussolini, *The Fall of Mussolini: His Own Story*, tr. from the Italian (New York, 1948); Giorgio Pini, *Filo diretto con Palazzo Venezia* (Bologna, 1950); General Francesco Rossi, *Mussolini e lo Stato Maggiore: Avvenimenti del 1940* (Rome, 1951); Ruggero Zangrandi, *1943: 25 luglio–8 settembre* (Milan, 1964). Collected works: Benito Mussolini, *Opera omnia*, 36 vols. (Florence, 1951–1963), the final volumes being on the war period. Accounts of the so-called Salò Republic, mostly by participants, are numerous: e.g., Ermanno Amicucci, *I 600 Giorni di Mussolini* (Rome, 1949); Dino Campini, *Strano Gioco di Mussolini* (Milan, 1952); Edmondo Cione, *Storia della Repubblica Sociale Italiana*, 2d ed. (Rome, 1951); Ugo Manunta, *La caduta degli angeli* (Rome, 1947); Alberto Mellini Ponce de Leon, *Guerra diplomatica a Salò* (Bologna, 1950); Giorgio Pini, *Itinerario tragico, 1943–1945* (Milan, 1950); Bruno Spampanato, *Contromemoriale*, Vol. 2 (Rome, 1952); Attilio Tamaro, *Due anni di storia 1943–1945*, 3 vols. (Rome, 1948–1950).

The Balkans and Eastern Europe. General: Andreas Hillgruber, *Südosteuropa im Zweiten Weltkrieg: Literaturbericht* (Frankfurt, 1962); Robert M. Kennedy, *German Anti-Guerrilla Operations in the Balkans 1941–1944* (Washington, D.C., 1954). Hungary: E. A. Macartney, *October Fifteenth: a History of Modern Hungary 1929–1945*, 2 vols. (Edinburgh, 1956–1957); Miklos Szinai and Laszlo Szucs, *Confidential Papers of Admiral Miklos Horthy* (Budapest, 1965); Maria Galantai, *The Changing of the Guard: the Siege of Budapest 1944–1945* (London, 1962); Miklos Horthy, *The Admiral Horthy Memoirs*, tr. from the Magyar (London, 1956); M. Kallay, *Hungarian Premier*, tr. from the Magyar (New York, 1954). Yugoslavia: J. B. Hoptner, *Yugoslavia in Crisis, 1934–1941* (New York, 1962); Constantin Fotitch, *The War We Lost* (New York, 1948); Milutin Markovic *et al., Drugi Svetski Rat* (Belgrade, 1957); Peter II of Yugoslavia, *La vie d'un roi: mémoires*, tr. from the Serbian (Paris, 1955); Branko Lazitch, *Tito et la révolution yougoslave* (Paris, 1957); Major William Jones, *Twelve Months with Tito's Partisans* (Bedford, 1946); Brigadier Fitzroy Maclean, *Eastern Approaches* (London, 1949); Jasper Rootham, *Miss Fire: the Chronicle of a British Mission to Mikhailovich* (London, 1946); Sime Balen, *Pavelić* (Zagreb, 1952); Moše Pijade, *La fable de l'aide soviétique à l'insurrection nationale yougoslave*, tr. from the Serbian (Paris, 1950). Greece: Ehrengard Schramm-von Thadden, *Griechenland und die Grossmächte im zweiten Weltkrieg* (Wiesbaden, 1955); Robert Crisp, *The Gods Were Neutral* (New York, 1961); D. A. Kokkinos, *Duo polemoe 1940–1941* (Athens, 1965); D. G. Kousoulas, *Revolution and Defeat: the Story of the Greek Communist Party* (London, 1965); Alexandre Papagos, *La Grèce en guerre 1940–1944*, tr. from the Greek (Athens, 1951). Rumania: Ion Popescu-Puturi *et al., La Roumanie pendant la deuxième guerre mondiale: études* (Bucharest, 1964), and *La contribution de la Roumanie à la victoire sur le fascisme* (Bucharest, 1965); Alexandre Cretzianu, *The Lost Opportunity* (London, 1957). Bulgaria: L. B. Walew, *Aus der Geschichte der Vaterländischen Front Bulgariens 1942–1944* (Berlin, 1952). Czechoslovakia: Václav Král, *Otázky Hospodarského a Socialniko vyvoje v Českych zemich, 1938–1945*, 3 vols. (Prague, 1957–1959), on economic and social developments; Wilhelm Dennler, *Die böhmische Passion: Prager Tagebuch, 1939–1947* (Freiburg, 1953); Václav Beneš, "Pan-Slavism and Czechoslovak Policy during World War II," *Indiana Slavic Studies*, I (1956), 137–64; see also the works of Eduard Beneš, Josef Korbel, and Paul Zinner, listed above. Poland: Institut Zachodni, *Documenta Occupationis Teutonicae*, Vol. 3 (Poznań, 1946), reminiscences about the war period by teen-agers; Jerzy Kirchmayer, *1939–1944: Kilka Zagadnien Polskich* (Warsaw, 1959); Jerzy Klimkowski, *Bylem adjutantem Gen. Andersa* (Warsaw, 1959); Ludwik Landau, *Kronika lat wojny i okupacji*, 3 vols. (Warsaw, 1962–1963); Jan Modzelewski *et al.* (eds.), *Pologne 1919–1939*, Vol. I (Neuchâtel, 1946); *Najnowsze Dzieje Polski: Materialy i Studia z Okresu II Wojny Swiatowej,*

Vol. 5 (Warsaw, 1961); Jerzy Putrament, *Pol wieku: Wojna* (Warsaw, 1962); Hans Roos, *A History of Modern Poland*, tr. from the Polish (New York, 1966); Wiktor Sukiennicki, "The Establishment of the Soviet Regime in Eastern Poland in 1939," *Journal of Central European Affairs*, XXIII (1963), 191–218.

The USSR: Alexander Werth, *Russia at War 1941–1945* (London, 1964), a lively firsthand record by a British war correspondent; John A. Armstrong, *Ukrainian Nationalism 1939–1945*, 2d ed. (New York, 1963); Leon Gouré and Herbert Dinerstein, *Moscow in Crisis* (Glencoe, Ill., 1955); N. J. Suprunenko, *Ukraina v Velikoi Otechestvennoi Voine* (Kiev, 1956); Ilya Ehrenburg, *Eve of War* (London, 1963) and *The War 1941–45* (London, 1964), the final volumes in the memoirs of the well-known Soviet journalist; Paolo Robotti, *La Prova* (Bari, 1965), memoirs of an Italian Communist in the USSR during the war.

Scandinavia: Bernard Ash, *Norway 1940* (London, 1964); S. Hartmann, *Förer uten folk: Quisling som politisk og psychologisk problem* (Oslo, 1959); Ralph Hewins, *Quisling, Prophet Without Honor* (London, 1965); Trygve Lie, *Leve eller dø: Norge in Krig* (Oslo, 1955); Magne Skodvin, *Striden om okkupasjionsstyret in Norge* (Oslo, 1956); Walther Hubatsch, *Unruhe des Nordens: Studien zur deutschskandinavischen Geschichte* (Göttingen, 1956); Aage Bertelsen, *Oktober 43* (Munich, 1960); L. B. Frederiksen, *Pressen under Besaettelsen* (Aarhus, 1960); Francis La Ruche, *La neutralité de la Suède* (Paris, 1953); Johan Scharffenberg, *Folke Bernadotte og det Svenske Redningskorps 1945* (Oslo, 1958); C. L. Lundin, *Finland in the Second World War* (Bloomington, Ind., 1956); Ernst Klink et al., *Operationsgebiet Östliche Ostsee und der Finnische-Baltische Raum, 1944* (Stuttgart, 1961); A. F. Upton, *Finland in Crisis, 1940–1941* (Ithaca, N.Y., 1965).

The Low Countries: J. Jacquemyns, *La société belge sous l'occupation allemande*, 3 vols. (Brussels, 1950); Louise Narvaez, *Degrelle m'a dit* (Paris, 1961); General E. R. van Overstraeten, *Dans l'étau: au service de la Belgique* (Paris, 1960); P. Struye, *L'évolution du sentiment public en Belgique sous l'occupation* (Brussels, 1945); J. Wullers-Rudiger, *En marge de la politique belge, 1914–1956* (Paris, 1957); Henry L. Mason, "War Comes to the Netherlands: September 1939–May 1940," *Political Science Quarterly*, LXXVIII (1963), 548–80; H. C. Posthumus Meyjes, *De Enquetecommissie is van oordeel* (Amsterdam, 1958), a résumé of the 18-volume parliamentary inquiry after the war; Jan van den Tempel, *Nederland in London* (Haarlem, 1946). See also two special issues of the *Revue d'Histoire de la Deuxième Guerre Mondiale*: No. 31 (1958) on Belgium and No. 50 (1963) on the Netherlands.

Switzerland: Alice Meyer, *Anpassung oder Widerstand: die Schweiz zur Zeit des deutschen Nationalsozialismus* (Frauenfeld, 1966), the best work on the subject; Frederick H. Hartmann, *The Swiss Press and Foreign Affairs in World War II* (Gainesville, Fla., 1960); Fred Luchsinger, *Die Neue Zürcher Zeitung im Zeitalter des zweiten Weltkrieges* (Zürich, 1955); E. O. Maetzke, *Die Deutsche-Schweizerische Presse zu einigen Problemen des zweiten Weltkrieges* (Tübingen, 1955); Günter Lachmann, *Der National-sozialismus in der Schweiz 1931–1945* (Berlin, 1962).

INDEX

Abetz, Otto, 133
Advisory Council for Italy, 211
Air Ministry, British, 83, 87
Air offensive, Allied, 174–82
Albania, 36
Aleutian Islands, 41
Alexander, General Harold, 183, 192
Algeria, 34, 182, 183, 185, 187
Allied expeditionary force to Finland, 21–22
Alsace, 108
Anderson, Sir John, 106, 247
Anglo-American Control Commission, 211, 217, 225, 231
Anglo-Soviet treaty of alliance (1942), 207
Anti-Comintern Pact, 131, 136, 140
Anti-Semitism, 8; *see also* Jews, repression and extermination of
Antonescu, Marshal Ion, 33, 104, 135–36, 217
Anzio beachhead, 192, 193
Appeasement policy, 8
Archangel, Soviet Union, 170
Ardennes Forest, Battle of, 201
Atlantic Charter (1941), 205–06
Atlantic Conference (1941), 205–06
Attlee, Clement, 102, 231
Atomic bombs, 99, 233
Atomic development, 99–106
Auschwitz extermination camp, 127
Austria, 213, 230, 231
Aymé, Marcel, 260

Badoglio, Marshal Pietro, 153, 154, 191, 192
Baldwin, Stanley, 83
Barbarossa, Operation, 35, 36, 37–43
Battle of Britain, 29–32, 49, 83, 89, 175, 245
Battle of London, 98
Battle of Stalingrad, 70, 164, 194, 207, 240
Battle of the Atlantic, 86, 88
Bazooka, 90
Beck, Josef, 3
Beck, General Ludwig, 162, 163
Becker, Jacques, 257
Belgium, collaboration in, 132; economic exploitation of, 119; invasion and subjugation of, 23–27; neutral attitude and hope of, 11–12; resistance movement in, 145, 148, 149

Benelux countries, 266
Beneš, Edouard, 155, 208–09, 226–27
Bergen-Belsen concentration camp, 94
Berger, General Gottlob, 143
Berlin, Germany, Soviet capture of, 202–03, 230
Bermuda, 167
Bessarabia, 32, 217
Beveridge, Sir William, 246
Bichelonne, Jean, 122
Bierut, Boleslaw, 223, 232
Black market, 123
Blockade tactics, 53–54
Blum, Léon, 263
Bock, General Fedor von, 40
Bohemia-Moravia, 110, 135, 155
Bohlen, Charles E., 213
Bohr, Niels, 99, 100, 101, 105, 106
Bomber Command, British, 175, 176, 177, 178
Bombing, strategic, 174–82
Bonhoeffer, Dietrich, 165, 261
Bonnard, Abel, 260
Bonnet, Georges, 5
Bonomi, Ivanoe, 154
Bor-Komorowski, General Tadeusz, 158
Bordeaux, France, 28
Boris, King, 136
Bormann, Martin, 63, 64
Boulogne, France, 27
Brasillach, Robert, 259
Brauchitsch, Marshal Heinrich von, 40, 96
Braun, Eva, 203
Britain, *see* Great Britain
British Broadcasting Corporation, 74–75, 76
British Commonwealth, 1, 167, 231
Budapest, Hungary, 200, 201
Bukovina, 32, 217
Bulgaria, 12, 32, 36, 107, 196; collaboration in, 136; postwar settlement of, 220, 225–26, 232
Burma, 197
Burma Road, 197
Byelorussia, 113, 159
Byrnes, James, 231 n.

Caesar, Julius, 144
Cairo, Egypt, 43
Camus, Albert, 261, 262
Carné, Marcel, 257
Carol, King, 33

306

harper ✦ torchbooks

† The New American Nation Series, edited by Henry Steele Commager and Richard B. Morris.
‡ American Perspectives series, edited by Bernard Wishy and William E. Leuchtenburg.
α History of Europe series, edited by J. H. Plumb.
§ The Library of Religion and Culture, edited by Benjamin Nelson.
‖ Researches in the Social, Cultural, and Behavioral Sciences, edited by Benjamin Nelson.
⋕ Harper Modern Science Series, edited by James A. Newman.
° Not for sale in Canada.
+ Documentary History of the United States series, edited by Richard B. Morris.
# Documentary History of Western Civilization series, edited by Eugene C. Black and Leonard W. Levy.
Λ The Economic History of the United States series, edited by Henry David et al.
¶ European Perspectives series, edited by Eugene C. Black.
** Contemporary Essays series, edited by Leonard W. Levy.
* The Stratum Series, edited by John Hale.

LOUIS B. WRIGHT: Culture on the Moving Frontier TB/1053

American Studies: The Civil War to 1900

T. C. COCHRAN & WILLIAM MILLER: The Age of Enterprise: *A Social History of Industrial America* TB/1054
W. A. DUNNING: Reconstruction, Political and Economic: 1865-1877 TB/1073
HAROLD U. FAULKNER: Politics, Reform and Expansion: 1890-1900. † *Illus.* TB/3020
GEORGE M. FREDRICKSON: The Inner Civil War: *Northern Intellectuals and the Crisis of the Union* TB/1358
JOHN A. GARRATY: The New Commonwealth, 1877-1890 † TB/1410
HELEN HUNT JACKSON: A Century of Dishonor: *The Early Crusade for Indian Reform.* † *Edited by Andrew F. Rolle* TB/3063
WILLIAM G. MCLOUGHLIN, Ed.: The American Evangelicals, 1800-1900: An Anthology ‡ TB/1382
JAMES S. PIKE: The Prostrate State: *South Carolina under Negro Government.* ‡ *Intro. by Robert F. Durden* TB/3085
VERNON LANE WHARTON: The Negro in Mississippi, 1865-1890 TB/1178

American Studies: The Twentieth Century

RAY STANNARD BAKER: Following the Color Line: *American Negro Citizenship in Progressive Era.* ‡ *Edited by Dewey W. Grantham, Jr. Illus.* ‡ TB/3053
RANDOLPH S. BOURNE: War and the Intellectuals: *Collected Essays, 1915-1919.* ‡ *Edited by Carl Resek* TB/3043
A. RUSSELL BUCHANAN: The United States and World War II. † *Illus.*
    Vol. I TB/3044; Vol. II TB/3045
THOMAS C. COCHRAN: The American Business System: *A Historical Perspective, 1900-1955* TB/1080
FOSTER RHEA DULLES: America's Rise to World Power: 1898-1954. † *Illus.* TB/3021
HAROLD U. FAULKNER: The Decline of Laissez Faire, 1897-1917 TB/1397
JOHN D. HICKS: Republican Ascendancy: 1921-1933. † *Illus.* TB/3041
WILLIAM E. LEUCHTENBURG: Franklin D. Roosevelt and the New Deal: 1932-1940. † *Illus.* TB/3025
WILLIAM E. LEUCHTENBURG, Ed.: The New Deal: *A Documentary History* + HR/1354
ARTHUR S. LINK: Woodrow Wilson and the Progressive Era: 1910-1917. † *Illus.* TB/3023
BROADUS MITCHELL: Depression Decade: *From New Era through New Deal, 1929-1941* ∆ TB/1439
GEORGE E. MOWRY: The Era of Theodore Roosevelt and the Birth of Modern America: 1900-1912. † *Illus.* TB/3022
WILLIAM PRESTON, JR.: Aliens and Dissenters:
TWELVE SOUTHERNERS: I'll Take My Stand: *The South and the Agrarian Tradition. Intro. by Louis D. Rubin, Jr.; Biographical Essays by Virginia Rock* TB/1072

Art, Art History, Aesthetics

ERWIN PANOFSKY: Renaissance and Renascences in Western Art. *Illus.* TB/1447
ERWIN PANOFSKY: Studies in Iconology: *Humanistic Themes in the Art of the Renaissance. 180 illus.* TB/1077
HEINRICH ZIMMER: Myths and Symbols in Indian Art and Civilization. *70 illus.* TB/2005

Asian Studies

WOLFGANG FRANKE: China and the West: *The Cultural Encounter, 13th to 20th Centuries. Trans. by R. A. Wilson* TB/1326
L. CARRINGTON GOODRICH: A Short History of the Chinese People. *Illus.* TB/3015

Economics & Economic History

C. E. BLACK: The Dynamics of Modernization: *A Study in Comparative History* TB/1321
GILBERT BURCK & EDITORS OF Fortune: The Computer Age: *And its Potential for Management* TB/1179
ROBERT L. HEILBRONER: The Future as History: *The Historic Currents of Our Time and the Direction in Which They Are Taking America* TB/1386
ROBERT L. HEILBRONER: The Great Ascent: *The Struggle for Economic Development in Our Time* TB/3030
FRANK H. KNIGHT: The Economic Organization TB/1214
DAVID S. LANDES: Bankers and Pashas: *International Finance and Economic Imperialism in Egypt. New Preface by the Author* TB/1412
ROBERT LATOUCHE: The Birth of Western Economy: *Economic Aspects of the Dark Ages* TB/1290
W. ARTHUR LEWIS: The Principles of Economic Planning. *New Introduction by the Author°* TB/1436
WILLIAM MILLER, Ed.: Men in Business: *Essays on the Historical Role of the Entrepreneur* TB/1081
HERBERT A. SIMON: The Shape of Automation: *For Men and Management* TB/1245

Historiography and History of Ideas

J. BRONOWSKI & BRUCE MAZLISH: The Western Intellectual Tradition: *From Leonardo to Hegel* TB/3001
WILHELM DILTHEY: Pattern and Meaning in History: *Thoughts on History and Society.° Edited with an Intro. by H. P. Rickman* TB/1075
J. H. HEXTER: More's Utopia: *The Biography of an Idea. Epilogue by the Author* TB/1195
H. STUART HUGHES: History as Art and as Science: *Twin Vistas on the Past* TB/1207
ARTHUR O. LOVEJOY: The Great Chain of Being: *A Study of the History of an Idea* TB/1009
RICHARD H. POPKIN: The History of Scepticism from Erasmus to Descartes. *Revised Edition* TB/1391
BRUNO SNELL: The Discovery of the Mind: *The Greek Origins of European Thought* TB/1018

History: General

HANS KOHN: The Age of Nationalism: *The First Era of Global History* TB/1380
BERNARD LEWIS: The Arabs in History TB/1029
BERNARD LEWIS: The Middle East and the West ° TB/1274

History: Ancient

A. ANDREWS: The Greek Tyrants TB/1103
THEODOR H. GASTER: Thespis: *Ritual Myth and Drama in the Ancient Near East* TB/1281

2

A. H. M. JONES, Ed.: A History of Rome through the Fifth Century # *Vol. I: The Republic* HR/1364
Vol. II The Empire: HR/1460
SAMUEL NOAH KRAMER: Sumerian Mythology TB/1055
NAPHTALI LEWIS & MEYER REINHOLD, Eds.: Roman Civilization *Vol. I: The Republic* TB/1231
Vol. II: The Empire TB/1232

History: Medieval

NORMAN COHN: The Pursuit of the Millennium: *Revolutionary Messianism in Medieval and Reformation Europe* TB/1037
F. L. GANSHOF: Feudalism TB/1058
F. L. GANSHOF: The Middle Ages: *A History of International Relations. Translated by Rémy Hall* TB/1411
HENRY CHARLES LEA: The Inquisition of the Middle Ages. || *Introduction by Walter Ullmann* TB/1456

History: Renaissance & Reformation

JACOB BURCKHARDT: The Civilization of the Renaissance in Italy. *Introduction by Benjamin Nelson and Charles Trinkaus. Illus.* Vol. I TB/40; Vol. II TB/41
JOHN CALVIN & JACOPO SADOLETO: A Reformation Debate. *Edited by John C. Olin* TB/1239
J. H. ELLIOTT: Europe Divided, 1559-1598 a ° TB/1414
G. R. ELTON: Reformation Europe, 1517-1559 ° a TB/1270
HANS J. HILLERBRAND, Ed., The Protestant Reformation # HR/1342
JOHAN HUIZINGA: Erasmus and the Age of Reformation. *Illus.* TB/19
JOEL HURSTFIELD: The Elizabethan Nation TB/1312
JOEL HURSTFIELD, Ed.: The Reformation Crisis TB/1267
PAUL OSKAR KRISTELLER: Renaissance Thought: *The Classic, Scholastic, and Humanist Strains* TB/1048
DAVID LITTLE: Religion, Order and Law: *A Study in Pre-Revolutionary England.* § *Preface by R. Bellah* TB/1418
PAOLO ROSSI: Philosophy, Technology, and the Arts, in the Early Modern Era 1400-1700. || *Edited by Benjamin Nelson. Translated by Salvator Attanasio* TB/1458
H. R. TREVOR-ROPER: The European Witch-craze of the Sixteenth and Seventeenth Centuries and Other Essays ° TB/1416

History: Modern European

ALAN BULLOCK: Hitler, A Study in Tyranny. ° *Revised Edition. Illus.* TB/1123
JOHANN GOTTLIEB FICHTE: Addresses to the German Nation. *Ed. with Intro. by George A. Kelly* ¶ TB/1366
ALBERT GOODWIN: The French Revolution TB/1064
STANLEY HOFFMANN et al.: In Search of France: *The Economy, Society and Political System In the Twentieth Century* TB/1219
H. STUART HUGHES: The Obstructed Path: *French Social Thought in the Years of Desperation* TB/1451
JOHAN HUIZINGA: Dutch Civilisation in the 17th Century and Other Essays TB/1453

JOHN MCMANNERS: European History, 1789-1914: *Men, Machines and Freedom* TB/1419
HUGH SETON-WATSON: Eastern Europe Between the Wars, 1918-1941 TB/1330
ALBERT SOREL: Europe Under the Old Regime. *Translated by Francis H. Herrick* TB/1121
A. J. P. TAYLOR: From Napoleon to Lenin: *Historical Essays* ° TB/1268
A. J. P. TAYLOR: The Habsburg Monarchy, 1809-1918: *A History of the Austrian Empire and Austria-Hungary* ° TB/1187
J. M. THOMPSON: European History, 1494-1789 TB/1431
H. R. TREVOR-ROPER: Historical Essays TB/1269

Literature & Literary Criticism

W. J. BATE: From Classic to Romantic: *Premises of Taste in Eighteenth Century England* TB/1036
VAN WYCK BROOKS: Van Wyck Brooks: The Early Years: *A Selection from his Works, 1908-1921 Ed. with Intro. by Claire Sprague* TB/3082
RICHMOND LATTIMORE, Translator: The Odyssey of Homer TB/1389
ROBERT PREYER, Ed.: Victorian Literature ** TB/1302

Philosophy

HENRI BERGSON: Time and Free Will: *An Essay on the Immediate Data of Consciousness* ° TB/1021
H. J. BLACKHAM: Six Existentialist Thinkers: *Kierkegaard, Nietzsche, Jaspers, Marcel, Heidegger, Sartre* ° TB/1002
J. M. BOCHENSKI: The Methods of Contemporary Thought. *Trans. by Peter Caws* TB/1377
ERNST CASSIRER: Rousseau, Kant and Goethe. *Intro. by Peter Gay* TB/1092
MICHAEL GELVEN: A Commentary on Heidegger's "Being and Time" TB/1464
J. GLENN GRAY: Hegel and Greek Thought TB/1409
W. K. C. GUTHRIE: The Greek Philosophers: *From Thales to Aristotle* ° TB/1008
G. W. F. HEGEL: Phenomenology of Mind. ° || *Introduction by George Lichtheim* TB/1303
MARTIN HEIDEGGER: Discourse on Thinking. *Translated with a Preface by John M. Anderson and E. Hans Freund. Introduction by John M. Anderson* TB/1459
F. H. HEINEMANN: Existentialism and the Modern Predicament TB/28
WERER HEISENBERG: Physics and Philosophy: *The Revolution in Modern Science. Intro. by F. S. C. Northrop* TB/549
EDMUND HUSSERL: Phenomenology and the Crisis of Philosophy. § *Translated with an Introduction by Quentin Lauer* TB/1170
IMMANUEL KANT: Groundwork of the Metaphysic of Morals. *Translated and Analyzed by H. J. Paton* TB/1159
WALTER KAUFMANN, Ed.: Religion From Tolstoy to Camus: *Basic Writings on Religious Truth and Morals* TB/123
QUENTIN LAUER: Phenomenology: *Its Genesis and Prospect. Preface by Aron Gurwitsch* TB/1169
MICHAEL POLANYI: Personal Knowledge: *Towards a Post-Critical Philosophy* TB/1158
WILLARD VAN ORMAN QUINE: Elementary Logic *Revised Edition* TB/577
WILHELM WINDELBAND: A History of Philosophy *Vol. I: Greek, Roman, Medieval* TB/38

Vol. II: Renaissance, Enlightenment, Modern
TB/39
LUDWIG WITTGENSTEIN: The Blue and Brown
Books °   TB/1211
LUDWIG WITTGENSTEIN: Notebooks, 1914-1916
TB/1441

Political Science & Government

C. E. BLACK: The Dynamics of Modernization:
A Study in Comparative History   TB/1321
DENIS W. BROGAN: Politics in America. *New
Introduction by the Author*   TB/1469
ROBERT CONQUEST: Power and Policy in the
USSR: *The Study of Soviet Dynastics* °
TB/1307
JOHN B. MORRALL: Political Thought in Medieval
Times   TB/1076
KARL R. POPPER: The Open Society and Its
Enemies *Vol. I: The Spell of Plato* TB/1101
*Vol. II: The High Tide of Prophecy: Hegel,
Marx, and the Aftermath*   TB/1102
HENRI DE SAINT-SIMON: Social Organization, The
Science of Man, and Other Writings. ||
*Edited and Translated with an Introduction
by Felix Markham*   TB/1152
CHARLES SCHOTTLAND, Ed.: The Welfare State **
TB/1323
JOSEPH A. SCHUMPETER: Capitalism, Socialism
and Democracy   TB/3008

Psychology

LUDWIG BINSWANGER: Being-in-the-World: *Se-
lected Papers.* || *Trans. with Intro. by Jacob
Needleman*   TB/1365
MIRCEA ELIADE: Cosmos and History: *The Myth
of the Eternal Return* §   TB/2050
MIRCEA ELIADE: Myth and Reality   TB/1369
SIGMUND FREUD: On Creativity and the Uncon-
scious: *Papers on the Psychology of Art,
Literature, Love, Religion.* § *Intro. by Ben-
jamin Nelson*   TB/45
J. GLENN GRAY: The Warriors: *Reflections on
Men in Battle. Introduction by Hannah
Arendt*   TB/1294
WILLIAM JAMES: Psychology: *The Briefer
Course. Edited with an Intro. by Gordon
Allport*   TB/1034

Religion: Ancient and Classical, Biblical and Judaic Traditions

MARTIN BUBER: Eclipse of God: *Studies in the
Relation Between Religion and Philosophy*
TB/12
MARTIN BUBER: Hasidism and Modern Man.
Edited and Translated by Maurice Friedman
TB/839
MARTIN BUBER: The Knowledge of Man. *Edited
with an Introduction by Maurice Friedman.
Translated by Maurice Friedman and Ronald
Gregor Smith*   TB/135
MARTIN BUBER: Moses. *The Revelation and the
Covenant*   TB/837
MARTIN BUBER: The Origin and Meaning of
Hasidism. *Edited and Translated by Maurice
Friedman*   TB/835
MARTIN BUBER: The Prophetic Faith   TB/73
MARTIN BUBER: Two Types of Faith: *Interpene-
tration of Judaism and Christianity* ° TB/75
M. S. ENSLIN: Christian Beginnings   TB/5
M. S. ENSLIN: The Literature of the Christian
Movement   TB/6
HENRI FRANKFORT: Ancient Egyptian Religion:
An Interpretation   TB/77

Religion: Early Christianity Through Reformation

ANSELM OF CANTERBURY: Truth, Freedom, and
Evil: *Three Philosophical Dialogues. Edited
and Translated by Jasper Hopkins and Herbert Richardson*   TB/317
EDGAR J. GOODSPEED: A Life of Jesus   TB/1
ROBERT M. GRANT: Gnosticism and Early Christianity   TB/136

Religion: Oriental Religions

TOR ANDRAE: Mohammed: *The Man and His
Faith* §   TB/62
EDWARD CONZE: Buddhism: *Its Essence and De-
velopment.* ° *Foreword by Arthur Waley*
TB/58
H. G. CREEL: Confucius and the Chinese Way
TB/63
FRANKLIN EDGERTON, Trans. & Ed.: The Bhaga-
vad Gita   TB/115
SWAMI NIKHILANANDA, Trans. & Ed.: The
Upanishads   TB/114
D. T. SUZUKI: On Indian Mahayana Buddhism.
° *Ed. with Intro. by Edward Conze.* TB/1403

Science and Mathematics

W. E. LE GROS CLARK: The Antecedents of
Man: *An Introduction to the Evolution of
the Primates.* ° *Illus.*   TB/559
ROBERT E. COKER: Streams, Lakes, Ponds. *Illus.*
TB/586
ROBERT E. COKER: This Great and Wide Sea: *An
Introduction to Oceanography and Marine
Biology. Illus.*   TB/551
WILLARD VAN ORMAN QUINE: Mathematical Logic
TB/558

Sociology and Anthropology

REINHARD BENDIX: Work and Authority in In-
dustry: *Ideologies of Management in the
Course of Industrialization*   TB/3035
KENNETH B. CLARK: Dark Ghetto: *Dilemmas of
Social Power. Foreword by Gunnar Myrdal*
TB/1317
KENNETH CLARK & JEANNETTE HOPKINS: A Rele-
vant War Against Poverty: *A Study of Com-
munity Action Programs and Observable So-
cial Change*   TB/1480
LEWIS COSER, Ed.: Political Sociology TB/1293
GARY T. MARX: Protest and Prejudice: *A Study
of Belief in the Black Community*   TB/1435
ROBERT K. MERTON, LEONARD BROOM, LEONARD S.
COTTRELL, JR., Editors: Sociology Today:
Problems and Prospects ||
Vol. I TB/1173; Vol. II TB/1174
GILBERT OSOFSKY, Ed.: The Burden of Race: *A
Documentary History of Negro-White Rela-
tions in America*   TB/1405
GILBERT OSOFSKY: Harlem: The Making of a
Ghetto: *Negro New York 1890-1930*   TB/1381
PHILIP RIEFF: The Triumph of the Therapeutic:
Uses of Faith After Freud   TB/1360
ARNOLD ROSE: The Negro in America: *The Con-
densed Version of Gunnar Myrdal's* An
American Dilemma. *Second Edition*   TB/3048
GEORGE ROSEN: Madness in Society: *Chapters in
the Historical Sociology of Mental Illness.* ||
Preface by Benjamin Nelson   TB/1337
PITIRIM A. SOROKIN: Contemporary Sociological
Theories: *Through the First Quarter of the
Twentieth Century*   TB/3046
FLORIAN ZNANIECKI: The Social Role of the
Man of Knowledge. *Introduction by Lewis
A. Coser*   TB/1372